Hands-On Unity 2020 Game Development

Build, customize, and optimize professional games using Unity 2020 and C#

Nicolas Alejandro Borromeo

BIRMINGHAM—MUMBAI

Hands-On Unity 2020 Game Development

Commissioning Editor: Pavan Ramchandani
Acquisition Editor: Ashitosh Gupta
Senior Editor: Hayden Edwards
Content Development Editor: Akhil Nair
Technical Editor: Deepesh Patel
Copy Editor: Safis Editing
Project Coordinator: Kinjal Bari
Proofreader: Safis Editing
Indexer: Priyanka Dhadke
Production Designer: Shankar Kalbhor

First published: July 2020

Production reference: 1270720

Published by Packt Publishing Ltd.
Livery Place
35 Livery Street
Birmingham
B3 2PB, UK.

ISBN 978-1-83864-200-6

www.packt.com

To Dad, who spoiled me with computers to help me keep learning – I miss you. Also, to my wife, for reminding me what I am capable of.

Packt.com

Subscribe to our online digital library for full access to over 7,000 books and videos, as well as industry leading tools to help you plan your personal development and advance your career. For more information, please visit our website.

Why subscribe?

- Spend less time learning and more time coding with practical eBooks and Videos from over 4,000 industry professionals

- Improve your learning with Skill Plans built especially for you

- Get a free eBook or video every month

- Fully searchable for easy access to vital information

- Copy and paste, print, and bookmark content

Did you know that Packt offers eBook versions of every book published, with PDF and ePub files available? You can upgrade to the eBook version at packt.com and as a print book customer, you are entitled to a discount on the eBook copy. Get in touch with us at customercare@packtpub.com for more details.

At www.packt.com, you can also read a collection of free technical articles, sign up for a range of free newsletters, and receive exclusive discounts and offers on Packt books and eBooks.

Contributors

About the author

Nicolas Alejandro Borromeo is working as a Unity senior developer at Product Madness in London. He was a game development career coordinator at **Universidad Argentina de la Empresa (UADE)** and has been a game development teacher in many other Argentine universities, such as UADE, UTN, UAI, and USAL, and in institutions such as Image Campus and DaVinci, since 2012. Nicolas has been a Unity Certified Instructor since 2019, teaching for high-profile Unity clients all around the globe. He was an MMO client-side developer at Band of Coders in Argentina and has been a Unity freelance developer since 2012.

About the reviewer

Sungkuk Park is a game engineer based in Berlin. He has participated in multiple game jams around the world and has created indie games to polish his skills. He is currently interested in the area of technical art, mainly CG, animation, gameplay, and VFX. In his spare time, he spends most of his time learning new skills, including drawing, animation, and VFX, that might come in handy when he pursues his next goal: being a game director for the next gaming generation!

Packt is searching for authors like you

If you're interested in becoming an author for Packt, please visit `authors.packtpub.com` and apply today. We have worked with thousands of developers and tech professionals, just like you, to help them share their insight with the global tech community. You can make a general application, apply for a specific hot topic that we are recruiting an author for, or submit your own idea.

Table of Contents

3

Working with Scenes and GameObjects

4

Grayboxing with Terrain and ProBuilder

5

Importing and Integrating Assets

9

Fullscreen Effects with postprocessing

10

Sound and Music Integration

11

User Interface Design

12

Creating Animations with Animator, Cinemachine, and Timeline

13

Introduction to Unity Scripting with C#

14

Implementing Movement and Spawning

15

Physics Collisions and Health System

16

Win and Lose Conditions

17

Scripting the UI, Sounds, and Graphics

18

Implementing Game AI for Building Enemies

19

Scene Performance Optimization

Preface

I still remember that moment of my life when I was afraid of telling my parents that I was going to study game development. At that time and where I was, that was considered a childish desire by most parents, and a career with no future, but I was stubborn enough to not care and to follow my dream. Today, game development is one of the biggest industries, generating more revenue than even the film industry.

Of course, following my dream was more difficult than I thought. Sooner or later, people chasing this particular dream have to face the fact that developing games is a difficult task that requires a deep level of knowledge in different areas. Sadly, most people give up due to this difficulty level, but I strongly believe that with proper guidance and tools, you can make your career path easier for you to follow. In my case, what helped me to flatten the learning curve was learning using Unity.

Welcome to this book about Unity 2020. Here you will learn how to use the most recent Unity features to create your first video game in the simplest way possible. Unity is a tool that provides you with powerful but easy-to-use features to solve the most common problems in game development, such as rendering, animation, physics, sound, effects, and so on. We will be using all those features to create a simple but complete game, learning all the nuances needed to handle Unity.

By the end of this book, you will be able to use Unity in a way that will allow you to start studying in depth that area of game development that you are interested in starting your career in, or that will simply allow you to create hobby games just for the joy of doing it. Unity is a versatile tool that can be used both in professional and amateur projects, and every day it is being used by more and more people.

It is worth mentioning that Unity can be used to create not only games but any kind of interactive app, from simple mobile apps to complex training or education applications (known as serious gaming), using the latest technologies, such as augmented and virtual reality. So, even if we are creating a game here, you are starting a learning path that can end in lots of possible specializations.

Who this book is for

People with different backgrounds can take advantage of either the whole book or just parts of it, thanks to the way it is structured. If you have basic **object-oriented programming (OOP)** knowledge but have never created a game before, or have never created one in Unity, you will find the book to be a nice introduction to game development and Unity's concepts, from the basic to the advanced. You will also find most of this book useful even if you are a seasoned Unity developer who wants to learn how to use its latest features.

On the other hand, if you don't have any programming knowledge, you can also gain from the book, as most chapters don't require programming experience to learn from them. Those chapters will give you a robust basic skillset using which you can start learning how to code in Unity, and by the time you have learned those basics of coding, you can get into the scripting-focused chapters of this book.

What this book covers

Chapter 1, Designing a Game from Scratch, is where we will discuss the details of the game we are going to create in the book before even opening Unity for the first time.

Chapter 2, Setting Up Unity, is where you will learn how to install and set up Unity on your computer, and is also where you will create your first project.

Chapter 3, Working with Scenes and GameObjects, is where we will learn about the concepts of Scenes and GameObjects, which are part of Unity's way of describing what your game world is composed of.

Chapter 4, Grayboxing with Terrain and ProBuilder, is where we will be creating our first level layout and prototyping it with the Terrain and ProBuilder Unity features.

Chapter 5, Importing and Integrating Assets, introduces graphics. As Unity is not a tool for creating graphics, but for displaying them, we will learn how to improve our Scene art by importing graphics into Unity.

Chapter 6, Materials and Effects with URP and Shader Graph, is where we will see how to use one of the latest Unity Render Systems (Universal Render Pipeline) and how to create effects with the Shader Graph feature.

Chapter 7, Visual Effects with Particle Systems and VFX Graph, is where you will learn how to create visual effects, for things such as water and fire, using the two main Unity tools for doing so: Particle Systems and the VFX Graph.

Chapter 8, Lighting Using the Universal Render Pipeline, covers lighting. Lighting is a concept big enough to have its own chapter. Here we will deepen our knowledge of the Universal Render Pipeline, specifically looking at its lighting capabilities.

Chapter 9, Fullscreen Effects with Post-Processing, delves into effects and post-processing. To get that cinematic effect that most modern games have today, we will learn how to add a layer of effects on top of our Scene graphics using the post-processing feature of the Universal Render Pipeline.

Chapter 10, Sound and Music Integration, gets into an often-neglected area: sound. Being underestimated by most beginner developers, here we will learn how to properly add sound and music to our game, taking into consideration its impact on performance.

Chapter 11, User Interface Design, explores the use of the **user interface** (**UI**). Of all the graphic-based ways to communicate information to the user, the use of the UI is the most direct. We will learn how to display information in the form of text, images, and life bars using the Unity UI system.

Chapter 12, Creating Animations with Animator, Cinemachine, and Timeline, moves us on from our simple static Scene. In this chapter, we will start moving our characters with animations and creating cutscenes with the latest Unity features for doing so.

Chapter 13, Introduction to Unity Scripting with C#, is the first programming chapter of the book. We will learn how to create our first script using C# in the Unity way.

Chapter 14, Implementing Movement and Spawning, is where we will learn how to program the movement of our objects and how to spawn them. General programming knowledge is assumed from now on.

Chapter 15, Physics Collisions and Health System, is where you will learn how to configure the physics settings of objects to detect when two of them collide and react to the collision. To put this in practice, we'll be creating a health system.

Chapter 16, Win and Lose Conditions, is where we will be detecting when the game should end, which will be when the player either wins it or loses it.

Chapter 17, Scripting the UI, Sounds, and Graphics, is where we will be making the previously created UI to show the relevant and current information of the game, such as the player's health and the score. Also, we'll look at sounds being played when necessary and the use of visual effects to reflect the actions of the player.

Chapter 18, Implementing Game AI to Build Enemies, is where we will be creating basic AI using several Unity features to create challenging enemies in our game.

Chapter 19, Scene Performance Optimization, explores performance. Making our game perform well is no easy task, and it is certainly a requirement if we want to release it. Here we will be learning how to profile our game's performance and tackle the most common performance issues.

Chapter 20, Building the Project, is where we will learn how to convert our Unity project into an executable format to distribute it to other people and run it without Unity being installed.

Chapter 21, Finishing Touches, is where we will briefly discuss how to move forward with the development of our game after finishing this book, discussing topics such as how to iterate and release the game.

Chapter 22, Augmented Reality in Unity, gives you an introduction to **augmented reality** (**AR**). In this extra chapter, we will be learning how to create an AR application with Unity's AR Foundation package, one of the most recently released ways to create AR applications with Unity.

To get the most out of this book

You will be developing a full project throughout the chapters of this book, and while you can just read the chapters, I highly recommend that you practice all the steps in this project as you advance through the book, to get the experience needed to properly learn the concepts we look at here. The chapters are designed so that you can customize the game according to your preferences, but do consider not deviating too much from the main idea.

The project files are split into folders per chapter and are designed in a cumulative way, each folder having just the new files introduced by the chapter or the ones that are different from previous chapters. This means, for example, that if one file doesn't change since chapter 1, you won't find it in the folders for chapter 2 onwards. You can open the scene file in each chapter folder to see how the game should look like at the end of that chapter. This allows you to see just what gets changed in each chapter and means that you can easily identify necessary changes. If, for some reason, you can't finish chapter 3, for example, you can just pick things up again with chapter 4 solved folder.

Software/Hardware covered in the book	OS requirements
Unity 2020.1	Windows, macOS X, or Linux (any)
Visual Studio 2019 Community	Windows
Xcode 11	macOSX

We advise you to type the code yourself or access the code via the GitHub repository (link available in the next section). Doing the latter will help you avoid any potential errors related to the copying and pasting of code.

Take into account that this book and its examples has been written using Unity 2020.1.0f1, the latest version available at the moment. This is the first Unity 2020 release, and while there might be newer versions, consider that if you use them, there might be slight differences in screenshots or steps depicted in the book, but nothing hard to sort out.

Download the example code files

You can download the example code files for this book from your account at `www.packt.com`. If you purchased this book elsewhere, you can visit `www.packtpub.com/support` and register to have the files emailed directly to you.

You can download the code files by following these steps:

1. Log in or register at `www.packt.com`.
2. Select the **Support** tab.
3. Click on **Code Downloads**.
4. Enter the name of the book in the **Search** box and follow the onscreen instructions.

Once the file is downloaded, please make sure that you unzip or extract the folder using the latest version of:

- WinRAR/7-Zip for Windows
- Zipeg/iZip/UnRarX for Mac
- 7-Zip/PeaZip for Linux

The code bundle for the book is also hosted on GitHub at `https://github.com/PacktPublishing/Hands-On-Unity-2020-Game-Development`. In case there's an update to the code, it will be updated on the existing GitHub repository.

We also have other code bundles from our rich catalog of books and videos available at `https://github.com/PacktPublishing/`. Check them out!

Download the color images

We also provide a PDF file that has color images of the screenshots/diagrams used in this book. You can download it here:

```
https://static.packt-cdn.com/downloads/9781838642006_
ColorImages.pdf.
```

Conventions used

There are a number of text conventions used throughout this book.

`Code in text`: Indicates code words in text, database table names, folder names, filenames, file extensions, pathnames, dummy URLs, user input, and Twitter handles. Here is an example: "Set its shader to `Universal Render Pipeline/Particles/ Unlit`."

Bold: Indicates a new term, an important word, or words that you see onscreen. For example, words in menus or dialog boxes appear in the text like this. Here is an example: "Create a new empty GameObject (using **GameObject | Create Empty**)."

> **Tips or important notes**
> Appear like this.

Get in touch

Feedback from our readers is always welcome.

General feedback: If you have questions about any aspect of this book, mention the book title in the subject of your message and email us at `customercare@packtpub.com`.

Errata: Although we have taken every care to ensure the accuracy of our content, mistakes do happen. If you have found a mistake in this book, we would be grateful if you would report this to us. Please visit `www.packtpub.com/support/errata`, selecting your book, clicking on the **Errata Submission Form** link, and entering the details.

Piracy: If you come across any illegal copies of our works in any form on the Internet, we would be grateful if you would provide us with the location address or website name. Please contact us at `copyright@packt.com` with a link to the material.

If you are interested in becoming an author: If there is a topic that you have expertise in and you are interested in either writing or contributing to a book, please visit `authors. packtpub.com`.

Reviews

Please leave a review. Once you have read and used this book, why not leave a review on the site that you purchased it from? Potential readers can then see and use your unbiased opinion to make purchase decisions, we at Packt can understand what you think about our products, and our authors can see your feedback on their book. Thank you!

For more information about Packt, please visit `packt.com`.

1
Designing a Game from Scratch

Welcome to the first chapter of the book! I am sure you are as super excited as I am to start this amazing journey into game development with Unity. We will be approaching game development in four parts. First, we will be talking about the basics of game development, looking at topics such as how to design your game before you start coding, and then we will prototype a simple first level using Unity. Then, we will dive into graphics to find out the look and feel of a good game. Later, we will learn how to get everything moving through the use of scripting; and, finally, we will see how you can finish and publish your game. As you go through the chapters, you will apply every concept to a full game project, so you will end the book with a fully functional shooter game.

In this chapter, we will design our game, Super Shooter. This phase is known as pre-production, where we will create a development plan. Our game design will include all the functionality we want in our game: the player character, the non-player characters, game assets, animations, and more. We will use screen mock-ups, as well as a narrative, to document our game's design. We will look at related concepts regarding the use of Unity for our game along the way. We will be discussing which pieces of documentation are necessary for all the design work we will be doing throughout this chapter.

Specifically, we will examine the following concepts in this chapter:

- Game concept
- Game characters
- Gameplay
- The difficulty balance
- Documentation

Game concept

Why not just start developing our game instead of designing it? This question is spawned from the excitement of developing games, especially with the Unity game engine. All games start with an idea. That idea is translated into a design, and that design is the basis for development and, eventually, the final game.

A game's design is like a blueprint for a house. You would not consider building a house without a blueprint, and it is an equally bad idea to develop a game without designing it first. The reason for this is to save time and frustration. For larger projects, time wasted also means unnecessary funds are expended.

Imagine that you employed a project team of 12 developers, animators, and artists. If you shared your game idea, would they have enough to go on? Would they do great things, but not have a cohesive set of components for your game? All we are doing with our game design is documenting as much as we can in the beginning so that the development process is purposeful. Without question, you will continually modify your game's design during development, so having a strong base from which to start is critical to your success.

Our game design will serve as the foundation for the look of our game, what the player's objectives are, what the gameplay will be, and supporting user actions, animations, audio, **artificial intelligence** (**AI**), and victory conditions. That is a lot to think about and underscores the importance of translating the game idea into the game design.

Throughout the book, we will be covering a range of components. However, in this section, we will cover those that appear in the following list:

- Game idea
- Input controls
- Winning and losing

So, let's look at each component in more detail.

Game idea

The basic concept of our Super Shooter game is that it will be a 3D game featuring a Futuristic Hero Soldier as the player character. The character must fight against Enemy Soldiers. These Enemies are intent on destroying our Hero's base and anyone that gets in their way, including our Hero. He will have a limited number of bullets he must keep track of.

Now that we have a general idea of what the game is going to be, let's talk about how the player will control the character.

Input controls

It is important to consider how players will interact with our game. The player will control our Hero using the standard set of controls. Players have an expectation that the industry norms for user controls will be implemented in games. So, our default set of user input controls, as shown in the following screenshot, will consist of the keyboard and mouse:

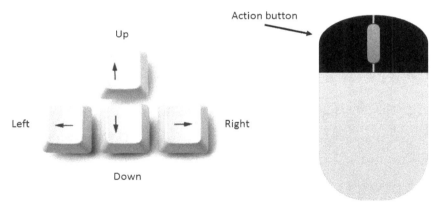

Figure 1.1 – Controls scheme

We will configure and program our game so that user input from the keyboard matches the key and action pairings shown in the following table:

Keyboard input	Action
Up arrow	Move forward
Down arrow	Move back
Left arrow	Move left
Right arrow	Move right
W	Move forward
S	Move back
A	Move left
D	Move right

Figure 1.2 – Keys mapping

The mouse will also be a significant source of user input. We will implement two components using the mouse, as indicated in the following table:

Mouse input	Action
Mouse movement	Rotate character
Left mouse button	Shoot bullet

Figure 1.3 – Mouse mapping

The left mouse button will be our action button. We will need to ensure bullets are shot only when the player has one or more bullets remaining.

That's how we handle input, but sometimes we need to end the game session! Let's talk about how the player will win and lose.

Winning and losing

Our winning condition will be when all the Enemy waves have been eliminated. There will be two different ways the player can lose the game. The first losing condition is when the base life becomes **0**. The second losing condition is if the Hero's life becomes **0**.

By this short description, you can tell that there will be several things to keep track of, including the following:

- Number of remaining Waves
- Number of our Base Life
- Number of our Hero Life

Now, we have defined what is called the game "core loop" (star a level, play it, win/lose it, and repeat). Let's dive deeper into the specific details, starting with our characters.

Game characters

Our game will feature several objects, but only two game characters. The first game character is our Hero and will be controlled by the player. The second type of game character is the Enemies. They are non-player characters that are controlled by AI. Let's look more closely at both of these characters.

Hero

The player will play our game as the Hero, our game's protagonist. This is a character that we will import for use in our game. So, what can our Hero player character do? We already know we will be able to move them throughout our game environment using a combination of keyboard and mouse inputs. We also know that the left mouse button—our action button—will cause him to shoot bullets.

> **Important Note:**
> Because the Hero is controlled by a human player, it is referred to as the Player Character.

We will implement the following animations for the Hero:

- **Idle**: This animation will play when the character is not being moved by the player.
- **Run**: This animation will play when the character is being moved by the player.
- **Shoot**: This is an animation that will cause the Hero to shoot a bullet.

That's our player. Now, let's discuss our enemy character.

Enemies

Our game's antagonist will be the Enemy Soldiers. We will control how many of them we want in our game and where they are placed. We will also control their behavior through AI. The Enemies will go straight to the base and, once there, they will start damaging it. We will determine how long it takes for our base to be completely destroyed.

> **Information Box:**
>
> Because the Enemy is controlled by AI and not a human player, it is referred to as a Non-Player Character.

We will implement the following animations for the Enemy soldiers:

- **Run**: The Enemies will be able to run toward the Hero when they see him and will stop when they are near enough to the player to start attacking him.
- **Attacking**: This animation will play when the Enemy is near enough to attack the base or the player.
- **Death**: This animation will play when the Enemy is defeated by the player.

We will require careful planning and scripting to create the desired Enemy behaviors. The number and placement of the Enemies are decisions we will need to make.

That defines our characters' details. Now, let's discuss how the game will be played, looking at the specific details.

Gameplay

The game will start with the player in the center of the game world. The Hero, controlled by the player, will need to defend the Base from the Enemies. To fend off the Enemies, the Hero will have a starting number of bullets. The goal is to defeat all the Enemies before the Base is completely destroyed by them.

Let's look at how we will make all this happen. The following gameplay components are covered in this section:

- Game-world layout
- Starting condition
- Ending condition
- Point system
- **Heads-up display** (HUD)

We will cover each of the preceding components and discuss how they change the game experience. Let's start by talking about how the game world will be designed.

Game-world layout

We will create our base environment, which consists of large metallic floor tiles, walls, doors where the enemies will be spawning, and our base building at the bottom part of the screen, where the enemies need to reach to start attacking it.

Here is a mock-up of the shape our game world will take:

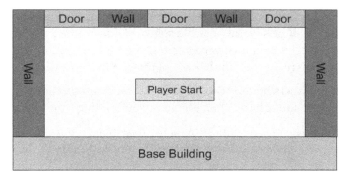

Figure 1.4 – Base layout

There are four basic things illustrated in the preceding mock-up, listed as follows:

- **Wall**: Impenetrable barriers that prevent the player from going outside the play area.

- **Door**: Impenetrable as the walls but will also serve as the Spawn Position of the Enemies. The Enemies will spawn behind them and can penetrate them to enter our Base Area.

- **Player Start**: Start Hero position.

- **Base Building**: Our Base. The enemies must be close enough to attack it.

With our base level design finished, let's discuss how the player will enter that world in a gentle way.

Starting condition

When our game is first launched, we will have several starting conditions set. Here is a list of those conditions:

- Number and placement of Enemies' Spawn Points (doors)
- Number of bullets held by the Hero
- Placement of the Base

Let's look at each of these starting conditions:

- The first starting condition is where to spawn Enemies. As you saw in our earlier mock-up, there will be several possible spawn points in the game (the doors). We will write a script to spawn waves of the enemies in random spots each time. Each wave will increase the number of enemies to increase the difficulty.
- The number of bullets held by the player must be carefully thought through. It needs to be big enough to defeat an enemy before they run out.
- Our third and final starting condition is the base placement. As you can see from the preceding screenshot, this is placed on the opposite side of the doors—so, the enemy must traverse the whole empty space between them, giving the player a chance to attack them.

We have defined the enemy spawning rules and how the player can play the game. Now, let's talk about how the game will end, looking at the exact implementation of this.

Ending condition

So far, we have established that we will track several components in the game. Let's remember them—they are as follows:

- Remaining Waves
- Base Health
- Player Health

Based on what we decided earlier regarding the end-of-game condition, we can apply the following mathematical checks to determine whether the game has ended and what the outcome is. Each end-of-game condition is listed in the following table, along with the outcome:

Condition number	End-of-game condition	Outcome
1	Remaining Waves == 0	Hero wins
2	Base Health == 0	Enemies win
3	Player Health == 0	Enemies win

Figure 1.5 – End-of-game conditions

In order to implement these three end-of-game conditions, we know we must track the number of waves, the player health, and the base health. This is mandatory.

Now that we have a full game, let's think about how we can make it more rewarding, by implementing a classic point system.

Point system

Since we are tracking key information that involves numbers, it makes it easy for us to implement a point system. We could, for example, give the player 50 points each time an Enemy is exterminated or we could also take away points each time an Enemy damages the base. In our case we will settle with just giving points when Enemies are killed, but you can feel free to expand this area if you want to.

Now, we have several systems that the player needs to be aware of, but right now, the player hasn't any way to make informed decisions about those. So, let's see how we can improve that, using an HUD.

HUD

We have decided to keep track of information during gameplay that has value beyond calculating points and the end of the game. The player will want to see this information as it tends to provide motivation and adds to the fun of the game. So, we will create an HUD for the player, and dynamically update the data in the game.

> **Information Box:**
> An HUD is a visual layer of information that is always present on the screen.

Here is a mock-up of what our HUD will look like in our Super Shooter game:

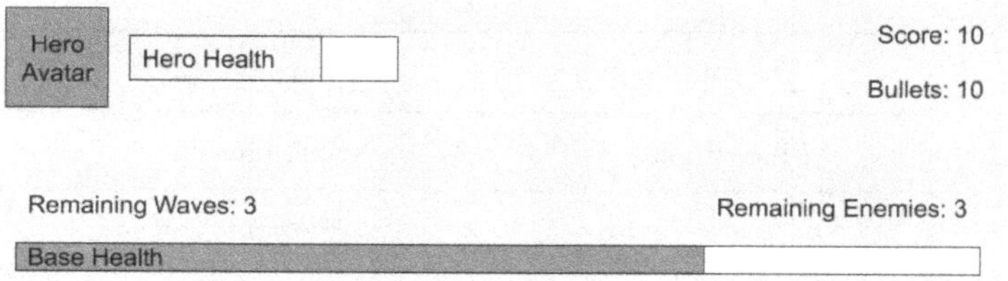

Figure 1.6 – UI layout

As you can see, there are several components to our HUD, as follows:

- **Hero Health**: A classic health bar that allows us to see visually the amount of life left. We choose a bar instead of a number because it is easier to see in the middle of an intense fight, instead of reading a number.

- **Hero Avatar**: An image next to the health bar just to show our Hero's face.

- **Score**: The number of points we have gathered.

- **Bullets**: The number of bullets remaining. The player must check this number frequently to avoid running out of bullets.

- **Remaining Waves/Enemies**: Info about the current state of the wave and game, just to let the player know when the game is going to end, putting some pressure on them in the process.

- **Base Health**: Another important piece of information. It's of sufficient size to let the player notice when the base is being attacked, and take action in that case.

Finally, we have a fully fledged game with lots of rules and specifications about how it will behave, and we can start creating our game right now. However, there's a good practice that it's never too soon to implement: balancing the game.

The difficulty balance

There are a lot of considerations to make when determining how difficult your game should be. If it is too difficult, players will lose interest, and if the game is too easy, it might not appeal to your intended audience. Some games include difficulty levels for users to select from. Other games have multiple levels, each with an increasing level of difficulty. There are several questions that we must contend with in order to achieve our desired difficulty balance.

In this section, we will first look at some questions relating to difficulty balance, followed by our implementation plan.

Difficulty balance questions

There are a lot of questions about our game that we need to consider in our game design. A review of the questions in this section will help us gain an appreciation of the issues that even a simple game such as ours must contend with, in order to achieve the desired difficulty balance.

The first set of questions, listed here, relates to the overall implementation of difficulty in our game:

- Should we have different levels of difficulty, selectable by the player?
- What specifically will be different with each difficulty level?
- Should we have multiple game levels, each with an increased amount of difficulty?
- What specifically will be different with each game level?

Consider the following questions regarding the Enemies in our game:

- How many Enemies should be spawned on each wave?
- At what distance should an Enemy become aware of the Hero?
- How much damage should an Enemy inflict on the Player with each attack?
- How much damage can an Enemy endure before it dies?

The next set of questions listed here refers to our playable character, the Hero:

- How much life should the character have?
- How much damage will the character take from a single enemy attack?
- Should the character be able to outrun Enemies?

We also have the base and bullets to account for in our game. Here are a couple of questions for each of those game assets that we will implement in our game. In the case of the base, the questions are as follows:

- How many attacks should it take for an enemy to destroy a base?
- What is the ideal max number of enemies spawned in a Wave?
- Where should Doors and the Base be located in the game environment?

And now, let's talk about questions in the case of Bullets, as follows:

- At what pace should the player run out of bullets?

- What will be the maximum number of Bullets the Player can have?

- How much damage will the bullets inflict on the Enemies?

As you can see, there are several questions that we need to answer as part of our design. Some of the questions may seem redundant as they relate to more than one component in the game. Now, let's answer some of those.

Implementation plan

Based on the questions posed in the last section, we must come up with some answers. So, let's do that here. Our first set of decisions focuses on the overall game concept, as follows:

- Implement one game level.

- Provide the user with three game difficulty settings: **easy**, **normal**, and **hard**.

Now that we've decided to create three game levels, we must determine how they will be different. This is easily managed by using a matrix. As we fill in the matrix, we will be able to document answers to most of the previously listed questions. Here is what we will refer to as the Difficulty Implementation Matrix:

Component	Easy	Normal	Hard
Number of Enemies on First Wave	X	X * 2	X * 4
Increase of Enemies per Each Wave	2	3	4
Damage from Enemies to Hero	-5 health points	-10 health points	-20 health points
Damage from Enemies to Base	-5 points	-7 points	- 9 points
Enemy Starting Health	X	X * 2	X * 5
Player Starting Health	X	X * .75	X * .5
Base Starting Health	300	400	500
Damage of Bullets to Enemies	X	X * .75	X *.50

Figure 1.7 – Difficulty pass per level

There will also be a set of decisions that will not change based on the user-selected difficulty level. Here is a list of those decisions:

- The aggressiveness of the Enemies will not change. We will script them so that if they are aware of the Hero, they will attack him.

- We will establish a pretty small vision area for the Enemies, making it easy for the Hero to sneak past them and, perhaps more importantly, outrun them.

- Respawning will be randomized between the spawn points previously identified in the game's mock-up.

It's important to take into account that this is the first balance pass, and we will surely change this based on the testing we will carry out when the game is implemented.

Now, we can say the game design is completed or can we? Actually, the game design never ends; it will keep evolving as the game is developed, but let's keep that for later. Now, let's talk about how we can communicate our great ideas with everyone in our team, using documentation.

Documentation

Now that we have covered all the main aspects of our game, it is important to prepare them to be shared with others. Through this book you will probably work alone, but in real-life productions you will likely work with others, so sharing your vision is a crucial skill you need to earn in order to create successful games. You will not be sharing your vision only with your teammates, but also with potential investors that want to put money into your game project (if you convince them to do so). In this section, we will give recommendations about how to properly format your game info into comprehensible documents.

Game Design Document (GDD)

This document is basically the Bible of your game. It contains a breakdown of all the aspects of it, each one with detailed explanations about how the different game systems should work. Here, you will put the questions and answers we previously answered in the Implementation Plan, and you will deep dive into them. Remember that you have an idea in your head, and making sure that others grasp that idea is complicated, so don't underestimate this important task.

Maybe you are making a game all by yourself and are saying you don't need a GDD because all the ideas can fit in your head, and that can be true for very small games, but any size of game and team can benefit from a GDD. It will serve as your notebook to put down your own ideas and read them. This is important because in your head everything makes sense, but once you read your own ideas and review them, you will find lots of blind spots that can be easily fixed instead of discovering them when coding the entire game.

Let's start talking about how a GDD can be structured.

GDD formats

Sadly, there's no standard or unique way of creating a GDD. Every company and team has its own way of doing this, not only in terms of which tool they use to create it but also the content of the document. This varies a lot according to the size of the team (or teams), the type of game, and the general culture of the company behind the game. As a matter of fact, some companies actually believe that there's no need to create a GDD.

A good idea to start creating them is to check out existing published GDDs of several games. There are lots of them out there, including big, well-known games (such as DOOM). Most of them are, generally, Word documents with sections explaining the game systems (such as weapons, inventory, and so on) and a list of all characters, while some can be just a list of bulletpoints explaining certain facts of the different pieces of the game. After that, you can start experimenting with different GDD formats that fit well with your project and your team.

Once you have decided on a good format, you must actually decide how you will write that format, and besides using pen and paper, a better idea is to use all those great digital tools out there. Let's see some of them.

GDD creation tools

After reviewing the existing GDDs, the next step is to pick a proper tool to write it. The first matter you need to take into account is that the GDD will change a lot very often all the time. In the process of creating the game, you will validate or discard ideas you wrote in the GDD, so using a dynamic tool is a good idea. This can be accomplished with any text processor you are familiar with, but there are other problems you need to tackle, and maybe text processors won't be enough.

Your GDD will be big I mean, BIG, even for simple games, so it will have lots of sections, and you will find cases where whole sections will refer to other sections, generating a big net of links between several parts of the document. A good tool for managing this instead of a text processor is using any kind of wiki, those being extremely useful tools that I strongly recommend using in these cases. They allow you to break down the whole GDD into articles that can be easily edited and linked to others, and, also, lots of wikis allow you to edit articles collaboratively. There are other additional features, such as comments that allow a whole conversation about a feature inside the GDD, with this recorded for future reference. The *Wikipedia* page relating to GDDs can be seen in the following screenshot:

Figure 1.8 – Wikipedia site

Moreover, you can also use other tools, such as Google Drive, which allows you to mix different types of documents—from regular text documents to dynamic slides—to create presentations, communicating complex aspects in a simple yet powerful media. Also, Google Drive has lots of great collaborative tools that improve the way several people work on the GDD.

All the tools we described are generic solutions to writing documents in general, and they can work like a charm, but there are other tools specifically crafted for games.

Now, let's start writing our GDD. I know I said there's no standard format, but let's at least see what every GDD should have, starting with the elevator pitch.

Elevator pitch

Imagine you are in a building taking an elevator, and on the next floor, an important game investor just gets in. They push the tenth-floor button, so you have eight floors of time to convince them to throw money into your pocket to help you create the game. I know this is an improbable case, but in real life, when you are in front of an investor in a round table, you won't have too much time to convince them. Remember that behind you there's a queue of maybe thousands of developers wanting to do the same, so you must be quick and visceral, and that's why having a good elevator pitch is so important.

An elevator pitch is probably the first sentence you will find in your GDD, and the most important one. It needs to describe your game in no more than two lines and convince the person reading the GDD that your game is a great idea—you need to make them want to play your game right now. Yes—it sounds super ambitious, and it is, but this can separate you from the whole crowd of developers wanting to get some funding for their game.

Again, there's no standard formula to create a successful elevator pitch (we all would be rich if such a thing existed), but here are some tips to take into account:

- You must make your pitch in no more than 10 seconds. Any longer, and you will lose the interest of the person you are trying to convince.

- You must sound convincing about your own idea; nobody is going to invest in a game you are not sure is the next big release.

- Don't use any technical words (I'm looking at you, programmers).

- Include what differentiates your game from all the other games out there.

- Iterate it until you can convince any person close to you to play the game, trying to test it with the most honest person you can find—a person that won't be bothered about shattering your idea into pieces (if your idea really deserves that).

- Practice it, over and over again, in front of a mirror, until you can say it nicely, clearly, and in one shot.

Here are some examples of an elevator pitch:

- Imagine yourself slaughtering giant Greek gods with just your arms and your strength until you become the king of Olympus. You will feel that power in [INSERT NAME OF TOTALLY NOT EXISTING GAME HERE].

- Civilization has fallen. A horrendous infection turns people into zombies. You have the only cure, and must traverse the whole country to deliver it, or humankind will collapse.

Okay—nowadays, those pitches are not super original, but a few years ago they were. Imagine the power that those pitches had at that time; you must find something similar. I'm not saying it's easy, but look how just two lines can be the start of amazing experiences, so focus first on writing those two lines, and then the rest of the game.

Now that you have gained the attention of an investor, it's time to show all the gameplay systems and the little details to them to hype them up further well, no—not right now. You just gained their attention; you haven't already convinced them. It's time to start talking a little bit about your game, and a high concept is a good way of doing so.

A high concept

A high concept is a series of statements that further describe your game, but, again, in a simple and concise way. Even if you are not trying to convince an investor, those statements will outline the way your game will be defined.

A good high concept can include sections such as the following ones:

- **Elevator pitch**: As we explained in the previous section.

- **Genre**: Maybe you are creating something new that has never been seen before, but it will probably be inspired by several other games. Here, you will specify the type of games on which you are basing your idea, so the reader of this document can start imagining how the game will be played. Later, you will specify the differences, but it is better to put a well-known idea forward first to start constructing the concept in the mind of the reader. Also, you can specify here the point of view the player will have in the game and the setting—for example, *Top-Down Medieval Roguelike* **role-playing game** (**RPG**).

- **Platform and demographics**: You need to be very clear about who will play your game. It is not the same creating a game for adults in North America as creating a game for Chinese teenagers, or games for business people who want to spend a few minutes distracted on their way home, on the bus. Those profiles will want different experiences, with different levels of challenge and game session length. They will even use different devices to play games. Taking this into account will help you find the game mechanics and balance that best fit your target audience. It's very common to say that you are creating a game for yourself, but remember that you won't be buying that game, so also think about your wallet when creating the game—for example: *Casual Players of Mobile Platforms*.

- **Features**: Create a shortlist of no more than three or five features that your game will have. Put the features you will be using from the genre you choose—for example: *you will shoot waves of enemies with a giant array of weapons. You will level up your ship to improve its stats*.

- **Unique Selling Points (USPs)**: This is similar to the features list, but here, you will include the features that differentiate your game from the others out there (no more than three or five)—for example: *you can traverse the scene using parkour-style moves. You can craft brand new weapons using looted materials*. Think about how unique those features were years ago.

Again, there's no ideal high concept. Maybe you will find some other aspects of your game that can be highlighted here and added to the document, but try to keep this all on just one page.

Now that we have discussed what every GDD *should* have, let's talk about what a GDD *may* have.

Tips for creating GDDs

Now, it's time to define what the whole game is. We said there's no standard format for GDDs, but at least we can take into account several good practices when creating them. The following list highlights a few of them:

- **Readability**: Your GDD must be prepared to be read by anyone, including people without game development knowledge. Don't use any technical words (guess who I'm still looking at), and try to keep things simple. A good test of your GDD readability is to give it to your granny or anyone that you see as being as far from gaming as possible, and that person must be able to read it.

- **Setting and introduction**: Before you start describing the game mechanics, put the reader inside the game. Describe the world, the player character, their backstory, their motivations, and what the main problem is that the player needs to struggle with. Make the reader of the GDD interested in the setting of the game and want to keep reading, to see how they will be able to play the game and tackle all the quests the player will face in the game.

- **Gameplay sections**: These are sections that break the game into several systems and subsystems linked to each other. Some examples can be Inventory, Quests, Crafting, Battle, Movement, Shops, and so on. You will want to be super specific about every aspect of how those systems work because—remember—this document will be used by the team to craft the code and assets of your game. All the previous analysis we did in the previous sections of this chapter will be here and will be further explained and analyzed.

- **Content sections**: You will want to also create content sections, such as the ones we previously designed. These can be—but are not limited to—Characters, Story, World, Levels, Aesthetics, Art Assets, Sound and Music Assets, Economics, and Input.

- **Share your idea**: Before immortalizing your ideas on the GDD and making everyone start crafting them, discuss the different GDD sections before marking them as finished. Discuss with your team, people on the internet, friends—everyone can give you valuable feedback about your idea. I'm pretty sure you are thinking that your idea will be stolen by some random person on the internet who will release the same game before you—and that can happen—but I'm not saying share the whole GDD, just some details about certain implementations you are not sure about.

- **Keep control**: Everyone in the team is a game designer—some more than others. Everyone will have ideas and things they will do differently. Listen to them—doing so will be useful, but remember you are in charge and you will have the final say. You need to be open, but set some limits and don't deviate from your original idea and concept. Prevent the famous feature creep: know when enough is enough. Again, not an easy task—you will learn this the hard way, believe me, but remember this when that happens: I told you!

- **The game will change**: I already said that, but I like to stress this as far as I can. The game will change a lot due to many reasons you will find in the process of creating it. You may find that X mechanic is not that fun, you created a better way of handling Y system, you think it's worth the time to change already existing parts of your game after a test showing that the players don't understand how to use a brand new key feature in your game, and so on. Be open to change and pivot your game idea. If you do this the right way, your game won't be as you originally imagined, but will be a better version of it.

- **Graphics**: Use graphics, diagrams, charts, and so on. Try to prevent huge text walls. Remember that an image is worth a thousand words. You are communicating, and nobody wants to spend valuable minutes trying to understand what you want to say. Improve your visual communication skills, and you will have a focused team.

- **Paper prototypes**: You can test some ideas in your head on paper before putting them in the GDD. Even if your game is a frenetic "beat 'em up," you can have little paper characters moving around a table, seeing how they can attack the player, and which movement pattern they will have. Do some math to look at the perfect timing, damage and health values, and so on.

- **Regular prototypes**: While your game is being developed the GDD will constantly change based on players' feedback. You must test your game, even if it's not finished, and get feedback from players as early as you can. Of course, they will tell you lots of things that you already know, but they will see lots of problems you don't see because you are creating and playing your game every day. They have the advantage of playing the game for the first time, and that is a real change.

Game design and GDD creation is a complex topic that can be explored in several chapters, but there are lots of books out there that do exactly that, and game design is not the main topic of this book.

After this, we can start creating our GDD, and remember: you will need to find out what the format that works best for you is.

Summary

In this chapter, we fully designed our Super Shooter game, and we plan to use our design to drive our development efforts. Our game design includes functionality, the player character, the non-player characters, game assets, animations, and more. We used screen mock-ups to help document our game's design. In addition, we planned our game's difficulty balance to help ensure the game is appropriately difficult based on user selection. We talked about what a GDD is, how we can create it, and how it and the game design will change during game production.

Remember that this is important because you want to answer all the questions you can before coding your game. If you don't do this, you will pay for it by having to recode parts of your game over and over for each unforeseen problem. You cannot prevent all possible complications, but at least a good amount was sorted out with this analysis.

In the next chapter, you will learn how to start using Unity. You will gain knowledge of why Unity is a great option to start creating games. You will be creating your first game project, and analyzing how it is composed.

2
Setting Up Unity

In this chapter, we will learn why Unity is a good **game engine** to start out with. There are lots of ways to begin a game development career, so choosing the proper tool to do so is a huge first step. Then, we will see how to install Unity and create a project with Unity Hub, a tool that manages different Unity installations and projects, helping us to deal with a whole host of them.

Specifically, we will examine the following concepts in this chapter:

- Why use a game engine such as Unity?
- Installing Unity
- Creating projects

Let's start by talking about why you should choose Unity to start your game development career.

Why use a game engine such as Unity?

When you want to create a game, you have several ways to do so, each with their pros and cons. So, why choose Unity? In this section, we will discuss the reasons for this, providing an overview of the previous and the current industry state, and specifically seeing the following concepts:

- Past and present industry insight
- Game engines
- Positives of Unity

Past and present industry insight

At the beginning, users struggled with devices with limited resources but simple game designs. As the industry evolved, the hardware became more powerful and the games more complex than before. A big AAA game title requires almost 200 developers, working on different areas of the game. Each one of those roles requires years of experience, making games an expensive and risky task: you never know whether a game is going to be a success or a big waste of money. For these reasons, it was very difficult for a single person to make an entire game.

> **Important Note:**
> AAA games are created by lots of people working in big companies, and this usually costs millions of dollars. There are also AA games, which denote the difference in team size and budget.

In the past, a programmer needed to learn how to use lots of tools in order to solve different game development problems. Some tools stopped receiving support from their creators, leaving them with unresolved bugs and features. Because of that, big companies started to hire highly skilled developers to create all those tools, resulting in what is called a game engine. Let's review what this is.

Game engines

A game engine is a set of different pieces of software that solve game development problems, such as audio, graphics, and physics issues, but that are designed to work together, all operating on the same philosophy. This is important because every team and company has its own way of working. Creating a game engine from scratch is a great task, and only a few big companies are able to do this. The game engines that companies create are usually private, so only the company is allowed to use them. Some companies sell their engine, but the cost is too high. But another way of getting game engines became available a few years ago.

You have probably heard about indie games created by between 1 and 10 developers, but how can such a small team create games? The answer is **general-purpose** game engines. These are game engines just like the ones that companies create, but they are designed to be a good foundation for every game and provide a toolset ready to be used by anyone in any game. These kinds of engines created a whole generation of enthusiast developers who are now able to develop their own games more easily than before. There were lots of game-engine companies in the past but only a few of these survive today, Unity being one of the most influential ones. But why is that? Let's discuss this further.

> **Important Note:**
> Other examples of general-purpose engines are Unreal Engine, Godot, Torque, and CryEngine.

Positives of Unity

Well, there are lots of potential reasons why Unity is so popular. Let's enumerate a few of them, as follows:

- Unity was designed with simplicity in mind, featuring a very simple and polished interface, and tools with few—but powerful—settings. This helps newcomers to not immediately feel lost the very second they start the engine.

- The programming language of Unity, C#, is very well known to both beginner and advanced programmers, and the Unity way of coding with C# is sleek and easy to understand. Unity and C# handle most of the programming problems you may encounter in other languages, decreasing your production time greatly.

- Unity was there when the mobile-gaming market era started, and its creators just put all their efforts into creating all the features any mobile engine needed. In my opinion, this is one of the most important reasons why Unity became what it is today.

- With other new technologies such as **augmented reality** (**AR**) and **virtual reality** (**VR**), Unity has expanded their use not only to gaming, but also to applications, training simulations, architecture visualization the, automotive industry, films, and so on. Using Unity, you can create applications for a wide spectrum of industries, and their use out there is increasing year on year.

- Unity has a big community of developers using it, creating bibliographies and tutorials, asking and answering questions, and creating plugins for the engine. All this helps a lot when you start using Unity because the answer to your problem is just a Google search away (and, sometimes, just a few dollars away).

- Because of its growth, there are lots of Unity jobs worldwide, more than for other game engines, and some of those jobs are looking for junior developers, so there's a big chance for a newcomer to enter the industry.

Unity is not all good—it has its cons, and there are other engines out there (such as Unreal Engine 4 or Godot) that compete with Unity over several of those limitations, having some better features than Unity but also having their own caveats. In my opinion, picking Unity or another engine depends on what you are intending to do, and what the technologies are that you are used to using, but at the end of the day, you can do everything you need just with Unity and deal with any weaknesses with the help of their big community. Now that we know about Unity, let's see how to install the engine.

Installing Unity

Okay; after all of that, you've decided to go with Unity—great decision! Now, where do we start? Let's start with a simple but necessary first step: installing Unity. It seems like a straightforward first step, but we can discuss a little bit about the proper ways to install it. In this section, we will be looking at the following concepts:

- Unity technical requirements
- Unity versions
- Installing Unity

To run Unity 2020, your computer will need to met the next requirements:

- If you use Windows, you need Windows 7 SP1 or higher, 8 or 10. Unity will run only on 64-bit versions of those systems; there is no 32-bit support.
- For Mac you need macOS High Sierra 10.13 or higher.
- For Linux you need exactly Ubuntu 16.04 or 18.04 or CentOS 7.

- Your CPU needs to support 64 bits and SSE2 (most CPUs support it).
- A graphics card with DirectX 10 support (most modern GPUs support it) on Windows, Metal support on Mac and Open GL 3.2+ or Vulkan support on Linux.

Now that we know the requirements, let's discuss the Unity versioning system.

Unity versions

In previous versions of Unity, we used to simply download the installer of a specific Unity version and hit **Next** until it was installed. But when you use Unity professionally, you need to have several versions of Unity installed because you will be working on different projects made with different versions. You may be wondering why you can't just use the latest Unity version for every project, but there are some problems with that.

In new versions of Unity, there are usually lots of changes about how the engine works, so you may need to rework lots of pieces of the game to upgrade it. Also, you may be using plugins that just haven't adapted to updates yet, so those will stop working. In my personal projects, I am used to doing project upgrades; but just for learning purposes, in a project that has a specific release date, it can take lots of time to upgrade the whole project, and that can push the release date back a lot. Maybe you need a specific feature that comes with an update that will help you a lot. In such a case, the cost of upgrading may be worthwhile, but take into account that most of the time, this doesn't happen.

Managing different projects made with different Unity versions, installing and updating new Unity releases, and so on used to be a huge hassle, but Unity Hub was created just to help us with this, and it has become the default way to install Unity. Let's see more about it.

Installing Unity with Unity Hub

Unity Hub is a small piece of software you install before installing Unity. It centralizes the management of all your Unity projects and installations. You can get it from the Unity official site. The steps to download it change frequently, but at the time of writing this book, you need to do the following:

1. Go to unity.com.
2. Click on the **Get started** blue button, as shown in the following screenshot:

Figure 2.1 – The Get started button on the Unity site

3. Click on the **Individual** tab and on the **Get started** button under the **Personal** section, as illustrated in the following screenshot:

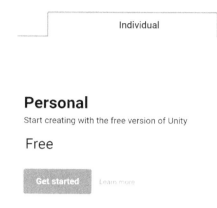

Figure 2.2 – Choosing an individual/free license

4. Click on the **Start here** button in the **New Users** section, as illustrated in the following screenshot:

Figure 2.3 – Starting the download

5. Accept the terms and conditions, as illustrated in the following screenshot:

Figure 2.4 – Agreeing to the privacy policy

6. Execute the downloaded installer.

Consider that we are using Unity Hub 2.3.2, the latest version at the moment of writing this book. If you use a newer one some steps might change, but the main concepts usually remain. Now that we have Unity Hub installed, we must use it to install a specific Unity version. You can do this with the following steps:

1. Start Unity Hub.

2. It may ask you to create a Unity account. If so, just create one and log in with that account. If not, click the person icon at the top-right part of the window and select **Sign in** to have the option to log in or create an account, as illustrated in the following screenshot:

Figure 2.5 – Logging in to Unity Hub

3. Follow the steps on the installer and then, you should see the following screen:

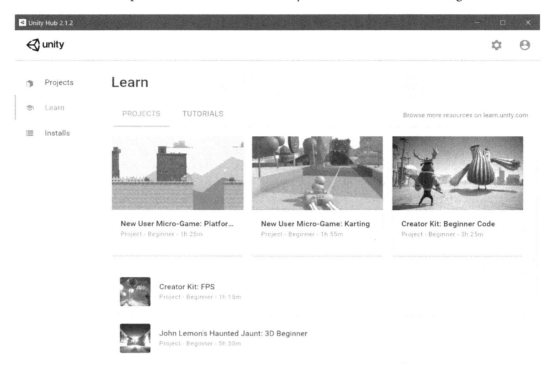

Figure 2.6 – Unity Hub window

4. Newer versions of Unity guides you through the Unity Installation and first project creation. In that case skip the next steps, but if you already have Unity installed, please follow them

5. Click on the **Installs** button and check if you have Unity 2020 listed there. If not press the **ADD** button. Make sure the latest Unity 2020 release (in my case Unity 2020.1.0f1) is selected, and then click on the **NEXT** button. Your screen may show a newer version than mine, so don't worry about that. The process is illustrated in the following screenshot:

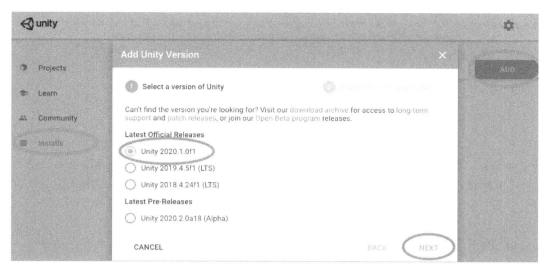

Figure 2.7 – Picking the Unity version to install

> **Important Note:**
> This is the program we will use in *Chapter 13, Introduction to Scripting with C#*, to create our code. We do not need the other Unity features right now, but you can go back later and install them if you need them.

6. A feature selection window will show up. Make sure **Microsoft Visual Studio Community** is checked. At the time of writing this book, the latest version is 2019, but a newer one could work just as well. Now, click the **NEXT** button. The process is illustrated in the following screenshot:

✓ Microsoft Visual Studio Community 2019	1.4 GB	1.3 GB
Platforms		
> ☐ Android Build Support	243.1 MB	1.1 GB
☐ iOS Build Support	365.8 MB	1.6 GB
☐ tvOS Build Support	362.2 MB	1.6 GB
☐ Linux Build Support (Mono)	59.0 MB	274.7 MB
☐ Mac Build Support (Mono)	92.4 MB	480.2 MB
CANCEL	BACK	NEXT

Figure 2.8 – Selecting Visual Studio

7. Accept Visual Studios terms and conditions, as illustrated in the following screenshot:

Figure 2.9 – Accepting Visual Studio's terms and conditions

8. You will see the selected Unity version downloading and installing in the list. Wait for this to finish. In the following screenshot, you will see that I have other Unity versions installed, but you will only be seeing one version, which is fine:

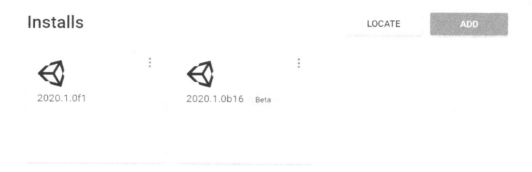

Figure 2.10 – All Unity installations I currently have on my machine

9. After Unity has finished installing, Visual Studio Installer will automatically execute. It will download an installer that will download and install Visual Studio Community 2019, as illustrated in the following screenshot:

Figure 2.11 – Installing Visual Studio

Remember that the preceding steps may be different in new Unity versions, so just try to follow the flow that Unity designed—most of the time, it is intuitive. Now is the time to create a project using Unity.

Creating projects

Now that we have Unity installed, we can start creating our game. To do so, we first need to create a project, which is basically a folder containing all the files that your game will be composed of. These files are called assets and there are different types of them, such as images, audio, 3D models, script files, and so on. In this section, we will see how to manage a project, addressing the following concepts:

- Creating a project
- Project structure

Creating a project

As with Unity installations, we will use Unity Hub to manage projects. We need to follow these steps to create one:

1. Open Unity Hub and click on the **Projects** button, and then click on **NEW**, as illustrated in the following screenshot:

Figure 2.12 – Creating a new project in Unity Hub

2. Pick the **Universal Render Pipeline** template, then a project name and a location, and hit **Create**. We will be creating a 3D game with simple graphics, prepared to run on every device Unity can be executed on, so the **Universal Render Pipeline** (or **URP**) is the better choice for that. In *Chapter 6, Materials and Effects with URP and Shader Graph*, we will be discussing exactly why. The process can be seen in the following screenshot:

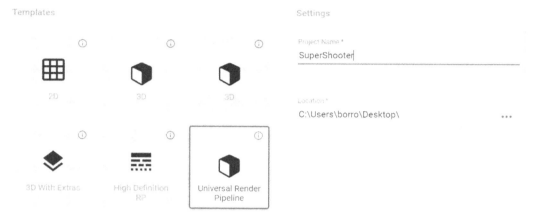

Figure 2.13 – Selecting the Universal Render Pipeline template

> **Important Note:**
>
> Try to put the project in Dropbox, Google Drive, or any cloud-synchronized folder to make sure you always have the project at hand. This project will grow, so make sure you have enough space in that folder. If you don't have enough space in your hosting service, just skip this. If you know how to use Git, that would be a better option.

3. Unity will create and automatically open the project. This can take a while, but after that, you will see a screen similar to the one shown in the following screenshot:

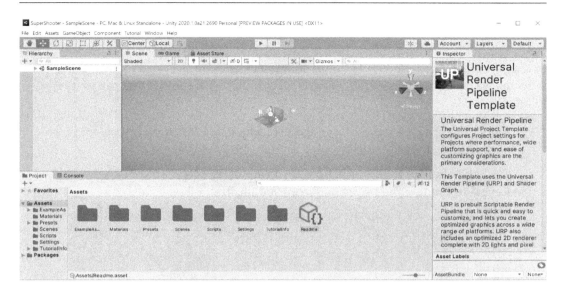

Figure 2.14 – The Unity Editor window

4. Try closing the window and opening it again, then going back to Unity Hub and picking the project from the list, as follows:

Figure 2.15 – Reopening the project

Now that we have created the project, let's explore its structure.

Project structure

We have just opened Unity but we won't start using it until the next chapter. Now, it's time to see how the project folder structure is composed. To do so, we need to open the folder in which we created the project. If you don't remember where this is, you can do the following:

1. Right-click the `Assets` folder in the **Project** panel, located in the bottom part of the editor.

2. Click the **Show in Explorer** option. If you are using a Mac, the option is called **Reveal in Finder**. The following screenshot illustrates this:

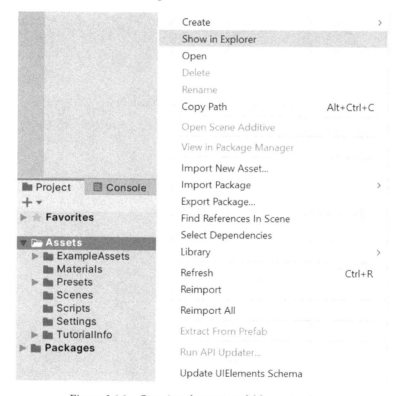

Figure 2.16 – Opening the project folder in Explorer

Then, you will see the following folder structure:

Figure 2.17 – Unity project folder structure

If anytime you want to move this project to another PC or send it to a colleague, you can just compress all those files and send it to them as a ZIP file, but not all the folders are necessary all of the time. The important folders are `Assets`, `Packages`, and `ProjectSettings`. The `Assets folder` will hold all the files we will create and use for our game, so this is a must. We will also configure different Unity systems to tailor the engine to our game. All the settings related to this are in the `ProjectSettings` folder. Finally, we will install different Unity modules or packages to expand its functionality, so the `Packages` folder will hold which ones we are using, for Unity to be aware of that. It's not necessary to copy the rest of the folders if you need to move the project elsewhere, but let's at least discuss what the `Library` folder is.

Unity needs to convert the files we will use into its own format in order to operate, and an example would be audio and graphics. Unity supports **MPEG Audio Layer 3 (MP3)**, **Waveform Audio File Format (WAV)**, **Portable Network Graphics (PNG)**, and **Joint Photographic Experts Group (JPG)** files (and much more), but prior to using them, they need to be converted into Unity's internal formats. Those converted files will be in the **Library** folder. If you copy the project without that folder, Unity will simply take the original files in the `Assets` folder and recreate the `Library` folder entirely. This process can take time, and the bigger the project, the more time involved.

Take into account that you want to have all the folders Unity created while you are working on the project, so don't delete any of them while doing so, but if you need to move an entire project, you now know exactly what you need to take with you.

Summary

In this chapter, we discussed why Unity is a great tool for creating games, comparing it with other engines in the market. This analysis has the intention of helping you choose Unity as your first game development tool. After that, we also reviewed how to install and manage different Unity versions using Unity Hub, and, finally, we saw how to create and manage multiple projects with the same tool. We will use Unity Hub a lot, so it is important to know how to use it initially. Now, we are prepared to dive into the Unity Editor.

In the next chapter, we will start learning the basic Unity tools to author our first-level prototype.

3
Working with Scenes and GameObjects

Welcome to the third chapter of the book—here is where the hard work starts! In this chapter, we will develop some base knowledge of Unity in order to edit a project. We will see how to use several Unity Editor windows to manipulate our first scene and its objects. Also, we will learn how an object or Game Object is created and composed and how to manage complex scenes with multiple objects using Hierarchies and Prefabs. Finally, we will review how we can properly save all our work to continue working on it later.

Specifically, we will examine the following concepts in this chapter:

- Manipulating scenes
- GameObjects and components
- Object hierarchies
- Prefabs
- Saving scenes and projects

Manipulating scenes

A **scene** is one of the several kinds of files (also known as **Assets**) in our project. A scene can mean different things according to the type of project or the way a company is used to working, but the most common use case is to separate your game into whole sections, the most common ones being the following:

- Main Menu
- Level 1, Level 2, Level 3, …, Level N
- Victory Screen, Lose Screen
- Splash Screen, Loading Screen

In this section, we will cover the following concepts related to scenes:

- The purpose of a scene
- The Scene View
- Our first GameObject
- Navigating the Scene View
- Manipulating GameObjects

The purpose of a scene

The idea of separating your game into scenes is that you will process and load just the data needed for the scene; so, if you are in the Main Menu you will have only the textures, music, and objects that that particular scene needs—there's no need to have the Level 10 Boss loaded in **random-access memory** (**RAM**) if you don't need it right now. That's why loading screens exist, just to fill the time between unloading the Assets needed in one scene and loading the ones needed in another. Maybe you are thinking that open-world games such as **Grand Theft Auto** (**GTA**) don't have loading screens while you roam around in the world, but they are actually loading and unloading chunks of the world in the background as you move, and those chunks are different scenes that are designed to be connected to each other.

The difference between the Main Menu and a regular level scene are the objects (also known as GameObjects) they have. In a menu, you will find objects such as a background, music, buttons, and logos, and in a level you will have the player, enemies, platforms, health boxes, and so on. So, it is up to you and the GameObjects you put in the scene to decide what that scene means for your game.

But how can we create a scene? Let's start with the Scene View.

The Scene View

When you open a Unity project, you will see the Unity Editor. It will be composed of several windows or **panels**, each one helping you to change different aspects of your game. In this chapter, we will be looking at the windows that help you author scenes. The Unity Editor is shown in the following screenshot:

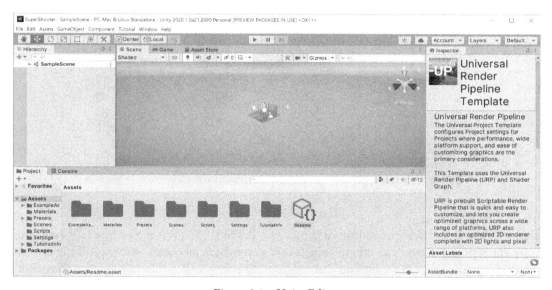

Figure 3.1 – Unity Editor

If you have ever programmed any kind of application before, you are probably used to having a starting function, such as **Main**, where you start writing code to create several objects needed for your app, and if we are talking about games, you probably create all the objects for the scene here. The problem with this approach is that in order to ensure all objects are created properly, you will need to run the program to see the results, and if something is misplaced you will need to manually change the coordinates of the object, which is a slow and painful process. Luckily, in Unity, we have the **Scene** View, an example of which is shown in the following screenshot:

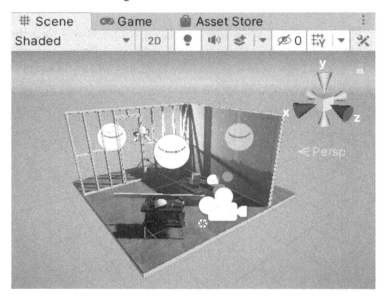

Figure 3.2 – Scene View

This window is an implementation of the classic **WYSIWYG (What You See Is What You Get)** concept. Here, you can create objects and place them all over the scene, all through a scene previsualization where you can see how the scene will look when you hit **Play**. But before learning how to use this scene, we need to have an object in the scene, so let's create our first object.

Our first GameObject

The Unity **Universal Render Pipeline (URP)** template comes with a construction site test scene, but let's create our own empty scene to start exploring this new concept. To do that, you can simply use the **File | New Scene** menu options to create an empty new scene, as illustrated in the following screenshot:

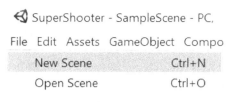

Figure 3.3 – Creating a new scene

We will learn several ways of creating GameObjects throughout the book, but now, let's start using some basic templates Unity provides us. In order to create them, we will need to open the **GameObject** menu at the top of the Unity window, and it will show us several template categories, such as **3D Object**, **2D Object**, **Effects**, and so on, as illustrated in the following screenshot:

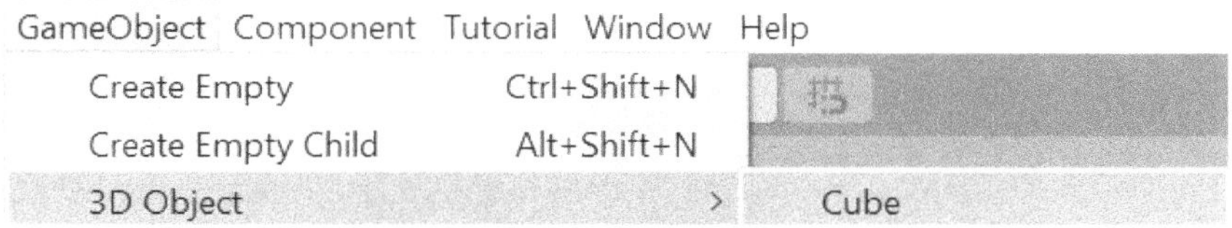

Figure 3.4 – Creating a cube

Under the **3D Object** category, we will see several 3D primitives such as **Cube**, **Sphere**, **Cylinder**, and so on, and while using them is not as exciting as using beautiful downloaded 3D models, remember that we are prototyping our level, also known as gray-boxing. This means that we will use lots of prototyping primitive shapes to model our level so that we can quickly test it and see whether our idea is good enough to start the complex work of converting it to a final version.

I recommend you pick the **Cube** object to start with because it is a versatile shape that can represent lots of objects. So, now that we have a scene with an object to edit, the first thing we need to learn to do with the scene view is to navigate through the scene.

Navigating the Scene View

In order to manipulate a scene, we need to learn how to move through it to view the results from different perspectives. There are several ways to navigate it, so let's start with the most common one: the first-person view. This view allows you to move through the scene using first-person-shooter-like navigation, using the mouse and the *WASD* keys. To navigate like this, you will need to press and hold the right mouse button, and while doing so, you can move the mouse to rotate the camera and press the *WASD* keys to move it. You can also press *Shift* to move faster and press the *Q* and *E* keys to move up and down.

Another common way of moving is to click an object to select it (the selected object will have an orange outline), and then press the *F* key to focus it, making the Scene View camera immediately move into a position where we to look at that object more closely. After that, we can press and hold the left *Alt* key and the left mouse button, and start moving the mouse to "orbit" around the object and see different angles to check that every part of it is properly placed, as demonstrated in the following screenshot:

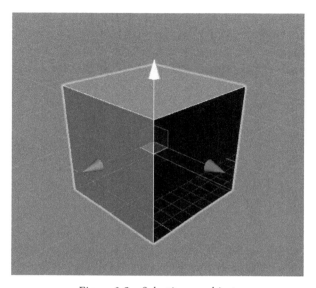

Figure 3.5 – Selecting an object

Now that we can move freely through the scene, we can start using the Scene View to manipulate GameObjects.

Manipulating GameObjects

Another use of the Scene View is to manipulate the locations of objects. In order to do so, we first need to select an object, and then press the *Y* key on the keyboard or the sixth button to the right in the top-left corner of the Unity Editor, shown in the following screenshot:

Figure 3.6 – Changing the transformation tool

This will show what is called the **Transform Gizmo** over the selected object, which allows us to change the position, rotation, and scale of the object, as illustrated in the following screenshot:

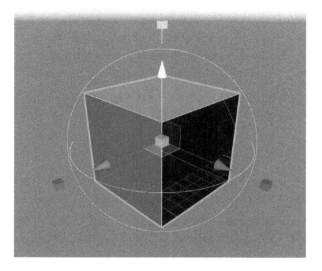

Figure 3.7 – Transform Gizmo

Let's start translating the object, which is accomplished by dragging the red, green, and blue arrows inside the Gizmo´s sphere. While you do this, you will see how the object will be moving along the selected axis. An interesting concept to explore here is the meaning of the color of those arrows. If you pay attention to the top-right area of the Scene View, you will see an axis Gizmo that serves as a reminder of those colors' meaning, as illustrated in the following screenshot:

Figure 3.8 – Axis Gizmo

Computer graphics use the classic 3D **Cartesian coordinate system** to represent objects' locations. The red color is associated with the *x* axis of the object, green with the *y* axis, and blue with the *z* axis. But what does each axis mean? If you come from another 3D authoring program, this can be different, but in Unity, the *z* axis (blue) represents the **Forward Vector**, which means that the arrow is pointing along the front of the object; the *x* axis is the **Right Vector**, and the *y* axis represents the **Up Vector**. Consider that those axes are **local**, meaning that if you rotate the object, they will change the direction they face because the orientation of the object changes the way the object is facing. Unity can show those axes in **global** coordinates if necessary, but for now, let's stick with local.

In order to be sure that we are working with local coordinates, make sure **Local** mode is activated, as shown in the following screenshot:

Figure 3.9 – Switching between pivot and local coordinates

If you see **Global** instead of **Local** as the right button, just click it and it will change. By the way, try to keep the left button as **Pivot**. If it says **Center**, just click it to change it.

I know—we are editing a cube, so there is no clear front or right side, but when you work with real 3D models such as cars and characters, they will certainly have those sides, and they must be properly aligned with those axes. If by any chance in the future you import a car into Unity and the front of the car is pointing along the red axis (X), you will need to fix that because our future moving code will rely on that convention, but let's keep that for later.

Now, let's use this Transform Gizmo to rotate the object using the three colored circles around it. If you click and drag, for example, the red circle, you will rotate the object along the *x* rotation axis. Here is another interesting tip to consider. If you want to rotate the object horizontally, based on the color-coding we previously discussed, you will probably pick the *x* axis—the one that is used to move horizontally—but, sadly, that's wrong.

A good way to look at rotation is like the accelerator of a bike: you need to take it and roll it. If you rotate the *x* axis like this, you will rotate the object up and down. So, in order to rotate horizontally, you would need to use the green circle or the *y* axis. The process is illustrated in the following screenshot:

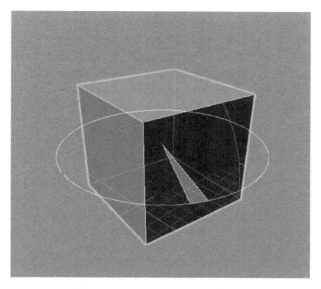

Figure 3.10 – Rotating an object

Finally, we have scaling, which is done through the colored cubes on the outer side of the Transform Gizmo sphere. If you click and drag those, you will see how our cube is stretched over those axes, allowing you to change the size of the object. Also, you will have a gray cube in the center of the gizmo that allows you to change the size of the object uniformly along all the axes. The process is illustrated in the following screenshot:

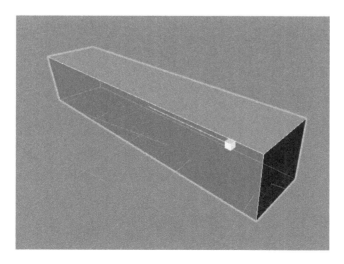

Figure 3.11 – Scaling an object

Remember that scaling objects is usually a bad practice in many cases. In the final versions of your scene, you will use models with the proper size and scale, and they will be designed in a modular way so that you can plug them one next to the other. If you scale them, several bad things can happen, such as textures being stretched and becoming pixelated, and modules that no longer plug properly. There are some exceptions to this rule, such as placing lots of instances of the same tree in a forest and changing its scale slightly to simulate variation, and, in the case of gray-boxing, it is perfectly fine to take cubes and change the scale to create floors, walls, ceilings, columns, and so on, because in the end, those cubes will be replaced with real 3D models.

CHALLENGE

Create a room composed of a floor, three regular walls, and a fourth wall with a hole for a door (three cubes). In the following screenshot, you can see how it should look:

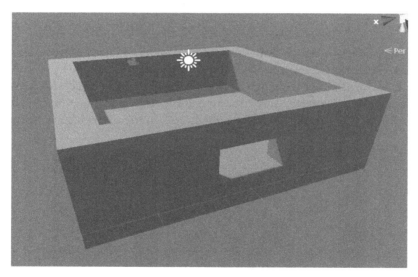

Figure 3.12 – Room task finished

Now that we can edit an object's location, let's see how we can edit all its other aspects.

GameObjects and components

We talked about our project being composed of Assets, and that a Scene (a specific type of Asset) is composed of GameObjects; so, how can we create an object? Through the composition of **components**.

In this section, we will cover the following concepts related to components:

- Components
- Manipulating components

Components

A **component** is one of several pieces a Game Object can be made of; each one is in charge of different features of the object. There are several components that solve different tasks, such as playing a sound, rendering a mesh, applying physics, and so on, and even if Unity has a large number of components, we will eventually need to create custom components, sooner or later. In the following screenshot, you can see what Unity shows us when we select a Game Object:

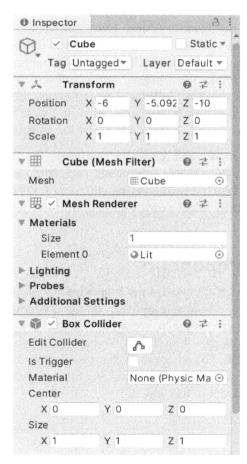

Figure 3.13 – The Inspector panel

In the previous screenshot, we can see the **Inspector** panel, and if we needed to guess what it does, right now we could say it is showing all the properties of the selected object and that we can configure them to change the behavior of the object, such as the position and rotation, whether it will project shadows or not, and so on. That is true, but we are missing a key element: those properties don't belong to the object; they belong to the components of the object. We can see some titles in bold before a group of properties, such as **Transform** and **Box Collider**, and so on. Those are the components of the object.

In this case, our object has a **Transform**, a **Mesh Filter**, a **Mesh Renderer**, and a **Box Collider** component, so let's review each one of those. **Transform** just has location information, such as the position, rotation, and scale of the object, and by itself it does nothing—it's just a point in our game—but as we add components to the object, that position starts to have more meaning. That's because some components will interact with **Transform** and other components, each one affecting the other.

An example of that would be the case of **Mesh Filter** and **Mesh Renderer**, both of those being in charge of rendering a 3D model. **Mesh Renderer** will render the mesh specified in the **Mesh Filter** in the position specified in the Transform component, so **Mesh Renderer** needs to get data from those other components and can't work without them. Another example would be the **Box Collider**. This represents the physical shape of the object, so when the physics calculates collisions between objects, it checks whether that shape is colliding with other shapes based on the position specified in the Transform.

We don't want to explore physics and rendering right now. The takeaway from this section is that a GameObject is a collection of components, each component adding a specific behavior to our object, and each one interacting with the others to accomplish the desired task. To further reinforce this, let's see how we can convert a cube into a sphere that falls using physics.

Manipulating components

The tool to edit an object's components is the **Inspector**. It not only allows us to change components' properties, but also lets us add and remove components. In this case, we want to convert a cube to a sphere, so we need to change several aspects of those components. We can start by changing the visual shape of the object, so we need to change the rendered model or **Mesh**. The component that specifies the Mesh to be rendered is the **MeshFilter** component. If we look at it, we can see a **Mesh** property that says **Cube** and that has a little circle with a dot to its right.

> **Important note**
>
> If you don't see any property such as the Mesh we just mentioned, try to click the triangle at the left of the component's name. Doing this will expand and collapse all the component's properties. This is illustrated in the following screenshot:

Box Collider
Edit Collider

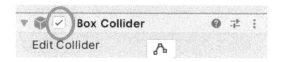

Figure 3.14 – Disabling a component

If we click it, the **Select Mesh** window will pop up, allowing us to pick several Mesh options; so, in this case, select the **Sphere** component. In the future, we will add more 3D models to our project so that the window will have more options. The mesh selector is shown in the following screenshot:

Select Mesh
Assets
Scene
safety_go...
safety_hat...
stud
stud_frame

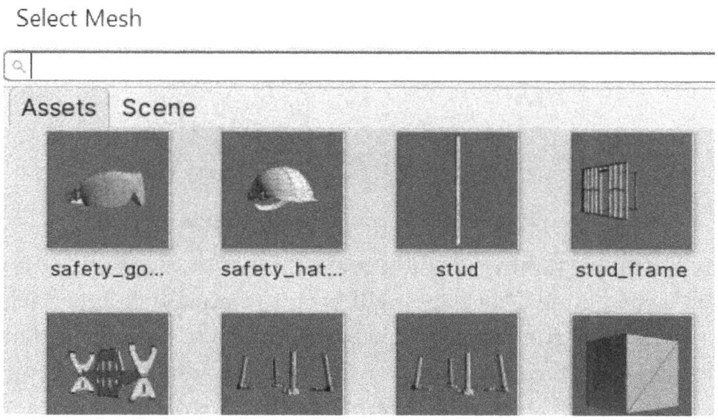

Figure 3.15 – Mesh selector

Okay—it looks like a sphere, but will it behave like a sphere? Let's find out. In order to do so, we can add a **Rigidbody** component to our sphere, which will add physics to it. In order to do so, we need to click the **Add Component** button at the bottom of the **Inspector**. It will show a **Component Selector** window with lots of categories, and, in this case, we need to click on the **Physics** category. The window will show all the Physics components, and there we can find the **Rigidbody**. Another option would be to type Rigidbody in the search box at the top of the window. The following screenshot illustrates how to add a component:

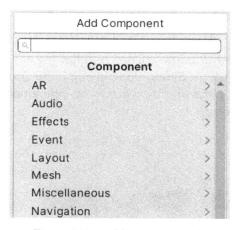

Figure 3.16 – Adding components

If you hit the Play button in the top-middle part of the editor, you can test your sphere physics using the **Game** panel. That panel will be automatically focused when you hit Play and will show you how the player will see the game. One problem that can happen here is that maybe you won't see anything, and that can happen if the game camera is not pointing to where our sphere is located. The playback controls are shown in the following screenshot:

Figure 3.17 – Playback controls

Here, you can just use the Transform Gizmo to rotate and position your camera in such a way that it looks at our sphere. While you are moving, you can check the little preview in the bottom-right part of the scene window to check out the new camera perspective. Another alternative would be to select the camera in the **Hierarchy** and use the shortcut *Ctrl + Shift + F* (or *command + Shift + F* on a Mac). The camera preview is shown in the following screenshot:

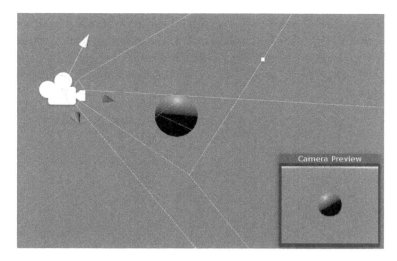

Figure 3.18 – Camera preview

Now, to test whether Physics collisions are executing properly, let's create a cube, scale it until it has the shape of a ramp, and put that ramp below our sphere, as follows:

Figure 3.19 – Ball and ramp objects

If you hit Play now, you will see the sphere colliding with our ramp, but in a strange way. It looks like it's bouncing, but that's not the case. If you expand the **Box Collider** component of our sphere, you will see that even if our object looks like a sphere, the green box gizmo is showing us that our sphere is actually a box in the Physics world, as illustrated in the following screenshot:

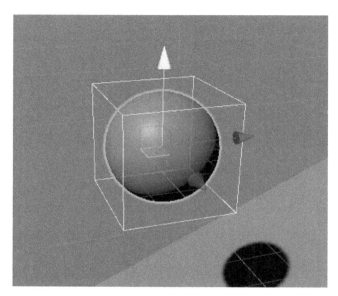

Figure 3.20 – Object with sphere graphic and box collider

Nowadays, video cards can handle rendering highly detailed models (with high polygon counts), but the Physics system is executed in the **central processing unit** (**CPU**) and it needs to do complex calculations in order to detect collisions. To get decent performance in our game (at least 30 **frames per second** (**FPS**)) the Physics system works using simplified collision shapes that may differ from the actual shape the player sees on the screen. That's why we have **Mesh Filter** and the different types of Collider components separated—one handles visual shape and the other the physics shape.

Again, the idea of this section is not to deep dive into those Unity systems, so let's just move on for now. How can we solve this? Simple: by modifying our components! In this case, **BoxCollider** can just represent a box shape, unlike **MeshFilter**, which supports any shape. So, first, we need to remove it by right-clicking the component's title and selecting the **Remove Component** option, as illustrated in the following screenshot:

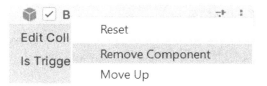

Figure 3.21 – Removing components

Now, we can again use the **Add Component** menu to select a **Physics** component, this time selecting the **Sphere Collider** component. If you look at the Physics components, you will see other types of colliders that can be used to represent other shapes, but we will look at them later in *Chapter 15, Physics Collisions and Health System*. The **Sphere Collider** component can be seen in the following screenshot:

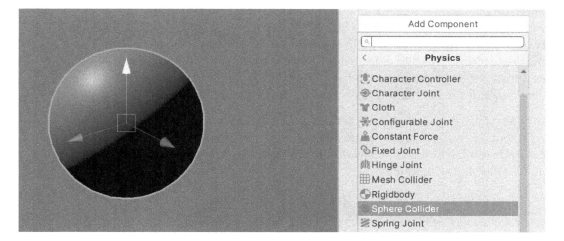

Figure 3.22 – Adding a Sphere Collider component

So, if you hit Play now, you will see that our sphere not only looks like a sphere, but also behaves as one. Remember: the main idea of this section of the book is understanding that in Unity you can create whatever object you want just by adding, removing, and modifying components, and we will be doing a lot of this throughout the book.

Now, components are not the only thing needed in order to create objects. Complex objects may be composed of several sub-objects, so let's see how that works.

Object hierarchies

Some complex objects may need to be separated in sub-objects, each one with its own components. Those sub-objects need to be somehow attached to the main object and work together to create the necessary object behavior.

In this section, we will cover the following concepts related to components:

- Parenting of objects
- Possible uses

Parenting of objects

Parenting consists of making an object the child of another, meaning that those objects will be related to each other. One type of relationship that happens is a **Transform relationship**, meaning that a child object will be affected by the parent's Transform. In simple terms, the child object will follow the parent, as if it is attached to it. In an example, imagine a player with a hat on their head. The hat can be a child of the player's head, making the hat follow the head while they are attached.

In order to try this, let's create a capsule that represents an enemy and a cube that represents the weapon of the enemy. Remember that in order to do, so you can use the **GameObject | 3D Object | Capsule** and **Box** options. An example capsule can be seen in the following screenshot:

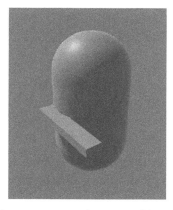

Figure 3.23 – A capsule representing a human and box representing a weapon

If you move the enemy object (the capsule), the weapon (the box) will keep its position, not following our enemy. So, in order to prevent that, we can simply drag the weapon to the enemy object in the **Hierarchy** window, as illustrated in the following screenshot:

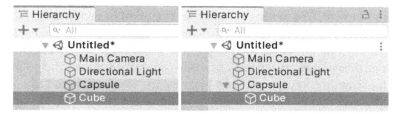

Figure 3.24 – Parenting the cube weapon to the capsule character

Now, if you move the enemy, you will see the gun moving, rotating, and being scaled along with it. So, basically, the gun transform also has the effects of the enemy Transform component.

Now that we have done some basic parenting, let's explore other possible uses.

Possible uses

There are some other uses of parenting aside from creating complex objects. Another common usage for it is to organize the project Hierarchy. Right now, our scene is simple, but in time it will grow, so keeping track of all the objects will become difficult. So, to prevent this, we can create empty GameObjects (in **GameObject | Create Empty**) to act as containers, putting objects into them just to organize our scene. Try to use this with caution, because this has a performance cost if you abuse it. Generally, having one or two levels of parenting when organizing a scene is fine, but more than that can have a performance hit. Consider that you can—and will—have deeper parenting for the creation of complex objects; the proposed limit is just for scene organization.

To keep improving on our previous example, duplicate the enemy a couple of times all around the scene, create an empty Game Object called **Enemies**, and drag all the enemies into it so that it will act as a container. This is illustrated in the following screenshot:

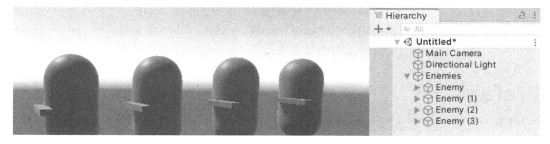

Figure 3.25 – Grouping enemies in a parent object

Another common usage of parenting is to change the **pivot** or center of an object. Right now, if we try to rotate our gun with the Transform Gizmo, it will rotate around its center because the creator of that cube decided to put the center there. Normally, that's okay, but let's consider the case where we need to make the weapon aim at the point where our enemy is looking. In this case, we need to rotate the weapon around the weapon handle; so, in the case of this "box" weapon, it would be the closest end to the enemy. The problem here is that we cannot change the center of an object, so one solution would be to create another "weapon" 3D model or mesh with another center, which will lead to lots of duplicated versions of the weapon if we consider other possible gameplay requirements such as a rotating weapon pickup. We can fix this easily using parenting.

The idea is to create an empty GameObject and locate it where we want the new pivot of our object to be. After that, we can simply drag our weapon inside this empty GameObject, and, from now on, consider the empty object as the actual weapon. If you rotate or scale this weapon container, you will see that the weapon mesh will apply those transformations around this container, so we can say the pivot of the weapon has changed (actually, it hasn't, but our container simulates the change). The process is illustrated in the following screenshot:

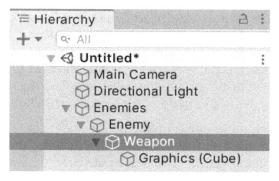

Figure 3.26 – Changing the weapon pivot

Now, let's continue seeing different ways of managing GameObjects, using Prefabs this time.

Prefabs

In the previous example, we created lots of copies of our enemy around the scene, but in doing so, we have created a new problem. Let's imagine we need to change our enemy and add a **Rigidbody** component to it, but because we have several copies of the same object, we need to take them one by one and add the same component to all of them. Maybe later, we will need to change the mass of each enemy, so again, we need to go over each one of the enemies and make the change, and here we can start to see a pattern.

One solution could be to select all the enemies using the *Ctrl* key (*option* on a Mac) and modify all of them at once, but that solution won't be of any use if we have enemy copies in other scenes. So, here is where Prefabs come in.

In this section, we will cover the following concepts related to Prefabs:

- Creating Prefabs
- Prefab-instance relationship
- Prefab variants

Creating Prefabs

A Prefab is a Unity tool that allows us to convert custom-made objects, such as our enemy, into an Asset that defines how they can be created. We can use them to create new copies of a custom object easily, without needing to create its components and sub-objects all over again.

In order to create a Prefab, we can simply drag our custom object from the **Hierarchy** window to the **Project** window, and after doing that you will see a new Asset in your project files. The **Project** window is where you can navigate and explore all your project files; so, in this case, our Prefab is the first Asset we ever created. Now, you can simply drag the Prefab from the **Project** window into the Scene to easily create new Prefab copies, as illustrated in the following screenshot:

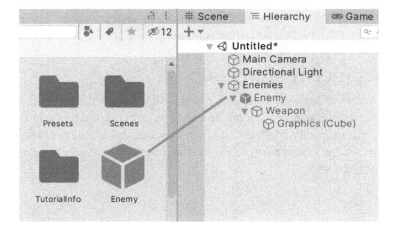

Figure 3.27 – Creating a Prefab

Now, we have a little problem here. If you pay attention to the **Hierarchy** window, you will see the original Prefab objects and all the new copies with its names in blue, while the enemies created before the Prefab will have its names in black. The blue in a name means that the object is an **instance** of a Prefab, meaning that the object was created based on a Prefab. We can select those blue named objects and click the **Select** button in the **Inspector** to select the original Prefab that created that object. This is illustrated in the following screenshot:

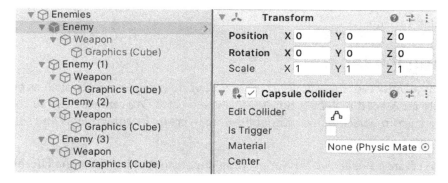

Figure 3.28 – Detecting Prefabs in the hierarchy

So, the problem here is that the previous copies of the Prefab are not instances of the original Prefab, and sadly there's no way to make them be connected to the Prefab. So, in order to make that happen, we need to simply destroy the old copies and replace them with copies created with the Prefab. At first, not having all copies as instances doesn't seem to be a problem, but it will be in the next section of this chapter, where we will explore the relationship between the Prefabs and their instances.

Prefab-instance relationship

An instance of a Prefab has a binding to the Prefab that helps to revert and apply changes easily between them. If you take a Prefab and make some modifications to it, those changes will be automatically applied to all instances across all the scenes in the project, so we can easily create a first version of the Prefab, use it all around the project, and then experiment with changes.

To practice this, let's say we want to add a **Rigidbody** component to the enemies so that they can fall. In order to do so, we can simply double-click the Prefab file and we will enter Prefab Edit Mode, where we can edit the Prefab isolated from the rest of the scene. Here, we can simply take the Prefab root object and add the **Rigidbody** component to it. After that, we can simply click on the **Scenes** button in the top-left part of the **Scene** window to get back to the scene we were editing, and now, we can see that all the Prefab instances of the enemy have a **Rigidbody** component, as illustrated in the following screenshot:

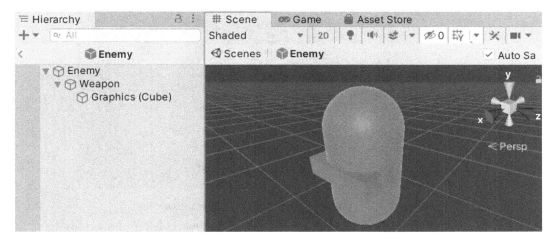

Figure 3.29 – Prefab Edit Mode

Now, what happens if we change a Prefab instance instead? Let's say we want one specific enemy to fly, so they won't suffer the effect of gravity. We can do that by simply selecting the specific Prefab and unchecking the **Use Gravity** checkbox in the **Rigidbody** component. After doing that, if we play the game, we will see that only that specific instance will float. That's because changes of an instance of a Prefab became an **override**, and we can see that clearly if you see how the **Use Gravity** property of that instance becomes bold in the **Inspector**. Let's take another object and change its **Scale** property to make it bigger. Again, we will see how the **Scale** property becomes bold, and with a little bar at its left. The **Use Gravity** checkbox can be seen in the following screenshot:

▼ 🌐 **Rigidbody**	
Mass	1
Drag	0
Angular Drag	0.05
Use Gravity	☐
Is Kinematic	☐

Figure 3.30 – Use Gravity being highlighted as an override

The overrides have precedence over the Prefab, so if we change the scale of the original Prefab, the one that has a scale override won't change, keeping its own version of the scale, as illustrated in the following screenshot:

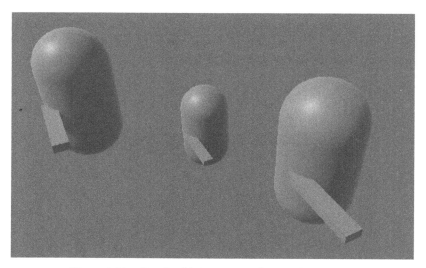

Figure 3.31 – One Prefab instance with an scale override

We can easily locate all overrides of an instance using the **Overrides** dropdown in the **Inspector**, locating all the changes our object has. It not only allows us to see all the overrides, but also reverts any override we don't want and applies the ones we want. Let's say we regretted the lack of gravity of that specific Prefab—no problem! We can just locate the override and revert it. The process is illustrated in the following screenshot:

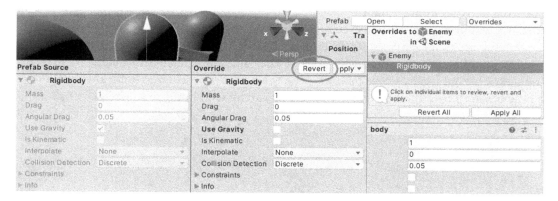

Figure 3.32 – Reverting a single override

Also, let's imagine that we really liked the new scale of that instance, so we want all instances to have that scale—great! We can simply hit the **Apply** button, select the specific change, and all instances will have that scale (except the ones with an override), as illustrated in the following screenshot:

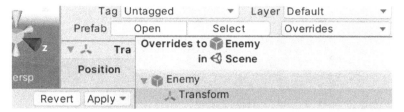

Figure 3.33 – The Apply button

Also, we have the **Revert All** and **Apply All** buttons, but use them with caution, because you can easily revert and apply changes that you are not aware of.

So, as you can see, Prefab is a really useful Unity tool to keep track of all similar objects and apply changes to all of them, and also have specific instances with few variations. Talking about variations, there are other cases where you will want to have several instances of a Prefab with the same set of variations—as an example, flying enemies and grounded enemies—but if you think about that, we will have the same problem we had when we didn't use Prefabs, so we need to manually update those varied versions one by one.

Here, we have two options: one is to create a brand new Prefab just to have another version with that variation. This leads to the problem that if we want all types of enemies to suffer changes, we need to manually apply the changes to each possible Prefab. The second option is to create a Prefab variant. Let's review the latter.

Prefab variants

A **Prefab variant** is the act of creating a new Prefab but based on an existing one, so the new one **inherits** the features of the base Prefab. This means that our new Prefab can have differences with the base one, but the features that they have in common are still connected.

To illustrate this, let's create a variation of the enemy Prefab that can fly: the flying enemy Prefab. In order to do that, we can select an existing enemy Prefab instance in the **Hierarchy** window, name it **Flying Enemy**, and drag it again to the **Project** window, and this time we will see a prompt, asking which kind of Prefab we want to create. This time, we need to choose **Prefab Variant**, as illustrated in the following screenshot:

Figure 3.34 – Creating Prefab variants

Now, we can enter the Prefab Edit Mode of the variant by double-clicking it, and then add a cube as the jet pack of our enemy, and also uncheck the **Use Gravity** property for the enemy. If we get back to the Scene, we will see the variant instance being changed, and the base enemies aren't changed. You can see this in the following screenshot:

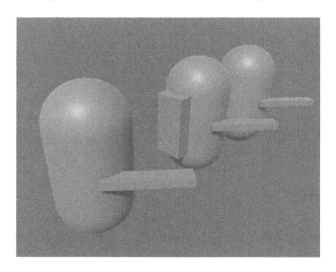

Figure 3.35 – Prefab variant instance

Now, imagine you want to add a hat to all our types of enemies. We can simply enter the Prefab Edit Mode of the base enemy Prefab by double-clicking it, and add a cube as a hat. Now, we will see that change applied to all the enemies, because remember: the **Flying Enemy** Prefab is a variant of the base enemy Prefab, meaning that it will inherit all the changes of that one.

We have created lots of content so far, but if our PC turns off for some reason, we will certainly lose it all, so let's see how we can save our progress.

Saving scenes and projects

As in any other program, we need to save our progress. The difference here is that we don't have just one giant file with all the project Assets, but several files for each Asset.

In this section, we will cover the following concepts related to saving:

- Saving our changes
- Project structure

Saving our changes

Let's start saving our progress by saving the scene, which is pretty straightforward. We can simply go to **File** | **Save Scene** or press *Ctrl + S* (*command + S* on a Mac). The first time we save our scene, a window will just ask us where we want to save our file, and you can save it wherever you want inside the Assets folder of our project, but never outside that folder. That will generate a new Asset in the **Project** window: a scene file, as illustrated in the following screenshot:

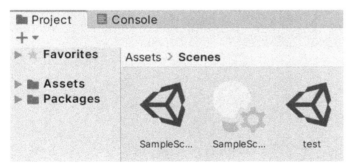

Figure 3.36 – Scene files

We can create a folder to save our scene in that dialog, or, if you already saved the scene, you can create a folder using the **Create** | **Folder** option in the **Project** window and drag the created scene to that folder. Now, if you create another Scene with the **File** | **New Scene** menu option, you can get back to the previous scene just by double-clicking the Asset in the **Project** window.

This only saved the Scene, but any change in Prefabs and another kind of Assets are not saved with that option. Instead, if you want to save every change on the Assets except Scenes, you can use the **File | Save Project** option. It can be a little bit confusing, but if you want to save all your changes, you need to both save the scenes and the project, as saving just the project won't save the changes on Scenes. Sometimes, the best way to be sure everything is saved is just by closing Unity, which is recommended when you try to move your project between computers or folders. Let's talk about that in the next section.

Project structure

Now that we have saved all our changes, we are ready to move the project between computers or to another folder (if you someday need to). You can close Unity to make sure everything is saved and just copy the entire project folder. If you don't remember where you saved your project, you can just right-click the Assets folder in the **Project** window and select **Show in Explorer** (**Reveal in Finder** on a Mac), as illustrated in the following screenshot:

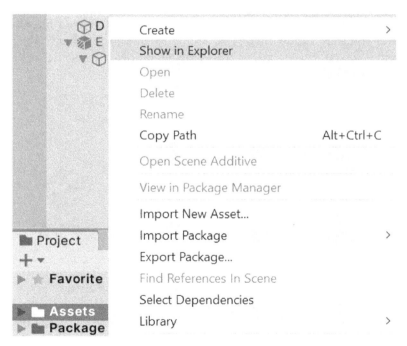

Figure 3.37 – Locating the project folder

Let's take the opportunity, now that we are in the project folder, to explore a little bit. We will find several folders and files in a full project, but not all the files are necessary to copy in order to move the project elsewhere. The most important folders are `Assets`, `ProjectSettings`, and `Packages`. These folders can be seen in the following screenshot:

Figure 3.38 – Project folder structure

Assets is where all our scenes, Prefabs, and other Asset files will live, so that folder and all its content is indispensable, including those metafiles automatically created per Asset. The `ProjectSettings` folder contains several configurations of different Unity systems we will fiddle with later in this book, but even if we didn't change any settings, it's always a good idea to bring that folder with us. **Packages** are a Unity feature that allows you to install official and custom Unity packages or plugins that extend the engine capabilities, this being a new different version of what the `.unitypackage` files used to be, but let's discuss that later. So far, it's important to note that that folder will have settings about which packages our project is using, so remember to also bring that one with you.

No other folders/files are necessary because some are them are temporary and others can be regenerated, such as **Library**, where all the converted versions of our Assets will live. By converted, we mean externally generated files, such as 3D models, images, sounds, and so on. Unity needs to convert those files to a Unity-compatible format. The original will live in **Assets** and the converted ones in **Library** so that they can be easily regenerated if necessary. Later, in *Chapter 5, Importing and Integrating Assets*, we will discuss integrating externally generated content.

Now, let's imagine you have compressed those three folders, copied them to a flash drive, and then decompressed the folders into another computer. How can we open the project again? As you can see, a project doesn't have a project file or anything like that—it's just a bunch of folders. In order to open a project, the easiest way would be to find a scene file in the `Assets` folder and double-click it so that Unity will open the project in that scene. Another option would be to use the **Add** button in Unity Hub and find the project folder (the one that contains the `Assets` folder). So, we will add that project to the list of our computer projects, and later, we can just click the name in that list to open it. The following screenshot illustrates this:

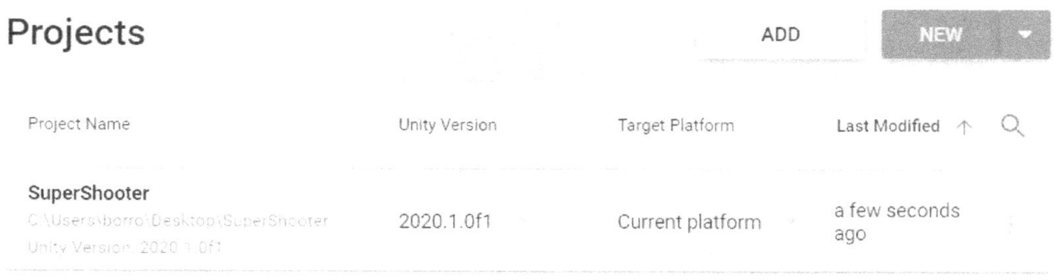

Figure 3.39 – Reopening a project

Now, we have all the base Unity knowledge we need in order to start diving into how to use the different Unity systems so that we can start creating a real game! Let's do that in the next chapter!

Summary

In this chapter, we saw a quick introduction of essential Unity concepts. We reviewed all the Unity windows and how we can use all of them to edit a full scene, from navigating it and creating premade objects, to manipulating them to create our own types of objects using GameObjects and Components. We also discussed how to use the **Hierarchy** window to parent GameObjects to create complex object hierarchies, as well as creating Prefabs to reutilize and manipulate large amounts of the same type of objects. Finally, we discussed how we can save our progress and move the project, reviewing the structure of it and which folders are the essential ones.

In the next chapter, we will learn about the different tools that we will use to create the first prototype of our game's level.

4

Grayboxing with Terrain and ProBuilder

Now that we have grasped all the necessary concepts to use Unity, let's start designing our first level. The idea in this chapter is to learn how to use the Terrain tool to create the Landscape of our game and then use ProBuilder to create the 3D mesh of the base with greater detail than using cubes. Using those tools, you will be able to create a prototype of any kind of scene and try out your idea before actually implementing it with final graphics.

Specifically, we will examine the following concepts in this chapter:

- Creating a Landscape with Terrain
- Creating Shapes with ProBuilder

Creating a Landscape with Terrain

So far, we have used Cubes to generate our level prototype, but we also learned that those shapes sometimes cannot represent all possible objects we could need. Imagine something irregular, such as a full terrain with hills, canyons, and rivers. This would be a nightmare to create using cubes. Another option would be to use 3D modeling software, but the problem with that is that the generated model will be so big and so detailed that it won't perform well, even on high-end PCs. In this scenario, we need to learn how to use Terrain, which we will do in this first section of this chapter.

In this section, we will cover the following concepts related to terrains:

- Discussing Height Maps
- Creating and configuring Height Maps
- Authoring Height Maps
- Adding Height Map details

Let's start talking about Height Maps, whose textures help us define the heights of our terrain.

Discussing Height Maps

If we create a giant area of the game with hills, canyons, craters, valleys, and rivers using regular 3D modeling tools, we will have the problem that we will use full detailed models for objects at all possible distances, thus wasting resources on details we won't see when the object is far away. We will see lots of terrain parts from a great distance, such as mountains and rivers, so this is a serious issue.

Unity Terrain tools use a technique called Height Maps to generate the terrain in a performant and dynamic way. Instead of generating large 3D models for the whole terrain, it uses an image called a Height Map, which looks like a top-down black and white photo of the terrain.

In the following figure, you can see a black and white top-down view of Scotland terrain heights, with white being a higher height and black being a lower height:

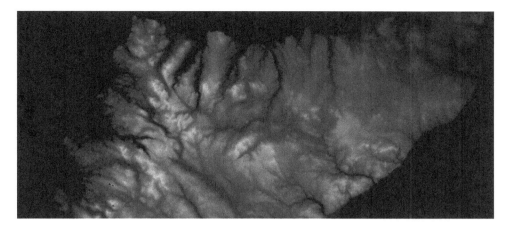

Figure 4.1 – Scotland's Height Map

In the preceding image, you can easily spot the peaks of the mountains while looking for the whitest areas of the image. Everything below sea level is black, while anything in the middle using gradients of gray represents different heights between the minimum and maximum heights. The idea is that each pixel of the image determines the height of that specific area of the terrain.

Unity Terrain tools can automatically generate a Terrain 3D mesh from that image, saving us the hard drive space of having full 3D models of that terrain. Also, Unity will create the terrain as we move, generating high-detail models for nearby areas and lower-detail models for faraway areas, making it a performant solution.

In the following figure, you can see the mesh that was generated for the terrain. You can appreciate that the nearer parts of the terrain have more polygons than the further-away parts:

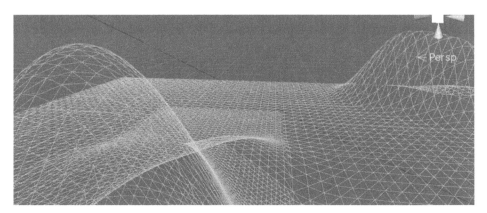

Figure 4.2 – Height Map generated mesh

Take into account that this technology also has its cons, such as the time it takes for Unity to generate those 3D models while we play and the inability to create caves, but for now, that's not a problem for us.

Now that we know what a Height Map is, let's see how we can use Unity Terrain tools to create our own Height Maps.

Creating and configuring Height Maps

If you click on **GameObject | 3D Object | Terrain**, you will see how a giant plane appears on your scene and that a Terrain object appears on your **Hierarchy** window. That's our terrain, and it is plain because its Height Map starts all black, so no height whatsoever is in its initial state. In the following screenshot, you can see what a brand new **Terrain** looks like:

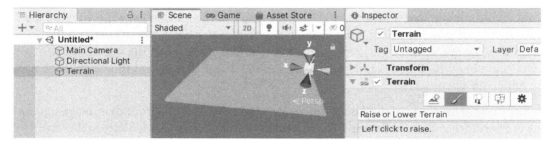

Figure 4.3 – Terrain with no heights painted yet

Before you start editing your terrain, you must configure different settings such as the size and resolution of the Terrain's Height Map, and that depends on what you are going to do with it. This is not the same as generating a whole world. Remember that our game will happen in the Player´s Base, so the terrain will be small. In this case, an area that's 200 x 200 meters in size surrounded by mountains will be enough.

In order to configure our terrain for those requirements, we need to do the following:

1. Select **Terrain** from the **Hierarchy** or **Scene** window.

2. Look at the **Inspector** for the **Terrain** component and expand it if it is collapsed.

3. Click on the wheel icon to switch to configuration mode. In the following screenshot, you can see where that button is located:

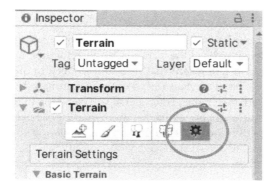

Figure 4.4 – Terrain settings button

4. Look for the **Mesh Resolution** section.

5. Change **Terrain Width** and **Terrain Length** to 200. This will say that the size of our terrain is going to be 200 x 200 meters.

6. **Terrain Height** determines the maximum height possible. The white areas of our Height Map are going to be that size. We can reduce it to 500 just to limit the maximum peak of our mountains:

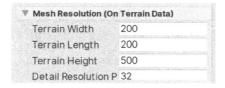

Figure 4.5 – Terrain resolution settings

7. Look for the **Texture Resolutions** section.

8. Change **Heightmap Resolut** to **257 x 257**:

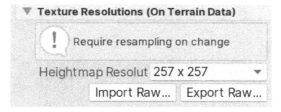

Figure 4.6 – Height Map resolution settings

> **Important Note**
>
> The Heightmap resolution is the size of the Heightmap image that will hold the heights of the different parts of the terrain. Using a resolution of 257 x 257 in our 200 x 200 meter terrain means that each square meter in the terrain will be covered by a little bit more than 1 pixel of the Heightmap. The higher the resolution per square meter, the greater detail you can draw in that area size. Usually, terrain features are big, so having more than 1 pixel per square meter is generally a waste of resources. Find the smallest resolution you can have that allows you to create the details you need.

Another initial setting you will want to set is the initial terrain height. By default, this is 0, so you can start painting heights from the bottom part, but this way, you can't make holes in the terrain because it's already at its lowest point. Setting up a little initial height allows you to paint river paths and holes in case you need them. In order to do so, do the following:

1. Select **Terrain**.

2. Click on the **Brush** button (second button).

3. Set the dropdown to **Set Height**.

4. Set the **Height** property to 50. This will state that we want all the terrain to start at 50 meters in height, allowing us to make holes with a maximum depth of 50 meters:

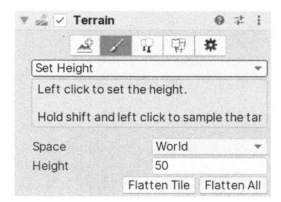

Figure 4.7 – Set Height terrain tool location

5. Click the **Flatten All** button. You will see all the terrain has been raised by those 50 meters we specified earlier.

Now that we have properly configured our Height Map, let's start editing it.

Authoring Height Maps

Remember that the Height Map is just an image with the heights, so in order to edit it, we would need to paint the heights in that image. Luckily, Unity has tools that allow us to edit the terrain directly in the Editor and see the results of the modified heights directly. In order to do this, we must follow these steps:

1. Select **Terrain**.

2. Click the **Brush** button.

3. Set the dropdown in **Raise or Lower Terrain** mode:

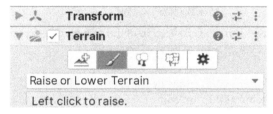

Figure 4.8 – Raise or Lower Terrain tool location

4. Select the second brush in the Brushes selector. This brush has blurred borders to allow us to create softer heights.

5. Set **Brush Size** to **30** so that we can create heights that span **30** meter areas. If you want to create subtler details, you can reduce this number.

6. Set **Opacity** to **10** to reduce the amount of height we paint per second or click:

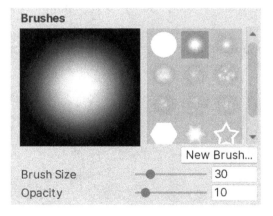

Figure 4.9 – Smooth edges brush

7. Now, if you move the mouse in the **Scene** view, you will see a little preview of the height you will paint if you click on that area. Maybe you will need to navigate closer to the terrain to see it in detail:

Figure 4.10 – Previsualization of the area to raise the terrain

---

Important Note

That checkered pattern you can see near the terrain allows you to see the actual size of the objects you are editing. Each cell represents a square meter. Remember that having a reference to see the actual size of the objects you are editing is useful to prevent creating too big or too small terrain features. Maybe you can put in other kinds of references, such as a big cube with accurate sizes representing a building to get a notion of the size of the mountain or lake you are creating. Remember that the cube has a default size of 1 x 1 x 1 meters, so scaling to (10,10,10) will give you a cube of 10 x 10 x 10 meters.

---

8. Hold left-click and drag the cursor over the terrain to start painting your terrain heights. Remember that you can press *Ctrl + Z (command+ Z* on Mac) to revert any undesired change.

9. Try to paint the mountains all around the borders of our area, which will represent the background hills of our base:

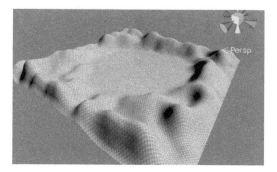

Figure 4.11 – Painted mountains around the edges of the terrain

Now, we have decent starter hills around our future base. We can also draw a river basin around our future base area. To do so, follow these steps:

1. Place a cube with a scale of (50, 10, 50) in the middle of the terrain. This will act as a placeholder for the base we are going to create:

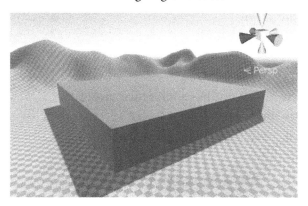

Figure 4.12 – Placeholder cube for the base area

2. Select **Terrain** and the **Brush** button once more.

3. Reduce **Brush Size** to **10**.

4. Holding the *Shift* key, left-click and drag the mouse over the terrain to paint the basin around our base placeholder. Doing this will lower the terrain instead of raising it:

Figure 4.13 – River basin around our placeholder base

Now, we have a simple but good starter terrain that gives us a basic idea of how it will look from our base's perspective. Before moving on, we will apply some finer details to make our terrain look a little bit better. In the next section, we will discuss how to simulate terrain erosion with different tools.

Adding Height Map details

In the previous section, we created a rough outline of the terrain. If you want to make it look a little bit realistic, then you need to start painting lots of tiny details here and there. Usually, this is done later in the level design process, but let's take a look now since we are exploring the Terrain tools. Right now, our mountains look very smooth. In real life, they are sharper, so let's improve that:

1. Select **Terrain** and enable the **Brush** button.

2. Set the dropdown in **Raise or Lower Terrain** mode.

3. Pick the fifth brush. This one has an irregular layout so that we can paint a little bit of noise here and there.

4. Set **Brush Size** to **50** so that we can cover a greater area:

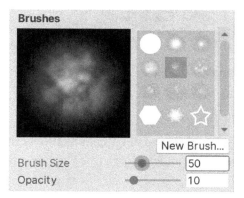

Figure 4.14 – Cloud pattern brush for randomness

5. Hold *Shift* and do small clicks over the hills of the terrain without dragging the mouse. Remember to zoom in to the areas you are applying finer details to because those can't be seen at great distances:

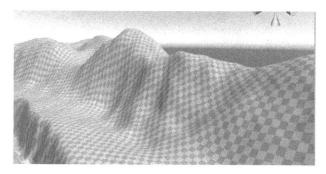

Figure 4.15 – Erosion generated with previous brush

This has added some irregularity to our hills. Now, let's imagine we want to have a flat area on the hills to put a decorative observatory or antenna. Follow these steps to do so:

1. Select **Terrain**, **Brush Tool**, and **Set Height** from the dropdown.

2. Set **Height** to **60**.

3. Paint an area over the hills. You will see how the terrain will raise if it's lower than **60** meters or became lower in areas greater than **60** meters:

Figure 4.16 – Flattened hill

4. You can see that the borders have some rough corners that need to be smoothed:

Figure 4.17 – Non-smoothed terrain edges

5. Change the dropdown to **Smooth Height** mode.

6.   Select the second brush with a size of **5** and an opacity of **10**:

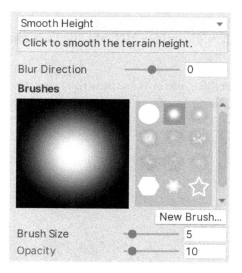

Figure 4.18 – Smooth Height brush

7.   Click and drag over the borders of our flat area to make them smoother:

Figure 4.19 – Smoothed terrain edges

We can keep adding details here and there, but we can settle with this for now. The next step is to create our Player's Base, but this time, let's explore ProBuilder in order to generate our geometry.

Creating Shapes with ProBuilder

So far, we have created simple scenes using cubes and primitive shapes, and that's enough for most of the prototypes you will create, but sometimes, you will have tricky areas of the game that would be difficult to model with regular cubes, or maybe you want to have some deeper details in certain parts of your game to get a visual of how the player will feel that area. In this case, we can use any 3D modeling tools for this, such as 3D studio, Maya, or Blender, but those can be difficult to learn and you probably won't need all their power at this stage of your development. Luckily, Unity has a simple 3D model creator called ProBuilder, so let's explore it.

In this section, we will cover the following concepts related to ProBuilder:

- Installing ProBuilder
- Creating a shape
- Manipulating the mesh
- Adding details

ProBuilder is not included by default in our Unity project, so let's start by learning how we can install it.

Installing ProBuilder

Unity is a powerful engine full of features, but having all those tools added to our project if we are not using all of them can make the engine run slower, so we need to manually specify which Unity tools we are using. To do so, we will use the Package Manager, a tool that we can use to see and select which Unity packages we are going to need. As you may recall, earlier, we talked about the `Packages` folder. This is basically what this Package Manager is modifying.

In order to install ProBuilder with this tool, we need to do the following:

1. Click the **Window | Package Manager** option:

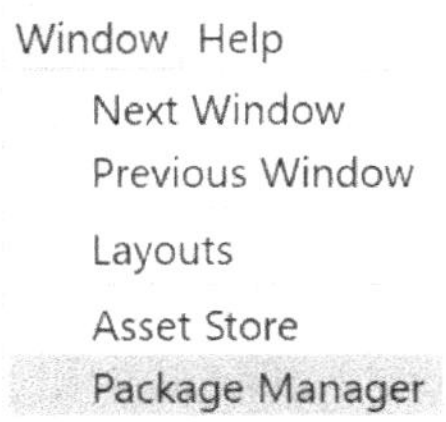

Figure 4.20 – Package Manager option

2. In the window that just opened, be sure that **Packages** is in **Unity Registry** mode by clicking on the button saying **Packages** at the top-left part of the window and selecting **Unity Registry**:

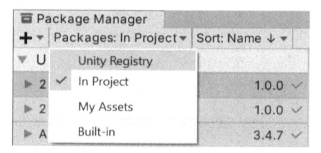

Figure 4.21 – Showing All Packages

3. Wait a moment for the left list of packages to fill. Make sure you are connected to the internet to download and install the packages.

4. Look at the **ProBuilder** package in that list and select it.

> **Important Note**
>
> Im using ProBuilder version 4.2.3, the newest version available at the moment of writing this book. While you can use a newer version, consider that the steps to use it may differ. You can look at older versions using the arrow at the left of the title.

Figure 4.22 – ProBuilder in the packages list

5. Click on the **Install** button at the bottom right-hand side of the **Package Manager**:

Figure 4.23 – Install button

6. Wait a moment for the package to install. You will notice the process has ended when the **Install** button has been replaced with an Up to Date label.

Now that we have installed ProBuilder in our project, let's use it!

Creating a Shape

We will start our base by creating a plane for our floor. We will do this by doing the following:

1. Open ProBuilder and go to the **Tools | ProBuilder | ProBuilder** window:

Figure 4.24 – ProBuilder Window option

2. In the window that has opened, click the plus icon (+) at the right of the **New Shape** button:

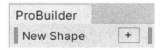

Figure 4.25 – New Shape option

3. In the **Shape Selector**, select **Plane**.

4. Set **Width** and **Length** to 50.

5. Set the **Width** and **Length** segments to 2. We will need those subdivisions later:

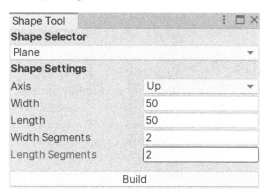

Figure 4.26 – New Shape settings

6. Click the **Build** button to confirm the **Plane**.

7. Click the first button of the four **ProBuilder** buttons in the **Scene** view to enable movement of the entire plane:

Figure 4.27 – Select object tool

8. Replace the placeholder cube with this floor:

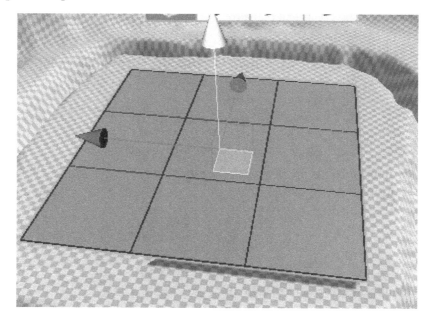

Figure 4.28 – Plane subdivided in a 3 x 3 grid

Now that we have created the floor, let's learn how we can manipulate its vertexes to change its shape.

Manipulating the mesh

If you select the plane, you will see that it is subdivided into a 3 x 3 grid because we set up the width and height segments to 2 (2 cuts). We have done that because we will use the outer cells to create our walls, thus raising them up. The idea is to modify the size of those cells to outline the wall length and width before creating the walls. In order to do so, we will do the following:

1. Select the plane.

2. Click the second button (showing the vertices) of the four new buttons that appeared in the Scene View:

Figure 4.29 – Selecting the vertices tool

3. Click and drag the mouse to create a selection box that picks the four vertices of the second row of vertexes:

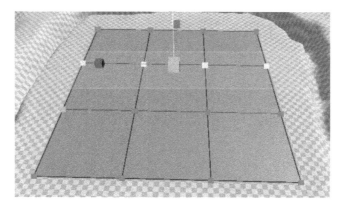

Figure 4.30 – Vertices selection

4. Click on the second button in the top-left of the buttons of the Unity Editor to enable the Move Tool:

Figure 4.31 – The Move Tool

5. Move the row of vertexes to make that subdivision of the plane thinner. You can use the checkered pattern on the terrain to get a notion of the size of the wall in meters:

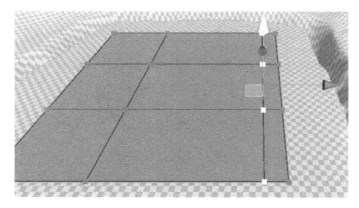

Figure 4.32 – Moved vertexes

6. Repeat *steps 3* to *5* for each row of vertexes until you get wall outlines with similar sizes:

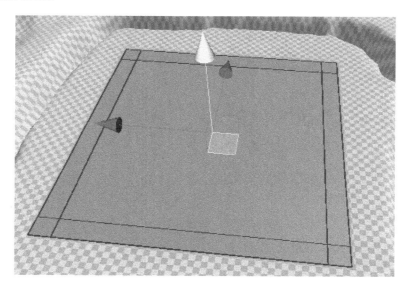

Figure 4.33 – Moved vertexes to reduce edge cell width

Important Note

If you want the vertexes to have exact positions, I recommend that you install and explore the ProGrids package. It is a position snapping system that works with regular Unity and ProBuilder.

Now that we have created the outline for our walls, let's add new faces to our mesh to create them. In order to use the subdivisions or "Faces" we have created to make our walls, we must pick and extrude them. Follow these steps to do so:

1. Select the plane.

2. Select the fourth button of the **ProBuilder** buttons in the Scene view:

Figure 4.34 – Select Face tool

3. While holding *Ctrl* (*command* on Mac), click over each of the faces of the wall outlines:

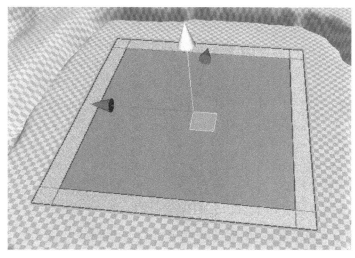

Figure 4.35 – Edge faces being selected

4. In the **ProBuilder** window, look for the plus icon (+) to the right of the Extrude Faces button. It will be located in the red section of the window:

Figure 4.36 – Extrude Faces option

5. Set **Distance** to 5 in the window that appeared after we clicked the plus button.

6. Click the **Extrude Faces** button in that window:

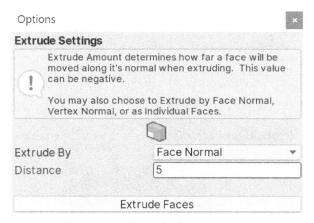

Figure 4.37 – Extrude distance option

7.   Now, you should see that the outline of the walls has just raised up from the ground:

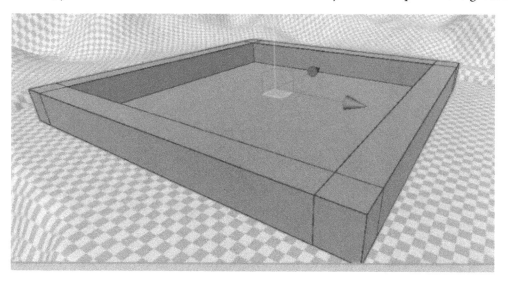

Figure 4.38 – Extruded grid edges

Now, if you pay attention to how the base floor and walls touch the terrain, there's a little gap. We can try to move the base downward, but the floor will probably disappear because it will be buried under the terrain. A little trick we can do here is just push the walls downward, without moving the floor, so that the walls will be buried in the terrain but our floor will keep a little distance from it. You can see an example of how it would look in the following figure:

Figure 4.39 – Slice of expected result

In order to do so, we need to do the following:

1.   Select the third **ProBuilder** button in the Scene view to enable edge selection:

Figure 4.40 – Select edges tool

2. While holding *Ctrl* (*command* on Mac), select all the bottom edges of the walls.

    If you selected undesired edges, just click them again while holding *Ctrl* (*command* on Mac) to deselect them, all while keeping the current selection:

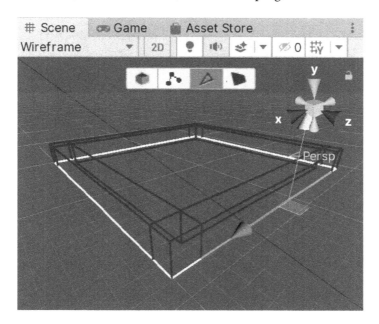

Figure 4.41 – Selecting floor edges

> **Information Box**
>
> If you want to use the Wireframe mode in the previous screenshot, click on the Shaded button in the top-left part of the Scene view and select the Wireframe option from the drop-down menu.

3. Enable the Move Tool pressing the second button in the top-left part of the Unity Editor:

Figure 4.42 – The Move Tool

4. Move the edges downward until they are fully buried under the terrain:

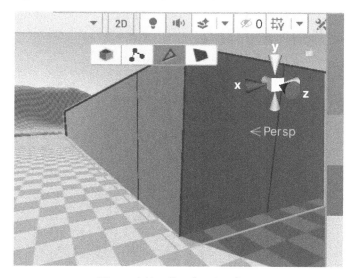

Figure 4.43 – Overlapping faces

Now that we have a base mesh, we can start adding details to it using several other ProBuilder tools.

Adding details

Let's start adding details to the base by applying a little bevel to the walls. Follow these steps:

1. Using the edge selection mode (the third button of the **ProBuilder** buttons), select the top edges of our model:

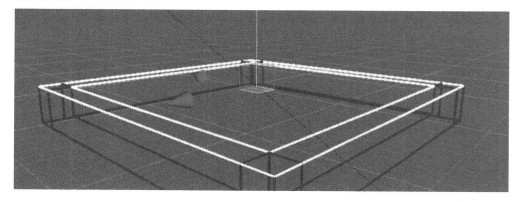

Figure 4.44 – Top wall edges being selected

2. In the **ProBuilder** window, click on the plus icon to the right of the **Bevel** button.

3. Set a distance of 0.5:

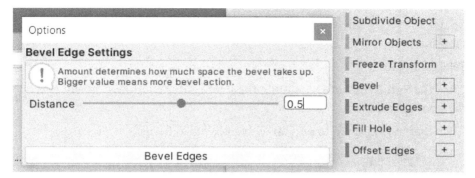

Figure 4.45 – Bevel distance to generate

4. Click on **Bevel Edges**. Now, you can see the top part of our walls with a little bevel:

Figure 4.46 – Result of the bevel process

5. Optionally, you can do that with the bottom part of the inner walls:

Figure 4.47 – Bevel being applied to floor-wall edges

Another detail to add could be a pit in the middle of the ground as a hazard we need to avoid falling into and to make the enemies avoid it using AI. In order to do that, follow these steps:

1. Enable the FACE selection mode by clicking the fourth ProBuilder Scene view button.

2. Select the floor.

3. Click the **Subdivide** faces option in the **ProBuilder** window. You will end up with the floor split into four.

4. Click that button again to end up with a 4 x 4 grid floor:

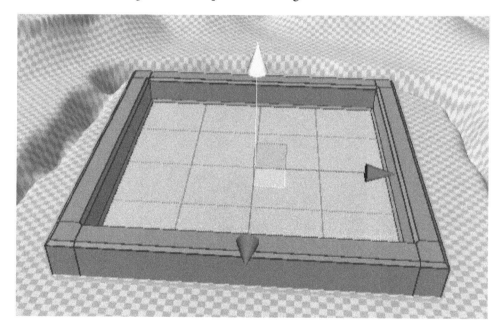

Figure 4.48 – Subdividing the floor

5. Select the four inner floor tiles.

6. Enable the Scale Tool by clicking the fourth button in the top-left part of the Unity Editor:

Figure 4.49 – Scale Tool

7. Using the gray cube at the center of the gizmo, scale down the center tiles:

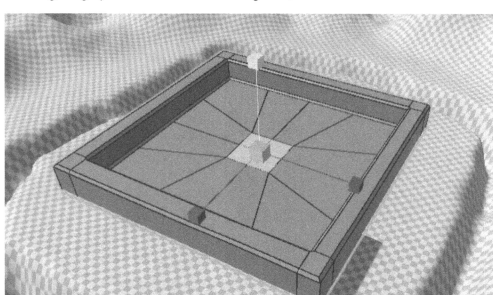

Figure 4.50 – Inner cells being shrunk

8. Click the Extrude Faces button in the **ProBuilder** window.

9. Push the extruded faces downward.

10. Right-click on the **ProBuilder** window tab and select **Close Tab**. We need to get back to terrain editing and having **ProBuilder** open won't allow us to do that comfortably:

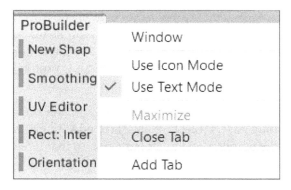

Figure 4.51 – Close Tab option

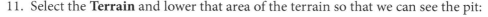

11. Select the **Terrain** and lower that area of the terrain so that we can see the pit:

Figure 4.52 – Terrain being lowered for the pit to be visible

I know we didn't plan the pit in the original level layout, but remember that the define acronym is a document that will constantly change in the middle of game development, so sometimes, we can be bold and change it in order to improve the game. Just take care to not go too far with never ending changes, which is a difficult-to-master art.

Summary

In this chapter, we learned how to create large Terrain meshes using Height Maps and Unity Terrain tools such as Paint Height and Set Height to create hills and river basins. Also, we saw how to create our own 3D meshes using ProBuilder, as well as how to manipulate the vertexes, edges, and faces of a model to create a prototype base model for our game. We didn't discuss some performance optimizations we can apply to our meshes or some advanced 3D modeling concepts as that would require entire chapters and that's outside the scope of this book. Right now, our main focus is prototyping, so we are fine with our level's current status.

In the next chapter, we will learn how to download and replace these prototyping models with final art by integrating Assets (files) we have created with external tools. This is the first step to improving the graphics quality of our game so that it reaches the final look, which we will finish by the end of Part 2.

5
Importing and Integrating Assets

In the previous chapter, we created the prototype of our level. Now, let's suppose that we have coded the game and tested it, validating the idea. With that, it's time to change the prototype art to the real finished art. Actually, we are going to code the game in Part 3, but for learning purposes, let's just skip that part for now. In order to use final assets, we need to learn how to get them (images, 3D models, and so on), how to import them into Unity, and how to use them in our scene.

In this chapter, we will examine the following topics:

- Importing assets
- Integrating assets
- Configuring assets

Importing assets

We have different sources of assets we can use in our project. We can simply get a file from our artist, download them from different free and paid assets sites, or we can use the Asset Store, Unity's official virtual asset store, where we can get free and paid assets ready to use with Unity. We will use a mix of downloading an asset from the internet and from the Asset Store, just to get all possible resources.

In this section, we will cover the following concepts related to importing assets:

- Importing assets from the internet
- Importing assets from the Asset Store
- Downloading and importing assets into our project from the internet

Importing assets from the internet

In terms of getting art assets for our project, let's start with our terrain textures. Remember that we have our terrain painted with a grid pattern, so the idea is to replace that with grass, mud, rock, and other kinds of textures. To do that, we must get images. In this case, these kinds of images are usually top-down views of different terrain patterns, and they have the requirement of being "tileable." You can see an example of this in the following screenshot:

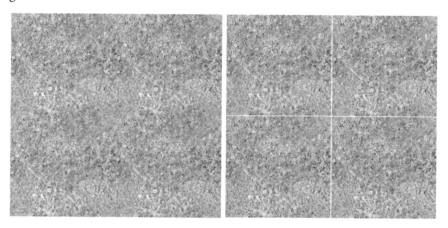

Figure 5.1 – Left: grass patch; right: the same grass patch separated to highlight the texture tiling

The grass on the left seems to be one single big image, but if you pay attention, you should be able to see some patterns repeating themselves. In this case, this grass is just a single image repeated four times in a grid, like the one on the right. This way, you can cover large areas by repeating a single small image, saving lots on RAM on your computer.

The idea is to get these kinds of images to paint our terrain. You can get them from several places, but the easiest way is to use Google Images or any Image Search Engine. To do this, follow these steps:

1. Open your browser (Chrome, Safari, Edge, and so on).
2. Go to your preferred search engine. In this case, I will use Google.

3. Use the keywords `PATTERN tileable texture`, replacing `PATTERN` with the kind of terrain you are looking for, such as `grass tileable texture` or `mud tileable texture`. In this case, I am going to type `grass tileable texture` and then press *Enter* to search.

4. Switch to image search mode:

Figure 5.2 – Google Search for images

5. Find any texture you find suitable for the kind of grass you need and click it. Remember that the texture must be a top-down view of the grass and must repeat.

> **Important Note**
> Try to check the image's resolution before picking it. Try to select squared images that have a resolution less than 1024 x 1024 for now.

6. Right-click the opened image and select **Save image as...**:

Figure 5.3 – Save image as... option

7. Save the image in any folder you will remember.

Now that you have downloaded the image, you can add it to your project in several ways. The simplest one would be doing the following:

1. Locate your image using **File Explorer** (**Finder** in Mac).

2. Locate or create the `Textures` folder in the Project window in Unity.

3. Put both File Explorer and Unity Project Window next to each other.

4. Drag the file from File Explorer to the `Textures` folder in the Unity Project Window:

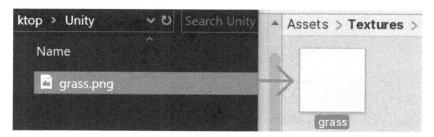

Figure 5.4 – Texture being dragged from File Explorer to Unity´s Project View

For simple textures like these ones, any search engine can be helpful, but if you want to replace the Player´s Base geometry with detailed walls and doors or place enemies in your scene, you need to get 3D models. If you search for those in any search engine using keywords such as "free zombie 3D model," you will find endless free and paid 3D models sites such as TurboSquid and Mixamo, but those sites can be problematic because those meshes are usually not prepared for being used in Unity, or even in games. You will find models with very high polygon counts, incorrect sizes or orientations, unoptimized textures, and so on. To prevent those problems, we'll want to use a better source, and in this case, we will use Unity´s Asset Store, so let's explore it.

Importing assets from the Asset Store

The Asset Store is Unity's official asset marketplace where you can find lots of models, textures, sounds, and even entire Unity plugins to extend the capabilities of the engine. In this case, we will limit ourselves to downloading 3D models to replace the Player´s Base prototype. You will want to get 3D models with a modular design, meaning that you will get several pieces such as walls, floors, corners, and so on. You can connect them to create any kind of scenario.

In order to do that, you must follow these steps:

1. Click on **Window | Asset Store** in Unity, which will open a new window saying the Asset Store has moved. In previous versions of Unity, you could see the Asset Store directly inside the editor, but now it is recommended to open it in a regular web browser, so just click the **Search online** button:

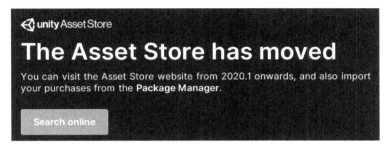

Figure 5.5 – Asset Store moved message

2. Your browser will open showing a site similar to the one in the following screenshot:

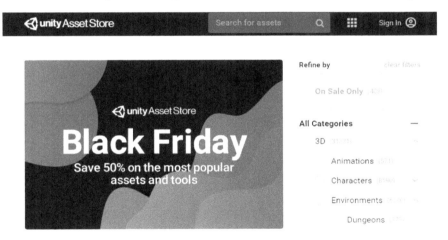

Figure 5.6 – Asset Store home page

3. In the right panel, open the 3D category by clicking the arrow to its right. Then, open **Environments** and check the **Sci-Fi** mark. As you can see, there are several categories for finding different types of assets, and you can pick another one if you want to. In **Environments**, you will find 3D models that can be used to generate the scenery for your game.

4. If you need to, you can pay for an asset, but let's hide the paid ones for now. You can do that by searching through the **Pricing** section on the sidebar, opening it using the plus (+) symbol on its right, and then checking the **Free Assets** checkbox:

Figure 5.7 – Free Assets option

5. In the search area, find any asset that seems to have the aesthetic you are looking for and click it. Remember to look out for outdoors assets, because most environment packs are usually interiors only. In my case, I have picked one called **Sci-Fi Styled Modular Pack** that serves for both interiors and exteriors. Take into account that that package might not exist by the time you are reading this, so you might need to choose another one. If you don't find a suitable package, you can download the asset files we used in the GitHub repository. Please refer to the preface instructions of how to access the it.

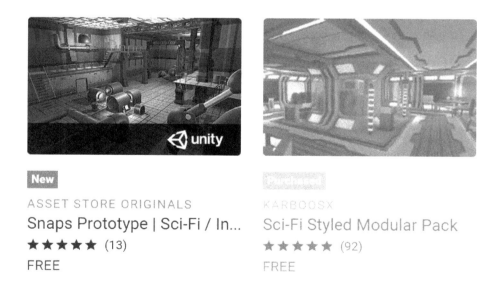

Figure 5.8 – Preview of Asset Store searched packages

> **Important Note**
> At the time of writing this book, Unity is releasing the "Snaps" packages, which are a set of official Unity 3D models that can be used for the modular design of different kinds of environments. Some of them are paid, while others are free – I recommend that you try them out.

6. Now, you will see the package details in the Asset Store window. Here, you can find information regarding the package's description, videos/images, the package's contents, and the most important part, the reviews, where you can check whether the package is worth buying if it's a paid one:

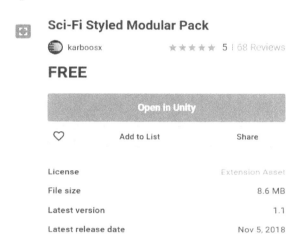

Figure 5.9 – Asset Store package details

7. If you are OK with this package, click the **Add To My Assets** button, log in to Unity if requested and then click **Open In Unity** button. You might be prompted to accept a switch of apps to Unity – just accept:

Figure 5.10 – Switching apps

8. This will open the **Package Manger** again, but this time in **My Assets** mode, showing a list of all the assets you have ever downloaded from the Asset Store, and the one you just selected highlighted in the list. You might need to log again in Unity clicking the Sign In button if you are not logged in Unity Hub.

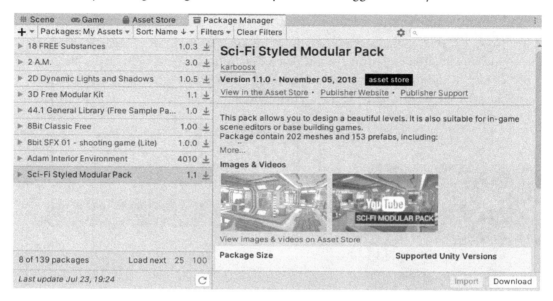

Figure 5.11 – Package Manager showing assets

9. Click on **Download** at the bottom-right part of the window and wait for it to end. Then hit **Import.** Double check that you have the proper asset package selected from the list.

10. After a while, the **Package Contents** Window will show up, allowing you to select exactly which assets of the package you want in your project. For now, leave it as-is and click **Import**:

Figure 5.12 – Assets to import

11. After some importing time, you will see all the package files in your
     Project Window.

Take into account that importing lots of full packages will increase your project's size
considerably, and that, later, you will probably want to remove the assets that you didn't
use. Also, if you import assets that generate errors that prevent you from playing the
scene, just delete all the .cs files that come with the package. They are usually in folders
called Scripts. Those are code files that might not be compatible with your Unity
version. In *Part 3*, we will learn how to make our own so that those are not necessary:

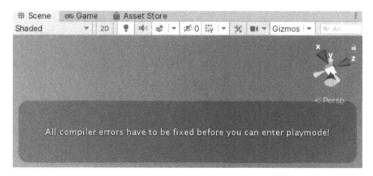

Figure 5.13 – Code error warning when hitting play

> **Important Note**
>
> The Asset Store is prone to changes, even if you are using the same Unity version I am using, so the previous steps may be changed by Unity without notice. Also, its contents change often, and you may not find the same packages used in this book. In such case, you can find another similar package, or take the files i used from the GitHub repo (links and instructions in the Preface).

Before you continue with this chapter, try to download an enemy character using the Asset Store, following the previous steps. In order to solve this exercise, you must complete the same steps as before but look in the **3D | Characters | Humanoid** category of the Asset Store.

Now that we have imported lots of art assets, let's learn how to use them in our scene.

Integrating assets

We have just imported lots of files that can be used in several ways, so the idea of this section is to see how Unity integrates those assets with the GameObjects and components that need them.

In this section, we will cover the following concepts related to importing assets:

- Integrating terrain textures
- Integrating meshes
- Integrating materials

Let's start using tileable textures to cover the terrain.

Integrating terrain textures

In order to apply textures to our terrain, do the following:

1. Select the **Terrain** object.
2. In the **Inspector**, click the brush icon of the **Terrain** component (second button).
3. From the drop-down menu, select **Paint Texture**:

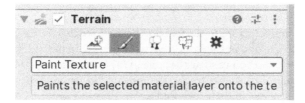

Figure 5.14 – The Paint Texture option

4. Click the **Edit Terrain Layers… | Create Layer** option.

5. Look for the terrain texture you downloaded previously in the texture picker window that appears:

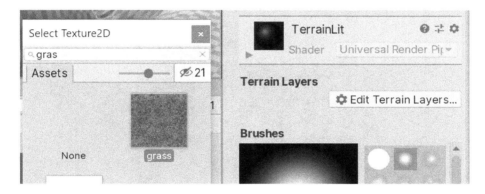

Figure 5.15 – Texture picker

6.   You will see how the texture will be immediately applied to the whole terrain.

7. Repeat *steps 4* and *5* to add other textures. This time, you will see that that texture is not immediately applied.

8. In the **Terrain Layers** section, select the new texture you have created to start painting with that. I used a mud texture in my case.

9. Like when you edited the terrain, in the **Brushes** section, you can select and configure a brush to paint the terrain.

10. In the Scene view, paint the areas you want to have that texture applied to.

11. If your texture patterns are too obvious, select your texture in the Terrains Layer box and then, open the **NewLayer N** where N is a number that depends on the layers you have created.

> **Important Note**
>
> Each time you add a texture to the terrain, you will see that a new asset called "NewLayer N" is created in the Project view. It holds data of the terrain layer you have created, and you can use that one in other terrains if you need to. You can also rename that asset to give it a meaningful name. Also, you can reorganize those assets in their own folder.

12. Open the section using the triangle to its left and increase the **Size** property in the **Tiling Settings** section until you find a suitable size where the pattern is not that obvious:

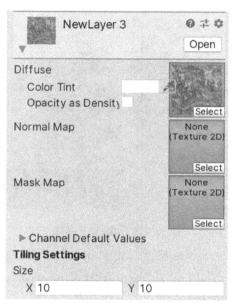

Figure 5.16 – Painting texture options

13. Repeat steps *4* to *12* until you have applied all the textures you wanted to add to your terrain. In my case, I applied the mud texture to the river basin and used a rock texture for the hills. For the texture of the rocks, I reduced the **Opacity** property of the brush to blend it better with the grass in the mountains. You can try to add a layer of snow at the top just for fun:

Figure 5.17 – Results of painting our terrain with three different textures

Of course, we can improve this a lot using lots of the advanced tools of the system, but let's keep things simple for now. Now, let's see how we can integrate the 3D models.

Integrating meshes

If you select one of the 3D assets we have configured previously and click the arrow to its right, one or more sub-assets will appear in the Project Window. This means that FBX is not a 3D model, but a container of assets that defines the 3D model:

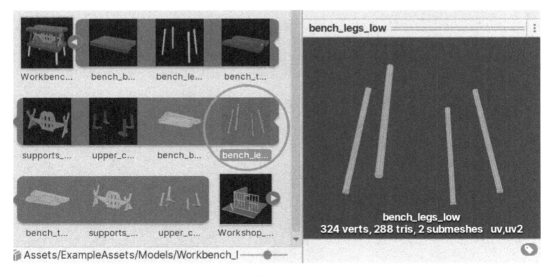

Figure 5.18 – Mesh picker

Some of those sub-assets are meshes, which is a collection of triangles that defines the geometry of your model. You can find at least one of those inside the file, but you can also find several, and that can happen if your model is composed of lots of pieces. For example, a car can be a single rigid mesh, but that won't allow you to rotate its wheels or open its doors; it will be just a static car, and that can be enough if the car is just a prop in the scene, but if the player will be able to control it, you will probably need to modify it. The idea is that all the pieces of your car are different GameObjects parented with one another, in such a way that if you move one, all of them will move, but you can still rotate the pieces independently.

When you drag the 3D model file to the scene, Unity will automatically create all the objects for each piece and its proper parenting based on how the artist created them. You can select the object in the **Hierarchy** and explore all its children to see this:

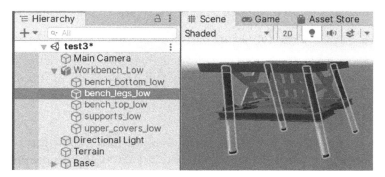

Figure 5.19 – Sub-object selection

Also, you will find that each of those objects will have their own `MeshFilter` and `MeshRenderer` components, each one rendering just that piece of the car. Remember that the mesh filter is a component that has a reference to the mesh asset to render, so the Mesh Filter is the one using those mesh Sub-Assets we talked about previously:

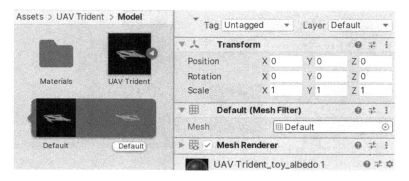

Figure 5.20 – Mesh Filter current mesh selection

Now, if you drag the 3D model file into the scene, you will get a similar result as if the model were a Prefab and you were instancing it. But 3D model files are more limited than Prefabs, because you can't apply changes to the model, so after you've dragged the object onto the scene and edited it to have the behavior you want, I suggest that you create a Prefab to get all the benefits we discussed in *Chapter 3*, *Working with Scenes and GameObjects*, such as applying changes to all the instances of the Prefab and so on. Never create lots of instances of a model from its model file – always create them from the Prefab you created based on that file.

That's the basic usage of 3D meshes. Now, let's explore the texture integration process, which will make our 3D models have more detail.

Integrating textures

Maybe your model already has a texture applied, or maybe it has magenta applied to it. In the latter case, that means the asset wasn't prepared to work with the URP template you selected when creating the project. Some assets in the Asset Store are meant to be used in older versions of Unity:

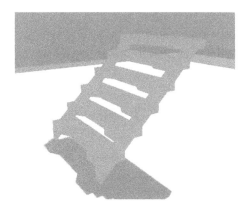

Figure 5.21 – Mesh being rendered with erroneous or no material at all

One option to fix that is using **Edit | Render Pipeline | Universal Render Pipeline | Upgrade Project Materials to UniversalRP Materials**. This will try to upgrade all your materials to the current version of Unity:

Clear All PlayerPrefs		Upgrade Project Materials to UniversalRP Materials
Render Pipeline >	Generate Shader Includes	Upgrade Selected Materials to UniversalRP Materials
Graphics Tier >	Universal Render Pipeline >	2D Renderer >

Figure 5.22 – Upgrading materials to URP

The con of this method is that, sometimes, it won't upgrade the materials properly. Luckily, we can fix this by reapplying the textures of the objects in this new way. Even if your assets work just fine, I suggest that you reapply your textures anyway, just to learn more about the concept of materials.

A texture is applied directly to an object. That's because the texture is just one single configuration of all the ones that control the aspect of your model. In order to change the appearance of a model, you must create a material. A material is a separate asset that contains lots of settings about how Unity should render your object. You can apply that asset to several objects that share the same graphics settings, and if you change the settings of the material, it will affect all the objects that are using it. It works like a graphics profile.

In order to create a material to apply the textures of your object, you need to follow these steps:

1. In the Project Window, click the plus (+) button at the top-left part of the window.

2. Find the **Material** option in that menu and click it.

3. Name your material. This is usually the name of the asset you are creating (for example, Car, Ship, Character, and so on).

4. Drag this material asset you created to the model instance on your scene. At the moment, if you move the mouse with the dragged asset over the object, you will be able to see a preview of how it will look with that material. You can confirm this by releasing the mouse.

5. Maybe your object has several parts. In that case, you will need to drag the material to each part of the object.

> **Important Note**
> Dragging the material will just change the materials property of the
> MeshRenderer component of the object you have dragged.

6. Select the material and click the circle to the left of the **Base Map** property.

7. In the **Texture Selector**, click on the texture of your model. It can be complicated to locate the texture. Usually, the name of the texture will match the model name. If not, you will need to try different textures until you see one that fits your object. Also, you may find several textures with the same name as your model. Just pick the one that seems to have the proper colors instead of the ones that look black and white or light blue; we will use those later:

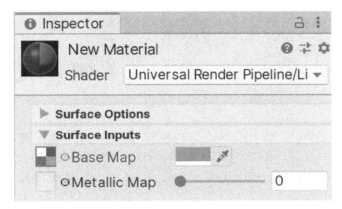

Figure 5.23 – Base Map property of URP materials

With this, you have successfully applied the texture to the object through a material. For each object that uses the same texture, just drag the same material. Now that we have a basic understanding of how to apply the model textures, let's learn how to properly configure the import settings before spreading models all over the scene.

Configuring assets

As we mentioned earlier, artists are used to creating art assets outside Unity, and that can cause differences between how the asset is seen from that tool and how Unity will import it. As an example, 3D Studio can work in centimetres, inches, and so on, while Unity works in meters. We have just downloaded and used lots of assets, but we have skipped the configuration step to solve those discrepancies, so let's take a look at this now.

In this section, we will cover the following concepts related to importing assets:

- Configuring meshes
- Configuring textures

Let's start discussing how to configure 3D meshes.

Configuring meshes

In order to change the model's import settings, you need to locate the model file you have downloaded. There are several file extensions that contain 3D models, with the most common one being the `.fbx` file, but you can encounter others such as `.obj`, `.3ds`, `.blender`, `.mb`, and so on. You can identify whether the file is a 3D mesh via its extension:

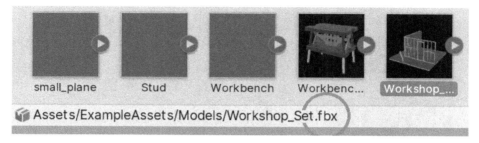

Assets/ExampleAssets/Models/Workshop_Set.fbx

Figure 5.24 – Selected asset path extension

Also, you can click the **Asset** and check in the Inspector for the tabs you can see in the following screenshot:

Figure 5.25 – Mesh materials settings

Now that you have located the 3D mesh files, you can configure them properly. Right now, the only thing we should take into account is the proper scale of the model. Artists are used to working with different software with different setups; maybe one artist created the model using meters as its metric unit, while other artists used inches, feet, and so on. When importing assets that have been created in different units, they will probably be unproportioned, which means we will get results such as humans being bigger than buildings and so on.

The best solution is to just ask the artist to fix that. If all the assets were authored in your company, or if you used an external asset, you can ask the artist to fix it to the way your company works, but right now, you are probably a single developer learning Unity by yourself. Luckily, Unity has a setting that allows you to rescale the original asset before using it in Unity. In order to change the scale factor of an object, you must do the following:

1. Locate the 3D mesh in your Project Window.

2. Drag it to the scene. You will see that an object will appear in your scene.

3. Create a capsule using the **GameObject | 3D Object | Capsule** option.

4. Put the capsule next to the model you dragged into the Editor. See whether the scale makes sense. The idea is that the capsule is representing a human being (2 meters tall) so that you have a reference for the scale:

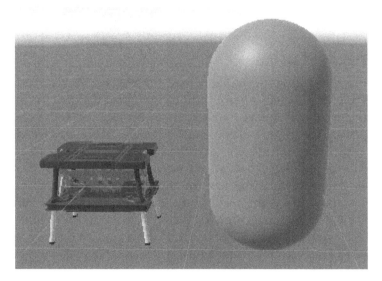

Figure 5.26 – Unproportioned asset

5. If the model is bigger or smaller than expected, select the mesh again in the Project Window (not the GameObject instance you dragged to the Editor) and you will see some import settings in the Inspector.

6. Look for the **Scale Factor** property and modify it, increasing it if your model is smaller than expected or reducing it in the opposite case:

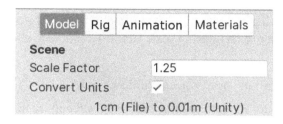

Figure 5.27 – Model mesh options

7. Click the **Apply** button at the bottom of the Inspector.

8. Repeat *steps* 6 and 7 until you get the desired result.

There are plenty of other options to configure, but let's stop here for now. Now, let's discuss how to properly configure the textures of our models.

Configuring textures

Again, there are several settings to configure here, but let's focus on the texture size for now. The idea is to use the size that best fits the usage of that texture, and that depends on lots of factors. The first factor to take into account is the distance from which the object will be seen. If you are creating a first person game, you will probably see lots of objects near enough to justify a big texture, but maybe you have lots of distant objects, such as billboards at the top of buildings, that you will never be near enough to see the details of, so you can use smaller textures for that. Another thing to take into account is the importance of the object. If you are creating a racing game, you will probably have lots of 3D models that will be on-screen for a few seconds and the player will never focus on them; they will be paying attention to the road and other cars. In this case, an object such as a trash can on the street can have a little texture and a low-polygon model and the user will never notice that (unless they stop to appreciate the scenery, but that's acceptable). Finally, you can have a game with a top-down view that will never zoom in on the scene, so the same object that has a big texture in first person games would have a less detailed texture here. In the next figure, you can see that the smaller ship could use a smaller texture:

Figure 5.28 – The same model being seen at different distances

The ideal size of the texture is relative. The usual way to find it is by changing its size until you find the smallest possible size with a decent quality when the object is seen from the nearest position possible in the game. This is a trial and error method. In order to do that, you can do the following:

1. Locate the 3D model and put it into the scene.

2. Put the Scene view camera in a position that shows the object at its biggest possible in-game size. As an example, in an FPS game, it would be almost right next to the object, while in a top-down game, it would be a few meters above the object. Again, that depends on your game.

3. Find and select the texture that the object is using in the folders that were imported with the package or from the material you created previously. They usually have the .png, .jpg, or .tif extensions.

4. In the Inspector, look at the **Max Size** property and reduce it, trying the next smallest value. For example, if the texture is at 2,048, try 1,024.

5. Click **Apply** and check the Scene view to see whether the quality has decreased dramatically or if the change isn't noticeable. You will be surprised.

6. Repeat *steps 4* to *5* until you get a bad-quality result. In that case, just increase the previous resolution to get an acceptable quality. Of course, if you are targeting PC games, you can expect higher resolutions than mobile games.

Now that you have imported, integrated, and configured your objects, let's just create our Player's Base with those assets.

Assembling the scene

Let's start replacing our prototype base using the environment pack we have downloaded. To do that, you must do the following:

1. In the **Environment** pack, locate the folder that contains all the models for the different pieces of the scene and try to find a corner. You can use the search bar in the Project Window to search for the `corner` keyword:

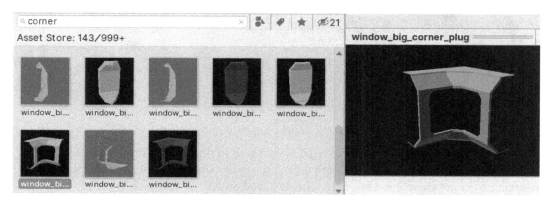

Figure 5.29 – Mesh picker

2. In my specific case, I have the outer and inner side of the corner as separate models, so I need to put them together.

3. Position it in the same position as any corner of your prototype base:

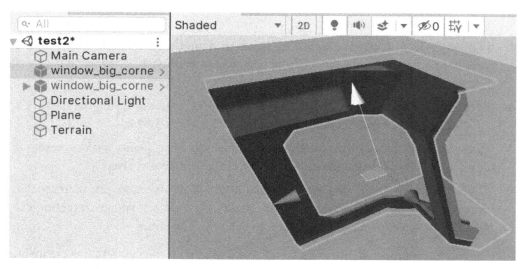

Figure 5.30 – Positioning the mesh on a placeholder for replacement

4. Find the proper model that will connect with that corner to create walls. Again, you can try searching for the `wall` keyword in the Project Window.

5. Instance it and position it so that it's connected to the corner. Don't worry if it doesn't fit perfectly; you will go over the scene when necessary later.

> **Important Note**
> You can select an object and press the *V* key to select a vertex of the selected object to drag it to a vertex of another object. This is called vertex snapping. It allows you to connect two pieces of a scene exactly as you intend:

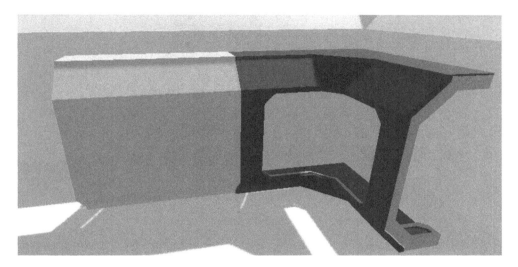

Figure 5.31 – Connecting two modules

6. Repeat the walls until you reach the other end of the Player Base and position another corner. You might get a wall that's a little bit larger or smaller than the original prototype, but that's fine:

Figure 5.32 – Chain of connected modules

7. Complete the rest of the walls and destroy the prototype. Remember that this process is slow and you will need to be patient.

8. Add floors by looking for floor tiles and repeating them all over the surface:

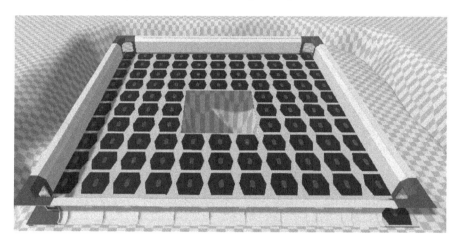

Figure 5.33 – Floor modules with a hole for the pit

9. Add whatever details you want to add with other modular pieces in the package.

10. Put all those pieces in a container object called `Base`. Remember to create an empty object and drag the base pieces into it:

Figure 5.34 – Mesh Sub-Assets

After a lot of practice doing this, you will slowly gain experience with the common pitfalls and good practices of modular scene design. All the packages have different modular designs in mind, so you will need to adapt to them.

Summary

In this chapter, we learned how to import models and textures and integrate them into our scene. We discussed how to apply textures to the terrain, how to replace our prototype mesh with modular models, how to apply textures to those, and how to properly configure the assets, all while taking several criteria into account according to the usage of the object.

With this, we have finished Part 1 of this book and have discussed several basic Unity concepts. In Part 2, we will start to deep dive into several Unity systems that allow us to improve the graphics and sound quality of our game. We will start to learn how to create custom material types to create interesting visual effects and animations.

6
Materials and Effects with URP and Shader Graph

Welcome to the first chapter of *Part 2*! I am super excited that you have reached this part of the book because here we will dive deep into different graphics and audio systems of Unity to dramatically improve the look and feel of the game. We will start this part with this chapter, where we will be discussing what the Shader of a Material is and how to create our own Shaders to achieve several custom effects that couldn't be accomplished using default Unity Shaders. We will be creating a simple water animation effect to learn this new concept.

In this chapter, we will examine the following Shader concepts:

- Introduction to Shaders
- Creating Shaders with Shader Graph

Introducing Shaders

We created Materials in the previous chapter, but we never discussed how they internally work and why the Shader property is super important. In this first section of the chapter, we will be exploring the concept of a Shader as a way to program the video card to achieve custom visual effects.

In this section, we will cover the following concepts related to Shaders:

- Shader Pipeline
- Render Pipeline and URP
- URP Built-in Shaders

Let's start by discussing how a Shader modifies the Shader Pipeline to achieve effects.

Shader Pipeline

Whenever a video card renders a 3D model, it needs input data to process, such as a Mesh, Textures, the transform of the object (position, rotation, and scale), and lights that affect that object. With that data, the video card must output the pixels of the object into the Back-Buffer, the image where the video card will be drawing our objects. That image will be shown when Unity finishes rendering all objects (and some effects) to display the finished scene. Basically, the Back-Buffer is the image the video card renders step by step, showing it when the drawing has finished (at that moment, it becomes the Front-Buffer, swapping with the previous one).

That's the usual way to render an object, but what happens between the input of the data and the output of the pixels can be handled through a myriad of different ways and techniques that depend on how you want your object to look; maybe you want it to be realistic or look like a hologram, maybe the object needs a disintegration effect or a toon effect—there are endless possibilities. The way to specify how our video card will handle the render of the object is through a Shader.

A Shader is a program coded in a specific video card language, such as CG, HLSL, or GLSL, that configures different stages of the render process, sometimes not only configuring them but also replacing them with completely custom code to achieve the exact effect we want. All of the stages of rendering form what we call the Shader Pipeline, a chain of modifications applied to the input data until it's transformed into pixels.

> **Important note**
> Sometimes, what we called the Shader Pipeline in this book can be also found in another bibliography as the Render Pipeline, and whereas the latter is also correct, in Unity, the term Render Pipeline refers to something different, so let's stick with this name.

Each stage of the pipeline is in charge of different modifications and depending on the video card Shader Model, this pipeline can vary a lot. In the next diagram, you can find a simplified Render Pipeline, skipping advanced/optional stages that are not important right now:

Figure 6.1 – Common Shader Pipeline

Let's discuss each of the stages:

- **Input Assembler**: Here is where all of the mesh data, such as the vertex position, UVs, and normals, are assembled to be prepared for the next stage. You can't do much here; this process is almost always the same.

- **Vertex Shader**: In the past, this stage was limited to applying the transformation of the object, the position and perspective of the camera, and some simple but limited lighting calculations. With modern GPUs, you are in charge of doing whatever you want. This stage receives each one of the vertexes of the object to render and outputs a modified one, so basically, you have the chance to modify the geometry of the object here. The usual code here is basically the same as old video cards had, applying the transform of the object, but you can do several effects such as inflating the object along its normals to apply the old toon effect technique or apply some distortions to make a hologram effect (look at the hologram effect in *Death Stranding*). There's also the opportunity to calculate data for the next stages, but we won't be going that deep for now.

- **Culling**: For most of the models you are going to render, you will never see the backside of the model's face. Let's take as an example a cube; there's no way to look at the back or inner side of any of its sides because they will be automatically occluded by the other sides. Knowing that, rendering both sides of each face of the cube, even if the backside can't be seen, makes no sense, and luckily this stage takes care of that. Culling will determine whether the face needs to be rendered based on the orientation of the face, saving lots of pixel calculation for occluded faces. You can change this to behave differently for specific cases; as an example, we can create a glass box that needs to be transparent to see all sides of the box.

- **Rasterizer**: Now that we have the modified and visible geometry of our model calculated, it's time to convert it into pixels. The Rasterizer creates all pixels for the triangles of our mesh. Lots of things happen here but again, we have very little control over that; the usual way to rasterize is just to create all pixels inside the edges of the mesh triangles. We have other modes that just render the pixels on the edges to see a wireframe effect, but this is usually used for debugging purposes:

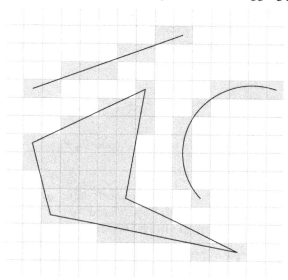

Figure 6.2 – Example of figures being rasterized

- **Fragment Shader**: This is one of the most customizable stages of all. Its purpose is simple: just determine the color of each one of the fragments (pixels) that the rasterizer has generated. Here, lots of things can happen, from simply outputting a plain color or sampling a texture to applying complex lighting calculations such as normal mapping and PBR. Also, you can use this stage to create special effects such as water animations, holograms, distortions, disintegrations, and other special effects that require you to modify what the pixels look like. We will explore how we can use this stage in the next sections of this chapter.

- **Depth Testing**: Before given the pixel as finished, we need to check whether the pixel can be seen. This stage checks whether the pixel's depth is behind or in front of the previously rendered pixel, guaranteeing that regardless of the rendering order of the objects, the nearest pixels to the camera are always being drawn on top of others. Again, usually, this stage is left in its default state, prioritizing pixels that are nearer to the camera, but some effects require different behavior. As an example, in the next screenshot, you can see an effect that allows you to see objects that are behind other objects, such as units and buildings in *Age of Empires*:

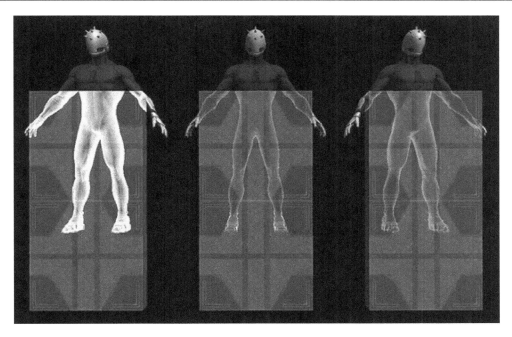

Figure 6.3 – Rendering the occluded parts of the character

- **Blending**: Once the color of the pixel is determined and we are sure the pixel is not occluded by a previous pixel, the final step is to put it in the Back-Buffer (the frame or image you are drawing). The usual way to do this is to just override whatever pixel was in that position (because our pixel is nearer to the camera), but if you think about transparent objects, we need to combine our pixel with the previous one to make the transparency effect. Transparencies have other things to take into account aside from the blending, but the main idea is that blending controls exactly how the pixel will be combined with the previously rendered pixel in the Back-Buffer.

Shader Pipelines is a subject that would require an entire book, but for the scope of this book, the previous description will give you a good idea of what a Shader does, and the possible effects that it can achieve. Now that we have discussed how a Shader renders a single object, it is worth discussing how Unity renders all objects using Render Pipelines.

Render Pipelines and URP

We have covered how the video card renders an object, but Unity is in charge of asking the video card to execute its Shader Pipeline per object. To do so, Unity needs to do lots of preparations and calculations to determine exactly how and when each Shader needs to be executed. The responsibility of doing this is given to what Unity calls a Render Pipeline.

A Render Pipeline is a way to draw the objects of a scene. At first, it sounds like there should be just one simple way of doing this, such as just iterating over all objects in the scene and executing the Shader Pipeline with the Shader specified in each object's Material, but it can be more complex than that. Usually, the main difference between one Render Pipeline and another is the way in which lighting and some advanced effects are calculated, but they can differ in other ways.

In previous Unity versions, there was just one single Render Pipeline, which is now called the Built-in Render Pipeline. It was a Pipeline that had all of the possible features you would need for all kinds of projects, from mobile 2D graphics and simple 3D graphics to cutting-edge 3D graphics what ones you can find on consoles or high-end PCs. This sounds ideal, but actually, it isn't; having one single giant renderer that needs to be highly customizable to adapt to all possible scenarios generates lots of overhead and limitations that cause more headaches than creating a custom Render Pipeline. Luckily, the latest version of Unity introduced the **Scriptable Render Pipelin**e (SRP), a way to create Render Pipelines adapted for your project.

Thankfully, Unity doesn't want you to create your own Render Pipeline for each project (a complex task), so it created two custom Pipelines for you that are ready to use: URP (formerly called LWRP), which stands for Universal Render Pipeline, and HDRP, which stands for High Definition Render Pipeline. The idea is that you must choose one or the other based on your project requirements (unless you really need to create your own). URP, the one we selected when creating the project for our game, is a Render Pipeline suitable for most games that don't require lots of advanced graphics features, such as mobile games or simple PC games, while HDRP is packed with lots of advanced rendering features for high-quality games. The latter requires high-end hardware to run, while URP runs in almost every relevant target device. It is worth mentioning that you can switch between Built-in Renderer, HDRP, and URP whenever you want, including after creating the project (not recommended):

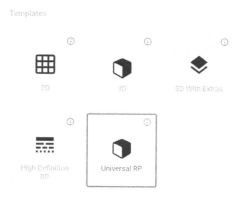

Figure 6.4 – Project wizard showing HDRP and URP templates

We can discuss how each one is implemented and the differences between each, but again, this can fill entire chapters; right now, the idea of this section is for you to know why we picked URP when we created our project because it has some restrictions we will encounter throughout this book that we will need to take into account, so it is good to know why we accepted those limitations (to run our game on all relevant hardware). Also, we need to know that we have chosen URP because it has support for Shader Graph, the Unity tool that we will be using in this chapter to create custom effects. Previous Unity Built-in Pipelines didn't provide us with such a tool (aside from third-party plugins). Finally, another reason to introduce the concept of URP is that it comes with lots of built-in Shaders that we will need to know about before creating our own to avoid reinventing the wheel, and to adapt ourselves to those Shaders, because if you came from previous versions of Unity, the ones you know won't work here, and actually this is exactly what we are going to discuss in the next section of this book: the differences between the different URP Built-in Shaders.

URP Built-in Shaders

Now that we know the difference between URP and other pipelines, let's discuss which Shaders come integrated into URP. Let's briefly describe the three most important Shaders in this Pipeline:

- **Lit**: This is the replacement of the old Standard Shader. This Shader is useful when creating all kinds of realistic Physics Materials such as wood, rubber, metal, skin, and combinations of them (such as a character with skin and metal armor). It supports Normal Mapping, Occlusion, Metallic and Specular Workflow, and transparencies.

- **Simple Lit**: This is the replacement of the old Mobile/Diffuse Shader. As the name suggests, this Shader is a simpler version of Lit, meaning that its lighting calculations are simpler approximations of how light works, getting fewer features than its counterpart. Basically, when you have simple graphics without realistic lighting effects, this is the best choice.

- **Unlit**: This is the replacement of the old Unlit/Texture Shader. Sometimes, you need objects without lighting whatsoever, and in that case, this is the Shader for you. No lighting doesn't mean an absence of light or complete darkness; it actually means that the object has no shadows at all, and it's fully visible without any shade. Some simplistic graphics can work with this, relying on shadowing being baked in the texture, meaning that the texture comes with the shadow. This is extremely performant, especially for low-end devices such as mobile phones. Also, you have other cases such as light tubes or screens, objects that can't receive shadows because they emit light, so they will be seen in full color even in complete darkness. In the following screenshot, you can see a 3D model using an Unlit Shader. It looks like it's being lit, but it's just the texture of the model with lighter and darker colors being applied in different parts of the object:

Figure 6.5 – Pod using an Unlit effect to simulate cheap lighting

Let's do an interesting disintegration effect with the Simple Lit Shader to demonstrate its capabilities. You must do the following:

1. Download and import a **Cloud Noise** Texture from any search engine:

Figure 6.6 – Noise Texture

2. Select the recently imported texture in the Project Panel.

3. In the Inspector, set the **Alpha Source** property to **From Gray Scale**. This will mean the alpha channel of the texture will be calculated based on the grayscale of the image:

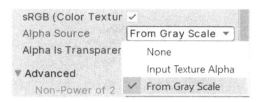

Figure 6.7 – Generate Alpha from Grayscale Texture setting

> **Important note**
>
> The alpha channel of a color is often associated with transparency, but you will notice that our object won't be transparent. The Alpha channel is extra color data that can be used for several purposes when doing effects. In this case, we will use it to determine which pixels are deintegrated first.

4. Create a Material by clicking on the + icon in the Project View and selecting **Material**:

Figure 6.8 – Material creation button

5. Create a cube with the **GameObject | 3d Object | Cube** option at the top menu of Unity:

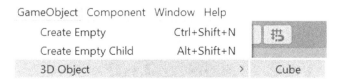

Figure 6.9 – Cube primitive creation

6. Drag the created Material from the Project Window to the cube to apply the Material.

7. Click in the drop-down menu at the right of the Shader property in the Inspector and look for the **Universal Render Pipeline | Simple Lit** option:

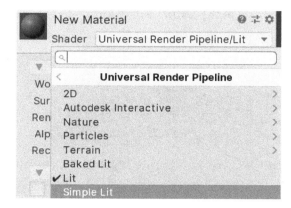

Figure 6.10 – Simple Lit Shader selection

8. Select the **Material** and in **Base Map,** set the recently downloaded Cloud Noise Texture.

9. Check the **Alpha Clipping** checkbox and set the **Threshold** slider to 0.5:

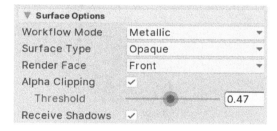

Figure 6.11 Alpha Clipping Threshold Material slider

10. You will see how as you move the Alpha Clipping slider, the object starts to disintegrate. Alpha Clipping discards pixels that have less Alpha intensity than the style value:

Figure 6.12 Disintegration effect with Alpha Clipping

11. Finally, set **Render Face** to **Both** to turn off the **Culling Shader Stage** and see both sides of the cube's faces:

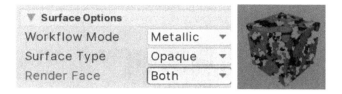

Figure 6.13 Double-sided Alpha Clipping

12. Take into account that the artist that creates the texture can configure the Alpha channel manually instead of calculating it from the grayscale, just to control exactly how the disintegration effect must look regardless of the texture´s color distribution.

The idea of this section is not to give a comprehensive guide to all of the properties of all URP Shaders, but to give you an idea of what a Shader can do when properly configured and when to use each one of the integrated Shaders. Sometimes, you can achieve the effect you need just by using existing Shaders. In fact, you can probably do so for probably 99% of the cases in simple games, so try to stick to them as much as you can. But if you really need to create a custom Shader to create a very specific effect, the next section will teach you how to use the URP tool called Shader Graph.

Creating Shaders with Shader Graph

Now that we know how Shaders work and the existing Shaders in URP, we have a basic notion of when it is necessary to create a custom Shader and when it is not necessary. In case you really need to create one, this section will cover the basics of effects creation with Shader Graph, a tool to create effects using a visual node-based editor, being an easy tool to use when you are not used to coding.

In this section, we will discuss the following concepts of the Shader Graph:

- Creating our first Shader Graph
- Using Textures
- Combining Textures
- Applying Transparency

Let's start seeing how we can create and use a Shader Graph.

Creating our first Shader Graph asset

Shader Graph is a tool that allows us to create custom effects using a node-based system. An effect in Shader Graph can look like the following screenshot, where you can see the nodes needed to create a hologram effect:

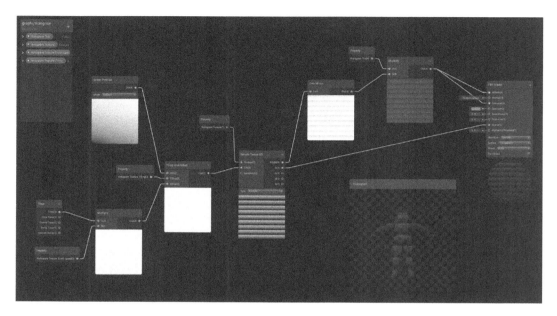

Figure 6.14 Shader Graph with nodes to create a custom effect

We will discuss later what those nodes do and will do a step-by-step effect example, but in the screenshot, you can see how the author created and connected several nodes, which are those interconnected boxes, each one doing a specific process to achieve the effect. The idea of creating effects with Shader Graph is to learn which specific nodes you need and how to connect them properly, to create an "algorithm" or a series of ordered steps to achieve a specific result. This is similar to the way we code the gameplay of the game, but this Graph is adapted and simplified just for effect purposes.

To create and edit our first Shader Graph asset, do the following:

1. In the Project Window, click the + icon and find the **Shader | PBR Graph** option. This will create a Shader Graph using PBR mode, meaning that this Shader will support lighting effects (unlike Unlit Graphs):

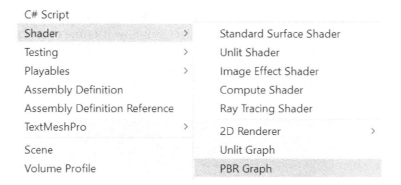

Figure 6.15 PBR Shader Graph creation

2. Name it `WaterGraph`. If you lose the opportunity to rename the asset, remember that you can select the asset, right-click, and select **Rename**:

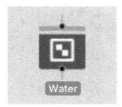

Figure 6.16 Shader Graph Asset

3. Create a new Material called `WaterMaterial` and set **Shader** to **Shader Graphs/Water**. If for some reason Unity doesn't allow you to do that, try right-clicking **WaterGraph** and clicking **Reimport**. As you can see, the created Shader Graph asset now appears as a Shader in the Material, meaning that we have already created a custom Shader:

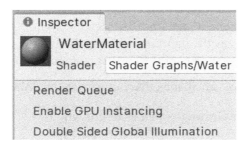

Figure 6.17 Setting a Shader Graph as a Material Shader

4. Create a Plane with the **GameObject | 3d Object | Plane** option.
5. Drag the **Material** to the **Plane** to apply it.

Now, you have created your first custom Shader and applied it to a Material. So far, it doesn't look interesting at all—it's just a gray effect, but now it's time to edit the graph to unlock its full potential. As the name of the Graph suggests, we will be creating a water effect in this chapter to illustrate several nodes of the Shader Graph toolset and how to connect them, so let's start by discussing the Master node. When you open the graph by double-clicking it, you will see the following:

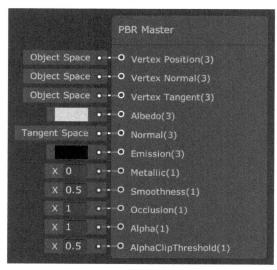

Figure 6.18 Master node with all of the properties needed to calculate object appearance

All nodes will have input pins, the data they need to work, and output pins, which are the results of its process. As an example, in a sum operation, we will have two input numbers and an output number, the result of the sum. In this case, you can see that the Master node just has inputs, and that's because all data that enters the Master node will be used by Unity to calculate the Rendering and Lighting of the object, things such as the desired object color or texture (the Albedo input pin), how smooth it is (the Smoothness input pin), or how much metal it contains (the Metallic input pin), so they are all of the properties that will affect how the lighting will be applied to the object. In a sense, the input of this node is the output data of the entire graph and the ones we need to fill.

Let's start exploring how we can change that output data by doing the following:

1.   Double-click **Shader Graph** to open its editor window.

2.   Click in the gray rectangle to the left of the **Albedo** input pin:

Figure 6.19 Albedo Master node input pin

3. In the color picker, select a light blue color, like water. Select the bluish part of the circle around the picker and then a shade of that color in the middle rectangle:

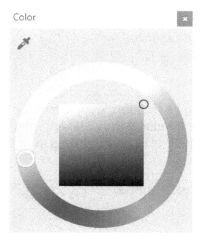

Figure 6.20 Color picker

4. Set **Smoothness** to 0.9:

Figure 6.21 Smoothness PBR Master node input pin

5. Click the **Save Asset** button at the top-left of the window:

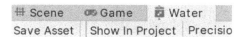

Figure 6.22 Shader Graph saving options

6. Go back to the Scene View and check the plane is light blue and with the sun reflected on it:

Figure 6.23 Initial Shader Graph results

As you can see, the behavior of the Shader varies according to the properties you set in the Master node, but so far, doing this is no different than creating an Unlit Shader and setting up its properties; the real power of Shader Graph is when you use nodes that do specific calculations as inputs of the Master node. We will start seeing the texturing nodes, which allow us to apply Textures to our model.

Using Textures

The idea of using Textures is to have an image applied to the model in a way that means we can paint different parts of the model with different colors. Remember that the model has the UV map, which allows Unity to know which part of the Texture will be applied to which part of the model:

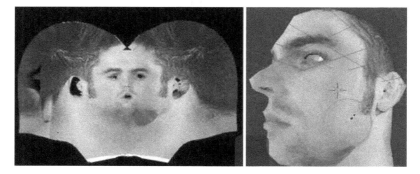

Figure 6.24 On the left, a face texture; on the right, the same texture applied to a face mesh

We have several nodes to do this task, one of them being Sample Texture 2D, a node that has two main inputs. First, it asks us for the texture to sample or apply to the model and then the UV. You can see it in the following screenshot:

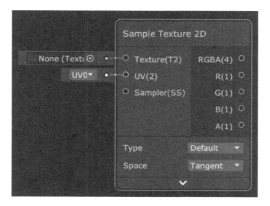

Figure 6.25 Sample Texture node

As you can see, the default value of the Texture input node is **None**, so there's no texture by default, and we need to manually specify that. For UV, the default value is UV0, meaning that, by default, the node will use the main UV channel of the model, and yes, a model can have several UVs set, but for now, we will stick with the main one. Let's try this node, doing the following:

1. Download and import a **Tileable Water Texture** from the internet:

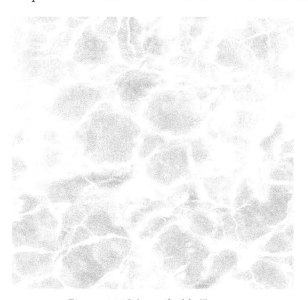

Figure 6.26 Water tileable Texture

2. Select the Texture and be sure that the **Wrap Mode** property of the Texture is on **Repeat**, which will allow us to repeat the Texture as we did in the terrain, because the idea is to use this Shader to cover large water areas:

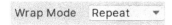

Figure 6.27 Texture Repeat mode

3. In the **Water Shader Graph**, right-click in an empty area of the **Shader Graph** and select **Create Node**:

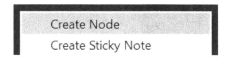

Figure 6.28 Shader Graph Create Node option

4. In the Search box, write `Sample texture` and all of the sample nodes will show up. Select **Sample Texture 2D** double clicking it:

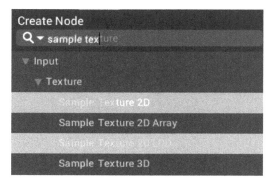

Figure 6.29 Sample texture node search

5. Click in the circle to the left of the Texture input pin of the Sample Texture 2D node. It will allow us to pick a Texture to sample—just select the water one. You can see that the Texture can be previewed in the bottom part of the node:

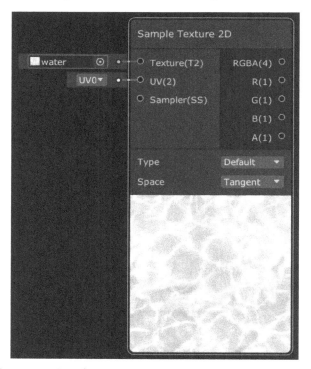

Figure 6.30 Sample Texture node with a Texture in its input pin

6. Drag the output pin **RGBA** from the **Sample Texture 2D** node to the **Albedo** input pin of the Master node:

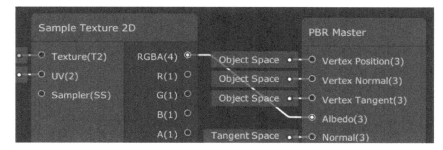

Figure 6.31 Connecting the results of a Texture sampling with the Albedo pin of the Master node

7. Click the **Save Asset** button at the top-left part of the Shader Graph editor and see the changes in the scene view:

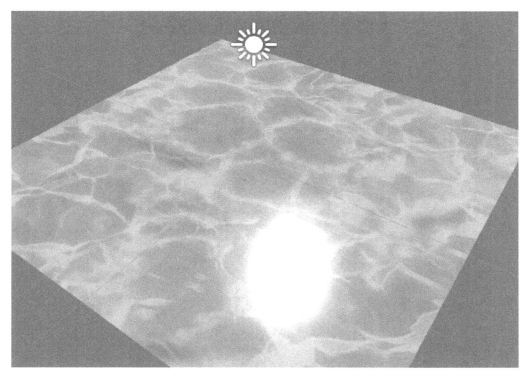

Figure 6.32 Results of applying a Texture in our Shader Graph

As you can see, the texture is properly applied to the model, but if you take into account that the default plane has a size of 10x10 meters, the ripples of the water seem too big, so let's tile the Texture! To do that, we need to change the UVs of the model, making them bigger. Bigger UVs sounds like the Texture should also get bigger, but take into account that we are not making the object bigger; we are just modifying the UV, so the same object size will read more of the texture, meaning that the bigger texture sample area will make repetitions of the texture and put them in the same object size, so that will be compressed inside the model area. To do so, follow the next steps:

1. Right-click in any empty space area and click **New Node** to search the UV node:

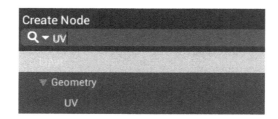

Figure 6.33 Searching for the UV node

2. Using the same method create a **Multiply** node.

3. Set the **B** pin input value to (4,4,4,4):

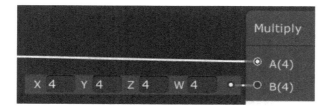

Figure 6.34 Multiplying the UVs by 4

4. Drag the **Out** pin of the UV node to the **A** pin of the **Multiply** node to connect them.

5. Drag the **Out** pin of the **Multiply** node to the **UV** pin of the **Sample Texture 2D** node to connect them:

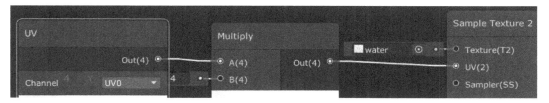

Figure 6.35 Using the multiplied UVs to sample the Texture

6. If you save the graph and go back to the Scene View, you can see that now the ripples are smaller, because we have tiled the UVs of our model. You can also see that in the preview of the **Sampler Texture 2D** node:

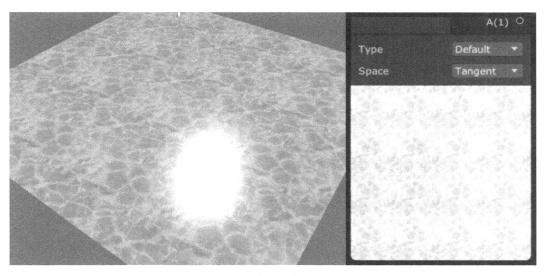

Figure 6.36 Results of the model's UV multiplication

Another interesting effect we can do now is to apply an Offset to the Texture to move it. The idea is that even if the plane is not actually moving, we will simulate the flow of the water through it, moving just the Texture. Remember, the responsibility of determining the part of the Texture to apply to each part of the model belongs to the UV, so if we add values to the UV coordinates, we will be moving them, generating a Texture sliding effect. To do so, let's do the following:

1. Create an **Add** node to the right of the **Multiply** node.

2. Connect the **Out** pin of the UV to the **A** pin of the **Add** node:

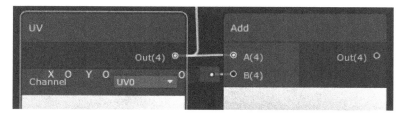

Figure 6.37 Adding values to the UVs

3. Create a **Time** node at the left of the **Add** node.

4. Connect the **Time** node to the **B** pin of the **Add** node:

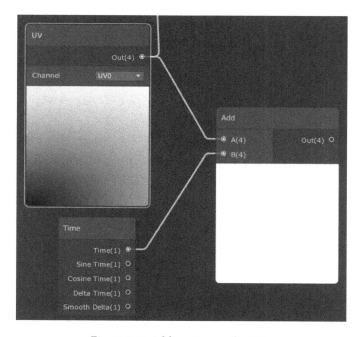

Figure 6.38 Adding time to the UVs

5.   Connect the **Out** pin of the **Add** node to the **A** input pin of the **Multiply** node:

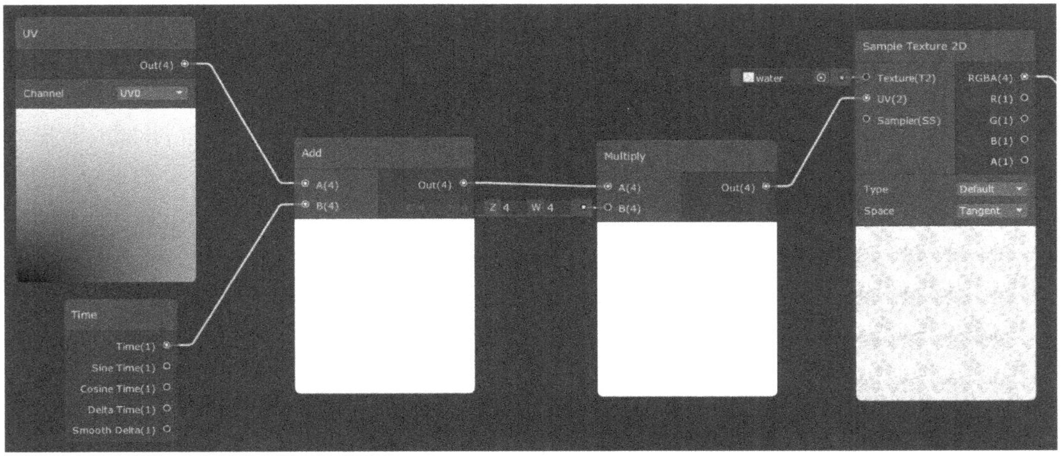

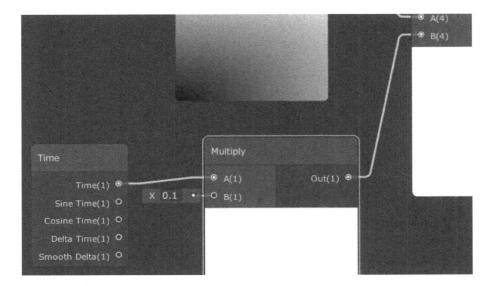

Figure 6.39 Added and multiplied UVs as an input of the Sample Texture

6.   Save and see the water moving in the Scene View.

7.   If you feel the water is moving too fast, try to use the multiplication node to make the time a smaller value. I recommend you try it by yourself before looking at the next screenshot, which has the answer:

Figure 6.40 Multiplication of time to move it faster

8. If you feel the graph is starting to get bigger, try to hide some of the node previews by clicking on the up arrow that appears on the preview when you move the mouse over it:

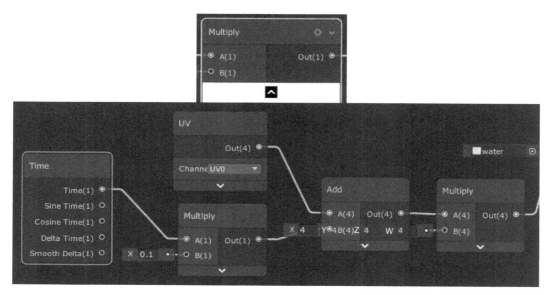

Figure 6.41 Hiding the preview and unused pins from the graph nodes

So, to recap, first we added the time to the UV to move it and then multiplied the result of the moved UV to make it bigger to tile the Texture. It is worth mentioning that there's a Tiling and Offset node that does all of this for us, but I wanted to show you how a simple multiplication to scale the UV and an add operation to move it generated a nice effect; you can't imagine all of the possible effects you can achieve with other simple mathematical nodes! Actually, let's explore other usages of mathematical nodes to combine Textures in the next section.

Combining Textures

Even though we have used nodes, we haven't created anything that can't be created using regular Shaders, but that's about to change. So far, we can see the water moving but it still look static, and that's because the ripples are always the same. We have several techniques to generate ripples, and the simplest one would be to combine two water Textures moving in different directions to mix their ripples, and actually, we can simply use the same Texture, just flipped, to save some memory. To combine the Textures, we will sum them and then divide them by 2, so basically, we are calculating the average of the textures! Let's do that by doing the following:

1. Select all of the nodes between **Time** and **Sampler 2D** (including them), creating a selection rectangle by clicking in any empty space in the graph, holding and dragging the click, and then releasing when all target nodes are covered:

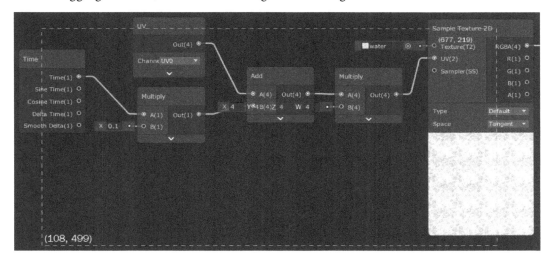

Figure 6.42 Selecting several nodes

2. Right-click and select **Copy**, and then again right-click and select **Paste**, or use the classic *Ctrl + C*, *Ctrl + V* commands (*command + C*, *command + V* in Mac), or just *Ctrl + D* (*command + D*).

3. Move the copied nodes below the original ones:

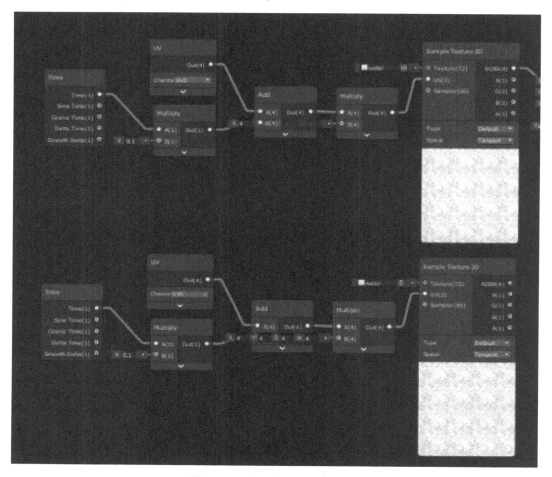

Figure 6.43 Duplication of nodes

4. For the copied nodes, set the **B** pin of the **Multiply** node connected to the **Sample Texture 2D** to (-4,-4,-4,-4). You can see that that flipped the texture.

5. Also, set the **B** pin of the **Multiply** node connected to the **Time** node in `-0.1`:

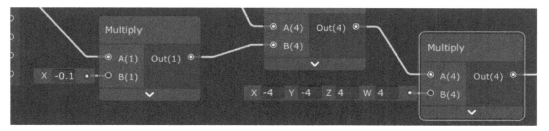

Figure 6.44 Multiplication of values

6. Create an **Add** node at the right of both Sampler Texture 2D nodes and connect the outputs of those nodes as the **A** and **B** input pins of the **Add** node:

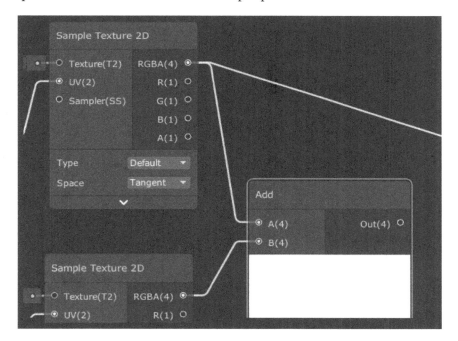

Figure 6.45 Adding two Textures

7. You can see that the resulting combination is too bright because we have summed up the intensity of both textures, so let's fix that by multiplying the **Out** of the **Add** node by (0.5,0.5,0.5,0.5), which will divide each resulting color channel by 2, averaging the color:

Figure 6.46 Dividing the sum of two Textures to get the average

8. Connect the **Out** pin of the **Multiply** node to the **Albedo** pin of the Master node to apply all of those calculations as the color of the object.

9. Save the **Asset** and see the results in the Scene View:

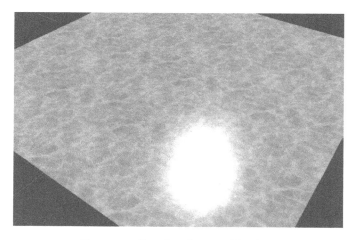

Figure 6.47 Results of texture blending

You can keep adding nodes to make the effect more diverse, such as using Sinus nodes to apply non-linear movements and so on, but I will let you learn that by experimenting with this by yourself. For now, we will stop here. As always, this topic deserves a full book, and the intention of this chapter is to give you a small taste of this powerful Unity tool. I recommend you look for other Shader Graphs examples on the internet to learn other usages of the same nodes and, of course, new nodes. One thing to consider here is that everything we just did is basically applied to the Fragment Shader stage of the Shader Pipeline we discussed earlier. Now, let's use the Blending Shader stage to apply some transparency to the water.

Applying transparency

Before declaring our effect finished, a little addition we can do is to make the water a little bit transparent. Remember that the Shader Pipeline has this Blending stage, which has the responsibility of blending each pixel of our model into the image being rendered in this frame. The idea is to make our Shader Graph modify that stage to apply an Alpha Blending, a blending that combines our model and the previous rendered models based on the Alpha value of our model. To get that effect, do the following steps:

1. Click the wheel at the top-right part of the Master node.

2. Set **Surface property** to **Transparent**.

3. Set the **Blend** property to **Alpha** if it isn't already at that value:

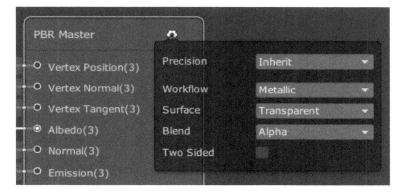

Figure 6.48 PBR Master node settings

4. Set the **Alpha** input pin of the Master to 0 . 5:

Figure 6.49 Setting the Alpha of the Master node

5. Save the graph and see the transparency being applied in the Scene View. If you can't see the effect, just put a cube in the water to make the effect more evident:

Figure 6.50 Shadows from the water being applied to a cube

6. You can see the shadows that the water is casting on our cube. That's because Unity doesn't detect that the object is transparent, so it thinks that it must cast shadows, so let's disable them. Click on the water plane and look for the Mesh Renderer component in the Inspector.

7. In the **Lighting** section, set **Cast Shadows** to **Off**; this will disable shadow casting from the Plane:

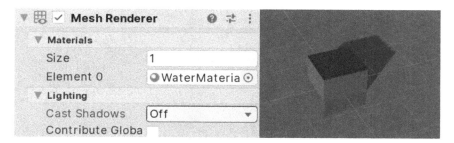

Figure 6.51 Disabling shadow casting

Adding transparency is a simple process but has its caveats, such as the shadow problem, and in more complex scenarios, it can have other problems, so I would suggest that you avoid using transparency unless it is necessary. Actually, our water can live without transparency, especially when we apply this water to the river basin around the base, because we don't need to see what's under the water, but the idea is for you to know all of your options. In the next screenshot, you can see how we have put a giant plane with this effect below our base, big enough to cover the entire basin:

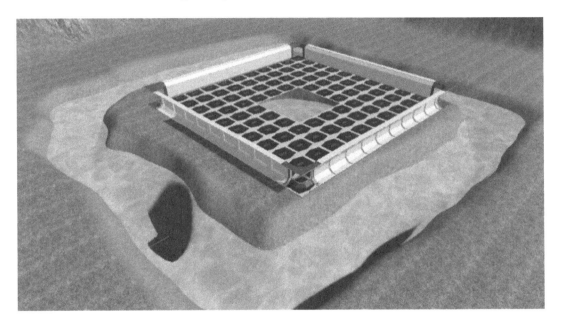

Figure 6.52 Using our water in the main scene

Summary

In this chapter, we discussed how a Shader works using a GPU and how to create our first simple Shader to achieve a nice water effect. Using Shaders is a complex and interesting job, and in a team, there are usually one or more people in charge of creating all of these effects, in a position called technical artist; so, as you can see, this topic can expand up to become a whole career. Remember, the intention of this book is to give you a small taste of all the possible roles you can take in the industry, so if you really liked this role, I suggest you start reading Shader-exclusive books. You have a long but super-interesting road in front of you.

But enough Shaders, for now—let's move to the next topic about improving graphics and creating visual effects with particle systems!

7
Visual Effects with Particle Systems and VFX Graph

Here, we will continue learning about visual effects for our game. We will be discussing particle systems, a way to simulate fire, waterfalls, smoke, and all kinds of fluids. Also, we will see the two Unity **particle systems** to create these kind of effects, **Shuriken** and **VFX Graph**, the latter being more powerful than the first, but requiring more hardware.

In this chapter, we will examine the following particle system concepts:

- Introduction to particle systems
- Creating fluid simulations
- Creating complex simulations with VFX Graph

Introduction to particle systems

All graphics and effects we have created so far use static meshes, 3D models that can't be skewed, bent, or deformed in any way. **Fluids** such as fire and smoke clearly can't be represented using this kind of mesh, but actually, we can simulate these effects with a combination of static meshes, and this is where particle systems are useful.

Particle systems are objects that emit and animates lots of **particles** or **billboards**, which are simple quad meshes that face the camera. Each particle is a static mesh, but rendering, animating, and combining lots of them can generate the illusion of a fluid. In the next image you can see on the left a smoke effect using particle systems, and on the right, the **Wireframe** view of the same particles. There you can see the quads that create the illusion of smoke, which is done by applying a smoke texture to each of the particles and animating them so they spawn at the bottom and move up in random directions:

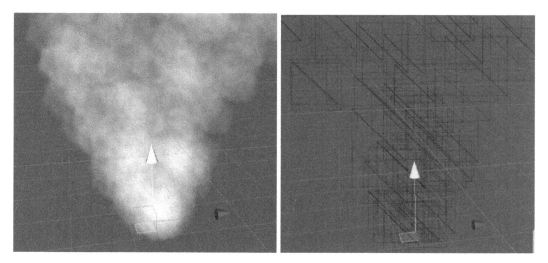

Figure 7.1 – Left side, a smoke particle system; right side, the wireframe of the same system

In this section, we will cover the following concepts related to particles:

- Creating a basic particle system
- Using advanced modules

Let's start discussing how to create our very first particle system.

Creating a basic particle system

To illustrate the creation of a particle system, let's create an explosion effect. The idea is to spawn lots of particles at once and spread them in all directions. Let's start creating the particle system and configuring the basic settings it provides to change its default behavior. To do so, follow these steps:

1. Select the **GameObject | Effects | Particle System** option:

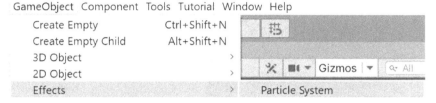

Figure 7.2 – Particle system creation button

2. You should see the effect in the following screenshot. The default behavior is a column of particles going up, like the smoke effect shown previously. Let's change that:

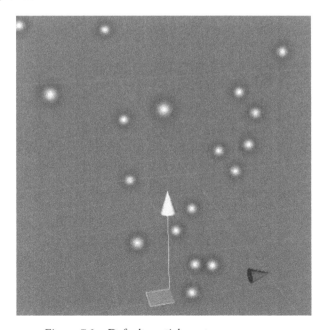

Figure 7.3 – Default particle system appearance

3. Click the created object in the scene and look at the inspector.

4. Open the **Shape** section by clicking on the title.

5. Change the **Shape** property to **Sphere**. Now the particles should move in all possible directions instead of following the default cone:

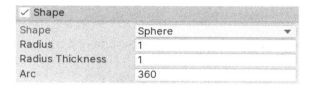

Figure 7.4 – Shape properties

6. In the particle system **module** (usually known as Main) set **Start Speed** to 10. This will make the particles move faster.

7. In the same module, set **Start Lifetime** to 0.5. This specifies how long a particle will live. In this case, we have given a lifetime of half a second. In combination with the speed (10 meters per second), this makes the particles disappear after moving 5 meters:

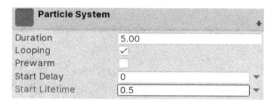

Figure 7.5 – Main Particle System module

8. Open the **Emission** module and set **Rate Over Time** to 0. This property specifies how many particles will be emitted per second, but for an explosion, we actually need a burst of particles, so we won't emit particles constantly over time in this case.

9. In the **Bursts** list, click the + button at the bottom and in the created item in the list, set the count column to 100:

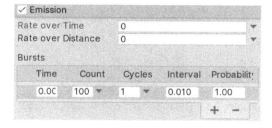

Figure 7.6 – Emission module

10. In the Main module (the one titled **Particle System**) set **Duration** to 1 and uncheck **Looping**. In our case, the explosion won't repeat constantly; we just need one explosion:

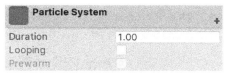

Figure 7.7 – Looping checkbox

11. Now that the particle isn't looping, you need to manually hit the **Play** button that is shown in the **Particle Effect** window in the bottom-right part of the Scene View to see the system:

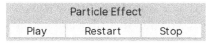

Figure 7.8 – Particle system playback controls

12. Set **Stop Action** to **Destroy**. This will destroy the object when the **Duration** time has passed. This will just work when you are running the game, so you can safely use this configuration while editing your scene:

Figure 7.9 – Stop Action set to Destroy

13. Set the **Start Size** of the Main module to 3. This will make the particles bigger so they seem denser:

Figure 7.10 – Particle system Start Size

14. Click on the down-pointing arrow at the right of the **Start Rotation** property of the Main module and select **Random Between Two Constants**.

15. Set the **Start Rotation** to 0 and 360 in the two input values that appeared after the previous step. This allows us to give the particles a random rotation when they spawn to make them look slightly different from each other:

Figure 7.11 – Random Start Rotation

16. Now the particles behave as expected, but they don't look as expected. Let's change that. Create a new material by clicking on the + icon in the Project View and selecting **Material**. Call it `Explosion`.

17. Set its shader to `Universal Render Pipeline/Particles/Unlit`. This is a special shader that is used to apply a texture to the Shuriken particle system:

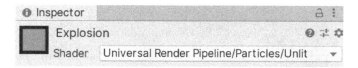

Figure 7.12 – Particle system material shader

18. Download a smoke particle texture from the internet or the **Asset Store**. In this case, it is important to download one with a black background; ignore the others:

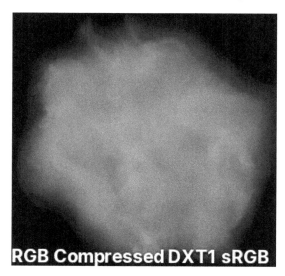

Figure 7.13 – Smoke particle texture

19. Set this texture as the **Base Map** of the material.

20. Set the **Surface Type** to **Transparent** and the **Blending Mode** to **Additive**. Doing this will make the particles blend with each other, instead of being drawn on each other, to simulate a big mass of smoke instead of individual smoke puffs. We use **Additive** mode because our texture has a black background and because we want to create a lighting effect (the explosion will brighten the scene):

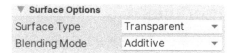

Figure 7.14 – Surface options for particles

21. Drag your material to the **Material** property of the **Renderer** module:

Figure 7.15 – Particle material settings

22. Now your system should look like this:

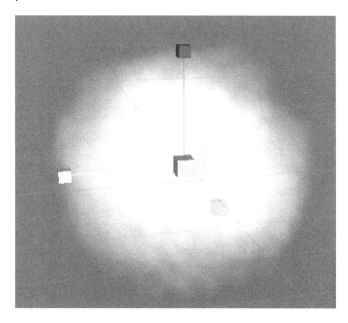

Figure 7.16 – Result of the previous settings

In the previous steps, we have changed how the particles or billboards will spawn (using the Emission module), in which direction they will move (using the Shape module), how fast they will move, how long they will last, how big they will be (using the Main module), and what they will look like (using the Renderer module). Creating particle systems is a simple case of properly configuring their different settings. Of course, doing it properly is an art on its own; it requires creativity and knowledge of how to use all the settings and configurations they provide. So, to increase our configurations toolbox, let's discuss some advanced modules.

Using advanced modules

Our system looks nice, but we can improve it a lot, so let's enable some new modules to increase its quality:

1. Check the checkbox on the left of the **Color over Lifetime** module to enable it:

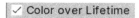

Figure 7.17 – Enabling the Color over Lifetime module

2. Open the module by clicking on the title and click the white bar on the right of the **Color** property. This will open the gradient editor.

3. Click slightly to the right of the top-left white marker in the bar to create a new marker. Also, click slightly to the left of the top-right white marker to create the fourth marker. These markers will allow us to specify the transparency of the particles during its life:

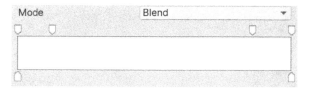

Figure 7.18 – Color over Lifetime gradient editor

4. If you created unwanted markers, just drag them outside the window to remove them.

5. Click on the top-left marker (not the one we created, the one that was already there) and set the **Alpha** slider at the bottom to 0. Do the same with the top-right marker, as shown in the following screenshot. Now you should see the particles fading away instead of popping out of existence when the explosion is finishing:

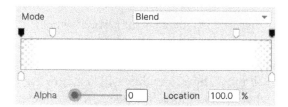

Figure 7.19 – Fade-in and fade-out gradient

6. Enable the **Limit Velocity over Lifetime** module by clicking on its checkbox.

7. Set the **Dampen** setting to 0.1. This will make the particles slowly stop instead of continuing to move:

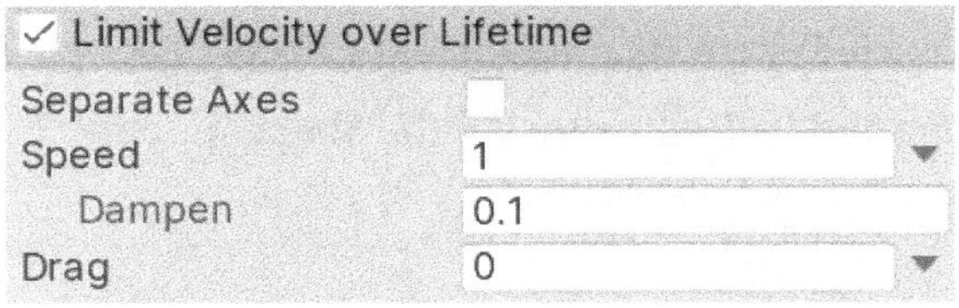

Figure 7.20 – Dampen the velocity to make the particles stop

8. Enable **Rotation over Lifetime** and set the **Angular Velocity** between -90 and 90. Remember that you should set the value in **Random Between Two Constants** by clicking on the down-pointing arrow to the right of the property. Now the particles should rotate slightly during their lives to simulate more motion:

Figure 7.21 – Random rotation velocity

As you can see, there are lots of extra modules that can be enabled and disabled to add layers of behavior on top of the existing ones, so again, use them creatively to create all kinds of effects. Remember that you can create Prefabs of these systems to replicate them all over your scene. I also recommend searching and downloading particle effects from the Asset Store to see how other people have used the same system to create amazing effects. That is the best way to learn how to create them, seeing a variety of different systems, and that is actually what we are going to do in the next section, create more systems!

Creating fluid simulations

As we said, the best way to learn how to create particle systems is to keep looking for already-created particle systems and explore how people have used the various system settings to create completely different simulations.

In this section, we will see how to create the following effects using particle systems:

- A waterfall effect
- A bonfire effect

Let's start with the simplest one, the waterfall effect.

Creating a waterfall effect

In order to do this, follow these steps:

1. Create a new particle system (**GameObject | Effects | Particle System**).

2. Set **Shape** to **Edge** and its **Radius** to 5 in the **Shape** module. This will make the particles spawn along a line of emission:

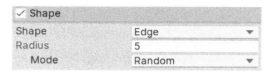

Figure 7.22 – Edge shape

3. Set the **Rate over Lifetime** of the **Emission** module to 50.

4. Set the **Start Size** of the Main module to 3 and the **Start Lifetime** to 3:

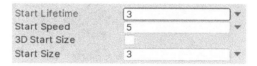

Figure 7.23 – Main module settings

5. Set the **Gravity Modifier** of the Main module to 0.5. This will make the particles fall down:

Figure 7.24 – Gravity Modifier in the Main module

6. Use the same **Explosion** material we created previously for this system:

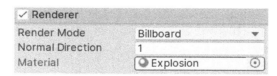

Figure 7.25 – Explosion particle material

7. Enable **Color Over Lifetime** and open the **Gradient** editor.

8. Click the bottom-right marker, and this time you should see a color picker instead of an alpha slider. The top markers allow you to change the transparency over time, while the bottom ones change the color of the particles over time. Set a light blue color in this marker:

Figure 7.26 – White to light blue gradient

As a challenge, I suggest you add a little particle system where this one ends to create some water splashes, simulating the water colliding with a lake at the bottom. Now we can add this particle system to one of the hills in our scene to decorate it, like in the following screenshot. I have adjusted the system a little bit to look better in this scenario. I challenge you to tweak it by yourself to make it look like this:

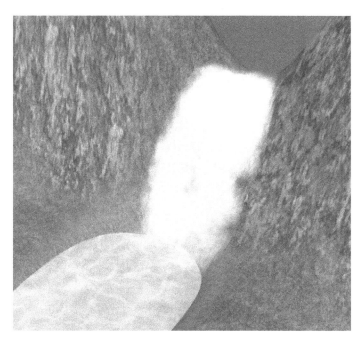

Figure 7.27 – The waterfall particle system being applied to our current scene

Now, let's create another effect, a bonfire.

Creating a bonfire effect

In order to create it, do the following:

1. Create a particle system.

2. Look for a **Fire Particle Texture Sheet** texture on the internet or the Asset Store. This kind of texture should look like a grid of different flame textures. The idea is to apply a flame animation to our particles swapping all those mini-textures:

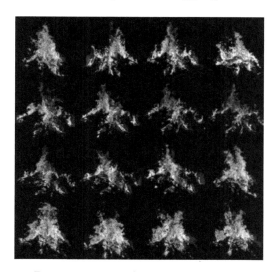

Figure 7.28 – Particles texture sprite sheet

3. Create a particle material and set this texture as the **Base Map**. Set the color at the right of the **Base Map** to white. Then set this material as the particle material. Remember to set **Surface Type** to **Transparent** and **Blending Mode** to **Additive**:

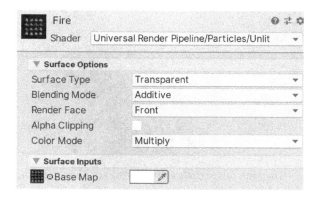

Figure 7.29 – A material with a particle sprite sheet

4. Enable the **Texture Sheet Animation** module and set the **Tiles** property according to your fire sheet. In my case, I have a grid of 4x4 sprites, so I put 4 in **X** and 4 in **Y**. After this, you should see the particles swapping textures:

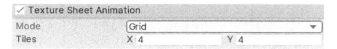

Figure 7.30 – Enabling Texture Sheet Animation

5. Set **Start Speed** to 0 and **Start Size** to 1.5 in the Main module.

6. Set **Radius** to 0.5 in **Shape**.

7. Create a second particle system and make it a child of the fire system:

Figure 7.31 – Parenting particle systems

8. Apply the Smoke material from the explosion example.

9. Set **Angle** to 0 and **Radius** to 0.5 in the Shape module.

10. The system should look like this:

Figure 7.32 – Result of combining fire and smoke particle systems

As you can see, you can combine several particle systems to create a single effect. Take care when doing this because it's easy to emit too many particles and affect the game's performance. Particles are not cheap and may cause a reduction in the game's **FPS (Frames Per Second)** if you are not cautious with them.

So far, we have explored one of the Unity systems that you can use to create these kinds of effects, and while this system is enough for most situations, Unity recently released a new one that can generate more complex effects, called **VFX Graph**. Let's see how to use it and see how it differs from Shuriken.

Creating complex simulations with VFX Graph

The particle system we have used so far is called Shuriken, and it handles all calculations in the CPU. This has both pros and cons. A pro is that it can run on all possible devices that Unity supports, regardless of their capabilities (all of them have CPUs), but a con is that we can exceed CPU capabilities easily if we are not cautious with the number of particles we emit. Modern games require more complex particle systems to generate believable effects, and this kind of CPU-based particle system solution has started to reach its limits. This is where the VFX Graph comes in:

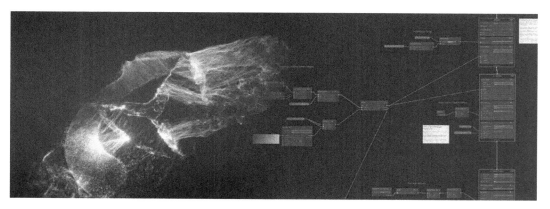

Figure 7.33 – On the left, a massive particle system, and on the right, an example of a VFX Graph

VFX Graph (Visual Effects Graph) is a GPU-based particle system solution, meaning that the system is executed on the video card instead of the CPU. That's because video cards are far more efficient at executing lots and lots of little simulations, like the ones each particle of a system needs, so we can reach far higher orders of magnitude in the number of particles with the GPU than we can with the CPU. The con here is that we need a fairly modern GPU that has **compute shader** capabilities to support this system, so we will exclude certain target platforms using this system (forget about most mobile phones), so only use it if your target platform supports it (mid to high-end PCs, consoles, and some high-end phones).

In this section, we will discuss the following concepts of VFX Graph:

- Installing VFX Graph
- Creating and analyzing a VFX Graph
- Creating a rain effect

Let's start seeing how we can add support for VFX Graph in our project.

Installing VFX Graph

So far, we have used lots of Unity features that were already installed in our project, but Unity can be extended with a myriad of plugins, both official and third-party. VFX Graph is one of those features that needs to be independently installed if you are using **Universal Render Pipeline (URP)**. We can do that using the Package Manager, a Unity window dedicated to managing official Unity plugins.

Something to think about when you are installing those packages is that each package or plugin has its own version, independent of the Unity version. That means that you can have Unity 2020.1 installed, but VFX Graph 7.1.5 or 7.1.2 or whatever version you want, and you can actually update the package to a newer version without upgrading Unity. This is important because some versions of these packages require a minimum version of Unity. Moreover, some packages depend on other packages, and actually specific versions of those packages, so we need to ensure we have the correct versions of every package to ensure compatibility. To be clear, the dependencies of a package are installed automatically, but sometimes we can have them installed separately, so in that scenario, we need to check the required version. It sounds complicated, but it is simpler than it sounds.

As the time of writing this book, I'm using get VFX Graph version 8.2.0, the same version as URP. Yes, URP is another feature you need to install using the Package Manager, but as we created the project using the URP template, it was already installed for us. Regarding versions, a piece of advice: never update your Unity version or a package version during the production of your game unless is really necessary. Upgrades generally come with lots of compatibility versions, meaning that some parts of your game may need to be fixed after the upgrade to comply with the way the new versions of those packages work. Also, consider that some packages has the Verified label, meaning that it was tested in our Unity version, and therefore is recommended to go with it.

Now, let's install the VFX Graph as follows:

1. In the top menu of Unity, go to **Window | Package Manager**:

Figure 7.34 – Package Manager location

2. Look for the **Visual Effects Graph** package on the left side of the window. Make sure you select version 8.2.0 or higher:

Figure 7.35 – Visual Effect Graph package

3. Click at the button **Install** at the bottom-right of the window and wait for the package to install:

Figure 7.36 – Install package button

4. It is recommended to restart Unity after installing packages, so save your changes and restart Unity.

Now that we have installed VFX Graph, let's create our first particle system using it.

Creating and analyzing a VFX Graph

The philosophy to create particle system using VFX Graph is similar to the regular Particle System. We will chain and configure modules as parts of the behavior of the particles, each module adding some specific behavior, but the way we do it is very different than with Shuriken. First, we need to create a **Visual Effect Graph**, an asset that will contain all the modules and configurations, and then make a GameObject play the Graph. Let's do that with the following steps:

1. In the Project window, click on the + button and look for **Visual Effects | Visual Effect Graph**:

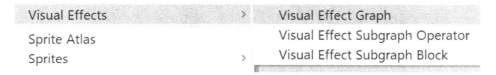

Figure 7.37 – Visual Effect Graph

2. Create an Empty GameObject using the **Game Object | Create Empty** option:

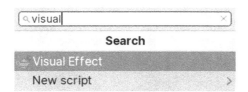

Figure 7.38 – Empty GameObject creation

3. Select the created object and look at the Inspector.

4. Using the **Add Component** search bar, look for the **Visual Effect** component and click on it to add it to the object:

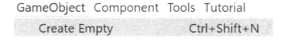

Figure 7.39 – Adding a component to the Visual Effect Graph

5. Drag the VFX asset we created to the **Asset Template** property of the **Visual Effect** component in our GameObject:

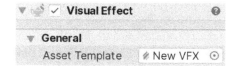

Figure 7.40 – Visual Effect using the previously created VFX asset

6. You should see clock particles being emitted from our object:

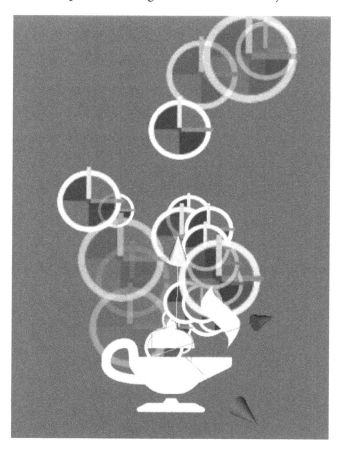

Figure 7.41 – Default VFX Asset results

Now that we have a base effect, let's create something that requires a lot of particles, such as dense rain. Before doing so, let's explore some core concepts of VFX Graph. If you double-click the Visual Effect asset, you will see the following editor:

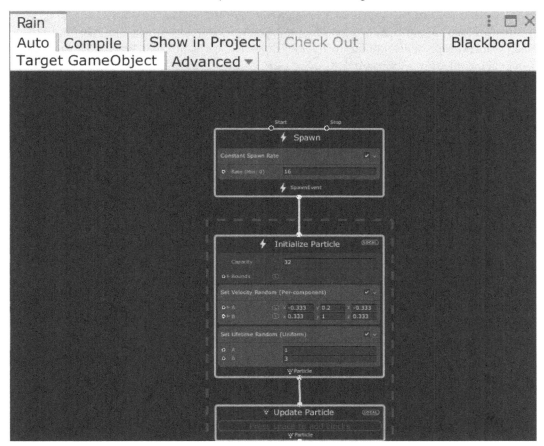

Figure 7.42 – Visual Effect Graph editor window

This window is composed of several interconnected nodes, generating a flow of actions to be executed. At first, it seems similar to the shader graph, but it works a little bit differently, so let's study each section of the default graph.

The first area to explore is the dotted one that contains three nodes. This is what Unity calls a **System**. A System is a set of nodes that defines how a particle will behave, and you can have as many as you want, which is the equivalent of having several particle system objects. Each System is composed of **Contexts**, the nodes inside the dotted area, and in this case, we have **Initialize Particle**, **Update Particle**, and **Output Particle Quad**. Each Context represents a different stage of the particle system logic flow, so let's define what each context in our graph does:

- **Initialize Particle**: This defines the initial data of each emitted particle, such as position, color, speed, and size. It is similar to the Start properties in the Main module of the particle system we saw at the beginning of this chapter. The logic in this node will only execute when a new particle is emitted.

- **Update Particle**: Here, we can apply modifications to the data of the living particles. We can change particle data such as the current velocity or size all the frames. This is similar to the Over Time nodes of the previous particle system.

- **Output Particle Quad**: This Context will be executed when the particle needs to be rendered. It will read the particle data to see where to render, how to render, which texture and color to use, and different visual settings. This is similar to the Renderer module of the previous particle system.

Inside each Context, apart from some base configurations, we can add **Blocks**. Each Block is an action that will be executed in the context. We have actions that can be executed in any Context and then some specific Context actions. As an example, we can use an Add Position Block in the Initialize Particle Context to move the initial particle position, but if we use the same Block in the Update Particle Context, it will move the particle constantly. So basically, Contexts are different situations that happen in the life of the particle, and Blocks are actions that are executed in those situations:

Figure 7.43 – A Set Velocity Random Block inside the Initialize Particle Context.
This sets the initial velocity of a particle

Also, we can have **Standalone Contexts**, Contexts outside systems, such as **Spawn**. This Context is responsible for telling the system that a new particle needs to be created. We can add Blocks to specify when the context will tell the system to create the particle, such as at a fixed rate over time, bursts, and so on. The idea is that spawn will create particles according to its blocks, while a System is responsible for initializing, updating, and rendering each of them, again, according to the blocks we set up inside each one of those Contexts.

So, we can see that there are lots of similarities with Shuriken, but the way to create a system here is quite different. Let's reinforce this by creating a rain effect, which will require lots of particles, a nice use case for VFX Graph.

Creating a rain effect

In order to create this effect, do the following:

1. Set the **Capacity** property of the **Initialize Particle** Context to 10000:

Figure 7.44 – Initialize Particle Context

2. Set the **Rate** of the **Constant Spawn Rate** of the **Spawn** context to 10000:

Figure 7.45 – Constant Spawn Rate Block

3. Set the **A** and **B** properties to (0, -50, 0) and (0, -75, 0) respectively in the **Set Velocity Random Block** in the **Initialize Particle** Context. This will set a random velocity pointing downward for our particles:

Figure 7.46 – Set Velocity Random Block

4. Click the **Initialize Particle** title to select the context, and once it's highlighted press the Spacebar to show the **Add Block** window.

5. Search for the **Set Position Random** block and click on it:

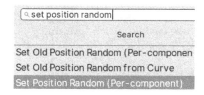

Figure 7.47 – Adding blocks

6. Set the **A** and **B** properties of the **Set Position Random** Block to (-50 , 0, -50) and (50, 0, 50) respectively. This will define an initial area in which to randomly spawn the particle.

7. Click the arrow at the left of the **Bounds** property of the **Initialize Particle** Block to display its properties, and set **Center** and **Size** to (0, -12.5, 0) and (100, 25, 100) respectively. This will define the area where the particles should live. Particles can actually move outside this area, but this is important for the system to work properly (search Frustum Culling on the internet for more information).

8. Select the GameObject that is executing the system, and in the bottom-right window in the Scene view check the **Show Bounds** checkbox to see the previously defined Bounds:

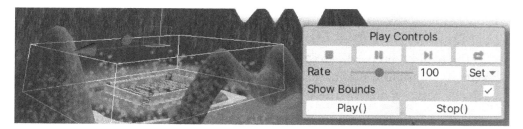

Figure 7.48 – Visual Effect Playback controls

9. Set the object position to cover the whole base area. In my case, the position is (100, 37, 100). Remember that you need to change the **Position** of the **Transform** component for this:

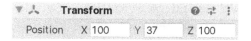

Figure 7.49 – Setting a transform position

10. Set the **A** and **B** properties of the **Set Lifetime Random** Block in the **Initialize Particle** to 0.5. This will make the particles have a shorter life, ensuring that they are always inside the bounds:

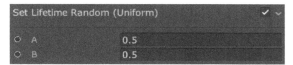

Figure 7.50 – Set Lifetime Random block

11. Change the **Main Texture** property of the **Output Particle Quad** Context to another texture. In this case, the previously downloaded smoke texture can work here, even though it's not water, because we will modify its appearance in a moment. Also, you can try to download a water droplet texture if you want to:

Figure 7.51 – VFX Graph Main Texture

12. Set **Blend Mode** of the **Output Particle Quad** Context to **Additive**:

Figure 7.52 – Additive mode of VFX Graph

13. If you can't see the last change being applied, click the **Compile** button in the top-left of the window. Also, you can save your changes using *Ctrl + S* (*Command + S* on Mac):

Figure 7.53 – VFX Asset Saving controls

14. Now we need to stretch our particles a little bit to look like actual raindrops instead of falling balls. To do so, first we need to change the orientation of our particles so they don't point at the camera all the time. In order to do this, right-click on the **Orient Block** in the **Output Particle Quad** Context and select **Delete** (or press *Delete* on PC or *Command + Backspace* on Mac):

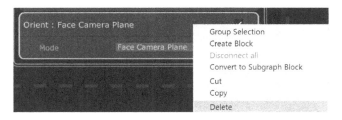

Figure 7.54 – Deleting a block

15. We want to stretch our particles according to their velocity direction. To do this, select the title of the **Output Particle Quad** context and hit the space bar to look for a block to add. In this case, we need to search for the **Orient Along Velocity** block.

16. Add a **Set Scale** Block to the **Initialize Particle** Context (click it and press the space bar) and set the **Scale** property to (0.25, 1.5, 0.25). This will stretch the particles to look like falling drops:

Figure 7.55 – Set Scale Block

17. Click the **Compile** button in the top-left window again to see the changes. Your system should look like this:

Figure 7.56 – Rain results

From here, you can experiment by adding and removing Blocks from the Contexts as you wish, and again, I recommend you look for already-created Visual Effects Graphs to find ideas for other systems. Actually, you can get ideas for VFX Graph by looking at effects made in Shuriken and using the analogous blocks. Also, I recommend you look for the VFX Graph documentation at `https://docs.unity3d.com/Packages/com.unity.visualeffectgraph@7.1/manual/index.html` to learn more about this system.

Summary

In this chapter, we discussed two different ways to create particle systems, using Shuriken and VFX Graph. We used them to simulate different fluid phenomena, such as fire, a waterfall, smoke, and rain. The idea is to combine particle systems with meshes to generate all the possible props needed for your scene. Also, as you can imagine, creating these kinds of effects professionally requires you to go deeper. If you want to dedicate yourself to this (another part of the job of a Technical Artist), you will need to learn how to create your own particle textures to get the exact look and feel you want, code scripts that control certain aspects of the systems, and several other aspects of particle creation. Again, that is outside the scope of the book.

Now that we have some rain in our scene, we can see that the sky and the lighting in the scene don't really reflect a rainy day, so let's fix that in the next chapter!

8
Lighting Using the Universal Render Pipeline

Lighting is a complex topic and there are several possible ways to handle it, with each one having its pros and cons. In order to get the best possible quality at the best performance, you need to know exactly how your renderer handles it, and that is exactly what we are going to do in this chapter. We will discuss how lighting is handled in Unity's **Universal Render Pipeline** (**URP**), as well as how to properly configure it to adapt our scene's mood with proper lighting effects.

In this chapter, we will examine the following lighting concepts:

- Applying lighting
- Applying shadows
- Optimizing lighting

Applying lighting

When discussing ways to process lighting in a game, there are two main ways we can do so, known as **Forward Rendering** and **Deferred Rendering**. Both handle lighting in a different order, with different techniques, requirements, pros, and cons. Forward Rendering is usually recommended for performance, while Deferred Rendering is usually recommended for quality. The latter is used by the **High Definition Render Pipeline** of Unity, the renderer used for high-quality graphics in high-end devices. At the time of writing this book, Unity is developing a performant version for URP. Also, in Unity, Forward Renderer comes in two flavors: **Multi-Pass Forward**, which is used in the built-in renderer (the old Unity renderer), and **Single Pass Forward,** which is used in URP. Again, each has its pros and cons.

Important information

Actually, there are other options available, both official and third-party, such as **Vertex Lit**, but for now, we will focus on the three main ones – the ones you use 95% of the time.

Choosing between one or another depends on the kind of game you are creating and the target platform you need to run the game on. Your chosen option will change a lot due to the way you apply lighting to your scene, so it's crucial you understand which system you are dealing with.

In this section, we will discuss the following Realtime lighting concepts:

- Discussing lighting methods
- Configuring ambient lighting with skyboxes
- Configuring lighting in URP

Let's start by comparing the previously mentioned lighting methods.

Discussing lighting methods

To recap, we mentioned three main ways of processing lighting:

- Forward Rendering (Single Pass)
- Forward Rendering (Multi-Pass)
- Deferred Rendering

Before we look at the differences between each, let's talk about the things they have in common. Those three renderers start drawing the scene by determining which objects can be seen by the camera; that is, the ones that fall inside the camera's frustum, and provide a giant pyramid that can be seen when you select the camera:

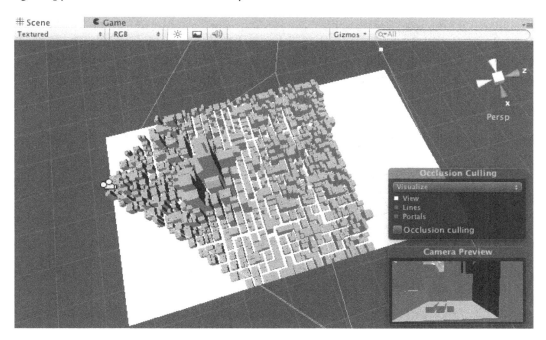

Figure 8.1 – The camera's frustum showing only the objects that can be seen by it

After that, Unity will order them from the nearest to the camera to the farthest (transparent objects are handled a little bit differently, but let's ignore that for now). It's done like this because it's more probable that objects nearer to the camera will cover most of the camera, so they will occlude others, preventing us from wasting resources calculating pixels for the occluded ones.

Finally, Unity will try to render the objects in that order. This is where differences start to arise between lighting methods, so let's start comparing the two Forward Rendering variants. For each object, Single Pass Forward Rendering will calculate the object´s appearance, including all the lights that are affecting the object, in one shot, or what we call a **Draw Call**. A Draw Call is the exact moment when Unity asks the video card to actually render the specified object. All the previous work was just preparation for this moment. In the case of the Multi-Pass Forward Renderer, by simplifying a little bit of the actual logic, Unity will render the object once per light that affects the object. So, if the object is being lit by three lights, Unity will render the object three times, meaning that three Draw Calls will be issued, and three calls to the GPU will be made to execute the rendering process:

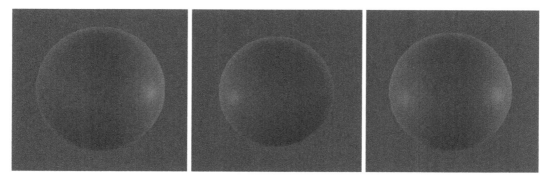

Figure 8.2 – Left image, first draw call of a sphere affected by two lights in Multi-Pass; middle image, second draw call of the sphere; right image, the combination of both Draw Calls

Now is when you are probably thinking, *"Why should I use Multi-Pass? Single-Pass is more performant!"* And yes, you are right! Single-Pass is way more performant than Multi-Pass, and here comes the great bit. A Draw Call in a GPU has a limited amount of operations that can be executed, so you have a limit to the complexity of the Draw Call. Calculating the appearance of an object and all the lights that affect it is very complex, and in order to make it fit in just one Draw Call, Single Pass executes simplified versions of lighting calculations, meaning less lighting quality and features. They also have a limit on how many lights can be handled in one shot, which, at the time of writing this book, is eight per object (four for low-end devices). This sounds like a small number, but it's usually just enough.

On the other side, Multi-Pass can apply any number of lights you want and can execute different logic for each light. Let's say our object has four lights that are affecting it, but there are two lights that are affecting it drastically because they are nearer or have higher intensity, while the remaining ones affecting the object are just enough to be noticeable. In this scenario, we can render the first two lights with higher quality and the remaining ones with cheap calculations – no one will be able to tell the difference. In this case, Multi-Pass can calculate the first two lights using **Pixel Lighting** and the remaining ones using **Vertex Lighting**. The difference is in their names; Pixel calculates light per object's pixel, while Vertex calculates light per object vertex and fills the pixels between these vertexes, thereby interpolating information between vertexes. You can clearly see the difference in the following images:

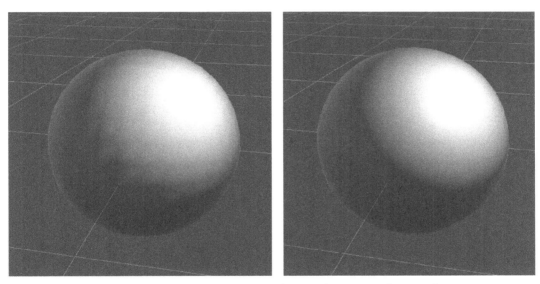

Figure 8.3 – Left image, a sphere being rendered with Vertex Lighting; right image, a sphere being rendered with Pixel Lighting)

In Single Pass, calculating everything in a single draw call forces you to use Vertex Lighting or Pixel Lighting; you cannot combine them.

So, to summarize the differences between Single and Multi-Pass, in Single Pass, you have better performance because each object is just drawn once, but you are limited to the number of lights that can be applied, while in Multi-Pass, you need to render the object several times, but with no limits on the number of lights, and you can specify the exact quality you want for each light. There are other things to consider, such as the actual cost of a Draw Call (one Draw Call can be more expensive than two simple ones), and special lighting effects such as toon shading, but let's keep things simple.

Finally, let's briefly discuss Deferred. Even though we are not going to use it, it's interesting to know why we are not doing that. After determining which objects fall inside the frustum and ordering them, Deferred will render the objects without any lighting, generating what is called a **G-Buffer**. A G-Buffer is a set of several images that contain different information about the objects of the scene, such as the colors of its pixels (without lighting), the direction of each pixel (known as **Normals**), and how far from the camera the pixels are. You can see a typical example of a G-Buffer in the following figure:

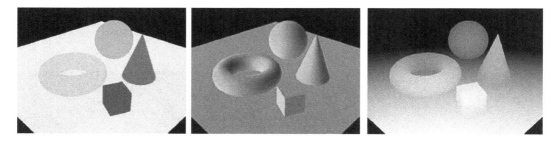

Figure 8.4 – Left image, plain colors of the object; middle image,
depths of each pixel; right image, normals of the pixels

> **Important information**
>
> Normals are directions, and the (X,Y,Z) components of the directions are encoded in the RGB components of the colors.

After rendering all the objects in the scene, Unity will iterate over all lights that can be seen in the camera, thus applying a layer of lighting over the G-Buffer, taking information from it to calculate that specific light. After all the lights have been processed, you will get the following result:

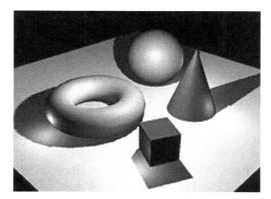

Figure 8.5 – Combination of the three lights that were applied to the
G-Buffer shown in the previous image

As you can see, the Deferred part of this method comes from the idea of calculating lighting as the last stage of the rendering process. This is better because you won't waste resources calculating lighting from objects that could potentially be occluded. If the floor of the image is being rendered first in Forward, the pixels that the rest of the objects are going to occlude were calculated in vain. Also, there's the detail that Deferred just calculates lighting in the exact pixels that the light can reach. As an example, if you are using a flashlight, Unity will calculate lighting only in the pixels that fall inside the cone of the flashlight. The con here is that Deferred is not supported by some relatively old video cards and that you can't calculate lighting with Vertex Lighting quality, so you will need to pay the price of Pixel Lighting, which is not recommended on low-end devices (or even necessary in simple graphics games).

So, why are we using URP with Single Pass Forward? Because it offers the best balance between performance, quality, and simplicity. In this game, we won't be using too many lights, so we won't worry about the light number limitations of Single Pass, and we won't take advantage of the Deferred benefits too much, so it makes no sense to use more hardware to run the game.

Now that we have a very basic notion of how URP handles lighting, let's start using it!

Configuring ambient lighting with skyboxes

There are different light sources that can affect the scene, such as the sun, torches, light bulbs, and more. Those are known as **Direct Lights**; that is, objects that emit light rays. Then, we have **Indirect Light**, light that usually represents bounces of Direct Lights. However calculating all the bounces of all the rays emitted by all the lights is impossible if you want to get a game running at least 30 FPS (or simply running). The problem is that not having Indirect Light will generate unrealistic results since our current scene lighting, where you can observe places where the sunlight doesn't reach, is completely dark because no light is bouncing from other places where light hits:

Figure 8.6 – Shadows projected on a mountain without ambient lighting

To solve this problem, we can use approximations of those bounces. These are what we call **ambient light**. This represents a base layer of lighting that usually applies a little bit of light based on the color of the sky, but you can choose whatever color you want. As an example, on a clear night, we can pick a dark blue color to represent the tint from the moonlight.

By default, Unity won't calculate ambient light from the sky, so we need to manually do that doing the following:

1. Select the Terrain in the Hierarchy and uncheck Static at the top right part of the Inspector. Later we will explain why we did this:

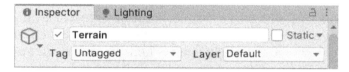

Figure 8.7 – Terrain in Hierarchy

2. Click on **Window | Rendering | Lighting Settings**. This will open the **Scene Lighting Settings** window:

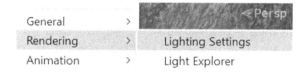

Figure 8.8 – Lighting Settings location

3. Click the **Generate Lighting** button at the bottom of the window. If you haven't saved the scene so far, a prompt will ask you to save it, which is necessary:

Figure 8.9 – Generate Lighting button

4. See the bottom-right part of the Unity window to check the progress calculation bar to check when the process has finished:

Figure 8.10 – Lighting generation progress bar

5. You can now see how completely dark areas now have a little effect shown on them from the light being emitted by the sky:

Figure 8.11 – Shadows with ambient lighting

Now, by doing this, we have better lighting, but it still looks like a sunny day. Remember, we want to have rainy weather. In order to do that, we need to change the default sky so that it's cloudy. You can do that by downloading a **skybox**. The current sky you can see around the scene is just a big cube containing textures on each side, and those have a special projection to prevent us from detecting the edges of the cube. We can download six images for each side of the cube and apply them to have whatever sky we want, so let's do that:

1. You can download skybox textures from wherever you want, but here, I will choose the Asset Store. Open it by going to **Window | Asset Store** and going to the Asset Store website.

2. Look for **2D | Textures & Materials | Sky** in the category list on the right. Remember that you need to make that window wider if you can't see the category list:

Figure 8.12 – Skybox category

3. Remember to check the **Free Assets** checkbox in the **Pricing** section:

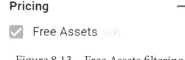

Figure 8.13 – Free Assets filtering

4. Pick any skybox you like for a rainy day. Take into account that there are different formats for skyboxes. We are using the six-image format, so check that before downloading one. In my case, I have chosen the skybox pack shown in the following figure. Download and import it, as we did in *Chapter 5, Importing and Integrating Assets*:

Figure 8.14 –Selected skybox set for this book

5. Create a new material by using the + icon in the **Project** window and selecting **Material**.

6. Set the **Shader** option of that material to **Skybox/6 sided**. Remember that the skybox is just a cube, so we can apply a material to change how it looks. The skybox shader is prepared to apply the six textures.

7. Drag the six textures to the **Front**, **Back**, **Left**, **Right**, **Up**, and **Down** properties of the material. The six downloaded textures will have descriptive names so that you know which textures go where:

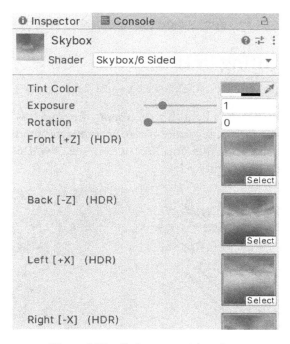

Figure 8.15 – Skybox material settings

8. Drag the material directly into the sky in the Scene View. Be sure you don't drag the material into an object because the material will be applied to it.

9. Repeat *steps 1* to *4* of the ambient light calculation (**Lighting Settings | Generate Lighting**) to recalculate it based on the new skybox. In the following figure, you can see the result of my project so far:

Figure 8.16 – Applied skybox

Now that we have a good base layer of lighting, we can start adding light objects.

Configuring lighting in URP

We have three main types of Direct Lights we can add to our scene:

- **Directional Light**: This is a light that represents the sun. This object emits light rays in the direction it is facing, regardless of its position; the sun moving 100 meters to the right won't make a big difference. As an example, if you slowly rotate this object, you can generate a day/night cycle:

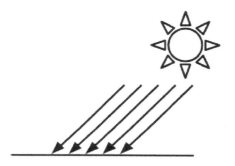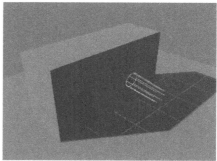

Figure 8.17 – Directional Light results

- **Point Light**: This light represents a light bulb, which emits rays in an omnidirectional way. The difference it has on the sun is that its position matters because it's closer. Also, because it's a weaker light, the intensity of this light varies according to the distance, so its effect has a range – the further the object from the light, the weaker the received intensity:

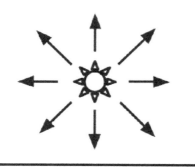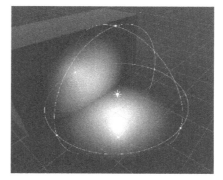

Figure 8.18 – Point Light results

- **Spotlight**: This kind of light represents a light cone, such as the one emitted by a flashlight. It behaves similarly to point lights in that its position and direction matters, and the light intensity decays over a certain distance:

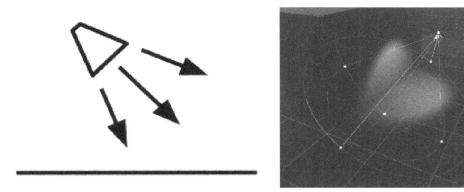

Figure 8.19 – Spotlight results

So far, we have a nice, rainy, ambient lighting, but the only Direct Light we have in the scene, the Directional Light, won't look like this, so let's change that:

1. Select the **Directional Light** object in the **Hierarchy** window and then look at the **Inspector** window.

2. Click the **Colour** property to open the Color Picker.

3. Select a dark gray color to achieve sun rays partially occluded by clouds.

4. Set **Shadow Type** to **No Shadows**. Now that we have a cloudy day, the sun does not project clear shadows, but we will talk more about shadows in a moment:

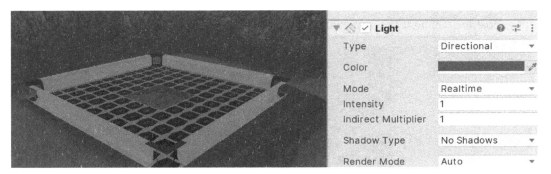

Figure 8.20 – Soft directional light with no shadows

Now that the scene is darker, we can add some lights to light up the scene, as follows:

1. Create a Spotlight by going to **GameObject | Light | Spotlight**:

Figure 8.21 – Creating a Spotlight

2. Select it. Then, in the **Inspector** window, set **Inner/Output Spot Angle** to 90 and 120, which will increase the angle of the cone.

3. Set **Range** to 50, meaning that the light can reach up to 50 meters, decaying along the way.

4. Set **Intensity** to 1000:

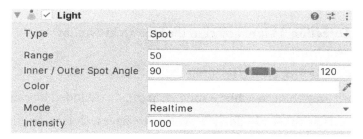

Figure 8.22 – Spotlight settings

5. Position the light at one corner of the base, pointing it at the center:

Figure 8.23 – Spotlight placement

6. Duplicate that light by selecting it and pressing *Ctrl + D* (*command + D* on Mac).

7. Put it in the opposite corner of the base:

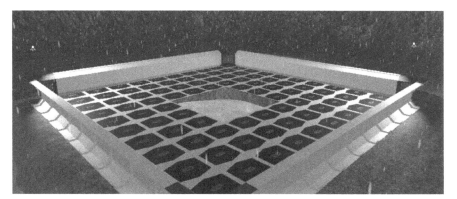

Figure 8.24 –Two Spotlight results

You can keep adding lights to the scene but take care that you don't go too far – remember the light limits. Also, you can download some light posts to put in where the lights are located to visually justify the origin of the light. Now that we have achieved proper lighting, we can talk about shadows.

Applying shadows

Maybe you are thinking that we already have shadows in the scene, but actually, we don't. The darker areas of the object, the ones that are not facing the lights, don't have shadows – they are not being lit, and that's quite different from a shadow. In this case, we are referring to the shadows that are projected from one object to another; for example, the shadow of the player being projected on the floor, or from the mountains to other objects. Shadows can increase the quality of our scene, but they also cost a lot to calculate, so we have two options: not using shadows (recommended for low-end devices such as mobiles) or finding a balance between performance and quality according to our game and the target device. In the first case, you can skip this whole section, but if you want to achieve performant shadows (as much as possible), keep reading.

In this section, we are going to discuss the following topics about shadows:

- Understanding shadow calculations

- Configuring performant shadows

Let's start by discussing how Unity calculates shadows.

Understanding shadow calculations

In game development, it is well-known that shadows are costly in terms of performance, but why? An object has a shadow when a light ray hits another object before reaching it. In that case, no lighting is applied to that pixel from that light. The problem here is the same problem we have with the light that ambient lighting simulates – it would be too costly to calculate all possible rays and its collisions. So, again, we need an approximation, and here is where Shadow Maps kick in.

A Shadow Map is an image that's rendered from the point of view of the light, but instead of drawing the full scene with all the color and lighting calculations, it will render all the objects in grayscale, where black means that the pixel is very far from the camera and whiter means that the pixel is nearer to the camera. If you think about it, each pixel contains information about where a **ray** of the light hits. By knowing the position and orientation of the light, you can calculate the position where each "ray" hit using the **Shadow Map**. In the following figure, you can see the Shadow Map of our Directional Light:

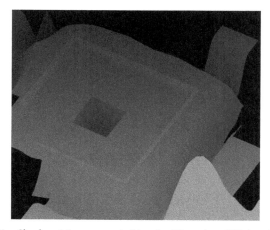

Figure 8.25 – Shadow Map generated by the Directional Light of our scene

Each type of light calculates Shadow Maps slightly differently, especially the Point Light. Since it's omnidirectional, it needs to render the scene several times in all its directions (front, back, up, down, right, and left) in order to gather information about all the rays it emits. We won't talk about this in detail here, though, as we could talk about it all day.

Now, something important to highlight here is that Shadow Maps are textures, and hence they have a resolution. The higher the resolution, the more "rays" our Shadow Map calculates. You are probably wondering what a low-resolution shadow map looks like when it has only a few rays in it. Take a look at the following figure to see one:

Figure 8.26 – Hard Shadow rendered with a low-resolution Shadow Map

The problem here is that having fewer rays generates bigger shadow pixels, resulting in a pixelated shadow. Here, we have our first configuration to consider: what is the ideal resolution for our shadows? You will be tempted to just increase it until the shadows look smooth, but of course, that will increase how long it will take to calculate it, so it will impact the performance considerably unless your target platform can handle it (mobiles definitely can't). Here, we can use the **Soft Shadows** trick, where we can apply a blurring effect over the shadows to hide the pixelated edges, as shown in the following figure:

Figure 8.27 – Soft Shadows rendered with a low-resolution Shadow Map

Of course, the blurry effect is not free, but combining it with low-resolution shadow maps, if you accept its blurry result, can generate a nice balance between quality and performance.

Now, low-resolution Shadow Maps have another problem, which is called **Shadow Acne**. This is the lighting error you can see in the following figure:

Figure 8.28 – Shadow Acne from a low-resolution Shadow Map

A low-resolution shadow map generates false positives because it has fewer "rays" calculated. The pixels to be shaded between the rays need to interpolate information from the nearest ones. The lower the Shadow Map's resolution, the larger the gap between the rays, which means less precision and more false positives. One solution would be to increase the resolution, but again, there will be performance issues (as always). We have some clever solutions to this, such as using **depth bias**. An example of this can be seen in the following figure:

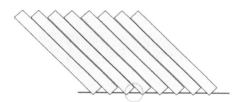

Figure 8.29 – A false positive between two far "rays." The highlighted area thinks the ray hit an object before reaching it.

The concept of **depth bias** is simple – so simple that it seems like a big cheat, and actually, it is, but game development is full of them! To prevent false positives, we "push" the rays a little bit further, just enough to make the interpolated rays reach the hitting surface:

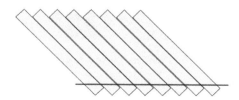

Figure 8.30 – Rays with a depth bias to eliminate false positives

Of course, as you are probably expecting, they don't solve this problem easily without having a caveat. Pushing depth generates false negatives in other areas, as shown in the following figure. It looks like the cube is floating, but actually, it is touching the ground – the false negatives generate the illusion that it is floating:

Figure 8.31 – False negatives due to a high depth bias

Of course, we have a counter trick to this situation known as **normal bias**. It still pushes objects, but along the direction they are facing. This one is a little bit tricky, so we won't go into too much detail here, but the idea is that combining a little bit of depth bias and another bit of normal bias will reduce the false positives, but not completely eliminate them. Therefore, we need to learn how to live with that and hide it by cleverly positioning objects:

Figure 8.32 – Reduced false negatives, which is the result of combining depth and normal bias

There are several other aspects that affect how Shadow Map works, with one of them being the light range. The smaller the light range, the less area the shadows will cover. The same Shadow Map resolution can add more detail to that area, so try to reduce the light ranges as much as you can.

I can imagine your face right now, and yes, lighting is complicated, and we've only just scratched the surface! But keep your spirits up! After a little trial and error fiddling with the settings, you will understand it better. We'll do that in the next section.

> **Important information**
>
> If you are really interested in learning more about the internals of the shadow system, I recommend that you look at the concept of **Shadow Cascades**, an advanced topic about Directional Lights and Shadow Map generation.

Configuring performant shadows

Because we are targeting mid-end devices, we will try to achieve a good balance of quality and performance here, so let's start enabling shadows just for the spotlights. The Directional Light shadow won't be that noticeable, and actually, a rainy sky doesn't generate clear shadows, so we will use that as an excuse to not calculate those shadows. In order to do this, do the following:

1. Select both Point Lights by clicking them in the Hierarchy while pressing *Ctrl* (*Command* on Mac). This will ensure that any changes made in the **Inspector** window will be applied to both:

Figure 8.33 – Selecting multiple objects

2. In the **Inspector** window, set **Shadow Type** to **Soft Shadows**. We will be using low-resolution shadow maps here:

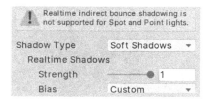

Figure 8.34 – Soft Shadows setting

3. Select **Directional light** and set **Shadow Type** to **No Shadows** to prevent it from casting shadows:

Figure 8.35 – No Shadows setting

4. Create a cube (**GameObject | 3D Object | Cube**) and place it near one of the lights, just to have an object that we can cast shadows on for testing purposes.

Now that we have a base test scenario, let's fiddle with the Shadow Maps resolution settings, preventing Shadow Acne in the process:

1. Go to **Edit | Project Settings**.

2. In the left-hand side list, look for **Graphics** and click it:

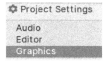

Figure 8.36 – Graphics settings

In the properties that appear after selecting this option, click in the box below **Scriptable Render Pipeline Settings** – the one that contains a name. In my case, this is **LWRP-HighQuality**, but yours may be different due to you having a different version of Unity:

Figure 8.37 – Current Render Pipeline setting

3. Doing that will highlight an asset in the Project window, so be sure that window is visible before selecting it. Select the highlighted asset:

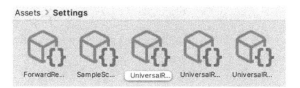

Figure 8.38 – Current pipeline highlighted

4. This asset has several graphics settings related to how URP will handle its rendering, including lighting and shadows. Expand the **Lighting** section to reveal its settings:

Figure 8.39 – Pipeline lighting settings

5. The **Shadow Resolution** setting under the **Additional Lights** subsection represents the Shadow Map resolution for all the lights that aren't the Directional Light (since it's the **Main Light**). Set it to **1024** if it's not already at that value.

6. Under the **Shadows** section, you can see the **Depth** and **Normal Bias** settings, but those only work for the Directional Light. So, instead, select both spotlights, set Bias mode to custom, and set the **Depth** and **Normal Bias** to 0.25 in order to reduce them as much as we can before we remove the Shadow Acne:

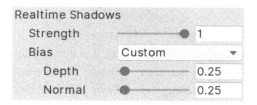

Figure 8.40 – Light shadows settings

7. This isn't entirely related to shadows, but here, you can change the **Per Object Light** limit to increase or reduce the number of lights that can affect the object (no more than eight).

8. In case you followed the shadow cascades tip presented earlier, you can play with the **Cascades** value a little bit to enable shadows for Directional Light to notice the effect. Remember that those shadow settings only work for Directional Light.

9. Set both lights so that they have a 40-meter range. See how the shadows improve in quality before and after the change:

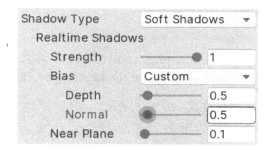

Figure 8.41 – Bias settings

Remember that those values only work in my case, so try to fiddle with the values a little bit to see how that changes the result – you may find a better setup for your PC. Also, remember that not having shadows is always an option, so always consider that in case your game is running low on FPS (and there isn't another performance problem lurking).

You probably think that that is all we can do about performance in terms of lighting, but luckily, that's not the case! We have another resource we can use to improve it further known as static lighting.

Optimizing lighting

We mentioned previously that not calculating lighting is good for performance, but what about not calculating lights, but still having them? Yes, its sounds too good to be true, but it is actually possible (and, of course, tricky). We can use a technique called static lighting or baking, which allows us to calculate lighting once and use the cached result.

In this section, we will cover the following concepts related to Static Lighting:

- Understanding static lighting
- Baking lightmaps
- Applying static lighting to dynamic objects

Understanding static lighting

The idea is pretty simple: just do the lighting calculations once, save the results, and then use those instead of calculating lighting all the time. You may be wondering why this isn't the default technique to use. This is because it has some limitations, with the big one being dynamic objects. **Precalculating shadows** means that they can't change once they've been calculated, but if an object that is casting a shadow is moved, the shadow will still be there, so the main thing to take into account here is that you can't use this technique with moving objects. Instead, you will need to mix **static** or **baked lighting** for static objects and **Realtime lighting** for dynamic (moving) objects. Also, consider that aside from this technique being only valid for static objects, it is also only valid for static lights. Again, if a light moves, the precalculated data becomes invalid.

Another limitation you need to take into account is that that precalculated data can have a huge impact on memory. That data occupies space in RAM, maybe hundreds of MBs, so you need to consider whether your target platform has enough space. Of course, you can reduce the precalculated lighting quality to reduce the size of that data, but you need to consider whether the loss of quality deteriorates the look and feel of your game too much. As with all options regarding optimization, you need to balance two factors: performance and quality.

We have several kinds of precalculated data in our process, but the most important one is what we call **lightmaps**. A lightmap is a texture that contains all the shadows and lighting for all the objects in the scene, so when Unity applies the precalculated or baked data, it will look at this texture to know which parts of the static objects are lit and which aren't. You can see an example of a lightmap in the following figure:

Figure 8.42 – Left, a scene with no lighting; middle, a lightmap holding precalculated data from that scene; right, the lightmap being applied to the scene

Anyway, having lightmaps has its own benefits. The baking process is executed in Unity, before the game is shipped to users, so you can spend plenty of time calculating stuff that you can't do at runtime, such as improved accuracy, light bounces, light occlusion in corners, and light from emissive objects. However, that can also be a problem. Remember, dynamic objects still need to rely on Realtime lighting, and that lighting will look very different compared to the static lighting, so we need to tweak them a lot for the user to not notice the difference.

Now that we have a basic notion of what static lighting is, let's dive into how to use it.

Baking lightmaps

To use lightmaps, we need to make some preparations regarding the 3D models. Remember that meshes have **UVs**, which contain information about which part of the texture needs to be applied to each part of the model. Sometimes, to save texture memory you can apply the same piece of texture to different parts. For example, in a car's texture, you wouldn't have four wheels, you'd just have one, and you can apply that same piece of texture to all the wheels. The problem here is that static lighting uses textures the same way, but here, it will apply the lightmaps to light the object. In the wheel scenario, the problem would be that if one wheel receives shadows, all of them will have them, because all the wheels are sharing the same texture space. The usual solution is to have a second set of UVs in the model with no texture space being shared, just to use for lightmapping.

Sometimes, downloaded models are already prepared for lightmapping, and sometimes they aren't, but luckily, Unity has us covered in those scenarios. To be sure a model will calculate lightmapping properly, let's make Unity automatically generate the **Lightmapping UV** set by doing the following:

1. Select the mesh asset (FBX) in the **Project** window.

2. In the **Model** tab, look for the **Generate Lightmap** checkbox at the bottom and check it.

3. Click the **Apply** button at the bottom:

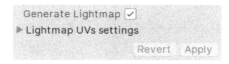

Figure 8.43 – Generate Lightmap setting

4. Repeat this process for every model. Technically, you can only do this in the models where you get artifacts and weird results after baking lightmaps, but for now, let's do this in all the models just in case.

After preparing the models for being lightmapped, the next step is to tell Unity which objects are not going to move. To do so, do the following:

1. Select the object that won't move.

2. Check the **Static** checkbox in the topright of the **Inspector** window:

Figure 8.44 – Static checkbox

3. Repeat this for every static object (this isn't necessary for lights; we will deal with those later).

Consider that you may not want every object, even if it's static, to be lightmapped, because the more objects you lightmap, the more texture size you will require. As an example, the terrain is too large and will consume most of the lightmapping's size. Usually, this is necessary, but in our case, the Spotlights are barely touching the terrain. Here, we have two options: leave the terrain as dynamic, or better, directly tell the Spotlights to not affect the terrain since one is only lit by ambient lighting and the Directional Light (which is not casting shadows). Remember that this is something we can do because of our type of scene; however, you may need to use other settings in other scenarios. You can exclude an object from both Realtime and Static lighting calculations by doing the following:

1. Select the object to exclude.

2. In the **Inspector** window, click the **Layer** dropdown and click on **Add Layer**:

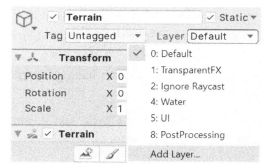

Figure 8.45 – Layer creation button

3. Here, you can create a layer, which is a group of objects that's used to identify which objects are not going to be affected by lighting. In the **Layers** list, look for an empty space and type in any name for those kinds of objects. In my case, I will only exclude the terrain, so I have just named it **Terrain**:

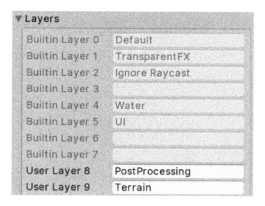

Figure 8.46 – Layers list

4. Once again, select the terrain, go to the **Layer** dropdown, and select the layer you created in the previous step. This way, you can specify that this object belongs to that group of objects:

Figure 8.47 – Changing a GameObject's layer

5. Select all the Spotlights lights, look for the **Culling Mask** in the **Inspector** window, click it, and uncheck the layer you created previously. This way, you can specify that those lights won't affect that group of objects:

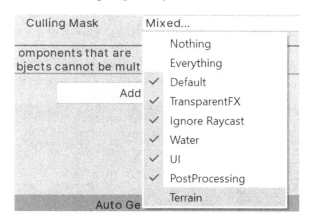

Figure 8.48 – Light Culling Mask

6. Now, you can see how those selected lights are not illuminating or applying shadows to the terrain.

Now, it's time for the lights since the **Static** checkbox won't work for them. For them, we have the following three modes:

- **Realtime**: A light in Realtime mode will affect all objects, both static and dynamic, using Realtime lighting, meaning there's no precalculation. This is useful for lights that are not static, such as the player's flashlight, a lamp that is moving due to the wind, and so on.

- **Baked**: The opposite of Realtime, this kind of light will only affect static objects with lightmaps. This means that if the player (dynamic) moves under a baked light on the street (static), the street will look lit, but the player will still be dark and won't cast any shadows on the street. The idea is to use this on lights that won't affect any dynamic object, or on lights that are barely noticeable on them, so that we can increase performance by not calculating them.

- **Mixed**: This is the preferred mode if you are not sure which one to use. This kind of light will calculate lightmaps for static objects, but will also affect dynamic objects, combining its Realtime lighting with the baked one (like Realtime lights also do).

In our case, our Directional Light will only affect the terrain, and because we don't have shadows, applying lighting to it is relatively cheap in URP, so we can leave the Directional Light in Realtime so that it won't take up any lightmap texture area. Our spotlights are affecting the base, but actually, they are only applying lighting to it – we have no shadows because our base is empty. In this case, it is preferable to not calculate lightmapping whatsoever, but for learning purposes, I will add a few objects as obstacles to the base to cast some shadows and justify the use of lightmapping, as shown in the following figure:

Figure 8.49 – Adding objects to project light

Here, you can see how the original design of our level changes constantly during the development of the game, and that's something you can't avoid – bigger parts of the game will change in time. Now, we are ready to set up the Light Modes and execute the baking process, as follows:

1. Select **Directional Light**.

2. Set **Render Mode** in the Inspector window to **Realtime** (if it's not already in that mode).

3. Select both Spotlights.

4. Set their **Render Mode** to **Mixed**:

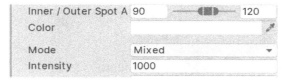

Figure 8.50 – Mixed lighting setting

5. Open the **Lighting Settings** window (**Window | Rendering | Lighting Settings**).

6. Click **Generate Lighting**, which is the same button we used previously to generate ambient lighting.

7. Wait for the process to complete. You can do this by checking the progress bar at the bottom-right of the Unity Editor. Note that this process could take hours in large scenes, so be patient:

Figure 8.51 – Baking progress bar

8. We want to change some of the settings of the baking process. In order to enable the controls for this, click the **New Lighting Settings** button. This will create an asset with lightmapping settings that can be applied to several scenes in case we want to share the same settings multiple times:

Figure 8.52 – Creating lighting settings

9. Reduce the quality of lightmapping, just to make the process go faster. Just to iterate, the lighting can easily be reduced by using settings such as **Lightmap Resolution**, **Direct**, **Indirect,** and **Environment Samples**. In my case, I have those settings applied, as shown in the following figure. Note that even reducing those will take time; we have too many objects in the scene due to the modular level design:

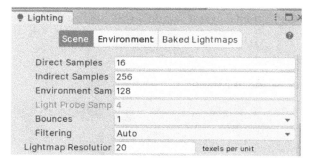

Figure 8.53 – Scene lighting settings

10. After the process has completed, you can check the bottom part of the **Lighting Settings** window, where you can see how many lightmaps need to be generated. We have a maximum lightmap resolution, so we probably need several of them to cover the entire scene. Also, it informs us of their size so that we can consider their impact in terms of RAM. Finally, you can check out the **Baked Lightmaps** section to see them:

Figure 8.54 – Generated lightmaps

11. Now, based on the results, you can move objects, modify light intensities, or make whatever correction you would need in order to make the scene look the way you want and recalculate the lighting every time you need to. In my case, those settings gave me good enough results, which you can see in the following figure:

Figure 8.55 – Lightmap result

We still have plenty of small settings to touch on, but I will leave you to discover those through trial and error or by reading the Unity documentation about lightmapping at this link. Reading the Unity manual is a good source of knowledge and I recommend that you start using it – any good developer, no matter how experienced, should read the manual.

Applying static lighting to static objects

When marking objects as static in your scene, you've probably figured out that all the objects in the scene won't move, so you probably checked the static checkbox for every one. That's OK, but you should always put a dynamic object into the scene to really be sure that everything works OK – no games have totally static scenes. Try adding a capsule and moving it around to simulate our player, as shown in the following figure. If you pay attention to it, you will notice something odd – the shadows being generated by the lightmapping process are not being applied to our dynamic object:

Figure 8.56 – Dynamic object under a lightmap's precalculated shadow

You may be thinking that Mixed Light Mode was supposed to affect both dynamic and static objects, and that is exactly what it's doing. The problem here is that everything related to static objects is precalculated into those lightmap textures, including the shadows they cast, and because our capsule is dynamic, it wasn't there when the precalculation process was executed. So, in this case, because the object that cast the shadow was static, its shadow won't affect any dynamic object.

Here, we have several solutions. The first would be to change the Static and Realtime mixing algorithm to make everything near the camera use Realtime lighting and prevent this problem (at least near the focus of attention of the player), which would have a big impact on performance. The alternative is to use **Light Probes**. When we baked information, we only did that on lightmaps, meaning that we have information on lighting just over surfaces, not in empty spaces. Because our player is traversing the empty spaces between those surfaces, we don't know exactly how the lighting would look in those spaces, such as the middle of a corridor. Light Probes are a set of points in those empty spaces where Unity also pre-calculates information, so when some dynamic object passes through it, it will sample information from it. In the following figure, you can see some Light Probes that have been applied to our scene. You will notice that the ones that are inside shadows are going to be dark, while the ones exposed to light will have a greater intensity. This effect will be applied to our dynamic objects:

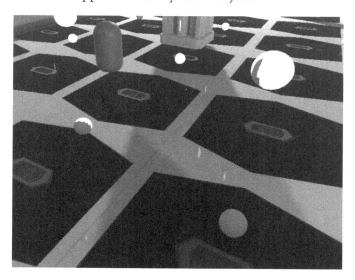

Figure 8.57 – Spheres representing Light Probes

If you move your object through the scene now, it will react to the shadows, as shown in the following two images, where you can see a dynamic object being lit outside a baked shadow and being dark inside:

Figure 8.58 – Dynamic object receiving baked lighting from Light Probes

In order to create Light Probes, do the following:

1. Create a group of **Light** Probes by going to **GameObject | Light | Light Probe Group**:

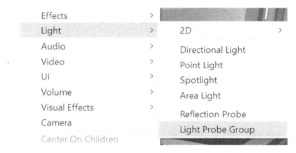

Figure 8.59 – Creating a Light Probe Group

2. Fortunately, we have some guidelines on how to locate them. It is recommended to place them where the lighting changes, such as inside and outside shadow borders. However, that is pretty complicated. The simplest and recommended approach is to just drop a grid of Light Probes all over your playable area. To do that, you can simply copy and paste the Light Grid Group several times to cover the entire base:

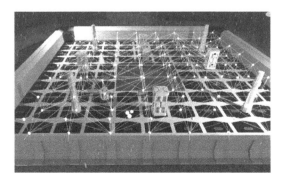

Figure 8.60 – Light Probe grid

3. Another approach would be to select one group and click the **Edit Light Probes** button to enter Light Probe edit mode:

Figure 8.61 – Light Probe Group edit button

4. Click the **Select All** button and then **Duplicate Selected** to duplicate all the previously existing probes.

5. Using the translate gizmo, move them next to the previous ones, extending the grid in the process. Consider that the nearer the probes are, you will need more to cover the terrain, which will generate more data. However, Light Probes data is relatively cheap, so you can have lots of them.

6. Repeat *steps 4* to *5* until you've covered the entire area.

7. Regenerate lighting with the **Generate Lighting** button in **Lighting Settings**.

With that, you have precalculated lighting on the Light Probes affecting our dynamic objects, combining both worlds to get cohesive lighting.

Summary

In this chapter, we discussed several lighting topics, such as how Unity calculates lights, shadows, how to deal with different light sources such as direct and indirect lighting, how to configure shadows, how to bake lighting to optimize performance, and how to combine dynamic and static lighting so that the lights aren't disconnected from the world they affect. This was a long chapter, but lighting deserves that. It is a complex subject that can improve the look and feel of your scene drastically, as well as reducing your performance dramatically. It requires a lot of practice and, here, we tried to summarize all the important knowledge you will need to start experimenting with it. Be patient with this topic; it is easy to get incorrect results, but you are probably just one checkbox away from solving it.

Now that we have improved all we can in the scene settings, in the next chapter, we will apply a final layer of graphic effects using the Unity Postprocessing Stack, which will apply full-screen image effects – ones that will give us that cinematic look and feel all games have nowadays.

9
Fullscreen Effects with postprocessing

So far, we have created different objects to alter the visuals of our scene, such as meshes, particles, and lights. We can tweak the settings of those objects here and there to improve our scene quality, but you will always feel that something is missing when comparing it with modern game scenes, and that is fullscreen or postprocessing effects. In this chapter, you will learn how to apply effects to the final rendered frame, which will alter the look of the overall scene.

- In this chapter, we will examine the following image effect concepts:
- Using postprocessing
- Using advanced effects

Using postprocessing

postprocessing is a Unity feature that allows us to apply several effects (a stack of effects) one on top of the other, which will alter the final look of an image. Each one will affect the finished frame, changing the colors in it based on different criteria. In the following screenshots, you can see a scene before and after applying image effects. You will notice a dramatic difference, but that scene doesn't have any change in its objects, including lights, particles, or meshes. The effects applied are based on pixel analysis. Have a look at both scenes here:

Figure 9.1 – A scene without image effects (left) and the same scene with effects (right)

Something to take into account is that the previous postprocessing solution, **postprocessing Stack version 2 (PPv2)** won't work on the **Universal Render Pipeline (URP)**; it has its own postprocessing implementation, so we will see that one in this chapter. Anyway, they are very similar, so even if you are using PPv2, you can still get something from this chapter.

In this section, we will discuss the following URP postprocessing concepts:

- Setting up a profile
- Using basic effects

Let's start preparing our scene to apply effects.

Setting up a profile

To start applying effects, we need to create a **Profile**, it being an Asset containing all the effects and settings we want to apply. This is a separated asset for the same reason the Material also is, because we can share the same post-processing profile across different scenes and parts of scenes. When we refer to parts of the scenes, we are referring to volumes or areas of the game that have certain effects applied. We can define a global area that applies effects regardless of the position of the player, or we can apply different effects—for example, when we are outdoors or indoors.

In this case, we will use a global volume, one that we will use to apply a profile with our first effect, by doing the following:

1. Create a new empty Game Object (**GameObject | Create Empty**).

2. Name it as PP Volume (meaning postprocessing Volume).

3. Add the **Volume** component to it.

4. Make sure the **Mode** is set to **Global**.

5. Click on the **New** button at the right of the **Profile** setting, which will generate a new Profile Asset named like our object (PPVolume Profile). You can later move that to its own folder, which is recommended for Asset organization purposes. The process is illustrated in the following screenshot:

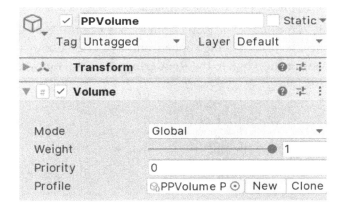

Figure 9.2 – Volume component

6. To test if the volume is working, let's add an effect. Click the **Add Override** button, and select the **postprocessing | Chromatic Aberration** option.

7. Check the **Intensity** checkbox in the **Chromatic Aberration** effect and set the intensity to 0.5, as illustrated in the following screenshot:

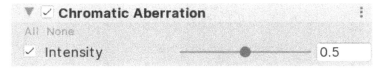

Figure 9.3 – C Chromatic aberration effect

8. Now, you will see an aberration effect being applied in the corners of the image. Remember to look at this in the Scene Panel; we will apply the effect to the Game View in the next step. This is illustrated in the following screenshot:

Figure 9.4 – Chromatic aberration applied to the scene

9. Now, if you hit **Play** and see the game from the view of the Main Camera, you will see that the effect is not being applied, and that's because we need to check the **postprocessing** checkbox in the **Rendering** section of our Main Camera, as illustrated in the following screenshot:

Figure 9.5 – Enabling post-processing

So, we have created a global volume, which will apply the effects specified as overrides to the entire scene regardless of the player position.

Now that we have prepared our scene to use postprocessing, we can start experimenting with different effects. Let's start with the simplest ones in the next section.

Using basic effects

Now that we have postprocessing in our scene, the only thing needed is to start adding effects and set them up until we have the desired look and feel. In order to do that, let's explore several simple effects included in the system.

Let's start with **Chromatic Aberration**, the one we just used, which, as with most image effects, tries to replicate a particular real-life effect. All game-engine rendering systems use a simple mathematical approximation of how eye vision really works, and because of that, we don't have some effects that occur in the human eyes or camera lenses. A real camera lens works by bending light rays to point them toward the camera sensors, but that bending is not perfect in some lenses (sometimes intentionally), and, hence, you can see a distortion, as shown in the following screenshot:

Figure 9.6 – I1mage without chromatic aberration (left) and
the same image with chromatic aberration (right)

This effect will be one of several that we will add to generate a cinematic feeling in our game, simulating the usage of real-life cameras. Of course, this effect won't look nice in every kind of game; maybe a simplistic cartoonish style won't benefit from this one, but you never know: art is subjective, so it's a matter of trial and error.

Also, we have exaggerated the intensity a little bit in the previous example to make the effect more noticeable, but I would recommend using an intensity of 0.25 in this scenario. It is usually recommended to be gentle with the intensity of the effects; it's tempting to have intense effects, but as you will be adding lots of them, after a while the image will be bloated, with too many distortions. So, try to add several subtle effects instead of a few intense ones. But, again, this depends on the target style you are looking for; there are no absolute truths here (but common sense still applies).

Finally, before moving on to discuss other effects, if you are used to using other kinds of postprocessing effects frameworks, you will notice that this version of chromatic aberration has fewer settings, and that's because the URP version seeks performance, so it will be as simple as possible.

The next effect we are going to discuss is **Vignette**. This is another camera-lens imperfection where the image intensity is lost at the edges of the lens. This can be applied not only to simulate older cameras but also to draw the attention of the user toward the center of the camera—for example, during cinematics. Also, if you are developing **virtual reality** (**VR**) applications, this can be used to reduce motion sickness by reducing the peripheral vision of the player. In the following screenshot, you can see an example of vignetting on an old camera:

Figure 9.7 – Photo taken with an old camera, with vignetting over the edges

Just to try it, let's apply some vignetting to our scene by doing the following:

1. Select the **PP Volume** GameObject.

2. Add the **postprocessing | Vignette** effect by clicking on the **Add Override** button.

3. Check the **Intensity** checkbox and set it to 0.3, increasing the effect.

4. Check the **Smoothness** checkbox and set it to 0.5; this will increase the spread of the effect. You can see the result in the following screenshot:

Figure 9.8 – Vignette effect

If you want, you can change the color by checking the **Color** checkbox and setting it to another value; in our case, black is okay to reinforce the rainy-day environment. Here, I invite you to check how other properties, such as **Center** and **Rounded**, work as **Particles**. You can create nice effects just playing with the values.

Another effect we are going to review in this basics section is **Motion Blur**, and again, it simulates the way the cameras work. A camera has an exposure time, the time it needs to capture photons to get each frame. When an object moves fast enough, the same object is placed in different positions during that brief exposure time, so it will appear blurred. In the following screenshot, you can see the effect applied to our scene. In the case of this image, we are rotating the camera up and down fast, with the following result:

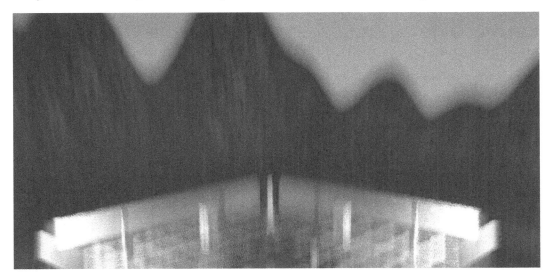

Figure 9.9 Motion Blur being applied to our scene

One thing to consider is that this blur will only be applied to the camera movement and not the movement of the objects (still camera, moving objects), due to the fact that this URP doesn't support motion vectors yet.

In order to use this effect, follow these next steps:

1. Add the **Post-processing | Motion Blur** override with the **Add override** button.

2. Check the **Intensity** checkbox and set it to 0.5.

3. Rotate the camera while seeing the Game View (not the Scene View). You can click and drag the **X** property of the **Transform** of the camera (not the value—the **X** label), as illustrated in the following screenshot:

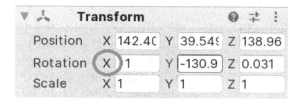

Figure 9.10 – Changing rotation

As you can see, this effect cannot be seen in the Scene View, as well as other effects, so take that into account before concluding the effect is not working. Unity does this because it would be very annoying to have that effect while working in the scene.

Finally, we are going to briefly discuss two final simple effects, **Film Grain** and **White Balance**. The first is pretty simple: add it, set the intensity to 1, and you will get the famous grain effect from the old movies. You can set the **Type** with different sizes to make it more subtle or obvious. White Balance allows you to change the color temperature, making colors warmer or cooler depending on how you configure it. In our case, we are working in a cold dark scene, so you can add it and set the temperature to -20 to adjust the appearance just slightly, and improve the look and feel in this kind of scene.

Now that we have seen a few of the simple effects, let's check out a few of the remaining ones, which are affected by some advanced rendering features.

Using advanced effects

The effects we are going to see in this section don't differ a lot from the previous ones; they are just a little bit trickier and need some background to properly use them. So, let's dive into them!

In this section, we are going to see the advanced effect concepts of

High Dynamic Range (HDR) and Depth Maps.

Advanced effects

Let's start by discussing some requirements for some of these effects to work properly.

HDR and Depth Map

Some effects not only work with the rendered image but also need additional data. We can first discuss the **Depth Map**, a concept we already discussed in the previous chapter. To do a recap, a Depth Map is an image rendered from the point of view of the camera, but instead of generating a final image of the scene, it renders the scene objects' depth, rendering the objects in shades of gray. The darker the color, the further from the camera the pixel is, and vice versa. In the following screenshot, you can see an example of a depth map:

Figure 9.11 – Depth map of a few primitive shapes

We will see some effects such as **Depth of Field**, which will blur some parts of the image based on the distance of the camera, but it can be used for several purposes on custom effects (not in the base URP package).

Another concept to discuss here that will alter how colors are treated and, hence, how some effects work is HDR. In older hardware, color channels (red, green, and blue) were encoded in a 0 to 1 range, 0 being no intensity and 1 being full intensity (per channel), so all lighting and color calculations were done in that range. That seems okay but doesn't reflect how light actually works. You can see full white (all channels set to 1) in a piece of paper being lit by sunlight, and you can see full white when you look directly at a light bulb, but even if both light and paper are of the same color, the latter will, first, irritate the eye after a while, and secondly, will have some overglow due to an excess of light. The problem here is that the maximum value (1) is not enough to represent the most intense color, so if you have a high-intensity light and another with even more intensity, both will generate the same color (1 in each channel) because calculations cannot go further than 1. So, that's why **HDR Rendering** was created.

HDR is a way for colors to exceed the 0.1 range, so lighting and effects that work based on color intensity have better accuracy in this mode. It is the same idea of the new TV feature with the same name, although in this case, Unity will do the calculations in HDR, but the final image will still work using the previous color space (0 to 1, or **Low Dynamic Range (LDR)**, so don't confuse Unity's **HDR Rendering** with the **Display's HDR**. To convert the HDR calculations back to LDR, Unity (and also TVs) uses a concept called **tonemapping**. You can see an example of an LDR-rendered scene and tonemapping being used in an HDR scene in the following screenshots:

Figure 9.12 – An LDR-rendered scene (left) and
an HDR scene with corrected overbrights using tonemapping (right)

Tonemapping is a way to bring colors outside the 0.1 range back to it. It basically uses some formulas and curves to determine how each color channel should be mapped back. You can clearly see this in the typical darker-to-lighter scene transition, such as when you exit a building without windows to go out into a bright day. For a time, you will see everything lighter until everything goes back to normal. The idea here is that calculations are not different when you are inside or outside the building; a white wall inside the building will have a color near the 1 intensity, while the same white wall outside will have a higher value (due to sunlight). The difference is that tonemapping will take the higher-than-1 color back to 1 when you are outside the building, and maybe it will increase the lighting of the wall inside if all the scene is darker, depending on how you set it.

Even if HDR is enabled by default, let's just see how we can check that, by doing the following:

1. Go to **Edit | Project Settings**.

2. Click on the **Graphics Settings** section in the left panel.

3. Click the asset referenced under the **Scriptable Render Pipeline Settings** property.

4. Click on the highlighted asset in the Project Panel. Ensure that this panel is visible before clicking the property in the **Graphics** settings.

5. Under the **Quality** section, ensure that **HDR** is checked, as illustrated in the following screenshot:

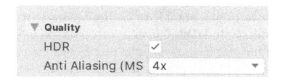

Figure 9.13 – Enabling HDR

Of course, the fact that HDR is togglable means that there are scenarios where you don't want to use it. As you can guess, not all hardware supports HDR, and using it incurs a performance overhead, so take that into account. Luckily, most effects work with both HDR and LDR color ranges, so if you have HDR enabled but the user device doesn't support it, you won't get any errors, just different results.

Now that we are sure we have HDR enabled, let's explore some advanced effects that use this and Depth Mapping.

Let's see certain effects that use the previously described techniques, starting with the commonly used Bloom. This effect, as usual, emulates the overglow that happens around a heavily lit object on a camera lens or even the human eye. In the following screenshots, you can see the difference between the default version of our scene and an exaggerated Bloom version. You can observe how the effect is only applied to the brightest areas of our scene. Have a look at both effects here:

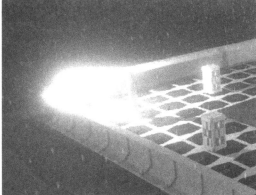

Figure 9.14 – The default scene (left) and the same scene with a high-intensity Bloom (right)

This effect is actually very common and simple, but I considered it advanced because the results are drastically affected by HDR. This effect relies on calculating the intensity of each pixel's color to detect areas where it can be applied. In LDR, we can have a white object that isn't actually overbright, but due to the limitations in this color range, Bloom may cause an overglow over it. In HDR, due to its increased color range, we can detect if an object is white or if the object is maybe light blue but just overbright, generating the illusion that it is white (such as objects near a high-intensity lamp). In the following screenshot, you can see the difference between our scene with HDR and without it. You will notice that the LDR version will have overglow in areas that are not necessarily overlit. The difference may be very subtle, but pay attention to the little details to note the difference. And remember, I exaggerated the effect here. Have a look at both scenes here:

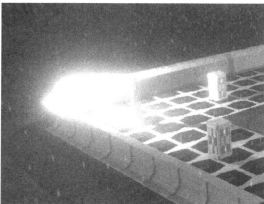

Figure 9.15 – Bloom in an LDR scene (left) and Bloom in an HDR scene (right).
Notice that the Bloom settings were changed to try to approximate them as much as possible

For now, let's stick with the HDR version of the scene. In order to enable Bloom, do the following:

1. Add the **Bloom** override to the profile, as usual.

2. Enable the **Intensity** checkbox by checking it, and set the value to 1.5. This controls how much overglow will be applied.

3. Enable **Threshold** and set it to 0.7. This value indicates the minimum intensity a color needs to have to be considered for overglow. In our case, our scene is somewhat dark, so we need to reduce this value in the Bloom effect settings to have more pixels included. As usual, those values need to be adjusted to your specific scenario.

4. You will notice that the difference is very subtle, but again, remember that you will have several effects, so all those little differences will sum up. You can see both effects in the following screenshots:

Figure 9.16 – Bloom effect

As usual, it is recommended for you to fiddle with the other values. Some interesting settings I recommend you to test are the **Dirt Texture** and **Dirt Intensity** values.

Now, let's move to another common effect, **Depth of Field**. This one relies on the depth map we discussed earlier. It is not that obvious to the naked eye, but when you focus on an object within your sight, the surrounding objects became blurred because they are out of focus. We can use this to focus the attention of the player in key moments of the gameplay. This effect will sample the Depth Map to see if the object is within the focus range; if it is, no blur will be applied, and vice versa. In order to use it, do the following:

1. This effect depends on the camera positioning of your game. To test it, in this case, we will put the camera near a column to try to focus on that specific object, as illustrated in the following screenshot:

Figure 9.17 – Camera positioning

2. Add the **Depth of Field** override.

3. Enable and set the **Mode** setting to **Gaussian**: the simplest one to use.

4. In my case, I have set **Start** to 10 and **End** to 20, which will make the effect start at a distance behind the target object. The **End** setting will control how the blur's intensity will increase, reaching its maximum at a distance of 20 meters. Remember to tweak these values to your case.

5. If you want to exaggerate the effect a little bit, set **Max Radius** to 1.5. The result is shown in the following screenshot:

Figure 9.18 – Exaggerated effect

Something to consider here is that our particular game will have a top-down perspective, and unlike the first-person camera, where you can see distant objects, here we will have objects near enough to not notice the effect, so we can limit the use of this effect just for cutscenes in our scenario.

Now, most of the remaining effects are different ways to alter the actual colors of the scene. The idea is that the real color sometimes doesn't give you the exact look and feel you are seeking. Maybe you need the dark zones to be darker to reinforce the sensation of a horror ambience, or maybe you want to do the opposite: increase the lightness of dark areas to represent an open scene. Maybe you want to tint the highlights a little bit to get a neon effect if you are creating a futuristic game, or perhaps you want a sepia effect temporarily, to do a flashback. We have a myriad ways to do this, and in this case, I will use a simple but powerful effect called **Shadow, Midtones, Highlights**.

This effect will apply different color corrections to—well —Shadows, Midtones, and Highlights, meaning that we can modify darker, lighter, and medium areas separately. Let's try it by doing the following:

1.   Add the **Shadow, Midtones, Highlights** override.

2.   Let's start doing some testing. Check the three **Shadows**, **Midtones**, and **Highlights** checkboxes.

3.   Move the **Shadow** and **Midtones** sliders all the way to the left and the one for **Highlights** to the right. This will reduce the intensity of Shadows and Midtones and increase the intensity of Highlights. We did this so that you can see the areas that **Highlights** will alter, based on their intensity (this can also be an interesting effect in a horror game). You can do the same with the rest of the sliders to check the other two areas. You can see the result in the following screenshot:

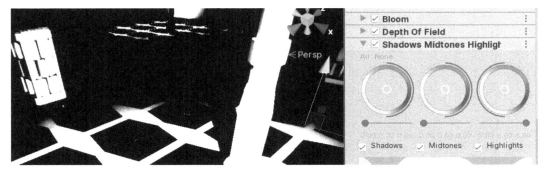

Figure 9.19 – Isolating highlights

4. Also, you can test moving the white circle at the center of the colored circle to apply a little bit of tinting to those areas. Reduce the intensity of the highlights by moving the slider a little bit to the left to make the tinting more noticeable. You can see the result in the following screenshot:

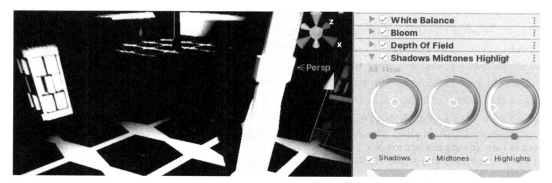

Figure 9.20 – Tinting highlights

5. By doing this, you can explore how those controls work, but of course, those extreme values are useful for some edge cases. In our scene, the settings you can see in the following screenshot worked best for me. As always, it is better to use subtler values to not distort too much the original result, as illustrated here:

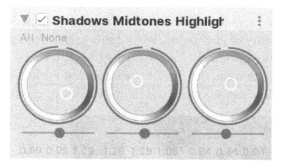

Figure 9.21 – Subtle changes

6. You can see the before-and-after effects in the following screenshots:

Figure 9.22 – Before-and-after effects

You have other simpler options such as **Split Toning**, which does something similar but just with Shadows and Highlights, or **Color Curves**, which give you advanced control of how each color channel of the scene will be mapped, but the idea is the same—that is, to alter the actual color of the resulting scene to apply a specific color ambience to your scene. If you remember the movie series *The Matrix,* when the characters were in the Matrix, everything had subtle green tinting and, while outside it, the tinting was blue.

Remember that the results of using HDR and not using it regarding these effects is important, so it is better to decide sooner rather than later whether to use HDR, excluding certain target platforms (which may not be important to your target audience), or not to use it (using LDR) and have less control over your scene lighting levels.

Also, take into account that maybe you will need to tweak some object's settings, such as light intensities and material properties, because sometimes we use postprocessing to fix graphics errors that may be caused by wrongly set objects, and that's not okay. For example, increasing the Ambient Lighting in our scene will drastically change the output of the effects, and we can use that to increase the overall brightness instead of using an effect if we find the scene too dark.

This has covered the main image effects to use. Remember that the idea is not to use every single one but to use the ones that you feel are contributing to your scene; they are not free in terms of performance (although not that resource-intensive), so use them wisely. Also, you can check for the already created profiles to apply them to your game and see how little changes can make a huge difference.

Summary

In this chapter, we discussed basic and advanced fullscreen effects to apply in our scene, making it look more realistic in terms of camera-lens effects and more stylish in terms of color distortions. We also discussed the internals of HDR and Depth Maps and how they are important when using those effects, which can immediately increase your game's graphic quality with minimal effort.

Now that we have covered most of the common graphics found in Unity systems, let's start looking at how to increase the immersion of our scene, using sounds.

10
Sound and Music Integration

We just achieved good enough graphics quality, but we are missing an important part of the game aesthetics: the sound. Often relegated to being a final step in game development, sound is one of those things that if it's there, you won't notice its presence, but if you don't have it, you will feel that something is missing. It will help you to reinforce the ambience you want in your game and must match the graphics setting.

In this chapter, we will examine the following sound concepts:

- Importing audio
- Integrating and mixing audio

Importing audio

As with graphic assets, it is important to properly set up the import settings of audio assets, which can be resource-intensive if not done properly.

In this section, we will examine the following audio importing concepts:

- Audio types
- Configuring import settings

Let's start by discussing the different kinds of audio we can use.

Audio types

There are different types of audio present in video games, which are the following:

- **Music**: Music used to enhance the player's experience according to the situation.

- **Sound effects (SFX)**: Sounds that happen as a reaction to player or NPC actions, such as clicking a button, walking, opening a door, and shooting a gun.

- **Ambient sound**: A game that only has sounds as reactions to events would feel empty. If you are recreating an apartment in the middle of the city, even if the player is just idle in the middle of the room doing nothing, lots of sounds should be heard, and the sources of most of them will be outside the room, such as an aeroplane flying overhead, a construction site two blocks away, and cars in the street. Creating objects that won't be seen is a waste of resources. Instead, we can place individual sounds all over the scene to recreate the desired ambience, but that would be resource-intensive, requiring lots of CPU and RAM to achieve believable results. Considering that these sounds usually are in the second plane of the user's attention, we can just combine them all into a single looping track and just play one audio, and that's exactly what ambient sound is. If you want to create a café scene, you can simply go to a real café and record a few minutes of audio, using that as your ambient sound.

For almost all games, we will need at least one music track, one ambient track, and several SFX to start the production of the audio. As always, we have different sources of audio assets, but we will use the Asset Store. It has three audio categories to search for the assets we need:

Figure 10.1 – Audio categories in the Asset Store

In my case, I also used the search bar to further filter the categories, searching for weather to find a rain effect. Sometimes, you can't find the exact audio separately; in such cases, you will need to dig in **Packs and Libraries**, so have patience here. In my case, I picked the three packages you can see in the following figure, but importing just some of the included sounds, all of them would weight a lot in the project. For ambience, I picked rain. Then, I picked **Music – Sad Hope** for music, and for SFX, I picked one gun sound effect package for our future Player's Hero Character. Of course, you can pick other packages to better suit your game's needs:

Figure 10.2 – The packages for our game

Please remember that those exact packages might not available at the moment you read this. In that case, you can either download other ones, or pick the files I used from the GitHub repo. Now that we have the necessary audio packages, let's discuss how to import them.

Configuring import settings

We have several import settings we can tweak, but the problem is that we need to consider the usage of the audio to properly set it up, so let's see the ideal settings for each case. In order to see the import settings, as always, you can select the asset and see it in the Inspector panel, as in the following screenshot:

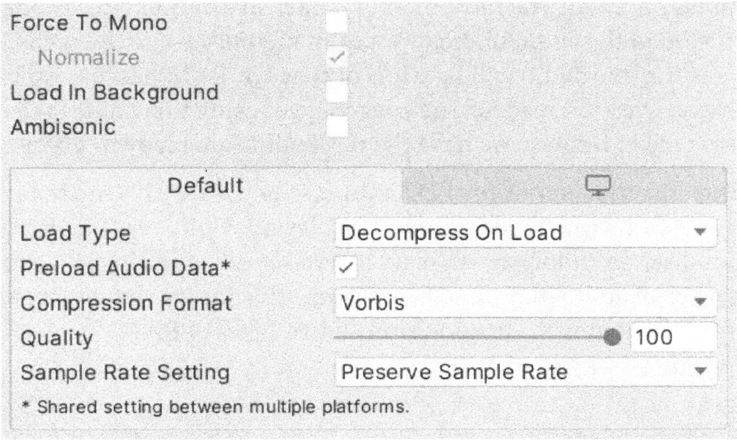

Figure 10.3 – Audio import settings

Let's discuss the most important ones, starting with **Force To Mono**. Some audio may come with stereo channels, meaning that we have one sound for the left ear and another one for the right ear. This means that one piece of audio can actually contain two different audio tracks. Stereo sound is useful for different effects and instrument spatialization in the case of music, so we want that in those scenarios, but there are other scenarios where stereo is not useful. Consider 3D sound effects such as a shooting gun or some walking-pace steps. In those cases, we need the sound to be heard in the direction to the source. If the shooting of a gun happened to my left, I need to hear it coming from my left. In these cases, we can convert stereo audio to mono audio by checking the **Force To Mono** checkbox in the audio import settings. This will make Unity combine the two channels into a single one, reducing the size of the audio usually to almost half its size (sometimes more, sometimes less, depending on various aspects).

You can verify the impact of that and other settings at the bottom of the Audio Asset inspector, where you can see the imported audio size:

Figure 10.4 – Left: audio imported without Force to Mono. Right: same audio with Force To Mono

The next setting to discuss, and an important one at that, is **Load Type**. In order to play some audio, Unity needs to read the audio from disk, decompress, and then play it. Load Type changes the way those three processes are handled. We have the following three options here:

- **Decompress on Load**: The most memory-intensive option. This mode will make Unity load the audio uncompressed in memory when the scene is loaded. That means that the audio will take lots of space in RAM because we have the uncompressed version loaded. The advantage of using this mode is that playing the audio is easier because we have the raw audio data ready to play in RAM.

- **Streaming**: The total opposite of **Decompress on Load**. This mode never loads audio in RAM. Instead, while the audio is playing, Unity reads a piece of the audio asset from disk, decompresses it, plays it, and repeats, running this process once for each piece of audio playing in **Streaming**. This means that this mode will be CPU - intensive, but will consume almost zero bytes of RAM.

- **Compressed in Memory**: The middle ground. This mode will load the audio from disk when the scene is loaded but will keep it compressed in memory. When Unity needs to play the audio, it will just take a piece from RAM, decompress it, and play it. Remember that reading pieces of the audio asset from RAM is considerably faster than reading from disk.

Maybe if you are an experienced developer you can easily determine which mode is better suited for which kind of audio, but if this is your first encounter with video games, it may sound confusing, so let's discuss the best modes for different cases:

- **Frequent short audio**: This could be a shooting gun or the sound of footsteps, which are sounds that last less than 1 second but can occur in several instances and play at the same time. In such cases, we can use Decompress On Load. Uncompressed short audio won't have a huge size difference from its compressed version. Also, since this is the most performant CPU option, having several instances won't have a huge impact on performance.

- **Infrequent large audio**: This includes music, ambient sound, and dialog. These kinds of audio usually have just one instance playing, and they are usually big. Those cases are better suited for Streaming mode because having them compressed or decompressed in RAM can have a huge impact in low-end devices such as mobile devices (on PCs, we can use Compressed in Memory sometimes). A CPU can handle having two or three bits of audio playing in Streaming, but try to have no more than that.

- **Frequent medium audio**: This includes pre-made voice chat dialog in multiplayer games, character emotes, long explosions, or any audio that is more than 500 KB (that is not a strict rule – this number depends a lot on the target device). Having this kind of audio decompressed in RAM can have a noticeable impact on performance, but due to the fact that this audio is fairly frequently used, we can have it compressed in memory. Their relatively smaller size means they usually won't make a huge difference in our game and we will avoid wasting CPU resources in reading from disk.

There are other cases to consider, but those can be extrapolated based on the previous ones. Remember that the previous analysis was made by taking into account the requirements of the standard game, but this can vary a lot according to your game and your target device. Maybe you are making a game that won't consume lots of RAM but is pretty intensive in terms of CPU resources, in which case you can just put everything in Decompress on Load. It's important to consider all aspects of your game and to balance your resources accordingly.

Finally, another thing to consider is the compression format, which will change the way Unity will encode the audio in the published game. Different compression formats will give different compression ratios in exchange for less fidelity with the original audio, or higher decompression times, and all this varies a lot based on the audio patterns and length. We have three compression formats:

- **PCM**: The uncompressed format will give you the highest audio quality, with no noise artifacts, but will result in a bigger asset file size.

- **ADPCM**: Compressing audio this way reduces file size and yields a fast uncompressing process, but this can introduce noise artifacts that can be noticeable in certain types of audio.

- **Vorbis**: A high-quality compression format that will yield almost zero artifacts but takes longer to decompress, so playing Vorbis audio will be slightly more intensive than for other formats. It also provides a quality slider to select the exact amount of compression aggressiveness.

Which one should you use? Again, that depends on the features of your audio. Short smooth audio can use PCM, while long noisy audio can use ADPCM; the artifacts introduced by this format will be hidden in the audio itself. Maybe long smooth audio where compression artifacts are noticeable could benefit from using Vorbis. Sometimes, it's just a matter of trial and error. Maybe use Vorbis by default and when performance is reduced, try to switch to ADPCM, and if that causes glitches, just switch to PCM. Of course, the problem here is being sure that the audio processing is really what's responsible for the performance issues – maybe switching all audio to ADPCM and checking whether that made a difference is a good way to detect that, but a better approach would be to use the Profiler, a performance measurement tool that we will see later in this book.

We have other settings, such as Sample Rate Setting, that again, with a little trial and error, you can use to detect the best setting.

I have set up the audio that I downloaded from the Asset Store as you can see in the following screenshots. The first one shows how I set up the music and ambient audio files (large files):

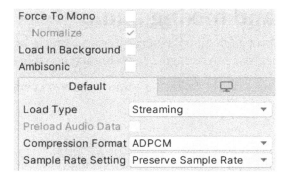

Figure 10.5 – Music and ambient settings

Should be stereo (Force To Mono unchecked), use **Streaming Load Type** because they are large and will have just one instance playing and **ADPCM Compression Format** because Vorbis didn't result in a huge size difference.

This second screenshot shows how I set up the SFX files (small files):

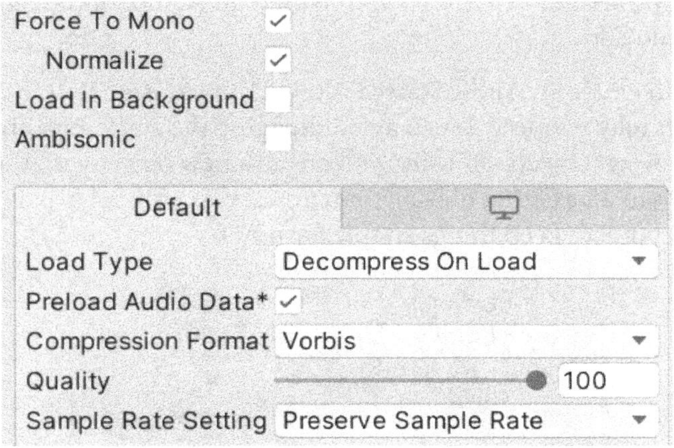

Figure 10.6 – Shooting SFX settings

Will be a 3D sound, so Force To Mono should be checked.. Will be short, so Decompress on Load Load Type works better. Vorbis Compression Format reduced the ADPCM size by more than a half

Now that we have our pieces of audio properly configured, we can start to use them in our scene.

Integrating and mixing audio

We can just drag our bits of audio into our scene to start using it, but we can dig a little bit further to explore the best ways to configure them to each possible scenario.

In this section, we will examine the following audio integration concepts:

- Using 2D and 3D AudioSources
- Using audio mixers

Let's start exploring AudioSources, objects that are in charge of audio playback.

Using 2D and 3D AudioSources

AudioSources are components that can be attached to GameObjects. They are responsible for emitting sound in our game based on **AudioClips**, which would be the audio assets we downloaded previously. It's important to differentiate an AudioClip from an **AudioSource**: we can have a single - explosion AudioClip, but lots of AudioSources playing it, simulating several explosions. In this way, an AudioSource can be seen as an instance of an AudioClip.

The simplest way to create an **AudioSource** is to pick an **AudioClip** (an audio asset) and drag it to the **Hierarchy** window. Try to avoid dragging the audio into an existing object; instead, drag it between objects, so Unity will create a new object with the **AudioSource** instead of adding it to an existing object (sometimes, you want an existing object to have the **AudioSource**, but let's keep things simple for now):

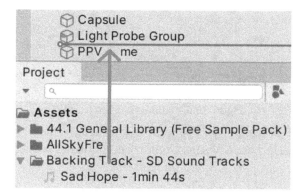

Figure 10.7 – Dragging an AudioClip to the Hierarchy window between objects

The following screenshot shows the **AudioSource** generated by dragging the music asset to the scene. You can see that the **AudioClip** field has a reference to the dragged audio:

Figure 10.8 – AudioSource configured to play our music asset

As you can see, the **AudioSource** has several settings, so let's review the common ones in the following list:

- **Play On Awake**: Determines whether the audio starts playing automatically when the game starts. We can uncheck that and play the audio via scripting, perhaps when the player shoots or jumps (more on that in Part 3 of the book).

- **Loop**: Will make the audio repeat automatically when it finishes playing. Remember to always check this setting on the music and ambient audio clips. It is easy to forget this because those tracks are long and we may never reach the end of them in our tests.

- **Volume**: Controls the audio intensity.

- **Pitch**: Controls the audio velocity. This is useful for simulating effects such as slow motion or the increasing revolutions of an engine.

- **Spatial Blend**: Controls whether our audio is 2D or 3D. In 2D mode, the audio will be heard at the same volume at all distances, while 3D will make the audio volume decrease as the distance from the camera increases.

In the case of our music track, I have configured it as shown in the following screenshot. You can drag the ambient rain sound to add it to the scene and use the same settings as these because we want the same ambient effect in all our scenes. In complex scenes, though, you can have different 3D ambient sounds scattered all over the scene to change the sound according to the current environment:

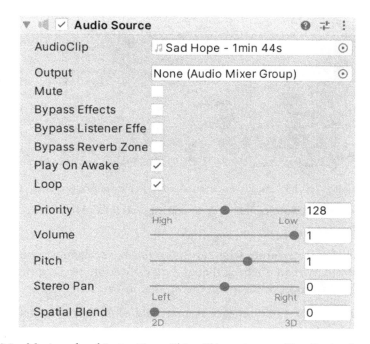

Figure 10.9 – Music and ambient settings. This will loop, is set to Play On Awake, and is 2D

Now, you can drag the shooting effect and configure it as shown in the following screenshot. As you can see, the audio, in this case, won't loop because we want the shooting effect to play once per bullet. Remember that, in our case, the bullet will be a prefab that will spawn each time we press the shoot key, so each bullet will have its own **AudioSource** that will play when the bullet is created. Also, the bullet is set to a 3D **Spatial Blend**, meaning that the effect will be transmitted through different speakers based on the position of the Audio Source relative to the position of the camera:

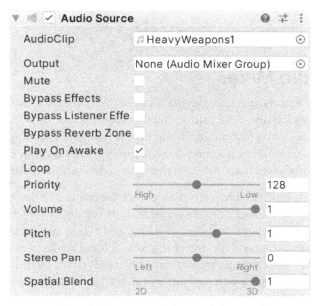

Figure 10.10 – Sound effect setting. This won't loop and is a 3D sound

Something to consider in the case of 3D sounds is the **Volume Rolloff** setting, which is inside the 3D sound settings section. This setting controls how the volume decays over distance to the camera. By default, you can see that this setting is set to **Logarithmic Rolloff**, the way real-life sound works, but sometimes you don't want real-life sound decay, because sounds in real life are usually heard slightly even if the source is very far away.

One option is to switch to **Linear Rolloff** and configure the exact maximum distance with the **Max Distance** setting:

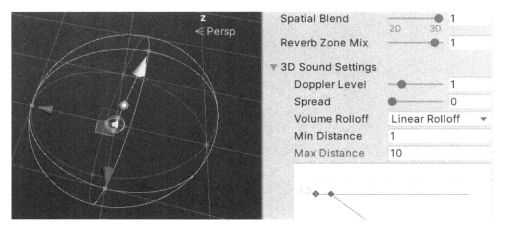

Figure 10.11 – A 3D sound with a maximum distance of 10 metres, using Linear Rolloff

Now that we can configure individual pieces of audio, let's see how to apply effects to groups of audio instances using an **Audio Mixer**.

Using an Audio Mixer

We will have several audio instances playing all over our game: the footsteps of characters, shooting, bonfires, explosions, rain, and so on. Controlling exactly which sounds are supposed to sound louder or lower depending on the case and applying effects to reinforce certain situations, such as being stunned due to a nearby explosion, is called audio mixing – the process of mixing several sounds together in a cohesive and controlled way.

In Unity, we can create an Audio Mixer, an asset that we can use to define groups of sounds. All changes to a group will affect all sounds inside it, by raising or lowering the volume, perhaps, or by applying an effect. You can have SFX and music groups to control sounds separately – as an example, you could lower the SFX volume while in the **Pause** menu but not the music volume. Also, groups are organized in a hierarchy, where a group can also contain other groups, so a change in a group will also apply changes to its sub-groups. As a matter of fact, every group you create will always be a child group of the master group, the group that will affect every single sound in the game (that uses that mixer).

Let's create a mixer with SFX and music groups:

1. In the Project window, using the + button, select the **Audio Mixer** option. Name the asset as you wish; in my case, I chose `Main Mixer`.

2. Double-click the created asset to open the **Audio Mixer** window:

Figure 10.12 – Audio Mixer window

3. Click the + button at the right of the **Groups** label to create a child group of the master node. Name it SFX:

Figure 10.13 – Group creation

4. Click on the **Master** group and click again on the + button to create another master node child group called Music. Remember to select the **Master** group before clicking the + button, because if another group is selected, the new group will be a child of that one. Anyway, you can rearrange a group child-parent relationship by dragging in the **Hierarchy** window:

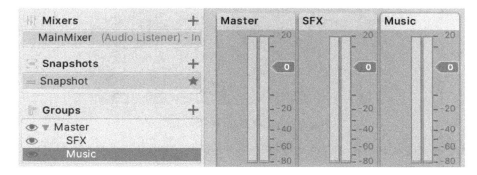

Figure 10.14 – The Master, SFX, and Music groups

5. Select the **Music** GameObject in the **Hierarchy** window and look for the **AudioSource** component in the Inspector window.

6. Click the circle to the right of the **Output** property and select the **Music** group in the **Audio Mixer** group selector. This will make that **AudioSource** be affected by the settings on the specified Mixer group:

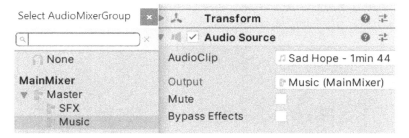

Figure 10.15 – Making an AudioSource belong to an Audio Mixer group

7. If you play the game now, you can see how the volume meters in the Audio Mixer start to move, indicating that the music is going through the **Music** group. You will also see that the **Master** group volume meter is also moving, indicating that the sound that is passing through the **Music** group is also passing through the **Master** group (the parent of the Music group) before going to the sound card of your computer:

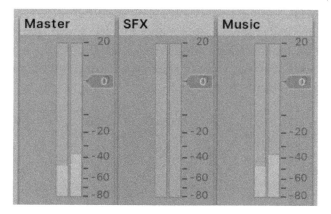

Figure 10.16 – Group volume levels

8. Repeat *steps 5* and *6* for the ambient and shooting sounds to make them belong to the **SFX** group.

Now that we have separated our sounds into groups, we can start adjusting the groups' settings. But, before doing that, we need to take into account the fact that we won't want the same settings all the time, as in the previously mentioned pause menu case, where the SFX volume should be lower. To handle those scenarios, we can create snapshots, which are presets of our mixer that can be activated via scripting during our game. We will deal with the scripting steps in Part 3 of this book, but we can create a normal snapshot for the in-game settings and a pause snapshot for the pause menu settings.

If you check the **Snapshots** list, you will see that a single snapshot has already been created – that can be our normal snapshot. So, let's create a pause snapshot by doing the following:

1. Click on the + button to the right of the **Snapshots** label and call the snapshot `Pause`. Remember to stop the game to edit the mixer or click the **Edit in Playmode** option to allow Unity to change the mixer during play. If you do the latter, remember that the changes will persist when you stop the game, unlike changes to GameObjects. Actually, if you change other assets during Play mode, those changes will also persist – only GameObject changes are reverted (and some other specific cases that we won't discuss right now):

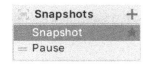

Figure 10.17 – Snapshot creation

2. Select the **Pause** snapshot and lower the volume slider of the **SFX** group:

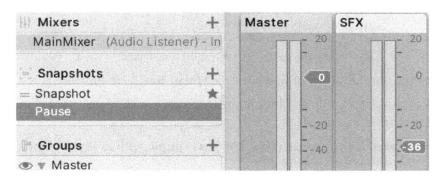

Figure 10.18 – Lowering the volume of the Pause snapshot

3. Play the game and hear how the sound is still at its normal volume. That's because the original snapshot is the default one – you can see that by checking for the star to its right. You can right-click any snapshot and make it the default one using the **Set as Start Snapshot** option.

4. Click on **Edit in Playmode** to enable **Audio Mixer** modification during runtime.

5. Click on the **Pause** snapshot to enable it and hear how the **Shooting** and **Ambient** sound volumes have decreased.

As you can see, one of the main uses of the mixer is to control group volume, especially when you see that the intensity of a group's volume is exceeding the 0 mark, indicating that the group is too loud. Anyway, there are other uses for the mixer, such as applying effects. If you've played any war game, you will have noticed that whenever a bomb explodes nearby, you hear the sound differently for a moment, as if the sound were located in another room. That can be accomplished using an effect called Low Pass, which blocks high-frequency sounds, and that's exactly what happens with our ears in those scenarios: the stress of the high-volume sound generated by an explosion irritates our ears, making them less sensitive to high frequencies for a while.

We can add effects to any channel and configure them according to the current snapshot, just as we did for the volume, by doing the following:

1. Click on the **Add...** button at the bottom of the **Master** group and select **Lowpass Simple**:

Figure 10.19 – The effects list of a channel

2. Select the normal snapshot (the one called **Snapshot**) to modify it.

3. Select the **Master** group and look at the Inspector panel, where you will see settings for the channel and its effects.

4. Set the **Cutoff freq** property of the **Lowpass Simple** settings to the highest value (22000); this will disable the effect.

5. Repeat *steps 3* and *4* for the **Pause** snapshot; we don't want this effect in that snapshot.

6. Create a new snapshot called **Bomb Stun** and select it to edit it.

7. Set **Cutoff freq** to 1000:

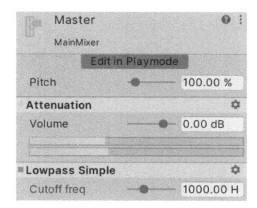

Figure 10.20 – Setting the cutoff frequency of the Lowpass Simple effect

8. Play the game and change between snapshots to check the difference.

Aside from the Low Pass filter, you can apply several other filters, such as Echo, to create an almost dreamy effect, or a combination of Send, Receive, and Duck to make a group lower its volume based on the intensity of another group (for instance, you may want to lower SFX volume when dialog is happening). I invite you to try those and other effects and check the results to identify potential uses.

Summary

In this chapter, we discussed how to import and integrate sounds, considering the memory impact of them and applying effects to generate different scenarios. Sound is a big part of achieving the desired game experience, so take the proper amount of time to get it right.

Now that we have covered almost all of the vital aesthetic aspects in our game, let's create another form of visual communication, the user interface.

11
User Interface Design

Everything that is shown on the screen and transmits through the speakers of a computer is forms of communication. In previous chapters, we used three-dimensional models to let the user know that they are in a base in the middle of the mountains, and we reinforced that idea with the appropriate sound and music. But for our game, we need to communicate other information, such as the amount of life the user has left, the current score, and so on, and sometimes, it is difficult to express these things using the in-game graphics (there are some successful cases that manage to do this, such as *Dead Space*, but let's keep things simple). In order to transmit this information, we will add another layer of graphics on top of our scene, which is usually called the **User Interface** (**UI**) or **Heads-Up Display** (**HUD**).

This will contain different visual elements, such as text fields, bars, and buttons, to prepare the user to take an informed decision based on things such as fleeing to a safe place when their life is low:

Figure 11.1 – Character creation UI displays info about the character stats with numbers

In this chapter, we will examine the following UI concepts:

- Understanding **Canvas** and **RectTransform**
- Canvas object types
- Creating a responsive UI

By the end of this chapter, you will be able to use the Unity UI system to create interfaces capable of informing the user about the state of the game and allowing them to take action by pressing buttons. Let's start discussing one of the basic concepts of the Unity UI system—RectTransform.

Understanding Canvas and RectTransform

Currently, there are three UI systems available in Unity for different purposes:

- **UI Elements**: A system to extend the Unity Editor with custom windows and tools. This uses several web concepts, such as stylesheets and XML-based language, to lay out your UI. In the future, it will be available to use in-game.

- **Unity UI**: A GameObject-based UI only applicable for in-game UIs (not editor extensions). You create it using GameObjects and components like any other object we have edited so far.

- **IMGUI**: A legacy code-based UI created entirely by using scripting. A long time ago, this was the only UI system used in both the editor and the in-game UI. Nowadays, it is only used to extend the editor and will soon be completely replaced by UI Elements.

In this chapter, we are only going to focus on in-game UI to communicate different information to the player regarding the state of the game, so we are going to use Unity UI. At the time of writing this book, there are plans to replace Unity UI with UI Elements, but there's no estimated date as to when this will happen. Anyway, even if Unity releases UI Elements as an in-game UI system soon, Unity UI will still be there for a while and is perfectly capable of handling all types of UI that you need to create.

If you are going to work with Unity UI, you first need to understand its two main concepts—Canvas and **RectTransform**. Canvas is the master object that will contain and render our UI and RectTransform is the feature in charge of positioning and adapting each UI element on our screen.

In this section, we will examine the following Unity UI concepts:

- Creating a UI with Canvas
- Positioning elements with RectTransform

Let's start using the Canvas component to create our UI.

Creating a UI with Canvas

In Unity UI, each image, text, and element you see in the UI is a GameObject with a set of proper components, but in order for them to work, they must be a child of a master GameObject with the Canvas component. This component is responsible for triggering the UI generation and drawing iterations over each child object. We can configure this component to specify exactly how that process works and adapt it to different possible requirements.

To start, you can simply create a canvas with the **GameObject | UI | Canvas** option. After doing that, you will see a rectangle in the scene, which represents the user screen, so you can put elements inside it and preview where they will be located relative to the user's monitor. You can see an example of this rectangle in the following screenshot:

Figure 11.2 – Canvas screen rectangle

You are probably wondering two things here. First, "why is the rectangle is in the middle of the scene? I want it to always be on the screen!". Don't worry because that will exactly be the case. When you edit the UI, you will see it as part of the level, as an object inside it, but when you play the game, it will be always projected over the screen, on top of every object. Also, you may be wondering why the rectangle is huge, and that's because one pixel of the screen maps to one meter on the scene. So again, don't worry about that; you will see all your UI elements in their proper size and position on the user's screen when you see the game in Game view.

Before adding elements to our UI, it's worth noting that when you created the UI, a second object is created alongside the canvas, called Event System. This object is not necessary to render a UI, but is necessary if you want the UI to be interactable, which means including actions such as clicking buttons, introducing text in fields, or navigating the UI with the joystick. The **EventSystem** component is responsible for sampling the user input, such as with a keyboard, mouse, or joystick, and sending that data to the UI to react accordingly. We can change the exact buttons to interact with the UI, but the defaults are OK for now, so just know that you need this object if you want to interact with the UI. If for some reason you delete the object, you can recreate it again in **GameObject | UI | Event System**.

Now that we have the base objects to create our UI, let's add elements to it.

Positioning elements with RectTransform

In Unity UI, each image, text, and element you see in the UI is a GameObject with a set of proper components according to its usage, but you will see that most of them have one component in common—**RectTransform**. Each piece of the UI is essentially a rectangle filled with text or images and has different behavior, so it is important to understand how the **RectTransform** component works and how to edit it.

In order to experiment with this component, let's create and edit the position of a simple white rectangle element for the UI by doing the following:

1. Go to **GameObject | UI | Image**. After that, you will see that a new GameObject is created within the **Canvas** element. Unity will take care of setting any new UI element as a child of **Canvas**; outside it, the element will not be visible:

Figure 11.3 – A default image UI element—a white box

2. Click on the 2D button in the top bar of the **Scene** view. This will just change the perspective of the Scene view to one that is better suited to edit the UI (and also two-dimensional games):

Figure 11.4 – The 2D button location

3. Double-click on the canvas in the **Hierarchy** window to make the UI fit entirely in the Scene view. This will allow us to edit the UI clearly. You can also navigate the UI using the mouse scroll wheel to zoom, and click and drag the scroll wheel to pan the camera:

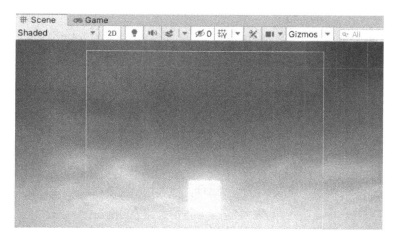

Figure 11.5 – The Scene view in 2D edit mode

4. Disable the **PPVolume** object to disable postprocessing. The final UI won't have postprocessing, but the editor view still applies it. Remember to re-enable it later:

Figure 11.6 – Disabling a game object—in this case, the postprocessing volume

5. Enable (if it is not already enabled) the **RectTrasform** tool, which is the fifth button in the top-left part of the Unity Editor (or press the *T* key). That will enable the rectangle gizmo, which allows you to move, rotate, and scale two-dimensional elements. You can use the usual transform, rotate, and scale gizmos, which were the ones we used in 3D mode, but the rectangle gizmo causes less trouble, especially with scaling:

Figure 11.7 – The rectangle gizmo button

6. Using the rectangle gizmo, drag the object to move it, use the blue dots to change its size, or locate the mouse in a tricky position near the blue dots to rotate it. Consider that resizing the object using this gizmo is not the same as scaling the object, but more on that in a moment:

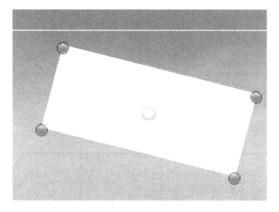

Figure 11.8 – The rectangle gizmo for editing two-dimensional elements

7. In the Inspector window, notice that after changing the size of the UI element, the **Rect Transform** setting's **Scale** property is still at (1, 1, 1), but you can see how the **Width** and **Height** properties changed. **Rect Transform** is essentially a classic transform but with **Width** and **Height** added (among other properties to explore later). You can set the exact values you want here expressed in pixels:

Figure 11.9 – The Rect Transform properties

Now that we know the very basics of how to position any UI object, let's explore the different types of elements you can add to Canvas.

Canvas objects types

So far, we have used the simplest Canvas object type—a white box—but there are plenty of other object types we can use, such as images, buttons, text, and much more. All of them use **RectTransform** to define their display area, but each one has its own concepts and configurations to understand.

In this section, we will explore the following Canvas object concepts:

- Integrating assets for the UI
- Creating UI controls

Let's first start exploring how we can integrate images and fonts to use in our canvas so that we can integrate them in our UI using the Images and Text UI object types.

Integrating assets for the UI

Before making our UI use nice graphics assets, we need, as always, to integrate them properly into Unity. In the following screenshot, you will find the UI design we proposed in *Chapter 1, Designing a Game From Scratch*:

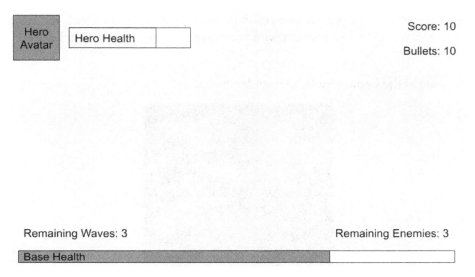

Figure 11.10 – Chapter 1's UI design

On top of that, we will add a Pause menu, which will be activated when the user presses *Esc*. It will look as in the following screenshot:

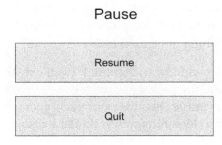

Figure 11.11 – The Pause menu design

Based on these designs, we can determine that we will need the following assets:

- The hero's avatar image
- A health bar image
- A Pause menu background image
- A Pause menu buttons image
- Font for the text

As always, we can find the required assets on the internet or on Asset Store. In my case, I will use a mixture of both. Let's start with the simplest one—the avatar. Take the following steps:

1. Download the avatar you want from the internet:

Figure 11.12 – Downloaded avatar asset

2. Add it into your project, either by dragging it to the Project window or by using the **Assets | Import New Asset** option. Add it to a `Sprites` folder.

3. Select the texture and in the Inspector window, set the **Texture Type** setting to **Sprite (2D and UI)**. All textures are prepared to be used in 3D by default. This option prepares everything to be used in 2D.

For the bars, buttons, and the window background, I will use Asset Store to look for a UI pack. In my case, I found the package in the following screenshot a good one to start my UI. As usual, remember that this exact package might not be available right now. In that case remember to look for another similar package, or pick the Sprites from the GitHub repo:

Figure 11.13 – Selected UI pack

At first, the pack contains lots of images configured the same way, as sprites, but we can further modify the import settings to achieve advanced behavior, as we will need for the buttons. The button asset comes with a fixed size, but what happens if you need a bigger button? One option is to use other button assets with different sizes, but this will lead to a lot of repetitions of the buttons and other assets, such as different-sized backgrounds for different windows, which will consume unnecessary RAM. Another option is to use the nine slices method, which consists of splitting an image so that the corners are separated from the other parts. This allows Unity to stretch the middle parts of the image to fit different sizes, keeping the corners at their original size, which, when combined with a clever image, can be used to create almost any size you need. In the following diagram, you can see a shape with nine slices in the bottom-left corner, and at the bottom-right corner of the same diagram, you can see the shape is stretched but keeps its corners at their original size. The top-right corner shows the shape stretched without slices. You can see that the non-sliced version is distorted, while the sliced version is not:

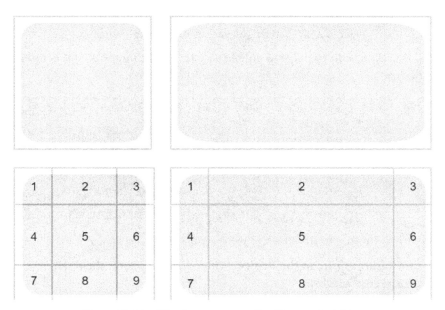

Figure 11.14 – Sliced versus non-sliced image stretching

In this case, we can apply the nine-slices to the button and the panel background images to use them in different parts of our game. In order to do this, do the following:

1. Open Package Manager using the **Window | Package Manager** option.

2. Verify that **Package Manager** is showing all the packages by setting the dropdown to the right of the + button in the top-left part of the window to **Unity Registry**:

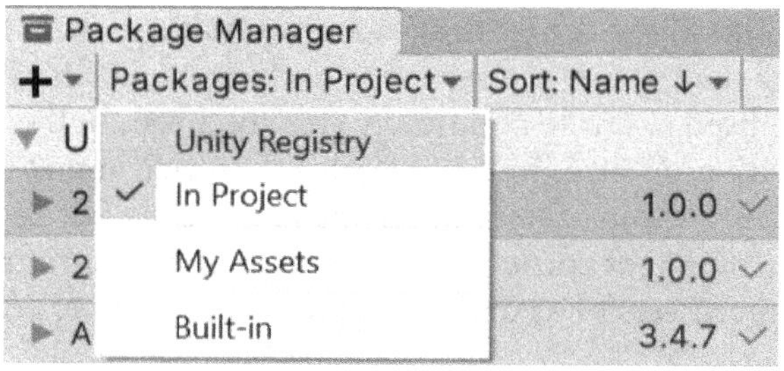

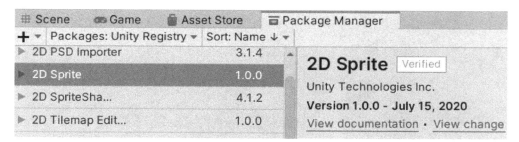

Figure 11.15 – Showing all packages in Package Manager

3. Install the **2D Sprite** package to enable the sprite editing tools (if it is not already installed):

Figure 11.16 – The 2D Sprite package in Package Manager

4. Select the button sprite in the **Project** window and click on the **Sprite Editor** button in the **Inspector** window:

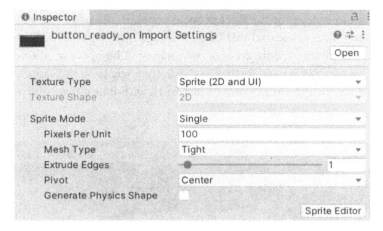

Figure 11.17 – The Sprite Editor button in the Inspector window

5. In the **Sprite Editor** window, locate and drag the green dots at the edges of the image to move the slice rulers. Try to ensure that the slices are not located in the middle of the edges of the button. One thing to notice is that in our case, we will work with three slices instead of nine because our button won't be stretched vertically.

6. Click on the **Apply** button in the top-right corner of the window and close it:

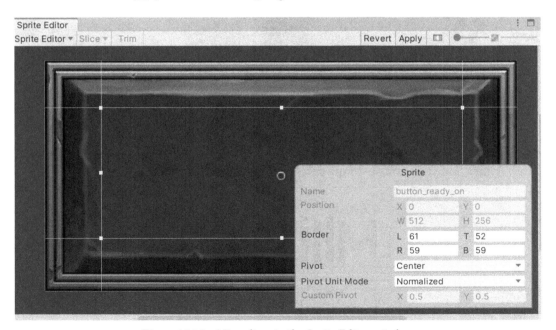

Figure 11.18 – Nine slices in the Sprite Editor window

7. Repeat the same steps for the **Background** panel. In my case, you can see in the following screenshot that this background is not prepared with nine slices in mind because all the middle areas of the image can be made smaller, and if the nine-slicing method is used to stretch them, they will look the same. So, we can edit it with any image editing tool or just work with it as it is for now:

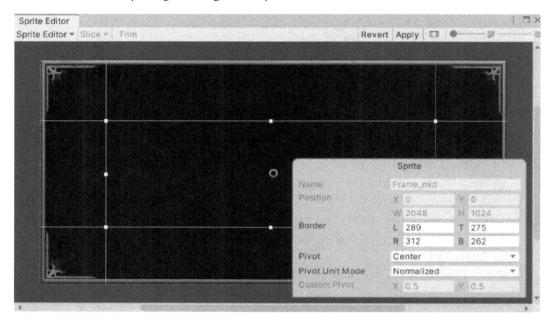

Figure 11.19 – Nine slices in the Sprite Editor window

Now that we have prepared our sprites, we can find a font, which is a pretty easy task. Just download any font in the `.ttf` or `.otf` formats and import it to Unity, and that's all—no further configuration required. You can find lots of good, free font websites on the internet. I am used to working with the classic `DaFont.com` site, but there's plenty of other sites that you can use. In my case, I will work with the following font:

Figure 11.20 – My chosen font from DaFont.com to use in the project

If the zipped file contains several font files, you can just drag them all into Unity and then use the one that you like the most. Also, as usual, try to put the font inside a folder called `Fonts`.

Now that we have all the required assets to create our UI, let's explore the different types of components to create all the required UI elements.

Creating UI controls

Almost every single part of the UI will be a combination of images and texts configured cleverly. In this section, we will explore the following components:

- Image
- Text
- Button

Let's start exploring **Image**. Actually, we have already an image in our UI—the white rectangle we created previously in this chapter. If you select it and look at the Inspector window, you will notice that it has an Image component, like the one in the following screenshot:

Figure 11.21 – The Image component's Inspector window

Let's start exploring the different settings of this component, starting with our hero's avatar. Take the following steps:

1. Using the rectangle gizmo, locate the white rectangle at the top-left part of the UI:

Figure 11.22 – The white rectangle located at the top-left part of the UI

2. In the **Inspector** window, click on the circle to the right of the Source Image property and pick the downloaded hero avatar sprite:

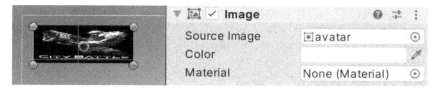

Figure 11.23 – Setting the sprite of our Image component

3. We need to correct the aspect ratio of the image to prevent distortion. One way to do this is to click the **Set Native Size** button at the bottom of the Image component to make the image use the same size as the original sprite. However, by doing this, the image can become too big, so you can reduce the image size by pressing *Shift* to modify both the **Width** and **Height** values. Another option is to check the **Preserve Aspect** checkbox to make sure the image fits the rectangle without stretching. In my case, I will use both:

Figure 11.24 – The Preserve Aspect and Set Native Size image options

Now, let's create the life bars by doing the following:

1. Create another Image component using the **GameObject | UI | Image** option.

2. Set the Source Image property to the life bar image you downloaded:

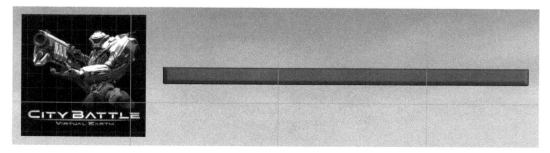

Figure 11.25 – The avatar and life bar

3. Set the **Image Type** property to **Filled**.

4. Set the **Fill Method** property to **Horizontal**.

5. Drag the Fill Amount slider to see how the bar is cut according to the value of the slider. We will change that value via scripting when we code the life system in *Part 3* of the book, where we will be code out own scripts:

Figure 11.26 – The Fill Amount slider, cutting the image width by 73% of its size

6. In my case, the bar image also comes with a bar frame, so I will create another image, set the sprite, and position it on top of the life bar to frame it. Bear in mind that the order the objects are in in the **Hierarchy** window determines the order in which they will be drawn. So, in my case, I need to be sure the frame GameObject is below the health bar image:

Figure 11.27 – Putting one image on top of the other to create a frame effect

7. Repeat steps *1 to 6* to create the base bar at the bottom, or just copy and paste the bar and the frame and locate it at the bottom of the screen:

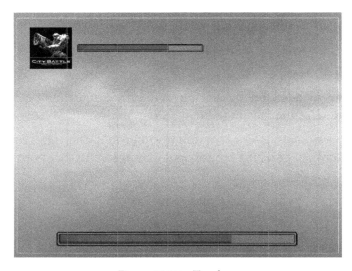

Figure 11.28 – Two bars

8. Click on the + button in the **Project** window and select the **Sprites | Square** option. This will create a simple squared sprite. This is the same as downloading a *4 x 4* resolution full-white image and importing it into Unity.

9. Set the sprite as the base bar instead of the downloaded bar sprite. This time, we will be using a plain-white image for the bar because in my case, the original one is red, and changing the color of a red image to green is not possible. However, a white image can be easily tinted. Take into account the detail of the original bar—for example, the little shadow in my original bar won't be present here, but if you want to preserve it, you should get a white bar with that detail.

10. Select the base health bar and set the **Color** property to green:

Figure 11.29 – A bar with a squared sprite and green tint

11. One optional step would be to convert the bar frame image into a nine-slices image to allow us to change the original width to fit the screen.

Now, let's add the text fields for the Score, Bullets, Remaining Waves, and Remaining Enemies labels by doing the following:

1. Create a text label using the **GameObject | UI | Text** option. This will be the Score label.

2. Position the label at the top-right part of the screen.

3. In the **Inspector** window, set the **Text** property to Score: 0.

4. Set the **Font Size** property to 20.

5. Apply the downloaded font by clicking on the circle to the right of the **Font** property and selecting the desired font.

6. Check the horizontal alignment option (the one on the far right) for the **Alignment** property and the central option for the vertical options:

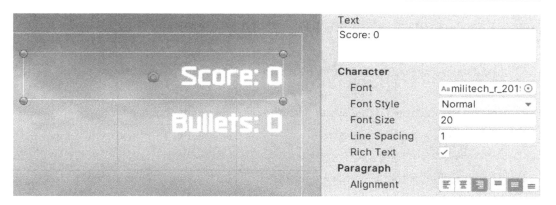

Figure 11.30 – The settings for a text label

7. Repeat *steps 1 to 6* to create the other three labels (or just copy and paste the score three times). For the **Remaining Waves** label, you can use the left alignment option to better match the original design:

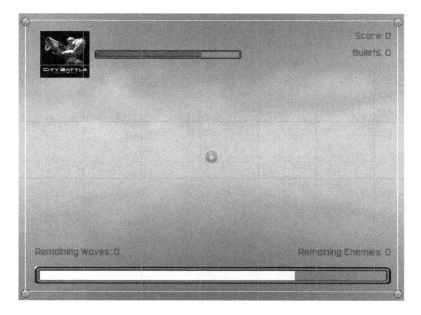

Figure 11.31 – All the labels for our UI

8. Set the color of all the labels to white as our scene will be mainly dark.

Now that we have completed the original UI design, let's create the Pause menu by doing the following:

1. Create an **Image** component for the menu's background (**GameObject | UI | Image**).

2. Set the **Background** panel sprite with the nine slices we made earlier.

3. Set the **Image Type** property to **Sliced** if it is not already. This mode will apply the nine-slices method to prevent the corners from stretching.

4. There's a chance that the image will stretch the corners anyway, which happens because sometimes the corners are quite big compared to the **RectTransform** setting's **Size** property that you are using, so Unity has no option other than to do that. In this scenario, the correct solution is to have an artist that creates assets tailored to your game, but sometimes we don't have that option. This time, we can just increase the **Pixels Per Unit** value of the sprite, which will reduce the scale of the original image while preserving its resolution.

   In the following two screenshots, you can see the background image with a **Pixels Per** Unit value of 100 and again with 700. Remember to only do this for the nine-slices or tiled-image types, or if you don't have an artist to adjust it for you:

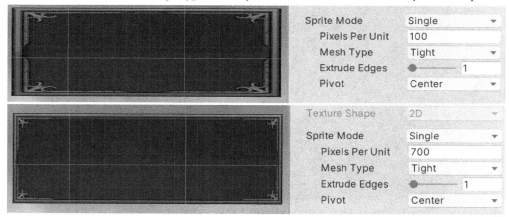

Figure 11.32 – On top, a large nine-slices image in a small RectTransform component, small enough to shrink the corners, on the bottom, the same image with Pixels Per Unit set to 700

5. Create a **Text** field, position it where you want the Pause label to be in your diagram, set it to display the Pause text, and set the font. Remember that you can change the text color with the **Color** property.

6. Drag the text field onto the background image. The parenting system in **Canvas** works the same—if you move the parent, the children will move with it. The idea is that if we disable the panel, it will also disable the buttons and all its content:

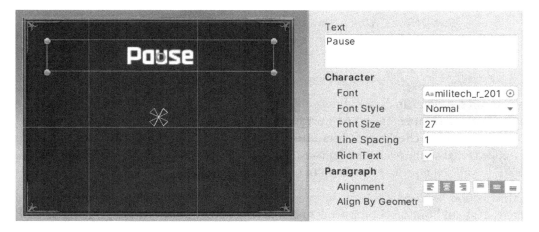

Figure 11.33 – The Pause label

7. Create two Buttons by going to **GameObject | UI | Button**. Position them where you want them on the background image.

8. Set them as children of the **Pause** background image by dragging them in the **Hierarchy** window.

9. Select the buttons and set the Source Image property of their Image components to use the button sprite that we downloaded earlier. Remember our **Pixels Per Unit** fix from earlier if you have the same problem as before.

10. You will notice that the button is essentially an image with a child Text object. Change the text of both buttons to Resume and Quit, respectively:

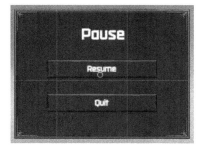

Figure 11.34 – The Pause menu implementation

11. Remember that you can hide the panel by unchecking the checkbox to the right of the name of the object in the top part of the **Inspector** window:

Figure 11.35 – Disabling a GameObject

As you can see, you can create almost any kind of UI just by using Image and Text components. Of course, there are more advanced components that enable you to create buttons, text fields, checkboxes, lists, and so on, but let's stick to the basics one. One thing to notice is that we have created buttons, but they do nothing so far. Later, in *Part 3* of the book, we will see how to script them to have a function.

In this section, we discussed how to import images and fonts to be integrated through the Image, Text, and Button components to create a rich and informative UI. Having done that, let's discuss how to make them adapt to different devices.

Creating a responsive UI

Nowadays, it is almost impossible to design a UI in a single resolution, and our target audience display devices can vary a lot. A PC has a variety of different kinds of monitors with different resolutions (such as 1080p, 4k, and so on) and aspect ratios (such as 16:9, 16:10, ultra-wide, and so one), and the same goes for mobile devices. We need to prepare our UI to adapt to the most common displays, and Unity UI has the tools needed to do so.

In this section, we will explore the following UI responsiveness concepts:

- Adapting objects' positions
- Adapting objects' sizes

We are going to explore how the UI elements can adapt their position and size to different screen sizes using advanced features of the Canvas and **RectTransform** components, such as Anchors and Scalers.

Adapting objects' positions

Right now, if we play our game, we will see how the UI fits nicely onto our screen. But if for some reason we change the **Game** view size, we will see how objects start to disappear from the screen. In the following screenshots, you can see different sized game windows and how the UI looks nice in one but bad in the others:

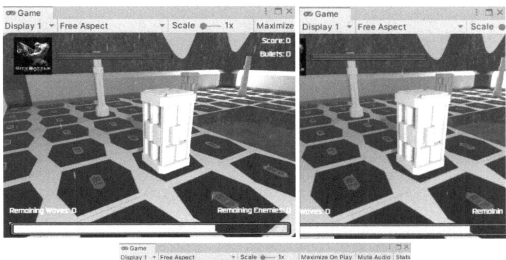

Figure 11.36 – The same UI but on different screen sizes

The problem is that we created the UI using whatever resolution we had in the editor, but as soon as we change it slightly, the UI keeps its design for the previous resolution. Also, if you look closely, you will notice that the UI is always centered, such as in the middle image, where the UI is cropped at its sides, or the third image, where extra space is visible along the borders of the screen. This happens because every single element in the UI has its own Anchor, a little cross you can see when you select an object, such as the one in the following screenshot:

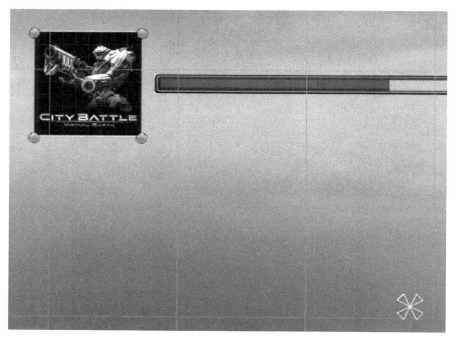

Figure 11.37 – An Anchor cross at the bottom-right part of the screen belonging
to the hero avatar in the top-left part of the screen

The X and Y position of the object is measured as a distance to that Anchor, and the Anchor has a position relative to the screen, with its default position being at the center of the screen. This means that on an 800 x 600 screen, the Anchor will be placed at the 400 x 300 position, and on a 1920 x 1080 screen, the Anchor will be located at the 960 x 540 position. If the X and Y position of the element (the one in RectTransform) is 0, the object will always be at a distance of 0 from the center. In the middle screenshot of the previous three examples, the hero avatar falls outside of the screen because its distance from the center is greater than half the screen, and the current distance was calculated based on the previous, bigger screen size. So, what we can do about that? Move the Anchor!

By setting a relative position, we can position the Anchor at different parts of our screen and make that part of the screen our reference position. In the case of our hero avatar, we can place the Anchor at the top-left corner of the screen to guarantee that our avatar will be at a fixed distance from that corner. We can do that by doing the following:

1. Select your hero avatar.

2. Drag the Anchor cross with your mouse to the top-left part of the screen. If for some reason the Anchor breaks into pieces when you drag it, undo the change (press *Ctrl + Z*, or *Command + Z* on macOS) and try to drag it by clicking in the center. We will break the Anchor later:

Figure 11.38 – An image with an Anchor at the top-left part of the screen

3. Put the Anchor of the **Health Bar** object and its frame in the same position. We want the bar to always be at the same distance from that corner so that it will move alongside the hero avatar if the screen size changes.

4. For the **Boss Bar** object, place the Anchor at the bottom-center part of the screen so that it will always be centered. Later, we will deal with adjusting its size.

5. Put the **Remaining Waves** label at the bottom-left corner and **Remaining Enemies** in the bottom-right corner:

Figure 11.39 – The Anchors for the life bar and the labels

6. Put the **Score** and **Bullets** Anchors at the top-right corner:

Figure 11.40 – The Anchors for the Score and Bullets labels

7. Select any element and drag the sides of the Canvas rectangle with your mouse to preview how the elements will adapt to their positions. Take into account that you must select any object that is a direct child of Canvas; the text within the buttons won't have that option:

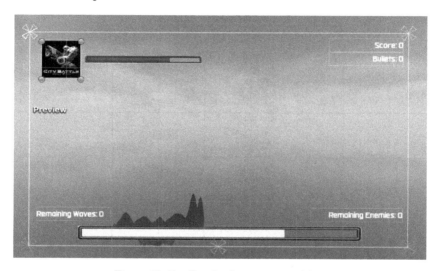

Figure 11.41 – Previewing canvas resizing

Now that our UI elements have adapted to their positions, let's consider scenarios where the object size must adapt as well.

Adapting objects' sizes

The first thing to consider when dealing with different aspect ratios is that our screen elements may not only move from their original design position (which we fixed in the previous section) but also they may not fit into the original design. In our UI, we have the case of the health bar, where the bar clearly doesn't adapt to the screen width when we previewed it on a wider screen. We can fix this by breaking our Anchors.

When we break our Anchors, the position and size of our object are calculated as a distance relative to the different Anchor parts. If we split the Anchor horizontally, instead of having an X and Width property, we will have a Left and Right property, representing the distance to the left and right Anchor. We can use this in the following way:

1. Select the health bar and drag the left part of the anchor all the way to the left part of the screen, and the right part to the right part of the screen.

2. Do the same for the health bar frame:

Figure 11.42 – The splitter Anchor in the health bar

3. Check the **Rect Transform** setting's **Left** and **Right** properties in the Inspector window, which represent the current distance to their respective Anchors. If you want, you can add a specific value, especially if your health bars are displaying outside the screen:

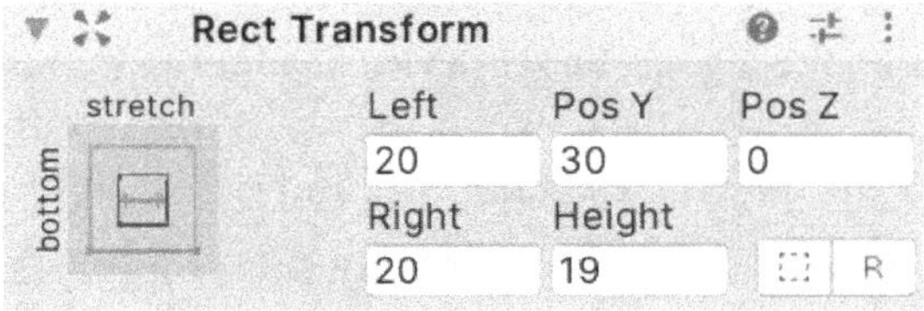

Figure 11.43 – The Left and Right properties of a split anchor

This way, the object will always be at a fixed distance of a relative position to the screen—in this case, the sides of the screen. If you are working with a child object, as is the case of the Text and Image components of the buttons, the Anchors are relative to the parent. If you pay attention to the Anchors of the text, they are not only split horizontally but also vertically. This allows the text to adapt its position to the size of the button, so you won't have to change it manually:

Figure 11.44 – The split Anchors of the text of the button

Now, this solution is not suitable for all scenarios. Let's consider a case where the hero avatar is displayed in higher resolution than what it was designed for. Even if the avatar is correctly placed, it will be displayed smaller because the screen has more pixels per inch that the other resolution. You consider using split Anchors, but the width and height Anchors could be scaled differently in different aspect ratio screens, so the original image becomes distorted. Instead, we can use the Canvas Scaler component.

The Canvas Scaler component defines what 1 pixel means in our scenario. If our UI design resolution is 1080p, but we see it in a 4k display (which is twice the resolution of 1080p), we can scale the UI so that a pixel becomes 2, adapting its size to keep the same proportional size as the original design. Basically, the idea is that if the screen is bigger, our elements should also be bigger.

We can use this component by doing the following:

1. Select the **Canvas** object and locate the **Canvas Scaler** component in the **Inspector** window.

2. Set the **UI Scale Mode** property to **Scale with Screen Size**.

3. This isn't the case for us, but if in the future you are working with an artist, set the reference resolution to the resolution in which the artist created the UI, keeping in mind that it must be the highest target device resolution. In our case, we are not sure which resolution the artist of the downloaded assets had in mind, so we can put 1920 x 1080, which is the full HD resolution size and is very common nowadays.

4. Set the **Match** property to **Height**. The idea of this property is that it sets which side of the resolution will be considered when carrying out the scaling calculation. In our case, if we are playing the game in 1080 resolution, 1 UI pixel equals 1 real screen pixel. However, if we are playing in 720p resolution, 1 UI pixel will be 0.6 real pixels, so the elements will be smaller on smaller resolution screens, keeping its correct size. We didn't choose a **Width** value in this case because we can have extreme widths in screens, such as ultra-wide, and if we picked that option, those screens would scale the UI unnecessarily. Another option is to set this value to 0.5 to consider the two values, but on a PC, this doesn't make too much sense. On a mobile device, you should choose this based on the orientation of the game, setting the height for landscape mode and the width for portrait mode. Try previewing a wider and higher screen and see how this setting works:

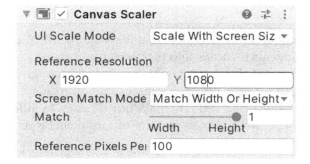

Figure 11.45 – Canvas Scaler with the correct settings for standard PC games

You will find that your UI will be smaller than your original design, which is because we should have set these properties before. Right now, the only fix is to resize everything again. Take this into account the next time you try this exercise; we only followed this order for learning purposes.

Before moving on, remember to reactivate the postprocessing volume object to show those effects again. You will notice that the UI is not affected by them in the Game view.

> **Important note:**
>
> If you want your UI to be affected by postprocessing effects, you can set **Canvas Render Mode** to **Screen Space – Camera**. Drag the main camera to the **Render Camera** property and set **Plane Distance** to 5. This will put the UI in the world with the rest of the objects, aligned to the camera view with a distance of 5 meters.

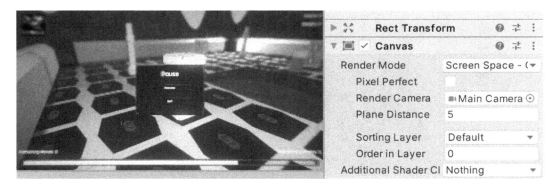

Figure 11.46 – Canvas Render Mode set to Camera mode to receive postprocessing effects

With this knowledge, you are now ready to start creating your firsts UIs by yourself.

Summary

In this chapter, we introduced the basics of UI, understanding the **Canvas** and **RectTransform** components to locate objects onscreen and create a UI layout. We also covered different kinds of UI elements, mainly **Image** and **Text**, to give life to our UI layout and make it appealing to the user. Finally, we discussed how to adapt UI objects to different resolutions and aspect ratios to make our UI adapt to different screen sizes, even though we cannot predict the exact monitor our user will be playing the game on.

In the next chapter, we will start seeing how to add animated characters to our game.

12
Creating Animations with Animator, Cinemachine, and Timeline

At our current game status, we mostly have a static Scene, without considering the Shader and particle animations. In the next chapter, when we will add scripting to our game, everything will start to move according to the behavior we want. But sometimes, we need to move objects in a predetermined way, such as with cutscenes, or specific character animations, such as jumping, running, and so on. The idea of this chapter is to go over several Unity animation systems to create all the possible movements of objects we can get without scripting.

In this chapter, we will examine the following animation concepts:

- Using skeletal animations with Animator
- Creating dynamic cameras with Cinemachine
- Creating cutscenes with Timeline

By the end of this chapter, you will be able to create cutscenes to tell the history of your game or highlight specific areas of your level, as well as create dynamic cameras that are capable of giving an accurate look of your game, regardless of the situation.

Using skeletal animations with Animator

So far, we have used what are called static meshes, which are solid three-dimensional models that are not supposed to bend or animate in any way (aside from moving separately, like the doors of a car). We also have another kind of mesh, called skinned meshes, which are meshes that have the ability to be bent based on a skeleton, so they can emulate the muscle movements of the human body. We are going to explore how to integrate animated humanoid characters into our project to create the enemy and player movements.

In this section, we will examine the following skeletal mesh concepts:

- Understanding skinning
- Importing skinned meshes
- Integration using Animator Controllers

We are going to explore the concept of skinning and how it allows you to animate characters. Then, we are going to bring animated meshes into our project to finally apply animations to them. Let's start by discussing how to bring skeletal animations into our project.

Understanding skinning

In order to get an animated mesh, we need to have four pieces, starting with the mesh itself and the model that will be animated, which is created the same way as any other mesh. Then, we need the skeleton, which is a set of bones that will match the desired mesh topology, such as the arms, fingers, feet, and so on. In *Figure 12.1*, you can see an example of a set of bones aligned with our target mesh. You will notice that these kinds of meshes are usually modeled with the *T* pose, which will facilitate the animation process:

Figure 12.1 – A ninja mesh with a skeleton matching its default pose

Once the artist has created the model and its bones, the next step is to do the skinning, which is the act of associating every vertex of the model to one or more bones. In this way, when you move a bone, the associated vertexes will move with it. This is done in such a way because it is easier to animate a reduced amount of bones instead of every single vertex of the model. In the next screenshot, you will see the triangles of a mesh being painted according to the color of the bone that affects it as a way to visualize the influence of the bones. You will notice blending between colors, meaning that those vertexes are affected differently by different bones to allow the vertexes near an articulation to bend nicely. Also, the screenshot illustrates an example of a two-dimensional mesh used for two-dimensional games, but the concept is the same:

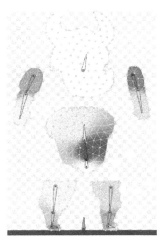

Figure 12.2 – Mesh skinning weights visually represented as colors

Finally, the last piece you need is the actual animation, which will simply consist of a blending of different poses of the meshes. The artist will create keyframes in an animation, determining which pose the model needs to have at different moments, and then the animation system will simply interpolate between them. Basically, the artist will animate the bones, and the skinning system will apply this animation to the whole mesh. You can have one or several animations, which you will later switch between according to the animation that you want to match the character's motion (such as idle, walking, falling, and so on).

In order to get the four parts, we need to get the proper assets containing them. The usual format in this scenario is **Filmbox** (**FBX**), which is the same that we have used so far to import 3D models. This format can contain every piece we need—the model, the skeleton with the skinning, and the animations—but usually, we will split the parts into several files to reutilize the pieces.

Imagine a city simulator game where we have several citizen meshes with different aspects and all of them must be animated. If we have a single FBX per citizen containing the mesh, the skinning, and the animation, it will cause each model to have its own animation, or at least a clone of the same one, repeating them. When we need to change that animation, we will need to update all the mesh citizens, which is a time-consuming process. Instead of this, we can have one FBX per citizen, containing the mesh and the bones with the proper skinning based on that mesh, as well as a separate FBX for each animation, containing the same bones that all the citizens have with the proper animation, but without the mesh. This will allow us to mix and match the citizen FBX with the animation's FBX files. You may be wondering why both the model FBX and the animation FBX must have the mesh. This is because they need to match in order to make both files compatible. In the next screenshot, you can see how the files should look:

Figure 12.3 – The animation and model FBX files of the package we will use in our project

Also, it is worth mentioning a concept called retargeting. As we said before, in order to mix a model and an animation file, we need them to have the same bone structure, which means the same amount of bones, hierarchy, and names. Sometimes, this is not possible, especially when we mix custom models created by our artist with external animation files that you can record from an actor using motion capture techniques or just by buying a Mocap library. In such cases, it is highly likely that you will encounter different bone structures between the one in the Mocap library and your character model, so here is where retargeting kicks in. This technique allows Unity to create a generic mapping between two different humanoid-only bone structures to make them compatible. In a moment, we will see how to enable this feature.

Now that we understand the basics behind skinned meshes, let's see how we can get the model's assets with bones and animations.

Importing skeletal animations

Let's start with how to import some animated models from the Asset Store, under the **3D | Characters | Humanoids** section. You can also use external sites, such as Mixamo, to download them. But for now, I will stick to the Asset Store as you will have less trouble making the assets work. In my case, I have downloaded a package, as you can see in the following screenshot, that contains both models and animations.

Note that sometimes you will need to download them separately because some assets will be model- or animation-only. Also, consider that the packages used in this book might not be available at the time you're reading; in that case, you can either look for another package with similar assets (characters and animations, in this case) or download the project files from the GitHub repository of the book and copy the required files from there:

VICX GAMES
SciFi Robots
★ ★ ★ ★ ☆ (14)
FREE

Figure 12.4 – Soldier models for our game

In my package content, I can find the animation's FBX files in the `Animations` folder and the single model FBX file in `Model`. Remember that sometimes you won't have them separated like this, and the animations may be located in the same FBX as the model, if any animations are present at all. Now that we have the required files, let's discuss how to properly configure them.

Let's start selecting the **Model** file and checking the **Rig** tab. Within this tab, you will find a setting called **Animation Type**, as in the following screenshot:

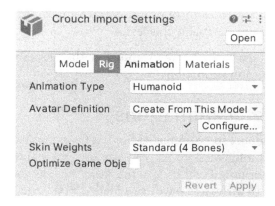

Figure 12.5 – The Rig properties

This property contains the following options:

- **None**: Mode for non-animated models; every static mesh in your game will use this mode.

- **Legacy**: The mode to be used in old Unity Projects and models; do not use this in new projects.

- **Generic**: A new animation system that can be used in all kinds of models but is commonly used in non-humanoid models, such as horses, octopuses, and so on. If you use this mode, both the model and animation FBX files must have the exact same bone names and structure, thereby reducing the possibility of combining animation from external sources.

- **Humanoid**: New animation systems designed to be used in humanoid models. It enables features such as retargeting and **Inverse Kinematics (IK)**. This allows you to combine models with different bones than the animation because Unity will create a mapping between those structures and a generic one, called the avatar. Take into account that sometimes the automatic mapping can fail, and you will need to correct it manually; so, if your generic model has everything you need, I would recommend you to stick to **Generic** if that's the default configuration of the FBX.

In my case, the FBX files in my package have the modes set to **Humanoid**, so that's good, but remember, only switch to other modes if it is absolutely necessary (for example, if you need to combine different models and animations). Now that we have discussed the **Rig** settings, let's talk about the **Animation** settings.

In order to do this, select any animation FBX file and look for the **Animation** section of the Inspector window. You will find several settings, such as the **Import Animation** checkbox, which must be marked if the file has an animation (not the model files), and the **Clips** list, where you will find all the animations in the file. In the following screenshot, you can see the **Clips** list for one of our animation files:

Clips	Start	End
HumanoidCrouchIdle	264.0	319.0
HumanoidCrouchWalk	105.0	159.0
HumanoidCrouchWalkRight	2193.0	2245.0
HumanoidCrouchWalkLeft	1542.0	1610.0
HumanoidCrouchTurnRight	1932.0	1976.0
HumanoidCrouchTurnLeft	1932.0	1976.0
HumanoidCrouchWalkRightl	1542.0	1610.0

+ −

Figure 12.6 – A Clips list in the Animation settings

An FBX file with animations usually contains a single large animation track, which can contain one or several animations. Either way, by default, Unity will create a single animation based on that track, but if that track contains several animations, you will need to split them manually. In our case, our FBX contains several animations already split by the package creator, but in order to learn how to do a manual split, do the following:

1. From the **Clips** list, select any animation that you want to recreate; in my case, I will choose HumanoidCrouchIdle.

2. Take a look at the **Start** and **End** values below the animation timeline and remember them; we will use them to recreate this clip:

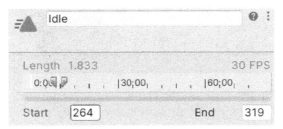

Figure 12.7 – The Clip settings

3.   Click on the minus button on the bottom-right part of the **Clips** list to delete the selected clip.

4.   Use the plus button to create a new clip and select it.

5.   Rename it to something similar to the original using the Take 001 input field. In my case, I will name it Idle.

6.   Set the **End** and **Start** properties with the values we needed to remember in *Step 2*. In my case, I have 319 for **End** and 264 for **Start**. This information usually comes from the artist, but you can just try the number that works best or simply drag the blue markers in the timeline on top of these properties.

7.   You can preview the clip by clicking on the bar titled for your animation (**HumanoidIdle**, in my case) at the very bottom of the Inspector window and click on the Play button. You will see the default Unity model, but you can see your own by dragging the model file to the preview window because it is important to check whether our models are properly configured. If the animation does not play, you will need to check whether the **Animation Type** setting matches the animation file:

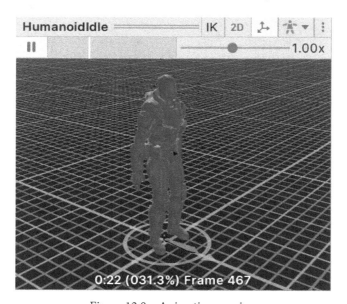

Figure 12.8 – Animation preview

Now, open the animation file, click on the arrow, and check the sub-assets. You will see that here, there is a file titled for your animation, alongside the other animations in the clip list, which contains the cut clips. In a moment, we will play them. In the following screenshot, you can see the animations in our .fbx file:

Figure 12.9 – Generated animation clips

Now that we covered the basic configuration, let's see how to integrate animations.

Integration using Animation Controllers

When adding animations to our characters, we need to think about the flow of the animations, which means thinking about which animations must be played, when each animation must be active, and how transitions between animations should happen. In previous Unity versions, you needed to code that manually, generating complicated scripts of C# code to handle complex scenarios; but now, we have Animation Controllers.

Animation Controllers are a state machine-based asset where we can diagram the transition logic between animations with a visual editor called **Animator**. The idea is that each animation is a state and our model will have several of them. Only one state can be active at a time, so we need to create transitions in order to change them, which will have conditions that must be met in order to trigger the transition process. Conditions are comparisons of data about the character to be animated, such as its velocity, whether it's shooting or crouched, and so on.

So, basically, an Animation Controller or state machine is a set of animations with transition rules that will dictate which animation should be active. Let's start creating a simple Animation Controller by doing the following:

1. Click the + button under the **Project** view, click on **Animator Controller**, and call it Player. Remember to locate your asset within a folder for proper organization; I will call mine Animators.

2. Double-click on the asset to open the **Animator** window. Don't confuse this window with the **Animation** window; the **Animation** window does something different.

3. Drag the **Idle** animation clip of your character into the **Animator** window. This will create a box in the Controller representing the animation that will be connected to the entry point of the Controller, indicating that the animation will be the default one because it is the first one that we dragged. If you don't have an **Idle** animation, I encourage you to find one. We will need at least one **Idle** and one walking/running animation clip:

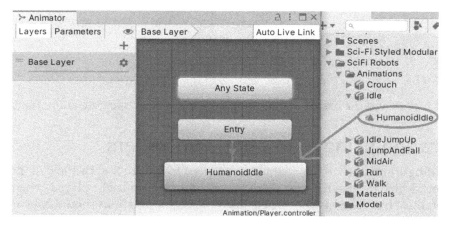

Figure 12.10 – Dragging an animation clip from an FBX asset into an Animator Controller

4. Drag the running animation in the same way.

5. Right-click on the **Idle** animation, select **Create Transition**, and left-click on the **Run** animation. This will create a transition between **Idle** and **Run**.

6. Create another transition from **Run** to **Idle** in the same way:

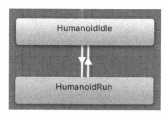

Figure 12.11 – Transitions between two animations

Transitions must have conditions in order to prevent animations from swapping constantly, but in order to create conditions, we need data to make comparisons. We will add properties to our Controller, which will represent data used by the transitions. Later, in *Part 3*, we will set that data to match the current state of our object. But for now, let's create the data and test how the Controller reacts with different values. In order to create conditions based on properties, do the following:

7. Click on the **Parameters** tab in the top-left part of the **Animator** window. If you don't see it, click on the crossed-eye button to display the tabs.

8. Click on the + button and select **Float** to create a number that will represent the velocity of our character, naming it `Velocity`. If you missed the renaming part, just left-click on the variable and rename it:

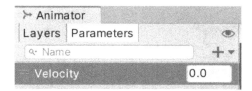

Figure 12.12 – The Parameters tab with a float Velocity property

9. Click on the **Idle to Run** transition (the white arrow) and look at the `Conditions` property in the Inspector window.

10. Click on the + button at the bottom of the list, which will create a condition that will rule the transition. The default setting will take the first parameter of our animator (in this case, it is **Velocity**) and will set the default comparer, in this case, **Greater**, to a value of 0. This tells us that the transition will execute from **Idle** to **Run** if **Idle** is the current animation and the velocity of the Player is greater than 0. I recommend you to set a slightly higher value, such as 0.01, to prevent any float rounding errors (a common CPU issue). Also, remember that the actual value of **Velocity** needs to be set manually via scripting, which we will do in *Part 3*:

Figure 12.13 – Condition to check whether the velocity is greater than 0.01

11. Do the same to the **Run to Idle** transition, but this time, change **Greater** to **Less** and again set the value to 0.01:

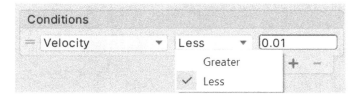

Figure 12.14 – Condition to check whether a value is less than 0.01

Now that we have our first Animator Controller set up, it's time to apply it to an object. In order to do that, we will need a series of components. First, when we have an animated character, rather than a regular Mesh Renderer, we use the Skinned Mesh Renderer. If you drag the model of the character to the scene and explore its children, you will see a component, as shown:

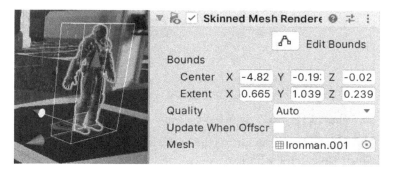

Figure 12.15 – A Skinned Mesh Renderer component

This component will be in charge of applying the bones' movements to the mesh. If you search the children of the model, you will find some bones; you can try rotating, moving, and scaling them to see the effect, as shown in the following screenshot. Consider the fact that your bone hierarchy might be different from mine if you downloaded another package from the Asset Store:

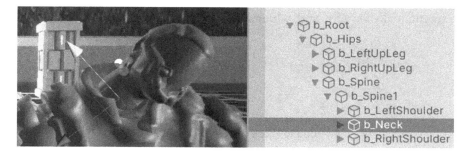

Figure 12.16 – Rotating the neckbone

The other component that we need is **Animator**, which is automatically added to skinned meshes at its root GameObject. This component will be in charge of applying the state machine that we created in the Animator Controller if the animation FBX files are properly configured as we mentioned earlier. In order to apply the Animator Controller, do the following:

1. Drag the model of the character to the Scene if it's not already there.

2. Select it and locate the **Animator** component in the root GameObject.

3. Click on the circle to the right of the **Controller** property and select the **Player** controller we created earlier. You can also just drag it from the Project window.

4. Make sure that the **Avatar** property is set to the avatar inside the FBX model; this will tell the animator that we will use that skeleton. You can identify the avatar asset by its icon of a person, as in the following screenshot. Usually, this property is correctly set automatically when you drag the FBX model to the Scene:

Figure 12.17 – Animator using the Player controller and the robot avatar

5. Set the **Camera** GameObject so that it's looking at the player and play the game, and you will see the character executing its **Idle** animation.

6. Without stopping the game, open the Animator Controller asset again by double-clicking it and selecting the character in the **Hierarchy** pane. By doing this, you should see the current state of the animation being played by that character, using a bar to represent the current part of the animation:

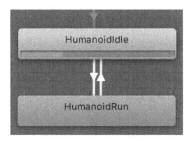

Figure 12.18 – The Animator Controller in Play mode while an object is selected, showing the current animation and its progress

7. Using the **Animator** window, change the value of **Velocity** to 1.0 and see how the transition will execute:

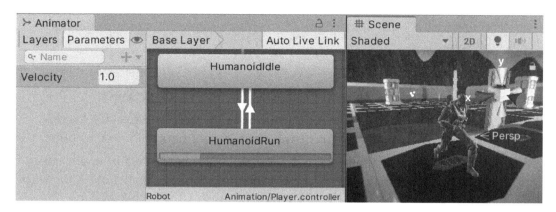

Figure 12.19 – Setting the velocity of the Controller to trigger a transition

Depending on how the **Run** animation was set, your character might start to move. This is caused by the root motion, a feature that will move the character based on the animation movement. Sometimes, this is useful, but due to the fact that we will fully move our character using scripting, we want that feature to be turned off. You can do that by unchecking the **Apply Root Motion** checkbox in the **Animator** component of the **Character** object:

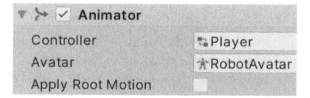

Figure 12.20 – Disabled root motion

8. You will also notice a delay between changing the **Velocity** value and the start of the animation transition. That's because, by default, Unity will wait for the original animation to end before executing a transition, but in this scenario, we don't want that. We need the transition to start immediately. In order to do this, select each transition of the Controller and in the Inspector window, uncheck the **Has Exit Time** checkbox:

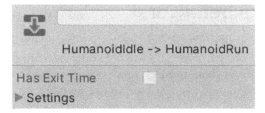

Figure 12.21 – Disabling the Has Exit Time checkbox to execute the transition immediately

You can start dragging other animations into the Controller and create complex animation logic, such as adding jumping, falling, or crouched animations. I invite you to try other parameter types, such as a Boolean, that use checkboxes instead of numbers. Also, as you develop your game further, your Controller will grow in its number of animations. To manage that, there are other features worth researching, such as Blend Trees and sub-state machines, but that's beyond the scope of this book.

Now that we understand the basics of character animations in Unity, let's discuss how to create dynamic camera animations to follow our player.

Creating dynamic cameras with Cinemachine

Cameras are a very important subject in video games. They allow the player to see their surroundings to make decisions based on what they see. The game designer usually defines how it behaves to get the exact gameplay experience they want, and that's no easy task. A lot of behaviors must be layered to get the exact feeling. Also, during cutscenes, it is important to control the path that the camera will be traversing and where the camera is looking to focus the action during those constantly moving scenes.

In this chapter, we will use the Cinemachine package to create both of the dynamic cameras that will follow the player's movements, which we will code in *Part 3*, and also, the cameras to be used during cutscenes.

In this section, we will examine the following Cinemachine concepts:

- Creating camera behaviors
- Creating dolly tracks

Let's start by discussing how to create a Cinemachine controlled camera and configure behaviors in it.

Creating camera behaviors

Cinemachine is a collection of different behaviors that can be used in the camera, which when properly combined can generate all kinds of common camera types in video games, including following the player from behind, first-person cameras, top-down cameras, and so on. In order to use these behaviors, we need to understand the concept of brain and virtual cameras.

In Cinemachine, we will only keep one main camera, as we have done so far, and that camera will be controlled by virtual cameras, separated GameObjects that have the previously mentioned behaviors. We can have several virtual cameras and swap between them at will, but the active virtual camera will be the only one that will control our main camera. This is useful for switching cameras at different points of the game, such as switching between our player's first-person camera. In order to control the main camera with the virtual cameras, it must have a **Brain** component.

To start using Cinemachine, first, we need to install it from the Package Manager, as we did previously with other packages. If you don't remember how to do this, just do the following:

1. Go to **Window | Package Manager**.

2. Ensure that the **Packages** option in the top-left part of the window is set to **Unity Registry**:

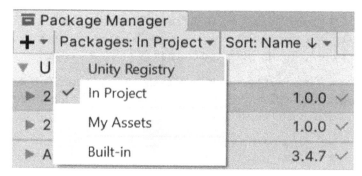

Figure 12.22 – The Packages filter mode

3. Wait a moment for the left panel to populate all packages from the servers (internet is required).

4. Look for the **Cinemachine** package from the list and select it. At the moment of writing this book, we are using Cinemachine 2.6.0.

5. Click the **Install** button in the bottom-right corner of the screen.

Let's start creating a virtual camera to follow the character we animated previously, which will be our player hero. Do the following:

1. Click **Cinemachine | Create Virtual Camera**. This will create a new object called CM vcam1:

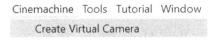

Figure 12.23 – Virtual camera creation

2. If you select the main camera from the **Hierarchy** pane, you will also notice that a CinemachineBrain component has been automatically added to it, making our main camera follow the virtual camera. Try to move the created virtual camera, and you will see how the main camera follows it:

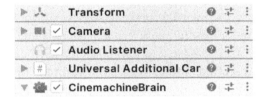

Figure 12.24 – The CinemachineBrain component

3. Select the virtual camera and drag the character to the **Follow** and **Look At** properties of the Cinemachine virtual camera component. This will make the movement and looking behaviors use that object to do their jobs:

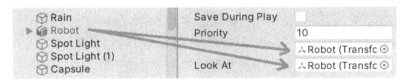

Figure 12.25 – Setting the target of our camera

4. You can see how the **Body** property of the virtual camera is set to **Transposer**, which will move the camera relative to the target set at the **Follow** property; in our case the character. You can change the **Follow Offset** property and set it to the desired distance you want the camera to have from the target. In my case, I used the (0, 3, and -3) values:

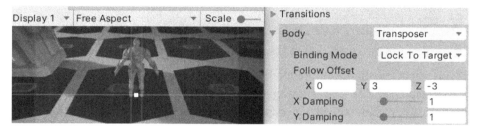

Figure 12.26 – The camera following the character from behind

5. *Figure 12.26* shows the **Game** view; you can see a small, yellow rectangle indicating the target position to look at the character, and it's currently pointing at the pivot of the character—its feet. We can apply an offset in the **Tracked Object Offset** property of the **Aim** section of the virtual camera. In my case, a value of 0, 1.5, and 0 worked well to make the camera look at the chest instead:

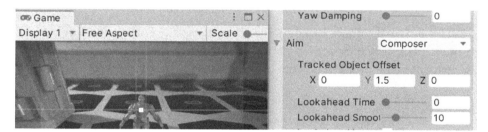

Figure 12.27 – Changing the Aim offset

As you can see, using Cinemachine is pretty simple, and in our case, the default settings were mostly enough for the kind of behavior we needed. However, if you explore the other **Body** and **Aim** modes, you will find that you can create any type of camera for any type of game. We won't cover the other modes in this book, but I strongly recommend you look at the documentation for Cinemachine to check what the other modes do. To open the documentation, do the following:

1. Open the Package Manager by going to **Window | Package Manger**.

2. Find **Cinemachine** in the left-hand side list. Wait a moment if it doesn't show up. Remember that you need an internet connection for it to work.

3. Once **Cinemachine** is selected, look for the **View documentation** link in blue. Click on it:

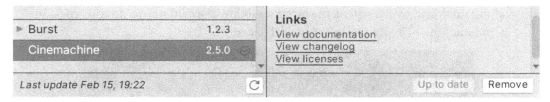

Figure 12.28 – The Cinemachine documentation link

4. You can explore the documentation using the navigation menu on the left:

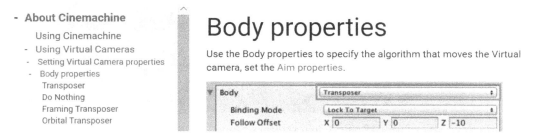

Figure 12.29 – The Cinemachine documentation

As you did with Cinemachine, you can find other packages' documentation in the same way. Now that we have achieved the basic camera behavior that we need, let's explore how we can use Cinemachine to create a camera for our intro cutscene.

Creating dolly tracks

When the player starts the level, we want a little cutscene with a pan over our scene and the base before entering the battle. This will require the camera to follow a fixed path, and that's exactly what Cinemachine's dolly camera does. It creates a path where we can attach a virtual camera so that it will follow it. We can set Cinemachine to move automatically through the track or follow a target to the closest point to the track; in our case, we will use the first option.

In order to create a dolly camera, do the following:

1. Let's start creating the track with a cart, which is a little object that will move along the track, which will be the target to follow the camera. To do this, click on **Cinemachine | Create Dolly Track with Cart**:

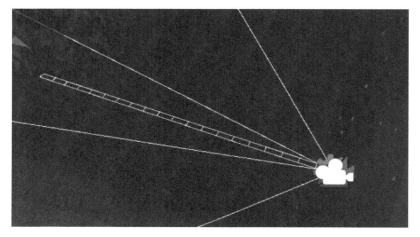

Figure 12.30 – A dolly camera with a default straight path

2. If you select the `DollyTrack1` object, you can see two circles with the numbers `0` and `1`. These are the control points of the track. Select one of them and move it as you move other objects using the arrows of the translation gizmo.

3. You can create more control points by clicking the + button at the bottom of the **Waypoints** list of the `CinemachineSmoothPath` component of the `DollyTrack1` object:

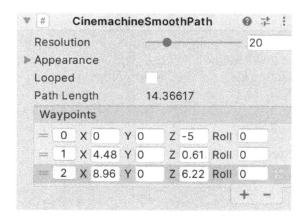

Figure 12.31 – Adding a path control point

4. Create as many waypoints as you need to create a path that will traverse the areas you want the camera to oversee in the intro cutscene. Remember, you can move the waypoints by clicking on them and using the translation gizmo:

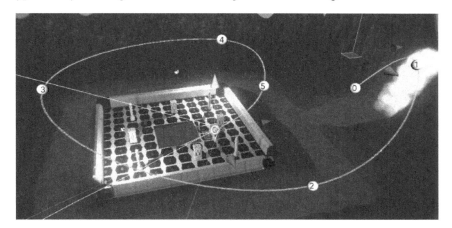

Figure 12.32 – A dolly track for our scene. It ends right behind the character

5. Create a new virtual camera. If you go to the **Game** view after creating it, you will notice that the character camera will be active. In order to test how the new camera looks, select it and click on the **Solo** button in the Inspector window:

Figure 12.33 – The Solo button to temporarily enable this virtual camera while editing

6. Set the **Follow** target this time to the `DollyCart1` object that we previously created with the track.

7. Set **Follow Offset** to 0, 0, and 0 to keep the camera in the same position as the cart.

8. Set **Aim** to **Same As Follow Target** to make the camera look in the same direction as the cart, which will follow the track curves:

Figure 12.34 – Configuration to make the virtual camera follow the dolly track

9. Select the **DollyCart1** object and change the **Position** value to see how the cart moves along the track. Do this while the game window is focused and **CM vcam2** is in solo mode to see how the camera will look:

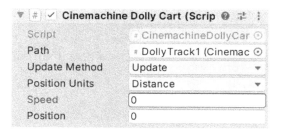

Figure 12.35 – The Dolly Cart component

With the dolly track properly set, we can create our cutscene using **Timeline** to sequence it.

Creating cutscenes with Timeline

We have our intro camera, but that's not enough to create a cutscene. A proper cutscene is a sequence of actions happening at the exact moment that they should happen, coordinating several objects to act as intended. We can have actions such as enabling and disabling objects, switching cameras, playing sounds, moving objects, and so on. To do this, Unity offers **Timeline**, which is a sequencer of actions to coordinate that kind of cutscenes. We will use **Timeline** to create an intro cutscene for our scene, showing the level before starting the game.

In this section, we will examine the following Timeline concepts:

- Creating animation clips
- Sequencing our intro cutscene

We are going to see how to create our own animation clips in Unity to animate our GameObjects and then place them inside a cutscene to coordinate their activation using the Timeline sequencer tool. Let's start creating a camera animation to use later in Timeline.

Creating animation clips

This is actually not a Timeline-specific feature, but rather a Unity feature that works great with Timeline. When we downloaded the character, it came with animation clips that were created using external software, but you can create custom animation clips using Unity's **Animation** window. Don't confuse it with the **Animator** window, which allows us to create animation transitions that react to the game situation. This is useful to create small object-specific animations that you will coordinate later in Timeline with other objects' animations.

These animations can control any value of an object's component properties, such as the positions, colors, and so on. In our case, we want to animate the dolly track's **Position** property to make it go from start to finish in a given time. In order to this, do the following:

1. Select the `DollyCart1` object.
2. Open the **Animation** (not **Animator**) window by going to **Window** | **Animation** | **Animation**.

3. Click on the **Create** button at the center of the **Animation** window. Remember to do this while the dolly cart (not track) is selected:

Figure 12.36 – Creating a custom animation clip

4. After doing this, you will be prompted to save the animation clip somewhere. I recommend you create an `Animations` folder in the project (inside the `Assets` folder) and call it `IntroDollyTrack`.

If you pay attention, the dolly cart now has an **Animator** component with an Animator Controller created, which contains the animation we just created. As with any animation clip, you need to apply it to your object with an Animator Controller; custom animations are no exception. So, the **Animation** window created them for you.

Animating in this window consists of specifying the value of its properties at given moments. In our case, we want **Position** to have a value of 0 at the beginning of the animation at the second 0 at the timeline, and have a value of 240 at the end of the animation at second 5. I chose 240 because that's the last possible position in my cart, but that depends on the length of your dolly track. Just test which is the last possible position in yours. Also, I chose the second 5 because that's what I feel is the correct length for the animation, but feel free to change it as you wish. Now, whatever happens between the animation's 0 and 5 seconds is an interpolation of the 0 and 240 values, meaning that in 2.5 seconds, the value of **Position** will be 120. Animating always consists of interpolating different states of our object at different moments.

In order to do this, do the following:

1. In the **Animation** window, click on the record button (the red circle in the top-left section). This will make Unity detect any changes in our object and save it to the animation. Remember to do this while you have selected the dolly cart.

2. Set the **Position** setting of the dolly cart to 1 and then 0. Changing this to any value and then to 0 again will create a keyframe, which is a point in the animation that says that at 0 seconds, we want the **Position** value to be 0. We need to set it first to any other value if the value is already at 0. You will notice that the **Position** property has been added to the animation:

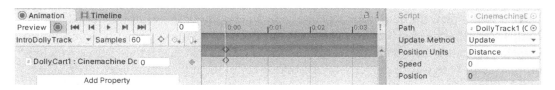

Figure 12.37 – The animation in Record mode after changing the Position value to 0

3. Using the mouse scroll wheel, zoom out the timeline to the right of the **Animation** window until you see 5 seconds in the top bar:

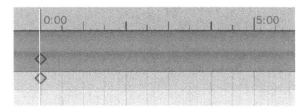

Figure 12.38 – The timeline of the Animation window showing 5 seconds

4. Click on the 5 second label in the top bar of the timeline to position the playback header at that moment. This will locate the next change we do at that moment.

5. Set the **Position** value of the dolly track to the highest value you can get; in my case, this is 240. Remember to have the **Animation** window in **Record** mode:

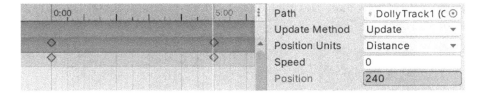

Figure 12.39 – Creating a keyframe with the 240 value at second 5 of the animation

6. Hit the play button in the top-left section of the **Animation** window to see the animation playing. Remember to view it in the **Game** view and while CM vcam2 is in solo mode.

Now, if we hit play, the animation will start playing, but that's something we don't want. In this scenario, the idea is to give control of the cutscene to the cutscene system, Timeline, because this animation won't be the only thing that needs to be sequenced in our cutscene. One way to prevent the **Animator** component from automatically playing the animation we created is to create an empty animation state in the Controller and set it as the default state by doing the following:

1. Search the Animator Controller that we created when we created the animation and open it. If you can't find it, just select the dolly cart and double-click on the **Controller** property of the **Animator** component on our Game Object to open the asset.

2. Right-click on an empty state in the Controller and select **Create State | Empty**. This will create a new state in the state machine as if we created a new animation, but it is empty this time:

Figure 12.40 – Creating an empty state in the Animator Controller

3. Right-click on **New State** and click on **Set as Layer Default State**. The state should become orange:

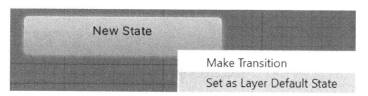

Figure 12.41 – Changing the default animation of the Controller to an empty state

4. Now, if you hit play, no animation will play as the default state of our dolly cart is empty.

Now that we have created our camera animation, let's start creating a cutscene that switches from the intro cutscene camera to the player camera by using Timeline.

Sequencing our intro cutscene

Timeline is already installed in your project, but if you go to the Package Manager of Timeline, you may see an **Update** button to get the latest version if you need some of the new features. In our case, we will keep the default version included in our project (1.3.4, at the time of writing this book).

The first thing we will do is create a cutscene asset and an object in the scene responsible for playing it. To do this, follow these steps:

1. Create an empty GameObject using the **GameObject | Create Empty** option.

2. Select the empty object and call it `Director`.

3. Go to **Window | Sequencing | Timeline** to open the **Timeline** editor.

4. Click the **Create** button in the middle of the **Timeline** window while the **Director** object is selected to convert that object into the cutscene player (or director).

5. After doing this, a window will pop up asking you to save a file. This file will be the cutscene or timeline; each cutscene will be saved in its own file. Save it in a `Cutscenes` folder in your project (the `Assets` folder).

6. Now, you can see that the **Director** object has a **Playable Director** component with the **Intro** cutscene asset saved in the previous step set for the **Playable** property, meaning this cutscene will be played by the director:

Figure 12.42 – Playable Director prepared to play the Intro Timeline asset

Now that we have the Timeline asset ready to work with, let's make it sequence actions. To start, we need to sequence two things—first, the cart position animation we did in the last step and then the camera swap between the dolly track camera (**CM vcam2**) and the player cameras (**CM vcam1**). As we said before, a cutscene is a sequence of actions executing at given moments, and in order to schedule actions, you will need tracks. In Timeline, we have different kinds of tracks, each one allowing you to execute certain actions on certain objects. We will start with the animation track.

The animation track will control which animation a specific object will play; we need one track per object to animate. In our case, we want the dolly track to play the **Intro** animation that we created, so let's do that doing the following:

1. Create an Animation Track doing right click in the left part of the Timeline editor and clicking Animation Track:

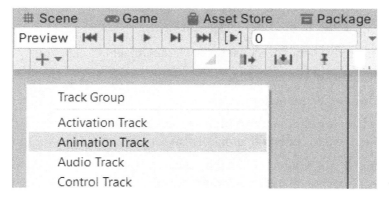

Figure 12.43 – Creating Animation Track

2. Select the **Director** object and check the **Bindings** list of the **Playable Director** component in the Inspector window.

3. Drag the **Cart** object to specify that we want the animation track to control its animation:

Figure 12.44 – Making the animation track control the dolly cart animation in this director

> **Important note:**
> Timeline is a generic asset that can be applied to any scene, but as the tracks control specifics objects, you need to manually bind them in every scene. In our case, we have an animation track that expects to control a single animator, so in every scene, if we want to apply this cutscene, we need to drag the specific animator to control in the **Bindings** list.

4. Drag the **Intro** animation asset that we created to the animation track in the **Timeline** window. This will create a clip in the track showing when and for how long the animation will play. You can drag many animations that the cart can play into the track to sequence different animations at different moments; but right now, we want just that one:

Figure 12.45 – Making the animator track play the intro clip

5. You can drag the animation to change the exact moment you want it to play. Drag it to the beginning of the track.

6. Hit the Play button in the top-left part of the **Timeline** window to see it in action. You can also manually drag the white arrow in the **Timeline** window to view the cutscene at different moments:

Figure 12.46 – Playing a timeline and dragging the playback header

> **Important note:**
> Remember that you don't need to use Timeline to play animations. In this case, we did it this way to control at exactly which moment we want the animation to play. You can control animators using scripting as well.

Now, we will make our Intro timeline asset tell the `CinemachineBrain` component (the main camera) which camera will be active during each part of the cutscene, switching to the player camera once the camera animation is over. We will create a second track—a Cinemachine track—which is specialized in making a specific `CinemachineBrain` component to switch between different virtual cameras. To do this, follow these steps:

1. Right-click on the empty space below the animation track and click on **Cinemachine Track**. Note that you can install Timeline without Cinemachine, but this kind of track won't show up in that case:

Figure 12.47 – Creating a new Cinemachine Track

2. In the **Playable Director** component's **Bindings** list, drag the main camera to **Cinemachine Track** to make that track control which virtual camera will be the one that controls the main camera at different moments of the cutscene:

Figure 12.48 – Making the Cinemachine Track control our Scene's Main Camera

3. The next step indicates which virtual camera will be active during specific moments of the timeline. To do so, our Cinemachine Track allows us to drag virtual cameras to it, which will create virtual camera clips. Drag both **CM vcam2** and **CM vcam1**, in that order, to the Cinemachine Track:

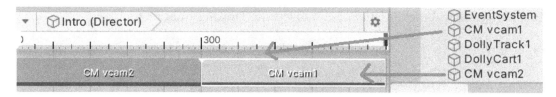

Figure 12.49 – Dragging virtual cameras to the Cinemachine Track

4. If you hit the play button or just drag the **Timeline Playback** header, you can see how the active virtual camera changes when the playback header reaches the second virtual camera clip. Remember to view this in the **Game** view.

5. If you place the mouse near the ends of the clips, a resize cursor will show up. If you drag them, you can resize the clips to specify their duration. In our case, we will need to match the length of the **CM vcam2** clip to the **Cart** animation clip and then put **CM vcam1** at the end of it by dragging it so that the camera will be active when the dolly cart animation ends. In my case, they were already the same length, but just try to change it anyway to practice. Also, you can make the **CM vcam1** clip be shorter; we just need that to play it for a few moments to execute the camera swap.

6. You can also overlap the clips a little bit to make a smooth transition between the two cameras, instead of a hard switch, which will look odd:

Figure 12.50 – Resizing and overlapping clips to interpolate them

If you wait for the full cutscene to end, you will notice how at the very end, **CM vcam2** becomes active again. You can configure how Timeline will deal with the end of the cutscene, as by default, it does nothing. This can cause different behavior according to the type of track; in our case, again giving the control to pick the virtual camera to the `CinemachineBrain` component, which will pick the virtual camera with the highest **Priority** value. We can change the **Priority** property of the virtual cameras to be sure that **CM vcam1** (the player camera) is always the more important one, or set **Wrap Mode** of the **Playable Director** component to **Hold**, which will keep everything, as the last frame of the timeline specifies.

In our case, we will use the latter option to test the Timeline-specific features:

Figure 12.51 – Wrap Mode set to the Hold mode

Most of the different kinds of tracks work under the same logic; each one will control a specific aspect of a specific object using clips that will execute during a set time. I encourage you to test different tracks to see what they do, such as **Activation**, which enables and disables objects during the cutscene. Remember, you can check out the documentation of the Timeline package in the Package Manager.

Summary

In this chapter, we introduced the different animation systems that Unity provides for different requirements. We discussed importing character animations and controlling them with Animation Controllers. We also saw how to make cameras that can react to the game's current situation, such as the player's position, or that can used during cutscenes. Finally, we looked at Timeline and the animation system to create an intro cutscene for our game. These tools are useful for making the animators in our team work directly in Unity without the hassle of integrating external assets (except for character animations) and also preventing the programmer from creating repetitive scripts to create animations, wasting time in the process.

Now, you are able to import and create animation clips in Unity, as well as apply them to GameObjects to make them move according the clips. Also, you can place them in the Timeline sequencer to coordinate them and create cutscenes for your game. Finally, you can create dynamic cameras to use in-game or in cutscenes.

So far, we have discussed lots of Unity systems that allow us to develop different aspects of our game without coding, but sooner or later, scripting will be needed. Unity provides generic tools for generic situations, but our game's unique gameplay must usually be coded manually. In the next chapter, the first chapter of *Part 3*, we will start learning how to code in Unity using C#.

13
Introduction to Unity Scripting with C#

Unity has a lot of great built-in tools to solve the most common problems in game development, such as the ones we have seen so far. Even two games of the same genre have their own little differences that make the games unique, and Unity cannot foresee that, so that's why we have scripting. Through coding, we can extend Unity's capabilities in several ways to achieve the exact behavior we need, all through a well-known language—C#. We will introduce how to create custom components using C# scripts.

One thing I should point out here is that this chapter is mainly a recap of C# scripting basics for Unity, but in one of the sections, I will explain some advanced tips for experienced programmers. So, try to not skip this chapter if you have programming experience but not in Unity.

In this chapter, we will examine the following scripting concepts:

- Creating C# scripts
- Using events and instructions

We are going to create our own Unity components, learning the basic structure of a class and the way that we can execute actions and expose properties to be configured. Let's start by discussing the basics of script creation.

Creating C# scripts

This book is intended for readers with some programming knowledge, but in this first section, we are going to discuss the C# script structure to make sure you have a strong foundation for the behaviors we will code in the following chapters.

In this section, we will examine the following script creation concepts:

- Initial setup
- Creating a MonoBehaviour-based class
- Adding fields

We are going to create our first Unity script, which will serve to create our component, discussing the tools needed to do so and exploring how to expose our class fields to the editor. Let's start with the basics of script creation.

Initial setup

One thing to consider before creating our first script is how Unity compiles code. While coding, we are used to having an **Integrated Development Environment** (**IDE**), which is a program to create our code and compile or execute it. In Unity, we will just use an IDE as a tool to create scripts easily with coloring and auto-completion because Unity doesn't have a custom code editor, and if you have never coded before, these are valuable tools for beginners. The scripts will be created inside the Unity project and Unity will detect and compile them if any changes are made, so you won't compile in the IDE. Don't worry—you can still use breakpoints in this method.

We can use Visual Studio, Visual Studio Code, Rider, or whatever C# IDE you'd like to use, but when you install Unity, you will probably see an option to install Visual Studio automatically, which allows you to have a default IDE. This installs the free version of Visual Studio, so don't worry about the licenses here. If you don't have an IDE on your computer and didn't check the Visual Studio option while installing Unity, you can do the following:

1. Open **Unity Hub**.
2. Go to the **Installs** section.

3. Click on the three dots in the top-right area of the Unity version you are using and click on **Add Modules**:

Figure 13.1 – Adding a module to the Unity installation

4. Check the option that says **Visual Studio**; the description of the option will vary depending on the version of Unity you are using.

5. Hit the **NEXT** button at the bottom right:

✓	Microsoft Visual Studio Community 2019	1.4 GB	1.3 GB
Platforms			
> ☐	Android Build Support	243.1 MB	1.1 GB
☐	iOS Build Support	365.8 MB	1.6 GB
☐	tvOS Build Support	362.2 MB	1.6 GB
☐	Linux Build Support (Mono)	59.0 MB	274.7 MB
☐	Mac Build Support (Mono)	92.4 MB	480.2 MB
CANCEL		BACK	NEXT

Figure 13.2 – Installing Visual Studio

6. Wait for the operation to end. This might take a few minutes.

If you have a preferred IDE, you can install it yourself and configure Unity to use it. If you can afford it or you are a teacher or a student (as it is free in these cases), I recommend Rider. It is a great IDE with lots of C# and Unity features that you will love; however, it is not vital for this exercise. In order to set up Unity to use a custom IDE, do the following:

1. Open the project.

2. Go to **Edit | Preferences** in the top menu of the editor.

3. Select the **External Tools** menu from the left panel.

4. From the external script editor, select your preferred IDE; Unity will automatically detect the supported IDEs:

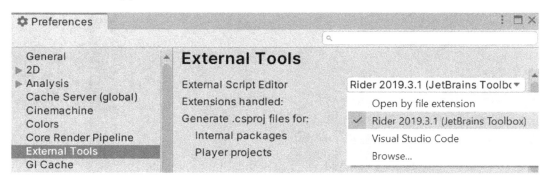

Figure 13.3 – Selecting a custom IDE

5. If you don't find your IDE in the list, you can use the **Browse...** option, but usually, IDEs that require you to use this option are not very well supported—but it's worth a shot.

Finally, some IDEs, such as Visual Studio, Visual Studio Code, and Rider, have Unity integration tools that you need to install in your project, which are optional but can be useful. Usually, Unity installs these automatically, but if you want to be sure that they are installed, do the following:

1. Open **Package Manager** (**Window | Package Manager**).

2. Search the list for your IDE or filter the list by using the search bar. In my case, I used Rider, and I can find a package called **JetBrains Rider Editor**:

Figure 13.4 – Custom IDE editor extension installation—in this case, the Rider one

3. Check whether your IDE integration package is installed by looking at the buttons in the bottom-right part of the package manager. If you see an **Install** or **Update** button, click on it, but if it says **Installed**, everything is set up.

Now that we have an IDE configured, let's create our first script.

Creating a MonoBehaviour-based class

C# is a heavily object-oriented language, and this is no different in Unity. Any time we want to extend Unity, we need to create our own class—a script with the instructions we want to add to Unity. If we want to create custom components, we need to create a class that inherits from MonoBehaviour, the base class of every custom component.

We can create C# script files directly within the Unity project using the editor, and you can arrange them in folders right next to other assets folders. The easiest way to create a script is by doing the following:

1. Select any game object that you want to have the component we are going to create. As we are just testing this out, select any object.

2. Click on the **Add Component** button at the bottom of the Inspector and look for the **New script** option at the bottom of the list, displayed after clicking on **Add Component**:

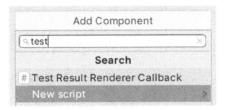

Figure 13.5 – The New script option

3. In the **Name** field, enter the desired script name. In my case, I will call it MyFirstScript, but for the scripts that you will use for your game, try to enter descriptive names, regardless of the length:

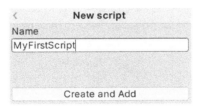

Figure 13.6 – Naming the script

> **Important note:**
> It is recommended that you use Pascal case for script naming. In Pascal case, a script for the player's shooting functionality would be called PlayerShoot. The first letter of each word of the name is in uppercase and you can't use spaces.

4. You can see how a new asset, called as the script was, is created in Project View. Remember that each component has its own asset, and I suggest you each component to a `Scripts` folder:

Figure 13.7 – Script asset

5. Now, you will also see that your Game Object has a new component in the Inspector window, which is named the same as your script. So, you have now created your first component class:

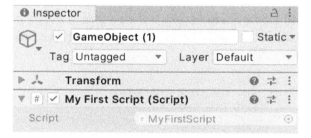

Figure 13.8 – Our script added to a game object

Now that we have created a `component` class, remember that a class is not the component itself. It is a description of what the component should be—a blueprint of how a component should work. To actually use the component, we need to instantiate it by creating a component based on the class. Each time we add a component to an object using the editor, we are instantiating it. Generally, we don't instantiate using new, but by using the editor or specialized functions. Now, you can add your component as you would any other component by using the **Add Component** button in the Inspector window and looking for it in the **Scripts** category or searching it by name:

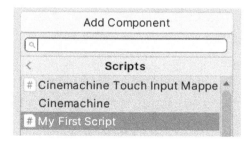

Figure 13.9 – Adding a custom component in the Scripts category

Something that you need to consider here is that we can add the same component to several game objects. We don't need to create a class for each game object that uses the component. I know this is basic programmers' knowledge, but remember that we are trying to recap the basics here. In the next chapter, we will look at more interesting topics.

Now that we have our component, let's explore how it looks and carry out a class structure recap by doing the following:

1. Locate the script asset in Project View and double-click on it. Remember that it should be located in the Scripts folder you created previously.

2. Wait for the IDE to open; this can take a while. You will know that the IDE has finished the initialization when you see your script code and its keywords properly colored, which varies according to the desired IDE. In Rider, it looks as in the following screenshot. In my case, I knew that Rider had finished initializing because the MonoBehaviour type and the script name are colored the same:

```csharp
using System.Collections;
using System.Collections.Generic;
using UnityEngine;

public class MyFirstScript : MonoBehaviour
{
    // Start is called before the first frame update
    void Start()
    {

    }
```

Figure 13.10 – A new script opened in the Rider IDE

3. The first three lines—the ones that start with the `using` keyword—include common namespaces. Namespaces are like code containers, which is, in this case, code created by others (such as Unity, C# creators, and so on). We will be using namespaces quite often to simplify our tasks; they already contain solved algorithms that we will use. We will be adding and removing the `using` component as we need; in my case, Rider is suggesting that the first two `using` components are not necessary because I am not using any code inside them, and so they are grayed out. But for now, keep them as you will use them in later chapters of this book. Remember, they should always be at the beginning of the class:

```
using System.Collections;
using System.Collections.Generic;
using UnityEngine;
```

Figure 13.11 – The using sections

4. The next line, the one that starts with `public class`, is where we declare that we are creating a new class that inherits from `MonoBehaviour`, the base class of every custom component. We know this because it ends with : `MonoBehaviour`. You can see how the rest of the code is located inside brackets right below that line, meaning that the code inside them belongs to the component:

```
public class MyFirstScript : MonoBehaviour
{
```

Figure 13.12 – The MyFirstScript class definition inherits from MonoBehaviour

Now that we have our first component, let's edit it, starting with the fields.

Adding fields

When we added components as `Rigidbody` or as different kinds of colliders, adding the components wasn't enough. We needed to properly configure them to achieve the exact behavior that we need. For example, `Rigidbody` has the `Mass` property to control the object's weight, and the colliders have the `Size` property to control their shape. This way, we can reuse the same component for different scenarios, preventing the duplication of similar components. With a `Box` collider, we can represent a square or rectangular box just by changing the size properties. Our components are no exception; if we have a component that moves an object and if we want two objects to move at different speeds, we can use the same component with different configurations.

Each configuration is a class field, a specific type variable where we can hold the parameter's value. We can create class fields that can be edited in the editor in two ways—by marking the field as `public`, but breaking the encapsulation principle, or by making a private field and exposing it with an attribute. Now, we are going to cover both methods, but if you are not familiar with **Object-Oriented Programming (OOP)** concepts, such as encapsulation, I recommend you use the first method.

Suppose we are creating a movement script. We will add an editable number field representing the velocity using the first method—that is, by adding the `public` field. We will do this by following these steps:

1. Open the script by double-clicking it as we did before.

2. Inside the class brackets, but outside any brackets within them, add the following code:

```
public class MyFirstScript : MonoBehaviour
{
    public float speed;
```

Figure 13.13 – Creating a speed field in our component

> **Important note:**
>
> The `public` keyword specifies that the variable can be seen and edited beyond the scope of the class. The `float` part of the code says that the variable is using the decimal number type, and `speed` is the name we chose for our field—this can be whatever you want. You can use other value types to represent other kinds of data, such as `bool` to represent checkboxes or Booleans and `string` to represent text.

3. To apply the changes, just save the file in the IDE (usually by pressing *Ctrl* + *S* or *command* + *S*) and return again to Unity. When you do this, you will notice a little loading wheel at the bottom-right part of the editor, indicating that Unity is compiling the code. You can't test the changes until the wheel finishes. Remember that Unity will compile the code; don't compile it in the IDE:

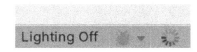

Figure 13.14 – The loading wheel

4. After the compilation is finished, you can see your component in the Inspector window and the **Speed** variable should be there, allowing you to set the speed you want. Of course, right now, the variables do nothing. Unity doesn't recognize your intention by the name of the variable; we need to set it for use in some way, but we will do that later:

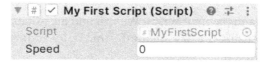

Figure 13.15 – A public field to edit data that the component will use later

5. Try adding the same component to other objects and set a different speed. This will show you how components in different game objects are independent, allowing you to change some of their behaviors via different settings.

The second way to define properties is similar, but instead of creating a `public` field, we create a `private` field, encouraging encapsulation and exposing it using the `SerializeField` attribute, as shown in the following screenshots. These screenshots show two ways of doing this—both will produce the same results; the only difference is the styling. Use the one that best fits your coding standards:

Figure 13.16 – Two ways to expose private attributes in the Inspector window

If you are not familiar with the OOP concept of encapsulation, just use the first method, which is more flexible for beginners. If you create a `private` field, it won't be accessible to other scripts because the `SerializeField` attribute only exposes the variable to the editor. Remember that Unity won't allow you to use constructors, so the only way to set initial data and inject dependencies is via serialized private fields or public fields and setting them in the editor (or using a dependency injection framework, but that is beyond the scope of this book). For simplicity, we will use the first method in most of the exercises in this book.

If you want, try to create other types of variables and see how they look in the inspector. Try replacing `float` with `bool` or `string`, as previously suggested. Now that we know how to configure our components through data, let's use that data to create some behaviour.

Using events and instructions

Now that we have a script, we are ready to do something with it. We won't implement anything useful in this chapter, but we will settle the concepts to add some types of behavior for the scripts we are going to create in the next chapters.

In this section, we are going to cover the following concepts:

- Events and instructions
- Using fields in instructions
- Common beginner errors

We are going to explore the Unity event system, which will allow us to respond to these situations by executing Unity functions. These functions will also be affected by the value of the editor, and fields exposed to our script will be configurable. Finally, we are going to discuss common scripting errors and how to solve them. Let's start by introducing the concept of Unity events.

Events and instructions

Unity allows us to create behavior in a cause-effect fashion, which is usually called an event system. An event is a situation that Unity is monitoring—for example, when two objects collide or are destroyed, Unity tells us about this situation, allowing us to react according to our needs. As an example, we can reduce the life of a player when it collides with a bullet. Here, we will explore how to listen to these events and test them by using some simple actions.

If you are used to event systems, you will know that they usually require us to subscribe to some kind of listener or delegate, but in Unity, there is a simpler method available. We just need to write the exact function for the event we are looking for exactly—and I mean *exactly*. If a letter of the name doesn't have the correct casing, it won't execute and no warning will be raised. This is the most common beginner's error that is made, so pay attention.

There are lots of events or messages to listen to in Unity, so let's start with the most common one—`Update`. This event will tell you when Unity wants you to update your object, depending on the purpose of your behavior; some don't need them. The `Update` logic is usually something that needs to be executed constantly; to be more precise, in every frame. Remember that every game is like a movie—a sequence of images that your screen switches through fast enough to look like we have continuous motion. A common action to do in the `Update` event is to move objects a little bit, and by doing this, every frame will make your object constantly move.

We will learn about the sorts of things we can do with Update and other events or messages later. Now, let's focus on how to make our component at least listen to this event. Actually, the base component already comes with two event functions that are ready to use, one being Update and the other one being in the script. If you are not familiar with the concept of functions in C#, we are referring to the snippet of code in the following screenshot, which is already included in our script. Try to find it in yours:

```
// Update is called once per frame
void Update()
{

}
```

Figure 13.17 – A function called Update, which will be executed with every frame

You will notice a (usually) green line of text (depending on the IDE) above the void Update() line—this is called a comment. These are basically ignored by Unity. They are just notes that you can leave to yourself and must always begin with // to prevent Unity from trying to execute them and failing. We will use this to temporarily disable lines of code later.

Now, to test whether this actually works, let's add an instruction to be executed all the time. There's no better test function than print. This is a simple instruction that tells Unity to print a message to the console, where all kinds of messages can be seen by the developers to check whether everything is properly working. The user will never see these messages. They are similar to the classic log files that developers sometimes ask you for when something goes wrong in the game and you are reporting an issue.

In order to test events using functions, do the following:

1. Open the script by double-clicking on it.

2. To test, add print("test"); within the event function. In the following screenshot, you can see an example of how to do that in the Update event. Remember to write the instruction *exactly*, including the correct casing, spaces, and quotes symbols:

```
void Update()
{
    print("test");
}
```

Figure 13.18 – Printing a message in all the frames

3. Save the file, go to Unity, and play the game.

> **Important note:**
> Remember to save the file before switching back to Unity from the IDE. This is the only way that Unity knows your file has changed. Some IDEs, such as Rider, save the file automatically for you, but I don't recommend you use auto-save, at least in big projects (you don't want accidental recompilations of unfinished work; that takes too long in projects with lots of scripts).

4. Look for the **Console** tab and select it. This is usually found next to the **Project View** tab. If you can't find it, go to **Window | General | Console**, or press *Ctrl + Shift + C* (*command + shift + C* on macOS).

5. You will see lots of messages saying `"test"` being printed in every frame of the **Console** tab. If you don't see this, remember to save the script file before playing the game.

6. Let's also test the `Start` function. Add `print("test Start");` to it, save the file, and play the game. The full script should look as follows:

```
public class MyFirstScript : MonoBehaviour
{
    [SerializeField] float speed;

    // Start is called before the first frame update
    void Start()
    {
        print("test Start");
    }

    // Update is called once per frame
    void Update()
    {
        print("test");
    }
}
```

Figure 13.19 – The script that tests the Start and Update functions

If you check the console now and scroll all the way up, you will see a single `"test Start"` message and lots of `"test"` messages following it. As you can guess, the `Start` event tells you that the game has started and allows you to execute the code that needs to happen just once at the beginning of the game. We will use this later in this book.

For the `void Update()` syntax, we will say to Unity that whatever is contained in the brackets below this line is a function that will be executed in all the frames. It is important to put the print instruction *inside* the `Update` brackets (the ones inside the brackets of the class). Also, the `print` function expects to receive text inside its parentheses, called an argument or parameter, and text in C# must be enclosed by quotation marks. Finally, all instructions inside functions such as `Update` or `Start` *must* end with a semicolon.

Here, I challenge you to try to add another event called `OnDestroy` using a `print function` to discover when it executes. A small suggestion is to play and stop the game and look at the bottom of the console to test this one.

For advanced users, you can also use breakpoints if your IDE allows you to do that. Breakpoints allow you to freeze Unity completely before executing a specific code line to see how our field's data changes over time and to detect errors. Here, I will show you the steps to use breakpoints in Rider, but the Visual Studio version should be similar:

1. Click on the vertical bar at the left of the line where you want to add the breakpoint:

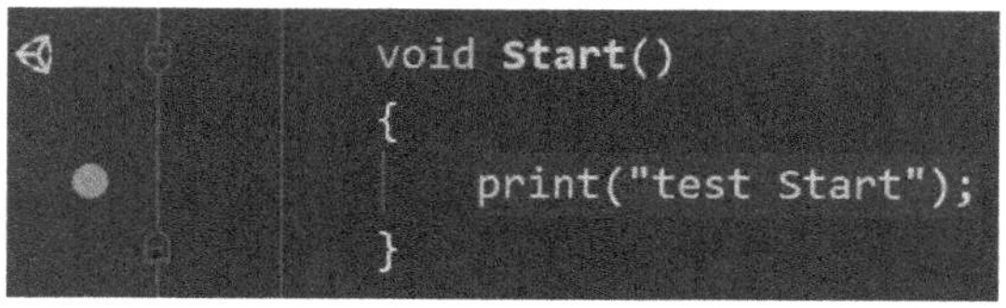

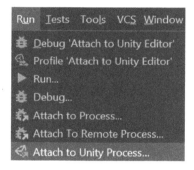

Figure 13.20 – A breakpoint in the print instruction

2. Go to **Run | Attach to Unity Process** (in Visual Studio, go to **Debug | Attack Unity Debugger**. Remember that you need the Visual Studio Unity plugin and the Visual Studio integration package of **Package Manager**):

Figure 13.21 – Attacking our IDE with a Unity process

3. From the list, look for the specific Unity instance you want to test. The list will show other opened editors or executing debugging builds.

Stopping the debugging process won't close Unity. It will just detach the IDE from the editor.

Now that we created both fields and instructions, let's combine them to make configurable components.

Using fields in instructions

We have created fields to configure our components' behavior, but we have not used them so far. We will create meaningful components in the next chapter, but one thing we will often need is to use the fields we have created to change the behavior of the object. So far, we have no real use of the speed field that we created. However, following the idea of testing whether our code is working (also known as debugging), we can learn how to use the data inside a field with a function to test whether the value is the expected one, changing the output of print in the console according to the field's value.

In our current script, our speed value doesn't change during runtime. However, as an example, if you are creating a life system with shield damage absorption and you want to test whether the reduced damage calculation is working properly, you might want to print the calculation values to the console and check whether they are correct. The idea here is to replace the fixed message inside the print functions with a field. When you do that, print will show the field's value in the console. So, if you set a value of 5 in speed and you print it, you will see lots of messages saying 5 in the console, and the output of the print function is governed by the field. To test this, your print message within the Update function should look as follows:

```
[SerializeField] float speed;

void Update()
{
    print(speed);
}
```

Figure 13.22 – Using a field as a print function parameter

As you can see, we just put the name of the field without quotation marks. If you use quotation marks, you will print a "speed" message. In other scenarios, you can use this speed value within some moving functions to control how fast the movement will be, or you can perhaps create a field called "fireRate" (fields use camel case instead of Pascal, with the first letter being in lowercase) to control the cooldown time between one bullet and the next:

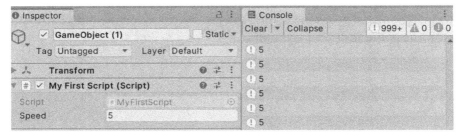

Figure 13.23 – Printing the current speed

> **Important note:**
>
> You can see that my editor is tinted in red, and thats because i configured it to be tinted in red when playing the game to easily detect that. You can do that going to Edit > Preferences > Colors and changing Playmode tint.

With all this, we now have the necessary tools to start creating actual components. Before moving on, let's recap some of the common errors that you will likely encounter if this is your first time creating scripts in C#.

Common beginner errors

If you are an experienced programmer, I bet you are quite familiar with these, but let's recap the common errors that will make you lose lots of time when you are starting with scripting. Most of them are caused by not copying the shown code *exactly*. If you have an error in the code, Unity will show a red message in the console and won't allow you to run the game, even if you are not using the script. So, never leave anything unfinished.

Let's start with a classic error, which is a missing semicolon, which has resulted in many programmer memes and jokes. All fields and most instructions inside functions (such as `print`), when called, need to have a semicolon at the end. If you don't add a semicolon, Unity will show an error, such as the one in the screenshot on the left in the following figure, in the console. You will also notice that the screenshot on the right in the following figure also has an example of bad code, where the IDE is showing a red icon suggesting something is wrong in that place:

Figure 13.24 – An error in the print line hinted by the IDE and the Unity console

You will notice that the error shows the exact script (`MyFirstScript.cs`), the exact line of code (`18`, in this case), and usually, a descriptive message—in this case, `;` `[semicolon]` `expected`. You can simply double-click the error and Unity will open the IDE highlighting the problematic line. You can even click on the links in the stack to jump to the line of the stack that you want.

I already mentioned why it is important to use the *exact* case for every letter of the instruction. However, based on my experience of teaching beginners, I need to stress this particular aspect more. The first scenario where this can happen is in instructions. In the following screenshots, you can see how a badly written `print` function looks—that is, you can see the error that the console will display and how the IDE will suggest that there is something wrong. First, in the case of Rider, the instruction is colored red, saying that the instruction is not recognized (in Visual Studio, it will show a red line instead). Then, the error message says that `Print` does not exist in the current context, meaning that Unity (or C#, actually) does not recognize any instruction named `Print`. In another type of script, `Print` in uppercase may be valid, but not in regular components, which is why the in the current context clarification exists:

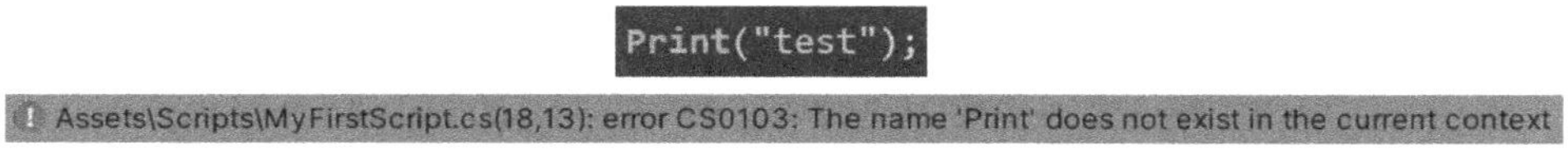

```
Print("test");
```

`! Assets\Scripts\MyFirstScript.cs(18,13): error CS0103: The name 'Print' does not exist in the current context`

Figure 13.25 – Error hints when writing an instruction wrong

Now, if you write an event with the wrong casing, the situation is worse. You can create functions such as `Start` and `Update` with whatever name you want for other purposes. Writing `update` or `start` is perfectly valid as C# will think that you are going to use those functions not as events but as regular functions. So, no error will be shown, and your code will just not work. Try to write `update` instead of `Update` and see what happens:

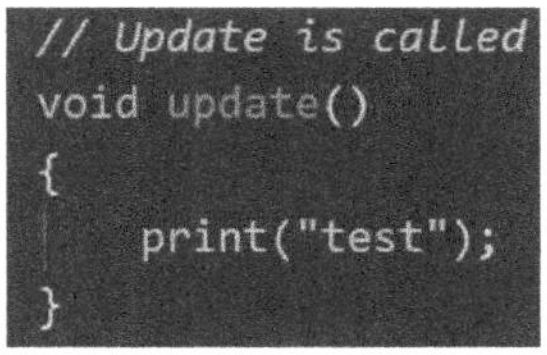

```
// Update is called
void update()
{
    print("test");
}
```

Figure 13.26 – The wrong casing in the Update function will compile the function but won't execute it

Another error is to put instructions outside the function brackets, such as inside the brackets of the class or outside them. Doing this will give no hint to the function as to when it needs to execute. So, a `print` function outside an `Event` function makes no sense, and it will show an error such as the ones in the following screenshots. This time, the error is not super descriptive. Identifier expected says that C# is expecting you to create a function or a field—the kind of structures that can be put directly inside a class:

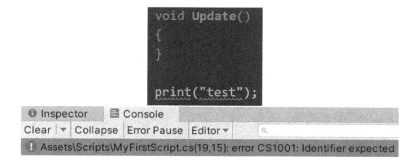

Figure 13.27 – Misplaced instruction or function call

Finally, another classic mistake is to forget to close open brackets. If you don't close a bracket, C# won't know where a function finishes and another starts or where the class function ends. This may sound redundant, but C# needs that to be perfectly defined. In the following screenshots, you can see how this would look:

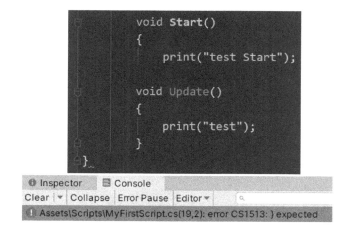

Figure 13.28 – Missing closed brackets

This one is a little bit difficult to catch because the error in the code is shown way after the actual error. This is caused by the fact that C# allows you to put functions inside functions (not used often) and so C# will detect the error later, asking you to add a closing bracket. However, as we don't want to put `update` inside `Start`, we need to fix the error before, at the end of `Start`. The error message will be descriptive in the console, but again, don't put the close bracket where the message suggests you do so unless you are 100% sure that position is correct.

You will likely face lots of errors aside from these ones, but they all work the same. The IDE will show you a hint and the console will display a message; you will learn them with time. Just have patience as every programmer experiences this. There are other kinds of errors, such as runtime errors, code that compiles but will fail when being executed due to some misconfiguration, or the worst—logic errors, where your code compiles and executes with no error but doesn't do what you intended.

Summary

In this chapter, we explored the basic concepts that you will use while creating scripts. We discussed the concepts of classes and instances and how they must inherit from MonoBehaviour to be accepted by Unity to create our own scripts. We also saw how to mix events and instructions to add behavior to an object and how to use fields in instructions to customize what they do.

We just explored the basics of C# scripting to ensure that everyone is on the same page. However, from now on, we will assume that you have basic coding experience in some programming language and you know how to use structures such as `if`, `for`, `array`, and so on. If not, you can still read through this book and try to complement the areas you don't understand with a C# introduction book as you need.

In the next chapter, we are going to start seeing how we can use what we have learned to create movement and spawning scripts.

14
Implementing Movement and Spawning

Now that we have prepared our project to start coding, let's create our first behavior. We will see the basics of how to move objects through scripting using the `Transform` component, which will be applied for the movement of our Player with the Keys, the constant movement of bullets, and other objects' movement. Also, we will see how to create and destroy objects during the game, such as bullets our Player and Enemy shoot and the Enemy Wave Spawners. These actions can be used in several other scenarios, so we will explore a few to reinforce the idea.

In this chapter, we will examine the following scripting concepts:

- Implementing movement
- Implementing spawning

We will start scripting components to do the previously mentioned movement behavior, and then we will continue with object creation and destruction.

Implementing movement

Almost every object in the game moves one way or another, the Player character with the keyboard, the Enemies through AI, the bullets simply move forward, and so on. There are several ways of moving objects in Unity, so we will start with the simplest one, that is, through the `Transform` component.

In this section, we will examine the following movement concepts:

- Moving objects through Transform
- Using Input
- Understanding Delta Time

First, we will explore how to access the Transform component in our script to drive the Player movement, to later apply movement based on the Player's keyboard Input. Finally, we are going to explore the concept of Delta Time to make sure the movement speeds are consistent in every computer. We are going to start learning about the Transform API to master simple movement.

Moving objects through Transform

`Transform` is the component that holds the Translation, Rotation, and Scale of an object, so every movement system such as Physics or Pathfinding will affect this component. Anyway, sometimes we want to move an object in a specific way according to our game by creating our own script, which will handle the movement calculations we need and modify Transform to apply them.

One concept implied here is that components alter other components. The main way of coding in Unity is to create components that interact with other components. Here, the idea is to create one that accesses another and tells it to do something, in this case, to move. To create a script that tells Transform to move, do the following:

1. Create and add a script called Player Movement to our character. In this case, it would be the animated robot object we created previously. Remember to move the script to the Scripts folder after creation:

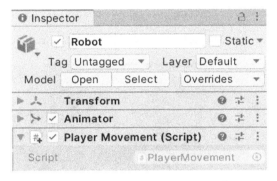

Figure 14.1 – Creating a Player Movement script for the character

2. Double-click the created script asset to open an IDE to edit the code.

3. We are moving, and the movement is applied every frame, so this script will use only the update function or method, and we can remove Start (it is a good practice to remove unused functions):

```
public class PlayerMovement : MonoBehaviour
{
    void Update()
    {

    }
}
```

Figure 14.2 – A component with just the update event function

4. To move our object along its forward axis (Z-axis), add the `transform.Translate(0,0,1);` line to the `update` function as shown in the following image.

Important Note

Every component inherits a `transform` field (to be specific, a getter) that is a reference to the Transform of the GameObject the component is placed, it represents the sibling Transform of our component. Through this field, we can access the `Translate` function of the Transform, which will receive the offset to apply in X, Y, Z local coordinates:

```
public class PlayerMovement : MonoBehaviour
{
    void Update()
    {
        transform.Translate(0, 0, 1);
    }
}
```

Figure 14.3 – A simple Move Forward script

5. Save the file and play the game to see the movement.

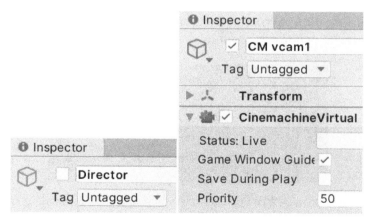

Figure 14.4 – Temporarily disabling the Director and increasing the Player Camera priority

> **Important Note**
>
> I recommend you temporarily disable the Playable Director object and increase
> the priority of CM vcam1, which will disable the introduction cutScene and
> make the Character Following Camera activated by default, reducing the time
> needed to test the game. Another option is to create a secondary Scene just to
> test the Player Movement, something that is actually done in real projects, but
> for now, let's keep things simple.

You will notice that the Player is moving too fast and that's because we are using a fixed
speed of 1 meter, and because `update` is executing all frames, we are moving 1 meter
per frame. In a standard 30 FPS game, the Player will move 30 meters per second, which
is too much. We can control the Player speed by adding a `speed` field and using the value
set in the editor instead of the fixed value of 1. You can see one way to do this in the next
screenshot, but remember the other options we discussed in the previous chapter
(using the Serialize Field attribute):

```
public float speed;

void Update()
{
    transform.Translate(0, 0, speed);
}
```

Figure 14.5 – Creating a speed field and using it as the Z speed of the movement script

Now if you save the script to apply the changes and set the **Speed** of the Player in the
Editor, you can play the game and see the results. In my case, I used 0.1, but you might
need another value (more on this later):

Figure 14.6 – Setting a speed of 0.1 meters per frame

You will notice that the Player will move automatically. Now let's see how to **execute** the
movement based on Player Input such as keyboard and mouse input.

Using Input

Unlike NPCs, we want the Player movement to be driven by the Player's Input, based on which keys they press, the mouse movement, and so on. We can recall the original key mapping we designed in *Chapter 1, Designing a Game from Scratch*, from the next two tables:

Keyboard input	Action
Up arrow	Move forward
Down arrow	Move back
Left arrow	Move left
Right arrow	Move right
W	Move forward
S	Move back
A	Move left
D	Move right

Table 14.1 – Keyboard mapping

Check out the mouse mapping in the following table:

Mouse input	Action
Mouse movement	Rotate character
Left mouse button	Shoot bullet

Table 14.2 – Mouse mapping

> **Important Note**
> The latest Unity version has a new Input system, but requires some settings before using it. For now we will use the default Input system to simplify our scripts

To know whether a certain key is pressed, such as the Up arrow, we can use the `Input.GetKey(KeyCode.W)` line, which will return a Boolean, indicating whether the key specified in the `KeyCode` enum is pressed. We can change the key to check the changing of the `KeyCode` enum value and combine the `GetKey` function with an `If` statement to make the translation execute only when that condition is met (the key is currently.

> **Important Note**
>
> The latest Unity version has a new Input system, but requires some settings before using it. For now we will use the default Input system to simplify our scripts.

Let's start implementing the keyboard movement by doing the following:

1. Make the forward movement execute only when the *W* key is pressed, as shown in the next screenshot:

```csharp
void Update()
{
    if (Input.GetKey(KeyCode.W))
    {
        transform.Translate(0, 0, speed);
    }
}
```

Figure 14.7 – Conditioning the movement until the W key is pressed

2. We can add other movement directions with more `If` statements. We can use *S* to move backward and *A* and *D* to move left and right, as shown in the following screenshot. Notice how we used the minus sign to invert the speed when we needed to move in the opposite axis direction:

```csharp
if (Input.GetKey(KeyCode.W))
    transform.Translate(0, 0, speed);

if (Input.GetKey(KeyCode.S))
    transform.Translate(0, 0, -speed);

if (Input.GetKey(KeyCode.A))
    transform.Translate(-speed, 0, 0);

if (Input.GetKey(KeyCode.D))
    transform.Translate(speed, 0, 0);
```

Figure 14.8 – Checking the W, A, S, and D keys' pressure

> **Important Note**
>
> Remember that using `If` without brackets means that only the line inside the `if` statement is going to be the one right next to the `if` statement, in this case, the `transform.Translate` calls. Anyway, in the final code, I recommend keeping the brackets.

3. If you also want to consider the arrow keys, you can use an OR inside `if`, as shown in the following screenshot:

```
if (Input.GetKey(KeyCode.W) || Input.GetKey(KeyCode.UpArrow))
    transform.Translate(0, 0, speed);

if (Input.GetKey(KeyCode.S) || Input.GetKey(KeyCode.DownArrow))
    transform.Translate(0, 0, -speed);

if (Input.GetKey(KeyCode.A) || Input.GetKey(KeyCode.LeftArrow))
    transform.Translate(-speed, 0, 0);

if (Input.GetKey(KeyCode.D) || Input.GetKey(KeyCode.RightArrow))
    transform.Translate(speed, 0, 0);
```

Figure 14.9 – Checking the W, A, S, D, and arrow keys' pressure

4. Save the changes and test the movement in Play Mode.

Something to take into account is that, first, we have another way to map several keys to a single action by configuring the Input Manager, a place where action mappings can be created, and second, at the time of writing this, Unity released an experimental new Input system that will replace this. For now, we will use this one because it is simple enough to start a basic game and because experimental Unity packages can have bugs or changes in the way they work. In games with complex input, controls are recommended to look for more advanced tools.

Now, let's implement the mouse controls. In this section, we will only cover rotation with mouse movement; we will shoot bullets in the next section. In the case of mouse movement, we can get a value by saying how much the mouse has moved both horizontally or vertically. This value isn't a Boolean but a number, a type of input usually known as Axis, a number that will indicate the intensity of the movement with bigger values, and the direction with the sign of the number. For example, if Unity's "Mouse X" axis says 0.5, it means that the mouse moved to the right with a moderate speed, but if it says -1, it moved quickly to the left, and if there is no movement, it will say 0. The same goes for sticks in gamepads; the **Horizontal** axis represents the horizontal movement of the left stick in common joysticks, so if the Player pulls the stick fully to the left, it will say -1.

We can create our own axes to map other common joysticks' pressure-based controls, but for our game, the default ones are enough. To detect mouse movement, do the following:

1. Use the `Input.GetAxis` function inside `update`, next to the movement `if` statements, as shown in the following screenshot, to store the value of this frame's mouse movement into a variable:

```
float mouseX = Input.GetAxis("Mouse X");
```

Figure 14.10 Getting the horizontal movement of the mouse

2. Use the `transform.Rotate` function to rotate the character. This function receives the degrees to rotate in the X-, Y-, Z-axis order. In this case, we need to rotate horizontally, so we will use the mouse movement value as the Y-axis rotation, as shown in the next screenshot:

```
float mouseX = Input.GetAxis("Mouse X");
transform.Rotate(0, mouseX, 0);
```

Figure 14.11 – Rotating the object horizontally based on mouse movement

3. If you save and test this, you will notice that the Player will rotate but very quickly or slowly, depending on your computer. Remember, this kind of value needs to be configurable, so let's create a `rotationSpeed` field to configure the speed of the Player in the Editor:

```
public float speed;
public float rotationSpeed;
```

Figure 14.12 – Speed and rotation speed fields

4. Now we need to multiply the mouse movement value by the speed, so, depending on `rotationSpeed`, we can increase or reduce the rotation amount. As an example, if we set a value of 0.5 in the rotation speed, multiplying that value by the mouse movement will make the object rotate at half the previous speed, as shown in the following screenshot:

```
float mouseX = Input.GetAxis("Mouse X");
transform.Rotate(0, mouseX * rotationSpeed, 0);
```

Figure 14.13 – Multiplying the mouse movement by the rotation speed

5. Save the code and go back to the Editor to set the rotation speed value. If you don't do this, the object won't rotate because the default value of the float type fields is 0:

Figure 14.14 – Setting the rotation speed

6. You might also notice that the camera controlled by Cinemachine might have a delay to adapt to the new Player position. You can adjust the interpolation speed as I did in the next screenshot to have more responsive behavior:

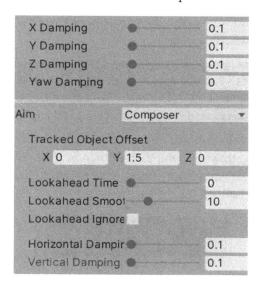

Figure 14.15 – Reduced damping of body and aim sections of the character virtual camera

Now that we have completed our movement script, we need to refine it to work in every machine by exploring the concept of Delta Time.

Understanding Delta Time

Unity's update loop executes as fast as the computer can. You can specify in Unity the desired frame rate but achieving that depends exclusively on whether your computer can reach that, which depends on lots of factors, not only hardware, so you cannot expect to always have consistent FPS. You must code your scripts to handle every possible scenario. Our current script is moving at a certain speed per frame, and the *per frame* part is important here.

We have set the movement speed to 0.1, so if my computer runs the game at 120 FPS, the Player will move 12 meters per second. Now, what happens in a computer where the game runs at 60 FPS? As you may guess, it will move only 6 meters per second, making our game to have inconsistent behavior across different computers. And here is where Delta Time saves the day.

Delta Time is a value that tells us how much time has passed since the previous frame. This time depends a lot on our game's graphics, amount of entities, physics bodies, audio, and countless aspects that will dictate how fast your computer can process a frame. As an example, if your game runs at 10 FPS, it means that, in a second, your computer can process the update loop 10 times, meaning that each loop takes approximately 0.1 seconds; in that frame, Delta Time will provide that value. In the next diagram, you can see an example of 4 frames taking different times to process, which can happen in real-life cases:

Figure 14.16 – Delta Time value varying on different frames of the game

Here, we need to code in such a way to change the *per frame* part of the movement to *per second*; we need to have consistent movement per second across different computers. A way to do that is to move proportionally to Delta Time: the higher the Delta Time value, the longer that frame is, and the greater the movement should be to match the real time that has passed since the last update. We can think about our speed field's current value in terms of 0.1 meters per second; our Delta Time saying 0.5 means that half a second has passed, so we should move half the speed, 0.05. After two frames, a second has passed, and the sum of the movements of the frames (2 x 0.05) matches the target speed, 0.1. Delta Time can be interpreted as the percentage of a second that has passed.

To make Delta Time affect our movement, we should simply multiply our speed by Delta Time every frame because Delta Time can be different every frame, so let's do that:

1. We access Delta Time using `Time.deltaTime`. We can start affecting the movement by multiplying Delta Time in every Translate:

```
if (Input.GetKey(KeyCode.W) || Input.GetKey(KeyCode.UpArrow))
    transform.Translate(0, 0, speed * Time.deltaTime);

if (Input.GetKey(KeyCode.S) || Input.GetKey(KeyCode.DownArrow))
    transform.Translate(0, 0, -speed * Time.deltaTime);

if (Input.GetKey(KeyCode.A) || Input.GetKey(KeyCode.LeftArrow))
    transform.Translate(-speed * Time.deltaTime, 0, 0);

if (Input.GetKey(KeyCode.D) || Input.GetKey(KeyCode.RightArrow))
    transform.Translate(speed * Time.deltaTime, 0, 0);
```

Figure 14.17 – Multiplying speed by Delta Time

2. We can do the same with the rotation speed, chaining the mouse and speed multiplications:

```
float mouseX = Input.GetAxis("Mouse X");
transform.Rotate(0, mouseX * rotationSpeed * Time.deltaTime, 0);
```

Figure 14.18 – Applying Delta Time to rotation code

3. If you save and play the game, you will notice that the movement will be slower than before and that's because now 0.1 is the movement per second, meaning 10 centimeters per second, which is pretty slow; try raising those values. In my case, 10 for speed and 180 for rotation speed was enough, but the rotation speed depends on the Player's preferred sensitivity, which can be configurable, but let's keep that for another time.

We just learned how to mix the Input system of Unity, which tells us about the state of the keyboard, mouse, and other input devices, with the basic Transform movement functions. This way, we can start making our game feel more dynamic.

Now that we have finished the Player's movement, let's discuss how to make the Player shoot bullets using Instantiate functions.

Implementing spawning

We have created lots of objects in the Editor that define our level, but once the game begins, and according to the Player actions, new objects must be created to better fit the scenarios generated by Player interaction. Enemies might need to appear after a while, or bullets must be created according to the Player input; even when enemies die there's a chance of spawning some power-up. This means that we cannot create all the necessary objects beforehand but should create them dynamically, and that's done through scripting.

In this section, we will examine the following spawning concepts:

- Spawning objects
- Timing actions
- Destroying objects

We will start seeing the Unity `Instantiate` function, which allows us to create instances of Prefabs on runtime, such as when pressing a key, or in a time-based fashion, such as making our enemy spawn bullets every certain amount of time. Also, we will learn how to destroy these objects to prevent our Scene from starting to perform badly due to too many objects being processed.

Let's start with how to shoot bullets according to the Player's Input.

Spawning objects

To spawn an Object in runtime or Play Mode, we need a description of the Object, which components it has, and its settings and possible sub-objects. You might be thinking about Prefabs here, and you are right, we will use an instruction that will tell Unity to create an instance of a Prefab via scripting. Remember that an instance of a Prefab is an Object created based on the Prefab, basically a clone of the original one.

We will start shooting the Player's bullets, so first let's create the bullet Prefab by doing the following:

1. Create a sphere in **GameObject | 3D Object | Sphere**. You can replace the sphere mesh with another bullet model if you want, but we will keep the sphere in this example for now.

2. Rename the sphere `Bullet`.

3. Create a material by clicking on the + button of the Project window and choosing the option **Material**, and call it `Bullet`. Remember to place it inside the `Materials` folder.

4. Check the **Emission** checkbox in the material and set the **emission Map** and **Base Map** colors to red. Remember, the Emission color will make the bullet shine, especially with the bloom effect in our post-processing volume:

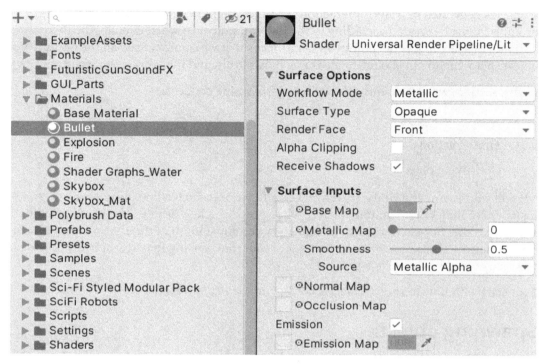

Figure 14.19 – Creating a red bullet material with emission color

5. Apply the Material to the Sphere by dragging the material to it.

6. Set the Scale to a smaller value—(0.3, 0.3, 0.3) worked in my case:

Figure 14.20 – Small red-colored bullet

7. Create a script called `ForwardMovement` to make the bullet constantly move forward at a fixed speed.

   I suggest you try to solve this by yourself first and look at the screenshot in the next step with the solution later as a little challenge to recap the movement concepts we saw previously. If you don't recall how to create a script, please read *Chapter 13, Introduction to Unity Scripting with C#*, and check the previous section to see how to move objects.

8. The next screenshot shows you what the script should look like:

```
using UnityEngine;

public class ForwardMovement : MonoBehaviour
{
    public float speed;

    void Update()
    {
        transform.Translate(0,0,speed * Time.deltaTime);
    }
}
```

Figure 14.21 – A simple Move Forward script

9. Add the script (if not already there) to the bullet, and set the speed to a value you see fit. Usually, bullets are faster than the Player, but that depends on the Player experience you want to get (remember the questions in *Chapter 1, Designing a Game from Scratch*). In my case, 20 worked fine. Test it by placing the bullet near the Player and playing the game:

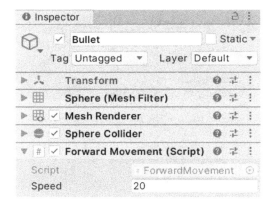

Figure 14.22 – Forward Movement script in the bullet

10. Drag the bullet GameObject instance to the Prefabs folder to create a **Bullet** Prefab. Remember that the Prefab is an asset that has a description of the created bullet, like a blueprint of how to create a bullet:

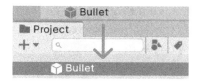

Figure 14.23 – Creating a Prefab

11. Remove the original bullet from the Scene; we will use the Prefab to create bullets when the Player presses a key (if ever).

Now that we have our bullet Prefab, it is time to instantiate it (clone it) when the Player presses a key. To do that, do the following:

1. Create and add a script to the Player's GameObject (the Robot) called PlayerShooting and open it.

   We need a way for the script to have access to the Prefab to know which Prefab to use from the probably dozens that we will have in our project. All of the data our script needs that depends on the desired game experience is in the form of a field, such as the speed field used so far, so in this case, we need a field of the GameObject type, a field that can reference or point to a specific Prefab, which can be set using the Editor.

2. Adding the field code would look like this:

```csharp
using UnityEngine;

public class PlayerShooting : MonoBehaviour
{
    public GameObject prefab;
}
```

Figure 14.24 – The Prefab reference field

> **Important Note**
>
> As you might guess, we can use the GameObject type to not only reference Prefabs but also other objects. Imagine an Enemy AI needing a reference to the Player object to get its position, using a GameObject to link the two objects. The trick here is considering that Prefabs are just regular Gameobjects that live outside the Scene; you cannot see them but they are in memory, ready to be copied or instantiated. You will only see them through copies or instances that are placed in the Scene with scripting or via the Editor as we have done so far.

3. In the Editor, click on the circle to the right of the property and select the Bullet Prefab. Another option is to just drag the Bullet Prefab to the property:

Figure 14.25 – Setting the Prefab reference to point the bullet

This way, we tell our script that the bullet to shoot will be that one. Remember to drag the Prefab and not the bullet in the Scene (that should be deleted by now).

We will shoot the bullet when the Player presses the left mouse button as specified in the design document, so let's place the proper if statement to handle that in the update event function, like the one shown in the next screenshot:

```
void Update()
{
    if (Input.GetKeyDown(KeyCode.Mouse0))
    {

    }
}
```

Figure 14.26 – Detecting the pressure of the left mouse button

You will notice that this time, we used GetKeyDown instead of GetKey, the former being a way to detect the exact frame the pressing of the key started; this if statement will execute its code only in that frame, and until the key is released and re-pressed, it won't enter again. This is one way to prevent bullets from spawning in every frame, but just for fun, you can try using GetKey instead to see how it would behave. Also, zero is the mouse button number that belongs to left-click, one being right-click and two middle-click.

We can use the `Instantiate` function to clone the Prefab, passing the reference to it as the first parameter. This will create a clone of the mentioned Prefab that will be placed in the Scene:

```
if (Input.GetKeyDown(KeyCode.Mouse0))
{
    Instantiate(prefab);
}
```

Figure 14.27 – Instantiating the Prefab

If you save the script and play the game, you will notice that when you press the mouse, a bullet spawn, but probably not in the place you are expecting, and if you don't see it, try to check the Hierarchy for new objects; it will be there. The problem here is that we didn't specify the desired spawn position, and we have two ways of settings that, which we will see in the next steps.

The first way is to use the `transform.position` and `transform.rotation` inherited fields from MonoBehaviour, which will tell us our current position and rotation. We can pass them as the second and third parameters of the `Instantiate` function, which will understand that this is the place we want our bullet to appear. Remember that it is important to set the rotation to make the bullet face the same direction as the Player, so it will move that way:

```
Instantiate(prefab, transform.position, transform.rotation);
```

Figure 14.28 – Instantiating the Prefab in our position and rotation

The second way, which will be longer but will give us more flexibility to change other aspects of the object, is by using the previous version of Instantiate, but saving the reference returned by the function, which will be pointing to the clone of the Prefab. Having a reference to the instantiated bullet allows us to change whatever we want from it, not only position but also rotation, but for now, let's limit ourselves to position and rotation. In this case, we will need the following three lines; the first will instantiate and capture the clone reference, the second will set the position of the clone, and the third will set the rotation. You will notice we will also use the `transform.position` field of the clone, but this time to change its value by using the = (assignment) operator:

```
GameObject clone = Instantiate(prefab);
clone.transform.position = transform.position;
clone.transform.rotation = transform.rotation;
```

Figure 14.29 – The longer version of instantiating a Prefab in a specific position

Use the version you like the most—both do the same. Remember that you can check the project repository to see the full script finished. Now you can save the file with one of the versions and try to shoot.

If you try the script so far, you should see the bullet spawn in the Player's position, but in our case, it will probably be the floor. The problem here is that the robot pivot is there, and usually, every humanoid character has the pivot there. We have several ways to fix that, the most flexible one being to create a shoot point, an empty Player's child Object placed in the position we want the bullet to spawn. We can use the position of that Object instead of the Player's position by doing the following:

1. Create an empty `GameObject` in **GameObject | Create Empty**. Rename it `ShootPoint`.

2. Make it a child of the Player's Robot Character Object, and place it where you want the bullet to appear, probably a little higher and further forward than the original spawn position:

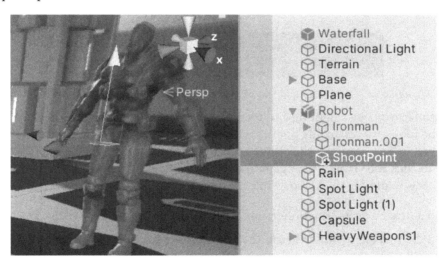

Figure 14.30 – An empty ShootPoint object placed inside the character

3. As usual, to access the data of another Object, we need a reference to it, such as the Prefab reference, but this time that one needs to point to our `ShootPoint`. We can create another `GameObject` type field, but this time drag `ShootPoint` instead of the Prefab. The script and the Object set would look as shown in the following screenshot:

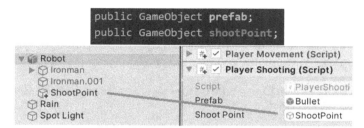

Figure 14.31 – The Prefab and Shoot Point fields and how they are set in the Editor

4. We can access the position of `shootPoint` by using the `transform.position` field of it again, as shown in the following screenshot:

```
GameObject clone = Instantiate(prefab);
clone.transform.position = shootPoint.transform.position;
clone.transform.rotation = shootPoint.transform.rotation;
```

Figure 14.32 – The Prefab and ShootPoint fields and how they are set in the Editor

You will notice that now shooting and rotating with the mouse has a problem; when moving the mouse to rotate, the pointer will fall outside the Game View, and when clicking, you will accidentally click the Editor, losing the focus on the Game View, so you will need to click the Game View again to regain focus and use Input again. A way to prevent this is to disable the cursor while playing. To do this, follow these steps:

1. Add a `Start` event function to our Player Movement Script.

2. Add the two lines you can see in the following screenshot to your script. The first one will make the cursor visible, and the second one will lock it in the middle of the screen, so it will never abandon the Game View. Consider that latter; you will need to reenable the cursor when you switch back to the main menu or the pause menu, to allow the mouse to click the UI buttons:

```
void Start()
{
    Cursor.visible = false;
    Cursor.lockState = CursorLockMode.Locked;
}
```

Figure 14.33 – Disabling the mouse cursor

3. Save and test this. If you want to stop the game, you could either press *Ctrl + Shift + P* (*command + Shift + P* on Mac) or press the *Esc* key to reenable the mouse. Both only work in the Editor; in the real game, you will need to reenable manually.

Now that we've covered the basics of object spawning, let's see an advanced example by combining it with timers.

Timing actions

Not entirely related to spawning, but usually used together, timing actions is a common task in videogames. The idea is to schedule something to happen later; maybe we want the bullet to be destroyed after a while to prevent memory overflow, or we want to control the spawn rate of enemies or when they should spawn, and that's exactly what we are going to do in this section, starting with the second, the Enemy waves.

The idea is that we want to spawn enemies at a certain rate at different moments of the game; maybe we want to spawn enemies from seconds 1 to 5 at a rate of 2 per second, getting 10 enemies, before giving the Player up to 20 seconds to finish them and programming another wave to start at second 25. Of course, this depends a lot on the exact game you want, and you can start with an idea like this one and modify it after some testing to find the exact way you want the wave system to work. In our case, we will exemplify timing with the previously mentioned logic.

First of all, we need an Enemy, and for now, we will simply use the same robot character as the Player, but adding a Forward Movement script to simply make it move forward; later in this book, we will add AI behavior to our enemies. I suggest you try to create this Prefab by yourself and look at the next steps once you have tried, to see the correct answer:

1. Drag the Robot FBX model to the Scene to create another Robot character, but rename it `Enemy` this time.

2. Add the `ForwardMovement` script created for the bullets but this time to `Enemy` and set it at a speed of 10 for now.

3. Drag the `Enemy` GameObject to the Project to create a Prefab based on that one; we will need to spawn it later. Remember to choose Prefab Variant, which will keep the Prefab linked with the original model to make the changes applied to the model automatically apply to the Prefab. Remember also to destroy the original Enemy from the Scene.

Now, to schedule actions, we will use the `Invoke` functions suite, a set of functions to create timers that are basic but enough for our requirements. Let's use it by doing the following:

1. Create an Empty GameObject at one end of the Base and call it `Wave1a`.

2. Create and add a script called `WaveSpawner` to it.

3. Our spawner will need four fields: the Enemy Prefab to spawn, the game time to start the wave, the `endTime` to end the wave spawning, and the spawn rate of the enemies—basically, how much time there should be between each spawn during the given spawning period. The script and the settings will look like the following screenshot:

```
public GameObject prefab; //Prefab to spawn
public float startTime; //Time to start the wave spawning
public float endTime; //Time to end the wave spawning
public float spawnRate; //Time between each spawn
```

Figure 14.34 – The fields of the wave spawner script

We will use the `InvokeRepeating` function to schedule a custom function to repeat periodically. You will need to schedule the repetition just once; Unity will remember that, so don't do it every frame. This is a good case to use the `Start` event function instead. The first argument of the function is a string (text between quotation marks) with the name of the other function to execute periodically, and unlike Start or update, you can name the function whatever you want. The second argument is the time to start repeating, our `startTime` field, in this case. Finally, the third argument is the repetition rate of the function, how much time needs to happen between each repetition, this being the `spawnRate` field. You can find how to call that function in the next screenshot, along with the custom `Spawn` function:

```
void Start()
{
    InvokeRepeating("Spawn", startTime, spawnRate);
}

void Spawn()
{

}
```

Figure 14.35 – Scheduling a Spawn function to repeat

4. Inside the Spawn function, we can put the spawning code as we know, using the
    Instantiate function. The idea is to call this function at a certain rate to spawn
    one Enemy per call. This time, the spawn position will be in the same position as
    the spawner, so place it carefully:

```
void Spawn()
{
    Instantiate(prefab, transform.position, transform.rotation);
}
```

Figure 14.36 – Instantiating in the Spawn function

If you test this script setting the Prefab startTime and spawnRate fields
to some test values, you will notice that the enemies will start spawning but
never stop, and you can see that we haven't used the endTime field so far. The
idea is to call the CancelInvoke function, one function that will cancel all
InvokeRepeating calls we made, but after a while to then use the Invoke
function, which works similarly to InvokeRepeating, but this one executes
just once. In the next screenshot, you can see how we added an Invoke call to
the CancelInvoke function in Start, using the endTime field as the time
to execute CancelInvoke. This will execute CancelInvoke after a while,
canceling the first InvokeRepeating call that spawns the prefab:

```
void Start()
{
    InvokeRepeating("Spawn", startTime, spawnRate);
    Invoke("CancelInvoke", endTime);
}
```

Figure 14.37 – Scheduling a Spawn repetition but canceling after a while with CancelInvoke

> **Important Note**
>
> This time, we used **Invoke** to delay the call to CancelInvoke. We didn't
> use a custom function because CancelInvoke doesn't receive arguments.
> If you need to schedule a function with arguments, you will need to create a
> parameterless wrapper function that calls the one desired and schedule that
> one, as we did with Spawn, where the only intention is to call Instantiate with
> specific arguments.

5. Now you can save and set some real values to our spawner. In my case, I used the ones shown in the following screenshot:

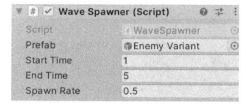

Figure 14.38 – Spawning enemies from seconds 1 to 5 of gameplay every 0.5 seconds, 2 per second

You should see the enemies being spawned one next to the other, and because they move forward, they will form a row of enemies. This behavior will change later with AI:

Figure 14.39 – Spawning enemies

If you want, you can create several Wave Spawner objects, scheduling waves for the later stages of the game. Remember the difficulty balance we discussed in *Chapter 1, Designing a Game from Scratch*; you will need to try this with the final AI for the enemies, but the number of waves, times, and spawn rates will determine the difficulty of the game, and that's why it is important to set those values properly. Also, there are plenty of methods to create waves of enemies; this is just the simplest one I could find. You may need to change it according to your game.

Now that we have discussed timing and spawning, let's discuss timing and destroying objects to prevent our bullets from living forever in memory.

Destroying objects

This is going to be super short but is a widely used function, so it deserves its own section. We can use the `Destroy` function to destroy Object instances. The idea is to make the bullets have a script that schedules their own auto-destruction after a while to prevent them from living forever. We will create the script by doing the following:

1. Select the Prefab of `Bullet` and add a script called `Autodestroy` to it as you did with other objects using the **Add Component | New Script** option. This time, the script will be added to the Prefab, and each instance of the Prefab you spawn will have it.

2. You can use the `Destroy` function as shown in the next screenshot to destroy the Object just once in `Start`.

    The `Destroy` function expects the object to destroy as the first argument, and here, we are using the `gameObject` reference, a way to point to our GameObject to destroy it. If you use the `this` pointer instead, we will be destroying only the `Autodestroy` component; remember that in Unity, you never create Gameobjects but components to add to them:

    ```
    void Start()
    {
        Destroy(gameObject);
    }
    ```

    Figure 14.40 – Destroying an Object when it starts

    Of course, we don't want the bullet to be destroyed as soon as it is spawned, so we need to delay the destruction. You may be thinking about using `Invoke`, but unlike most functions in Unity, `Destroy` can receive a second argument, which is the time to wait until destruction.

3. Create a `delay` field to use as the second argument of `Destroy`, as shown in the next screenshot:

    ```
    public float delay;

    void Start()
    {
        Destroy(gameObject, delay);
    }
    ```

    Figure 14.41 – Using a field to configure the delay to destroy the Object

4. Set the `delay` field to a proper value; in my case, 5 was enough. Now check how the bullets despawn after a while by looking at them being removed from the Hierarchy.

Now, we can create and destroy objects at will, which is something very common in Unity scripting.

> **Important Note**
>
> Look into the concept of object pooling; you will learn that sometimes creating and destroying objects is not that performant.

Summary

We have created our first real scripts, which provide useful behavior. We discussed how to instantiate Prefabs via scripting, to create objects at will according to the game situation. Also, we saw how to schedule actions, in this case, spawning, but this can be used to schedule anything. Finally, we saw how to destroy created objects, to prevent increasing the number of objects to an unmanageable level. We will be using these actions to create other kinds of objects, such as sounds and effects, later in this book.

Now you are able to create any type of movement or spawning logic your objects will need and make sure those objects are destroyed when needed. You might think that all games move and create shooting systems the same way, and while they are similar, being able to create your own movement and shooting scripts allows you to customize those aspects of the game to behave as intended and create the exact experience you are looking for.

In the next chapter, we will be discussing how to detect collisions to prevent the Player and bullets from passing through walls and much more.

15
Physics Collisions and Health System

As games try to simulate real-world behaviors, one important aspect to simulate is physics, which dictates how Objects move and how they collide with each other, such as the collision of players and walls or bullets and enemies. Physics can be difficult to control due to the myriad of reactions that can happen after a collision, so we will learn how to properly configure it to obtain a semi-accurate Physics, which will generate the desired arcade movement feeling but get collisions working—after all, sometimes, real life is not as interesting as videogames.

In this chapter, we will examine the following collision concepts:

- Configuring Physics
- Detecting collisions
- Moving with Physics

First, we will learn how to properly configure Physics, a step needed for the collisions between Objects to be detected by our scripts, using new events we are also going to learn. Then, we are going to discuss the difference between moving with `Transform`, as we have done so far, and moving with Rigidbody and the pros and cons of each version. Let's start discussing Physics settings.

Configuring Physics

The Unity's Physics system is prepared to cover a great range of possible gameplay applications, so properly configuring it is important to get the desired result.

In this section, we will examine the following Physics settings concepts:

- Setting shapes
- Physics Object types
- Filtering collisions

We are going to start learning about the different kinds of colliders that Unity offers, to then learn about different ways to configure those to detect different kinds of Physics reactions (collisions and triggers). Finally, we will discuss how to ignore collisions between specific Objects to prevent situations such as the Player's bullets damaging the Player.

Setting shapes

At the beginning of this book, we learned that Objects usually have two shapes, the visual shape, which is basically the 3D mesh, and the physical one, the collider, the one that the Physics system will use to calculate collisions. Remember that the idea of this is to allow you to have a highly detailed visual model while having a simplified Physics shape to increase the performance.

Unity has several types of colliders, so here we will recap the common ones, starting with the primitive types, that is, Box, Sphere, and Capsule. These shapes are the cheapest ones (in terms of performance) to detect collisions due to the fact that the collisions between them are done via mathematical formulas, unlike other colliders such as the Mesh Collider, which allows you to use any mesh as the physics body of the Object, but with a higher cost and some limitations. The idea is that you should use a primitive type to represent your Objects or a combination of them, for example, a plane could be done with two Box Colliders, one for the body and the other one for the wings. You can see an example of this in the following screenshot, where you can see a weapons collider made out of primitives:

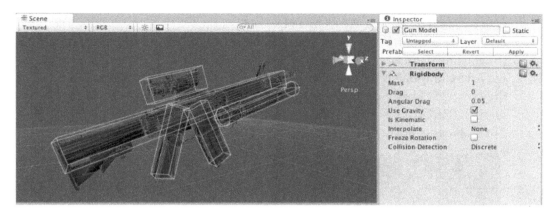

Figure 15.1 – Compound colliders

Anyway, try to avoid doing this; if we want the weapon to just fall to the ground, maybe a Box Collider covering the entire weapon can be enough, considering those kinds of collisions don't need to be accurate, thereby increasing performance. Also, some shapes cannot be represented even with a combination of primitive shapes, such as ramps or pyramids, where your only solution is to use a Mesh Collider, which asks for a 3D mesh to use for collisions, but we won't use them in this book; we will solve all of our Physics colliders with primitives.

Now, let's add the necessary colliders to our scene to prepare it to calculate collisions properly. Consider that if you used an Asset Store environment package other than mine, you may already have the scene modules with colliders; I will be showing the work I needed to do in my case, but try to extrapolate the main ideas here to your scene. To add the colliders, follow these steps:

1. Select a wall in the base and check the Object and possible child Objects for collider components; in my case, I have no colliders. If you detect any Mesh Collider, you can leave it, but I would suggest you remove it and replace it with another option in the next step. The idea is to add the collider to it, but the problem I detected here is that, due to the fact that my wall is not an instance of a Prefab, I need to add a collider to every wall.

2. One option is to create a Prefab and replace all of the walls for instances of the Prefab (the recommended solution) or to just select all walls in the Hierarchy (by clicking them while pressing *Ctrl* or *Cmd* on Mac) and, with them selected, use the **Add Component** button to add a collider to all of them. In my case, I will use the `Box Collider` component, which will adapt the size of the collider to the mesh. If it doesn't adapt, you can just change the Size and Center properties of the Box Collider to cover the entire wall:

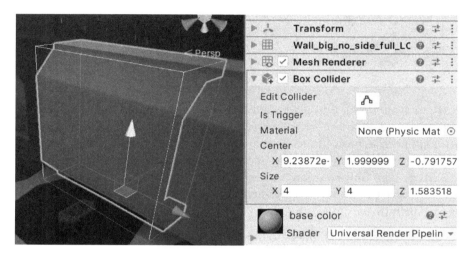

Figure 15.2 – A Box Collider added to a wall

3. Repeat *steps 1 and 2* for the corners, floor tiles, and any other obstacle that will block Player and Enemy movement.

For our Enemy and Player, we will be adding the Capsule Collider, the usual collider to use in movable characters due to the fact that the rounded bottom will allow the Object to smoothly climb ramps, and being horizontally rounded allows the Object to easily rotate in corners without getting stuck, along with other conveniences of that shape. Remember that the Enemy is a Prefab, so you will need to add the collider to the Prefab, while our Player is a simple Object in the scene, so you will need to add the collider to that one.

> **Important Note**
> You may be tempted to add several Box Colliders to the bones of the character to create a realistic shape of the Object, and while we can do that to apply different damage according to the part of the body where the enemies where shot, we are just creating movement colliders; the capsule is enough. In advanced damage systems, both capsule and bone colliders will coexist, one for the movement and the other for damage detection; but we will simplify this in our game.

Also, sometimes the collider won't adapt well to the visual shape of the Object, and in my case, the Capsule Collider didn't have a nice shape for the character. I needed to fix its shape to match the character by setting its values as shown in the following screenshot:

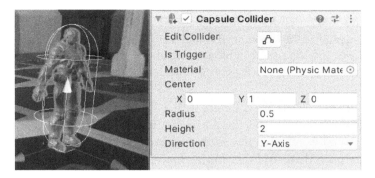

Figure 15.3 – Character Collider

The bullet we created with the Sphere already had a Sphere Collider, but if you replaced the mesh of the bullet with another one, you might want to change the collider. For now, we don't need other Objects in our game, so now that everyone has its proper collider, let's see how to set the different Physics settings to each Object to enable proper collision detection.

Physics Object types

Now that we have added colliders to every Object by making the Objects have a presence in the Physics Simulation, it is time to configure them to have the exact Physics behavior we want. We have a myriad of possible combinations of settings, but we will discuss a set of common profiles that cover most situations. Remember besides colliders, we saw the Rigidbody component at the beginning of this book, which is the one that applies physics to the Object. The following profiles are done with a combination of colliders and Rigidbody settings:

- **Static Collider**: As the name suggests, this kind of collider is the one that is not supposed to move by any means in the game, aside from some specific exceptions. Most of the environment Objects falls into this category, such as walls, floors, obstacles, and the Terrain. These kind of colliders are just colliders with no `Rigidbody` component, so they have a presence in the Physics Simulation, but don't have any Physics applied to them; they cannot be moved by other Objects, they won't have physics, and they will be fixed at their position no matter what. Take into account that this has nothing to do with the static checkbox at the top-right part of the Editor; those are for the previously seen systems (such as Lighting and others), so you can have a Static Collider with that checkbox unchecked if needed.

> **Important note**
>
> Take into account that these Objects can be moved via scripting, but you shouldn't. Unity applies an optimization technique to them, and every time a Static Collider is moved, the optimization becomes invalid, needing further calculation to update it, and doing that every frame is costly.
>
> We just mentioned Terrain as an example, and if you check the Terrain's components, you will see that it has its own kind of collider, the Terrain Collider. For Terrains, that's the only collider to use.

- **Physics Collider**: These are colliders with a `Rigidbody` component, like the example of the falling ball we did in the first part of this book. These are fully Physics-driven Objects that have gravity and can be moved through forces; other Objects can push them and they perform every other Physics reaction you can expect. You can use this for the Player, grenade movement, or falling crates or in all Objects in heavily physics-based games such as **The Incredible Machine**.

- **Kinematic Collider**: These are colliders that have a `Rigidbody` component but have the **Is Kinematic** checkbox checked. These don't have the same Physics reactions to collisions and forces as Static Colliders, but they can be moved via scripting (`transform.Translate`) with no performance penalty. Consider that due to the fact they don't have Physics, they won't have collisions either, so they can pass through walls. These can be used in Objects that need to move using animations or custom scripting movement such as moving platforms, considering that, in this case, the platform won't collide with other Objects, but the Player, having usually a Physics Collider, will collide against them; actually, the Physics Collider is the one that will collide with every kind of collider.

- **Trigger Static Collider**: This is a regular Static Collider but with the **Is Trigger** checkbox of the Collider checked. The difference is that Kinematic and Physics Objects pass through it but by generating a `Trigger` event, an event that can be captured via scripting, and tells us that something is inside the collider. This can be used to create buttons or trigger Objects, in areas of the game when the Player passes through something happening, such as a wave of enemies being spawned, a door being opened, or winning the game in case that area is the goal place of the Player. Consider that regular Static Colliders won't generate a trigger event when passing through this type because those aren't supposed to move.

- **Trigger Kinematic Collider**: Kinematic Colliders don't generate collisions, so they will pass through any other Object, but they will generate Trigger events, so we can react via scripting. This can be used to create moveable power-ups that, when touched, disappear and gives us points, or bullets that move with custom scripting movement and no physics, just straight like our bullets, but that damage other Objects on contact.

- We can have a Trigger Physics Collider, a collider with Rigidbody but with **Is Trigger** checked, usually, it has no real use; it will be an ever-falling Object that will generate trigger events in the world, but passing through everything. Of course, other profiles can exist aside from the specified ones to use in some games with specific gameplay requirements, but considering all possible combinations of Physics settings are up to you to experiment with to see whether some are useful for your case, the described profiles will cover 99% of cases.

- To recap the previous scenarios, I leave you with the following table showing the reaction of contact between all of the types of colliders. You will find a row per each profile that can move; remember that static profiles aren't supposed to move. Each column represents the reaction when they collide with the other types, "Nothing" meaning the Object will pass through with no effect, "Trigger" meaning the Object will pass through but raising Trigger events, and "Collision" meaning that the Object won't be able to pass through the Object:

	Collides with Static	**Collides with Dynamic**	**Collides with Kinematic**	**Collides with Trigger Static**	**Collides with Trigger Kinematic**
Dynamic	Collision	Collision	Collision	Trigger	Trigger
Kinematic	Nothing	Nothing	Nothing	Trigger	Trigger
Trigger Kinematic	Trigger	Trigger	Trigger	Trigger	Trigger

Table 15.4 Collision Reaction Matrix

Considering this, let's start configuring the physics of our Scene's Objects.

The walls, corners, floor tiles, and obstacles should use the Static Collider Profile, so they have no `Rigidbody` component on them and their colliders will have the **Is Trigger** checkbox unchecked:

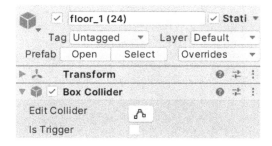

Figure 15.5 – Configuration for floor tiles; remember the static checkbox is for lighting only

The Player should move and generate collisions against Objects, so we need it to have a Dynamic Profile. This profile will generate a funny behavior with our current movement script (which I encourage you to test), especially when colliding against walls, so it won't behave as you expected. We will deal with this later in this chapter:

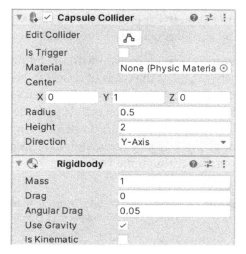

Figure 15.6 – Dynamic settings on the Player

For the Enemy Prefab, we will be using the Kinematic profile here because we will be moving this Object with Unity's AI systems later, so we don't need Physics here, and as we want the player to collide against them, we need a Collision reaction there, so there's no Trigger here:

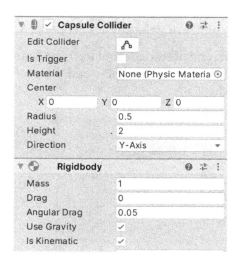

Figure 15.7 – Kinematic setting for the Enemy

For the `Bullet` Prefab, it will move but with simplistic movement via scripting (just move forward), and not Physics. We don't need collisions; we will code the bullet to destroy itself as soon as it touches something and will damage the collided Object (if possible), so a Kinematic Trigger profile is enough for this one; we will use the `Trigger` event to script the contact reactions:

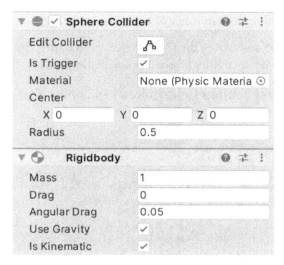

Figure 15.8 – The Kinematic Trigger setting for our bullet; Is Trigger and Is Kinematic are checked

Now that we have properly configured the Objects, let's check how to filter undesired collisions between certain Object types.

Filtering collisions

After all of the hassle of configuring Objects, do we want to prevent collisions? Actually, yes, sometimes we want certain Objects to ignore each other. As an example, the bullets shot by the Player shouldn't collide with the Player itself and the bullets from the enemies shouldn't hit them. We can always filter that with an `If` statement in the C# script, checking whether the hit Object is from the opposite team or whatever filtering logic you want, but by then, it is too late, the Physics system has already wasted resources by checking a collision between Objects that were never meant to collide. Here is where the Layer Collision Matrix can help us.

The Layer Collision Matrix sounds scary, but it is a simple setting of the Physics system that allows us to specify which groups of Objects should collide with other groups, for example, the Player's bullets should collide with enemies, and Enemy bullets should collide with the Player. The idea is to create those groups and put our Objects inside them, and in Unity, those groups are called **layers**. We can create layers and set the layer property of the GameObject (the top part of the Inspector) to assign the Object to that group or layer. Consider that you have a limited number of layers, so try to use them wisely.

Once we create the layers and assign the Object, we can go to the Physics settings and specify which layers will collide against other layers. We can achieve this by doing the following:

1. Go to **Edit | Project Settings** and, inside it, look for the **Tags and Layers** option from the left pane:

Figure 15.9 – Tags and Layers settings

2. From the **Layers** section, use the empty spaces from **Layer 10** onward to create the needed ones. In our case, we will use this for the bullet scenario, so we need four layers, Player, Enemy, PlayerBullet, and PlayerEnemy:

User Layer 8	PostProcessing
User Layer 9	Terrain
User Layer 10	Player
User Layer 11	Enemy
User Layer 12	PlayerBullet
User Layer 13	EnemyBullet

Figure 15.10 – Creating layers

3. Select the `Player` and, from the top part of the Inspector, change the layer property to `Player`. Also, change the `Enemy` Prefab to have the `Enemy` layer. A window will show asking you whether you want to change the child Objects also; select that option:

Figure 15.11 – Changing the layers of the Player and the Enemy Prefab

In the case of the bullet, we have a problem; we have one Prefab but two layers and a Prefab can only have one layer. We have two options, that is, changing the layer according to the shooter via scripting or have two bullet Prefabs with different layers. For simplicity, I will choose the latter, also taking the chance to apply another material to the Enemy bullet to make it look different.

We will be creating a Prefab Variant of the Player bullet. Remember that a Variant is a Prefab that is based on an original one like class inheritance. When the original Prefab changes, the Variant will change, but the Variant can have differences, which will make it unique:

1. Drop a bullet in to the Scene to create an instance.

2. Drag the instance again to the `Prefabs` folder, this time selecting the **Prefab Variant** option. Call it `Enemy Bullet`. Remember to destroy the Prefab instance in the scene.

3. Create a second material similar to the Player bullet, but yellow or whatever color you like, and put it on the Enemy Bullet Prefab Variant.

4. Select the Variant for the Enemy bullet, set its layer (`EnemyBullet`), and do the same for the original Prefab (`PlayerBullet`). Even if you changed the original Prefab layer, as the Variant modified it, the modified version (or override) will prevail, allowing each Prefab to have its own layer.

5. Go to **Edit | Project Settings** and look for the **Physics settings** (not Physics 2D).

6. Scroll down until you see the Layer Collision Matrix, a half grid of checkboxes. You will notice that each column and row is labeled with the names of the layers, so each checkbox in the cross of a row and column will allow us to specify whether these two should collide. In our case, we configured it as shown in the following screenshot:

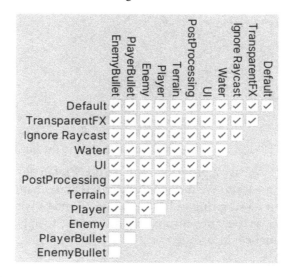

Figure 15.12 – Making Player bullets to collide with enemies and Enemy bullets with the Player

It is worth noticing that sometimes filtering logic won't be that fixed or predictable, for example, our bullet may only hit Objects that have a certain amount of life or Objects that don't have an invisibility temporal buff or conditions that can change during the game and are difficult to generate all possible layers for all possible groups. So, in these cases, we should rely on manual filtering after the Trigger or Collision event.

Now that we have filtered collisions, let's check whether our settings are working properly by reacting to collisions in the next section.

Detecting collisions

As you can see, proper Physics settings can be complicated and very important, but now that we have tackled that, let's do something with those settings by reacting to the contact in different ways and creating a Health System in the process.

In this section, we will examine the following collision concepts:

- Detecting Trigger events
- Modifying the other Object

First, we are going to explore the different collision and trigger events Unity offers to react to contact between two Objects through the Unity collision events. This allows us to execute any reaction code we want to place, but we are going to explore how to modify the contacted Object components using the GetComponent function.

Detecting Trigger events

If Objects are properly configured, as previously discussed, we can get two reactions, triggers and collisions. The Collision reaction has a default effect that is blocking the movement of the Objects, but we can add custom behavior on top of that using scripting, but with triggers, unless we add custom behavior, it won't produce any noticeable effect. Either way, we can script reactions to both possible scenarios such as adding a score, reducing health, and losing the game. To do so, we can use the suite of Physics events.

These events are split into two groups, Collision events and Trigger events, so according to your Object setting, you will need to pick the proper group. Both groups have three main events, **Enter**, **Stay**, and **Exit**, telling us when a collision or trigger began (Enter), whether they are still happening or are still in contact (Stay), and when they stopped contacting (Exit). For example, we can script a behavior such as playing a sound when two Objects start contact in the Enter event, such as a friction sound, and stop it when the contact ends, in the Exit event.

Let's test this by creating our first contact behavior, that is, the bullet being destroyed when contacting something. Remember that the bullets are configured to be triggers, so they will generate Trigger events on contact with anything. You can do this with the following steps:

1. Create and add a script called ContactDestroyer on the Bullet Player Prefab; as the Bullet Enemy Prefab is a Variant of it, it will have also the same script.

2. To detect when a trigger happens, such as with Start and Update, create an event function named OnTriggerEnter.

3. Inside the event, use the Destroy(gameObject); line to make the bullet destroy itself when touching something:

```
public class ContactDestroyer : MonoBehaviour
{
    void OnTriggerEnter()
    {
        Destroy(gameObject);
    }
}
```

Figure 15.13 – Auto destroying on contact with something

4. Save and shoot the bullets against the walls to see how they disappear instead of passing through it. Again, here, we don't have a collision but a trigger that destroys the bullet on contact. So, in this way, we are sure that the bullet will never pass through anything, but we are still not using Physics movement.

For now, we won't need the other Collision events, but in case you need them, they will work similarly; just put OnCollisionEnter instead. Now, let's explore another version of the same function. It not only tells us that we hit something but also what we contacted against. We will use this to make our Contact Destroyer also destroy the other Object. To do this, follow these steps:

1. Replace the OnTriggerEnter method signature with the one in the following screenshot. This one receives a parameter of the Collider type, indicating the exact collider that hit us:

```
void OnTriggerEnter(Collider other)
```

Figure 15.14 – Version of the trigger event that tells us which Object we collided with

2. We can access the entire Object of that collider using the gameObject setter, so we can use this to destroy the other one also, as shown in the following screenshot. If we just use Destroy by passing the other reference, it would only destroy the Collider component:

```
void OnTriggerEnter(Collider other)
{
    Destroy(gameObject);
    Destroy(other.gameObject);
}
```

Figure 15.15 – Destroying both Objects

3. Save and test the script. You will notice that the bullet will destroy everything it touches.

Of course, we don't want the bullet to destroy everything on contact, just itself and the other Object if it complies with certain criteria, such as being on the opposite team or something else, according to our game. In our case, we will move a step forward, and instead of directly destroying the Object on contact, we will make the Enemies and the Player have a life amount, so the bullets will reduce it until reaching 0.

Modifying the other Object

So far, we used the `transform` field to access a specific component of the Object, but what happens when we need to access others? In our scenario, for the bullet to damage the collided Object, it will need to access its `Life` component to change the amount of life. Remember that Unity doesn't have all kinds of possible behaviors for games. So, in our case, the `Life` component is the one that we are going to create just to hold a float field with the amount of life. Every Object that has this component will be considered as a damageable Object. Here is where the `GetComponent` function will help us.

If you have a reference to a GameObject or Component, you can use `GetComponent` to access a reference of a target component if the Object contains it (if not, it will return null). Let's see how to use that function to make the bullet lower the amount of life of the other Object if it is damaged by following these steps:

1. Create and add a `Life` component with a `public float` field called `amount` to both the Player and enemies. Remember to set the value in the amount field for both Objects in the Inspector:

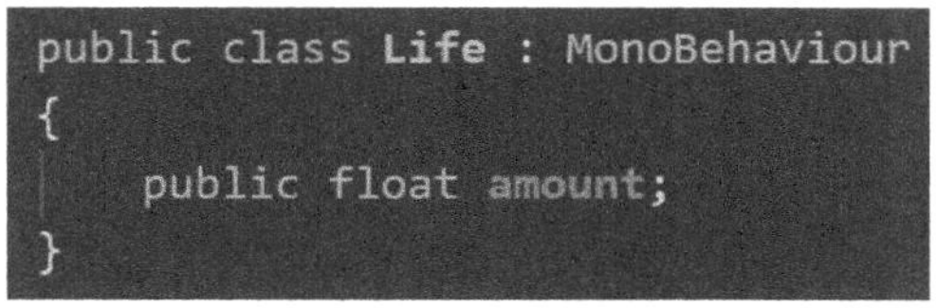

```
public class Life : MonoBehaviour
{
    public float amount;
}
```

Figure 15.16 – The Life component

2. Remove the `ContactDestroyer` component from the Player bullet, which will also remove it from the Enemy Bullet Variant, and instead add a new one called `ContactDamager`; you may need the `ContactDestroyer` behavior later. So, we are creating another component.

3. Add an `OnTriggerEnter` event that receives the other collider and just add the `Destroy` function call that auto destroys itself, not the one that destroyed the other Object; our script won't be responsible for destroying it, just reducing its life.

4. Add a float field called damage, so we can configure the amount of damage to inflict to the other Object. Remember to save the file and set a value before continuing.

5. Use `GetComponent` on the reference to the other collider to get a reference to its `life` component and save it in a variable:

```
Life life = other.GetComponent<Life>();
```

Figure 15.17 – Accessing the collided Object's Life component

6. Before reducing the life of the Object, we must check whether the life reference isn't null, which would happen if the other Object doesn't have the `Life` component, as in the case of walls and obstacles. The idea is that the bullet will destroy itself when anything collides with it and reduce the life of the other Object if it is a damageable Object that contains the `Life` component.

    In the following screenshot, you will find the full script finished:

```
using UnityEngine;

public class ContactDamager : MonoBehaviour
{
    public float damage;

    void OnTriggerEnter(Collider other)
    {
        Destroy(gameObject);

        Life life = other.GetComponent<Life>();
        if (life != null)
        {
            life.amount -= damage;
        }
    }
}
```

Figure 15.18 – Reducing the life of the collided Object

7. Place an Enemy in the scene based on a Prefab and set the instance speed (the one in the scene) to 0 to prevent it from moving.

8. Select it before hitting Play and start shooting at it.

You can see how the life value reduces in the Inspector. You can also press the *Esc* key to regain control of the mouse and select the Object while in Play Mode to see the life field change during the runtime in the Editor.

Now, you will notice that life is decreasing, but it will become negative; we want the Object to destroy itself when its life is below 0 instead. We can do this in two ways, one is to add an `Update` to the `Life` component, which will check all of the frames for whether life is below 0, destroying itself when that happens. The second way is by encapsulating the `life` field and checking that inside the setter to prevent checking all frames. I would prefer the second way, but we will implement the first one to make our scripts as simple as possible for beginners. To do this, follow these steps:

1. Add `Update` to the `Life` component.

2. Add `If` to check whether the `amount` field is below `0`.

3. Add `Destroy` in case the `if` condition is true.

4. The full `Life` script will look like the following screenshot:

```
public class Life : MonoBehaviour
{
    public float amount;

    void Update()
    {
        if (amount < 0)
        {
            Destroy(gameObject);
        }
    }
}
```

Figure 15.19 – The Life component

5. Save and see how the Object is destroyed once its life value becomes 0.

Optionally, you can instantiate an Object when this happens such as a sound, a particle, or maybe a power-up. I will leave this as a challenge for you.

By using a similar script, you can make a life power-up that increases the life value or a speed power-up that accesses the `PlayerMovement` script and increases the speed field; from now on, use your imagination to create exciting behaviors using this.

Now that we have explored how to detect collisions and react to them, let's explore how to fix the Player falling when hitting some wall.

Moving with Physics

So far, the Player, the only Object that moves with the Dynamic Collider Profile and the one that will move with Physics, is actually moving through custom scripting using the Transform API. Every dynamic Object should instead move using the Rigidbody API functions in a way the Physics system understands better, so here we will explore how to move Objects, this time through the Rigidbody component.

In this section, we will examine the following Physics movement concepts:

- Applying forces
- Tweaking Physics

We will start seeing how to move Objects the correct physical way, through forces, and we will apply this concept to the movement of our player. Then, we will explore why real physics is not always fun, and how we can tweak the Physics properties of our Objects to have a more responsive and appealing behavior.

Applying forces

The physically accurate way of moving an Object is through forces, which affect the Object's velocity. To apply force, we need to access `Rigidbody` instead of `Transform` and use the `AddForce` and `AddTorque` functions to move and rotate, respectively. These are functions where you can specify the amount of force to apply to each axis of position and rotation. This technique of movement will have full Physics reactions; the forces will accumulate on the velocity to start moving and will suffer drag effects that will make the speed slowly decrease, and the most important aspect here is that it will collide against walls, blocking the Object's way.

To get this kind of movement, we can do the following:

1. Create a `Rigidbody` field in the `PlayerMovement` script, but this time, make it `private`, meaning, do not write the `public` keyword in the field, which will make it disappear in the Editor; we will get the reference another way.

    Certain coding standards specify that you need to explicitly replace the `public` keyword with the `private` keyword, but in C#, putting `private` and not putting it have the same effect, so it's up to your preference:

    ```
    private Rigidbody rb;
    ```

Figure 15.20 – The private Rigidbody reference field

2. Using GetComponent in the Start event function, get our Rigidbody and save it in the field. We will use this field to cache the result of the GetComponent function; calling that function every frame to access the Rigidbody is not performant. Also, you can notice here that the GetComponent function can be used to retrieve not only components from other Objects (like the collision example) but also your own:

```
void Start()
{
    Cursor.visible = false;
    Cursor.lockState = CursorLockMode.Locked;


    rb = GetComponent<Rigidbody>();
}
```

Figure 15.21 – Caching the Rigidbody reference for future usage

3. Replace the transform.Translate calls with rb.AddRelativeForce. This will call the add force functions of the Rigidbody, specifically, the relative ones, which will consider the current rotation of the Object. For example, if you specify a force on the z axis (the third parameter), the Object will apply its force along with its forward vector.

4. Replace the transform.Rotate calls with rb.AddRelativeTorque, which will apply rotation forces:

```
if (Input.GetKey(KeyCode.W) || Input.GetKey(KeyCode.UpArrow))
    rb.AddRelativeForce(0, 0, speed * Time.deltaTime);

if (Input.GetKey(KeyCode.S) || Input.GetKey(KeyCode.DownArrow))
    rb.AddRelativeForce(0, 0, -speed * Time.deltaTime);

if (Input.GetKey(KeyCode.A) || Input.GetKey(KeyCode.LeftArrow))
    rb.AddRelativeForce(-speed * Time.deltaTime, 0, 0);

if (Input.GetKey(KeyCode.D) || Input.GetKey(KeyCode.RightArrow))
    rb.AddRelativeForce(speed * Time.deltaTime, 0, 0);

float mouseX = Input.GetAxis("Mouse X");
rb.AddRelativeTorque(0, mouseX * rotationSpeed * Time.deltaTime, 0);
```

Figure 15.22 – Using the Rigidbody forces API

> **Important note**
>
> If you are familiar with Unity, you might be thinking that I need to do this in a Fixed Update, and while that's correct, doing this in the Update won't have any noticeable effect. I prefer to use `Update` in beginners' scripts to prevent problems that can happen when using `GetKeyDown` and `GetKeyUp` in `FixedUpdate`.

Now, if you save and test the results, you will probably find the Player falling and that's because now we are using real physics, which contains floor friction, and due to the force being applied at the center of gravity, it will make the Object fall. Remember that, in terms of Physics, you are a Capsule; you don't have legs to move, and here is where standard physics is not suitable for our game. The solution is to tweak Physics to emulate the kind of behavior we need.

Tweaking Physics

To make our Player move like in a regular platformer game, we will need to freeze certain axes to prevent the Object from falling. Remove the friction to the ground and increase the air friction (drag) to make the Player reduce its speed automatically when releasing the keys. To do this, follow these steps:

1. In the `Rigidbody` component, look at the **Constraints** section at the bottom and check the **X** and **Z** axes of the **Freeze Rotation** property:

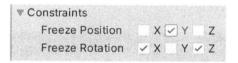

Figure 15.23 – Freezing rotation axes

This will prevent the Object from falling sideways but will allow the Object to rotate horizontally. You might also freeze the y axis of the **Freeze Position** property if you don't want the Player to jump, preventing some undesired vertical movement on collisions.

2. You will probably need to change the speed values because you changed from a meters-per-second value to newtons per second, the expected value of the **Add Force** and **Add Torque** functions. Using **1000** in speed and **45** in rotation speed was enough for me.

3. Now, you will probably notice that the speed will increase a lot over time, as will the rotation. Remember that you are using forces, which affects your velocity. When you stop applying forces, the velocity is preserved, and that's why the Player still keeps rotating even if you are not moving the mouse. The fix to this is to increase the **Drag** and **Angular Drag values**, which emulates air friction and which will reduce the movement and rotation respectively when no force is applied. Experiment with values that you see suitable; in my case, I used 2 for **Drag** and 10 for **Angular Drag**, needing to increase the **Rotation Speed** to 150 to compensate for the drag increase:

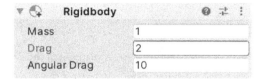

Figure 15.24 – Setting air friction for rotation and movement

4. Now, if you move while touching the wall, instead of sliding, like most games, your Player will stick to the obstacles due to contact friction. We can remove this by creating a Physics Material, an asset that can be assigned to the colliders to control how they react in those scenarios. Start creating one by clicking on the + button from the Project window and selecting **Physics Material** (not the 2D version). Call it Player and remember to put it in a folder for those kinds of assets.

5. Select it and set **Static Friction** and **Dynamic Friction** to 0, and **Friction Combine** to Minimum, which will make the Physics system pick the minimum friction of the two colliding Objects, being always the minimum—in our case, zero:

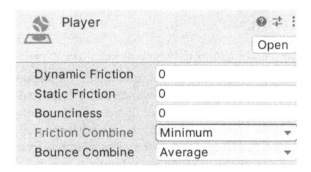

Figure 15.25 – Creating a Physics Material

6. Select the Player and drag this asset to the **Material** property of the
    Capsule Collider:

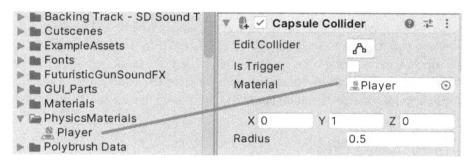

Figure 15.26 – Setting the Physics material of the Player

7. If you play the game now, you may notice that the Player will move faster than
    before because now we don't have any kind of friction on the floor, so you may need
    to reduce the movement force.

8. A little error you might find here is that the motion blur effect applied by the
    camera post-processing on the Player has some hiccups, such as frames where
    the Object is moving and others where it's not. The problem is that Physics is not
    executed in every frame due to the performance and determinism (by default, it is
    50 times per frame), but the rendering does, and that is affecting the postprocessing.
    You can set the **Interpolate** property of the Rigidbody to the **Interpolate** value to
    make the Rigidbody calculate Physics at its own rate but interpolate the position
    every frame to simulate fluidness:

Figure 15.27 – Making the Rigidbody interpolate its position

As you can see, we needed to bend the Physics rules to allow a responsive player
movement. You can get more responsiveness by increasing drags and forces, so the
speeds are applied faster and reduced faster, but that depends, again, on the experience
you want your game to have. Some games want an immediate response with no velocity
interpolation, going from 0 to full speed and vice versa from one frame to the other, and
in these cases, you can override the velocity and rotation vectors of the Player directly at
your will or even use other systems instead of Physics, such as the Character Controller
component, which have special physics for platformer characters; but let's keep things
simple for now.

Summary

Every game has physics one way or the other, for movement, collision detection, or both. In this chapter, we learned how to use the Physics system for both, being aware of proper settings to make the system work properly, reacting to collisions to generate gameplay systems, and moving the Player in such a way it collides with obstacles, keeping its physically-inaccurate movement. We used these concepts to create our Player and bullet movement and make our bullets damage the Enemies, but we can reuse the knowledge to create a myriad of other possible gameplay requirements, so I suggest you play a little bit with the physics concepts seen here; you can discover a lot of interesting use cases.

In the next chapter, we will be discussing how to program the visual aspects of the game, such as effects, and make the UI react to input.

16
Win and Lose Conditions

Now that we have a basic gameplay experience, it's time to make the game end sometime, both in the cases of winning and losing. One common way to implement this is through separated components with the responsibility of overseeing a set of Objects to detect certain situations that need to happen, such as the Player life becoming 0 or all of the waves being cleared. We will implement this through the concept of Managers, components that will manage several Objects, monitoring them.

In this chapter, we will examine the following Manager concepts:

- Creating Object Managers
- Creating Game Modes
- Improving our code with events

With this knowledge, you will be able to not only create the victory and loose condition of the game, but also do that in a properly structured way using design patterns such as Singleton and Event Listeners. These skills are not only useful for creating the code for the winning and losing functions of the game, but any code in general.

Creating Object Managers

Not every Object in the scene should be something that can be seen, heard, or collided with. Some Objects can also exist with a conceptual meaning, not something tangible. Imagine you need to keep a count of the number of enemies, where do you save that? You also need someplace to save the current score of the Player, and you may be thinking it could be on the Player itself, but what happens if the Player dies and respawns? The data would be lost! In such scenarios, the concept of a Manager can be a useful way of solving this in our first games, so let's explore it.

In this chapter, we are going to see the following Object Manager concepts:

- Implementing the Singleton design pattern
- Creating Managers with Singleton

We will start by discussing what the Singleton design pattern is and how it helps us simplify the communication of Objects. With it we will create Managers Objects, which will allow us to centralize information of a group of Objects, among other things. Let's start discussing the Singleton design pattern.

Implementing the Singleton design pattern

Design patterns are usually described as common solutions to common problems. There are several coding design decisions you will have to make while you code your game, but luckily, the way to tackle the most common situations are well known and documented. In this section, we are going to discuss one of the most common design patterns, the Singleton, a very controversial but convenient one to implement in simple projects.

A Singleton pattern is used when we need a single instance of an Object, meaning that there shouldn't be more than one instance of a class and that we want it to be easily accessible (not necessarily, but useful in our scenario). We have plenty of cases in our game where this can be applied, for example, `ScoreManager`, a component that will hold the current score. In this case, we will never have more than one score, so we can take advantage of the benefits of the Singleton Manager here.

One benefit is being sure that we won't have duplicated scores, which makes our code less error-prone. Also, so far, we have needed to create public references and drag Objects via the Editor to connect two Objects or look for them using `GetComponent`, but with this pattern, we will have global access to our Singleton component, meaning you can just write the name of the component and you will access it. In the end, there's just one `ScoreManager` component, so specifying which one via the Editor is redundant. This is similar to `Time.deltaTime`, the class responsible for managing time—we have just one time.

> **Important note**
>
> If you are an advanced programmer, you may be thinking about code testing and dependency injection now, and you are right, but remember, we are trying to write simple code so far, so we will stick to this simple solution.

Let's create a Score Manager Object, responsible for handling the score, to show an example of a Singleton by doing the following:

1. Create an empty GameObject (**GameObject | Create Empty**) and call it `ScoreManager`; usually, Managers are put in empty Objects, separated from the rest of the scene Objects.

2. Add a script called `ScoreManager` to this Object with an `int` field called `amount` that will hold the current score.

3. Add a field of the `ScoreManager` type called `instance`, but add the `static` keyword to it; this will make the variable global, meaning it can be accessed anywhere by just writing its name:

```csharp
using UnityEngine;

public class ScoreManager : MonoBehaviour
{
    public static ScoreManager instance;

    public int amount;
}
```

Figure 16.1 – A static field that can be accessed anywhere in the code

4. In `Awake`, check whether the `instance` field is not null, and in that case, set ourselves as the instance reference using the `this` reference.

5. In the `else` clause of the null checking `if` statement, print a message indicating that there's a second `ScoreManager` instance that must be destroyed:

```csharp
void Awake()
{
    if (instance == null)
    {
        instance = this;
    }
    else
    {
        print("Duplicated ScoreManager, ignoring this one");
    }
}
```

Figure 16.2 – Checking whether there's only one Singleton instance

The idea is to save the reference to the only `ScoreManager` instance in the instance static field, but if by mistake the user creates two objects with the `ScoreManager` component, this `if` statement will detect it and inform the user of the error, asking them to take action. In this scenario, the first `ScoreManager` instance to execute `Awake` will find that there's no instance set (the field is null) so it will set itself as the current instance, while the second `ScoreManager` instance will find the instance is already set and will print the message. Remember that `instance` is a static field, the one shared between all classes, unlike regular reference fields, where each component will have its own reference, so in this case, we have two `ScoreManagers` added to the scene, and both will share the same instance field.

To improve the example a little bit, it would be ideal to have a simple way to find the second `ScoreManager` in the game. It will be hidden somewhere in the Hierarchy and it would be difficult to find. We can replace `print` with `Debug.Log`, which is basically the same but allows us to pass a second argument to the function, which is an Object, to highlight when the message is clicked in the console. In this case, we will pass the `gameObject` reference to allow the console to highlight the duplicated Object:

```
Debug.Log("Duplicated ScoreManager, ignoring this one", gameObject);
```

Figure 16.3 – Printing messages in the console with Debug.Log

6. After clicking the log message, this GameObject will be highlighted in the Hierarchy:

Figure 16.4 – The highlighted Object after clicking the message

7. Finally, a little improvement can be made here by replacing `Debug.Log` with `Debug.LogError`, which will also print the message but with an error icon. In a real game, you will have lots of messages in the console, and highlighting the errors over the information messages will help us to identify them quickly:

```
Debug.LogError("Duplicated ScoreManager, ignoring this one", gameObject);
```

Figure 16.5 – Using LogError to print an error message

8. Try the code and observe the error message in the console:

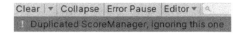

Figure 16.6 – An error message in the console

The next step would be to use this Singleton somewhere, so in this case, we will make the enemies give points when they are killed by doing the following:

1. Add a script to the Enemy Prefab called ScoreOnDeath with an int field called amount, which will indicate the number of points the Enemy will give when killed. Remember to set the value to something other than 0 in the Editor for the Prefab.

2. Create the OnDestroy event function, which will be automatically called by Unity when this Object is destroyed; in our case, the Enemy:

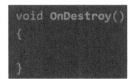

Figure 16.7 – The OnDestroy event function

> **Important note**
>
> Consider that the OnDestroy function is also called when we change scenes or the game is quitting, so in this scenario, maybe we will get points when changing scenes, which is not correct. So far, this is not a problem in our case, but later in this chapter, we will see a way to prevent this.

3. Access the Singleton reference in the OnDestroy function by writing ScoreManager.instance, and add the amount field of our script to the amount field of the Singleton to increase the score when an Enemy is killed:

```
public int amount;

void OnDestroy()
{
    ScoreManager.instance.amount += amount;
}
```

Figure 16.8 – Full ScoreOnDeath component class contents

4. Select the ScoreManager in the hierarchy, hit play, and kill some enemies to see the score increase with every kill. Remember to set the amount field of the ScoreOnDeath component of the Prefab.

As you can see, the Singleton simplified a lot the way to access `ScoreManager` and prevented us from having two versions of the same Object, which will help us to reduce errors in our code. Something to take into account is that now you will be tempted to just make everything a Singleton, such as the Player life or Player bullets and use it just to make your life easier to create gameplay such as power-ups, and while that will totally work, remember that your game will change, and I mean, change a lot; any real project will suffer that. Maybe today, the game will have just one Player, but maybe in the future, you will want to add a second Player or an AI companion, and you want the power-ups to affect them too, so if you abuse the Singleton pattern, you will have trouble handling those scenarios. Maybe the companion will try to get the pickup but the main Player will be healed instead!

The point here is to try to use the pattern as few times as you can, in cases where you don't have any other way to solve the problem. To be honest, there are always ways to solve problems without Singleton, but they are a little bit more difficult to implement for beginners, so I prefer to simplify your life a little bit to keep you motivated. With enough practice, you will reach a point where you will be ready to improve your coding standards.

Now that we know how to create Singletons, let's finish some other Managers that we will need later in the game.

Creating Managers with Singleton

Sometimes, we need a place to put together information about a group of similar Objects, for example, an Enemy Manager, to check the number of enemies and potentially access an array of them to iterate over them and do something, or maybe `MissionManager`, to have access to all of the active missions in our game. Again, these cases can be considered Singletons, single Objects that won't be repeated (in our current game design), so let's create the ones we will need in our game, that is, `EnemyManager` and `WaveManager`.

In our game, `EnemyManager` and `WaveManager` will just be places to save an array of references to the existent enemies and waves in our game, just as a way to know the current amount of them. There are ways to search all Objects of a certain type to calculate the count of them, but those functions are expensive and not recommended to use unless you really know what you are doing. So, having a Singleton with a separate updated list of references to the target Object type will require more code but will perform better. Also, as the game features increase, these Managers will have more functionality and helper functions to interact with those Objects.

Let's start with the enemies Manager by doing the following:

1. Add a script called `Enemy` to the Enemy Prefab; this will be the script that will connect this Object with `EnemyManager` in a moment.

2. Create an empty `GameObject` called `EnemyManager` and add a script to it called `EnemiesManager`.

3. Create a `public` static field of the `EnemiesManager` type called `instance` inside the script and add the Singleton repetition check in `Awake` as we did in `ScoreManager`.

4. Create a public field of the `List<Enemy>` type called `enemies`:

```
public List<Enemy> enemies;
```

Figure 16.9 – List of Enemy components

A list in C# represents a dynamic array, an array capable of adding and removing Objects. You will see that you can add and remove elements to this list in the Editor, but keep the list empty; we will add enemies another way. Take into account that `List` is in the `System.Collections.Generic` namespace; you will find the `using` sentence at the beginning of our script. Also, consider that you can make the list private and expose it to the code via a getter instead of making it a public field; but as usual, we will make our code as simple as possible for now.

Important note

Remember that `List` is a class type, so it must be instantiated, but as this type has exposing support in the Editor, Unity will automatically instantiate it. You must use the new keyword to instantiate it in cases where you want a non-Editor-exposed list, such as a private one or a list in a regular non-component C# class.

The C# list internally is implemented as an array. if you need a linked list, look at the `LinkedList` collection type.

---

5. In the `Start` function of the `Enemy` script, access the `EnemyManager` Singleton and using the `Add` function of the enemies list, add this Object to the list. This will "register" this Enemy as active in the Manager, so other Objects can access the Manager and check for the current enemies. The `Start` function is called after all of the `Awake` function calls, and this is important because we need to be sure that the `Awake` function of the Manager is executed prior to the `Start` function of the Enemy to ensure that there is a Manager set as the instance.

> **Important Note**
>
> The problem we solved with the `Start` function is called a race condition, that is, when two pieces of code are not guaranteed to be executed in the same order, whereas `Awake` execution order can change due to different reasons. There are plenty of situations in code where this will happen, so pay attention to the possible race conditions in your code. Also, you might consider using more advanced solutions such as lazy initialization here, which can give you better stability, but again, for the sake of simplicity and exploring the Unity API, we will use the `Start` function approach for now.

6. In the `OnDestroy` function, remove the Enemy from the list to keep the list updated with just the active ones:

```csharp
public class Enemy : MonoBehaviour
{
    void Start()
    {
        EnemyManager.instance.enemies.Add(this);
    }

    void OnDestroy()
    {
        EnemyManager.instance.enemies.Remove(this);
    }
}
```

Figure 16.10 – The Enemy script to register ourselves as an active Enemy

With this, now we have a centralized place to access all of the active enemies in a simple but efficient way. I challenge you to do the same with the waves, using `WaveManager`, which will have the collection of all active Waves to later check whether all waves finished their work to consider the game as won. Take some time to solve this; you will find the solution in the following screenshots, starting with `WavesManager`:

```csharp
using System.Collections.Generic;
using UnityEngine;

public class WavesManager : MonoBehaviour
{
    public static WavesManager instance;

    public List<WaveSpawner> waves;

    void Awake()
    {
        if (instance == null)
            instance = this;
        else
            Debug.LogError("Duplicated WavesManager", gameObject);
    }
}
```

Figure 16.11 – The full WavesManager script

You will need also the `WavesSpawner` script:

```
using UnityEngine;

public class WaveSpawner : MonoBehaviour
{
    public GameObject prefab;
    public float startTime;
    public float endTime;
    public float spawnRate;

    void Start()
    {
        WavesManager.instance.waves.Add(this);
        InvokeRepeating("Spawn", startTime, spawnRate);
        Invoke("EndSpawner", endTime);
    }

    void Spawn()
    {
        Instantiate(prefab, transform.position, transform.rotation);
    }

    void EndSpawner()
    {
        WavesManager.instance.waves.Remove(this);
        CancelInvoke();
    }
}
```

Figure 16.12 – The modified WaveSpawner script to support WavesManager

As you can see, `WaveManager` is created the same way `EnemyManager` was, just a Singleton with a list of `WaveSpawner` references, but `WaveSpawner` is different. We execute the `Add` function of the list in the `Start` event of `WaveSpawner` to register the wave as an active one, but the `Remove` function needs more work.

The idea is to deregister the wave from the active waves list when it finishes spawning all enemies when the spawner finishes its work. Before this modification, we used `Invoke` to call the `CancelIncoke` function after a while to stop the spawning, but now we need to do more after the end time. Instead of calling `CancelInvoke` after the specified wave end time, we will call a custom function called `EndSpawner`, which will call `CancelInvoke` to stop the spawner, `Invoke Repeating`, but also will call `Remove` from `WavesManager` list function to make sure the removing from the list is called exactly when `WaveSpawner` finishes its work.

Using Object Managers, we have now centralized information about a group of Objects, and we can add all sorts of Objects group logic here, but besides having this information for updating the UI (which we will do in the next chapter), we can use this information to detect whether the Victory and Lose conditions of our game are met, creating a Game Mode Object to detect that.

Creating Game Modes

We have created Objects to simulate lots of gameplay aspects of our game, but the game needs to end sometime, whether we win or lose. As always, the question is where to put this logic and that leads us to further questions. The main questions would be, will we always win or lose the game the same way? Will we have a special level with different criteria than to kill all of the waves, such as a timed survival? Only you know the answer to those questions, but if right now the answer is no, it doesn't mean that it won't change later, so it is advisable to prepare our code to adapt seamlessly to changes.

> **Important note**
>
> To be honest, preparing our code to adapt seamlessly to changes is almost impossible; there's no way to have perfect code that will consider every possible case, and we will always need to rewrite some code sooner or later. We will try to make the code as adaptable as possible to changes; always doing that doesn't consume lots of developing time and it's sometimes preferable to write simple code fast then complex code slow that might not be necessary, and so balance your time budget wisely.

To do this, we will separate the Victory and Lose conditions logic in its own Object, which I like to call the "Game Mode" (not necessarily an industry standard). This will be a component that will oversee the game, checking conditions that need to be met in order to consider the game over. It will be like the referee of our game. The Game Mode will constantly check the information in the Object Managers and maybe other sources of information to detect the needed conditions. Having this Object separated from other Objects allows us to create different levels with different Game Modes; just use another Game Mode script in that level and that's all.

In our case, we will have a single Game Mode for now, which will check whether the number of waves and enemies becomes 0, meaning that we have killed all of the possible enemies and the game is won. Also, it will check whether the life of the Player reaches 0, considering the game as lost in that situation. Let's create it by doing the following:

1. Create a `GameMode` empty Object and add a `WavesGameMode` script to it. As you can see, we called the script with a descriptive name considering that we can add other game modes.

2. In its `Update` function, check whether the number of enemies and waves reached 0 by using the Enemy and Wave Managers; in that case, just `print` a message in the console for now. All lists have a `Count` property, which will tell you the number of elements stored inside.

3. Add a `public` field of the `Life` type called `PlayerLife` and drag the Player to that one; the idea is to also detect the lose condition here.

4. In `Update`, add another check to detect whether the life amount of the `PlayerLife` reference has reached 0, and in that case, `print` a lose message in the console:

```
[SerializeField] Life playerLife;

void Update()
{
    if (EnemyManager.instance.enemies.Count <= 0 && WavesManager.instance.waves.Count <= 0)
    {
        print("You win!");
    }

    if (playerLife.amount <= 0)
    {
        print("You lose!");
    }
}
```

Figure 16.13 – Win and lose condition checks in WavesGameMode

5. Play the game and test both cases, whether the Player life reaches 0 or whether you have killed all enemies and waves.

> **Important note**
>
> Remember that we don't want two instances of this Object, so we can make it a Singleton also, but as this Object won't be accessed by others, that might be redundant; I will leave this up to you. Anyway, remember that this won't prevent you from having two different `GameModes` instantiated; for doing so, you can create a `GameMode` base class, with the Singleton functionality ready to prevent two `GameModes` in the same scene.

Now, it is time to replace the messages with something more interesting. For now, we will just change the current scene to a Win scene and Lose scene, which will only have a UI with a win and lose message and a button to play again. In the future, you can add a Main Menu scene and have an option to get back to it. Let's do that by doing the following:

1. Create a new scene (**File | New Scene**) and save it, calling it `WinScreen`.

2. Add a UI Text and center it with the text, `You won!`.

3. Add a UI Button right below the text and change its text to `Play Again`:

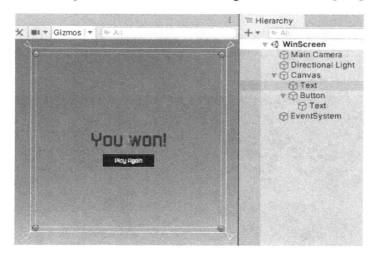

Figure 16.14 – WinScreen

4. Select the Scene in the Project View and press *Ctrl + D* (*Cmd + D* on Mac) to duplicate the scene. Rename it `LoseScreen`.

5. Double-click the `LoseScreen` scene to open it and just change the `You won!` text with a `You lose!` text.

6. Go to **File | Build Settings** to open the Scenes in the Build list inside this window.

    The idea is that Unity needs you to explicitly declare all scenes that must be included in the game. You might have test scenes or scenes that you don't want to release yet, so that's why we need to do this. In our case, our game will have `WinScreen`, `LoseScreen`, and the scene we have created so far with the game scenario, which I called `Game`, so just drag those scenes from the Project View to the list of the Build Settings window; we will need this to make the Game Mode script change the scenes properly. Also, consider that the first scene in this list will be the first scene to be opened when we play the game in its final version (known as the build), so you may want to rearrange the list according to that:

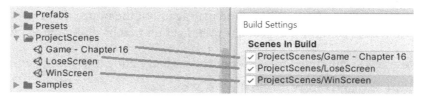

Figure 16.15 – Registering the scenes to be included in the build of the game

7. In `WavesGameMode`, add a `using` statement for the `UnityEngine.SceneManagement` namespace to enable the scene changing functions in this script.

8. Replace the console `print` messages with calls to the `SceneManager.LoadScene` function, which will receive a string with the name of the scene to load; in this case, it would be `WinScreen` and `LoseScreen`. You just need the scene name, not the entire path to the file.

    If you want to chain different levels, you can create a `public` string field to allow you to specify via the Editor which scenes to load. Remember to have the scenes added to the Build Settings, if not, you will receive an error message in the console when you try to change the scenes:

```csharp
using UnityEngine;
using UnityEngine.SceneManagement;

public class WavesGameMode : MonoBehaviour
{
    [SerializeField] Life playerLife;

    void Update()
    {
        if (EnemyManager.instance.enemies.Count <= 0 && WavesManager.instance.waves.Count <= 0)
        {
            SceneManager.LoadScene("WinScreen");
        }

        if (playerLife.amount <= 0)
        {
            SceneManager.LoadScene("LoseScreen");
        }
    }
}
```

Figure 16.16 – Changing scenes with `SceneManager`

9. Play the game and check whether the scenes change properly.

> **Important note**
> Right now, we picked the simplest way to show whether we lost or won, but maybe in the future, you will want something more gentle than a sudden change of the scene, such as maybe waiting a few moments with `Invoke` to delay that change or directly show the winning message inside the game without changing the scenes. Consider that when testing the game with people and checking whether they understood what happens while they play, game feedback is important to keep the Player aware of what is happening and is not an easy task to tackle.

Now we have a fully functional simple game, with mechanics and win and lose conditions, and while this is enough to start developing other aspects of our game, I want to discuss some issues with our current Manager approach and how to solve them with events.

Improving our code with events

So far, we used Unity event functions to detect situations that can happen in the game such as Awake and Update. These functions are ways for Unity to communicate two components, as in the case of OnTriggerEnter, which is a way for the Rigidbody to inform other components in the GameObject that a collision has happened. In our case, we are using ifs inside Updates to detect changes on other components, such as GameMode checking whether the number of enemies reached 0. But we can improve this if we are informed by the Enemy Manager when something has changed, and just do the check-in that moment, such as with the Rigidbody telling us the collisions instead of checking collisions every frame.

Also, sometimes, we rely on Unity events to execute logic, such as the score being given in the OnDestroy event, which informs us when the Object is destroyed, but due to the nature of the event, it can be called in situations we don't want to add to the score, such as when the scene is changed or the game is closed. Objects are destroyed in those cases, but not because the Player killed the Enemy, leading to the score being raised when it shouldn't. In this case, it would be great to have an event that tells us that the Player's lives have reached 0 to execute this logic, instead of relying on the general-purpose destroy event.

The idea of events is to improve the model of communication between our Objects, being sure that in the exact moment something happens, the interested parts in that situation are notified to react accordingly. Unity has lots of events, but we can create specific ones to our gameplay logic. Let's start seeing this applied in the Score scenario we discussed earlier; the idea is to make the Life component to have an event to communicate other components that the Object was destroyed because its life reached 0.

There are several ways to implement this, and we will use a little bit of a different approach than the Awake and Update methods; we will use the UnityEvent field type. This is a field type capable of holding references to functions to be executed when we want to, like C# delegates, but with other benefits, such as better Unity Editor integration. To implement this, do the following:

1. In the Life component, create a public field of the UnityEvent type called onDeath. This field will represent an event where other classes can subscribe to it to be aware of when Life reaches 0:

```
public class Life : MonoBehaviour
{
    public float amount;
    public UnityEvent onDeath;
```

Figure 16.17 – Creating a custom event field

2. If you save the script and go to the Editor, you can see the event in the Inspector. Unity Events support subscribing methods to them in the Editor so we can connect two Objects together. We will use this in the UI scripting chapter, so let's just ignore this for now:

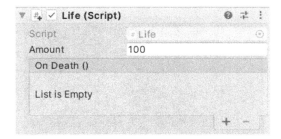

Figure 16.18 – UnityEvents showing up in the Inspector

> **Important note**
> You can use the generic delegate action or a custom delegate to create events instead of using UnityEvent, and aside from certain performance aspects, the only noticeable difference is that UnityEvent will show up in the Editor, as demonstrated in *step 2*.

3. When life reaches 0, call the Invoke function of the event, and this way, we will be telling anyone interested in the event that it has happened:

```
public float amount;
public UnityEvent onDeath;

void Update()
{
    if (amount <= 0)
    {
        onDeath.Invoke();
        Destroy(gameObject);
    }
}
```

Figure 16.19 – Executing the event

4. In `ScoreOnDeath`, rename the `OnDestroy` function to `GivePoints` or whatever name you prefer; the idea here is to stop giving points in the `OnDestroy` event.

5. In the `Awake` function of the `ScoreOnDeath` script, get the `Life` component using `GetComponent` and save it in a local variable.

6. Call the `AddListener` function of the `onDeath` field of the `Life` reference and pass the `GivePoints` function as the first argument. The idea is to tell `Life` to execute `GivePoints` when the `onDeath` event is invoked. This way, `Life` informs us about that situation. Remember that you don't need to call `GivePoints`, but just pass the function as a field:

```
void Awake()
{
    var life = GetComponent<Life>();
    life.onDeath.AddListener(GivePoints);
}

void GivePoints()
{
    ScoreManager.instance.amount += amount;
}
```

Figure 16.20 – Subscribing to the OnDeath event to give points in that scenario

> **Important note**
>
> Consider calling `RemoveListener` in `OnDestroy`; as usual, it is convenient to unsubscribe listeners when possible to prevent any memory leak (a reference preventing the GC from deallocating memory). In this scenario, it is not entirely necessary because both the `Life` and `ScoreOnDeath` components will be destroyed at the same time, but try to get used to that good practice.

7. Save, select `ScoreManager` in the Editor, and hit play to test this. Try deleting an Enemy from the Hierarchy while in Play Mode to check how the score doesn't rise because the Enemy was destroyed for any other reason than its life becoming 0; you must destroy an Enemy by shooting at them to see the score being raised.

    Now that `Life` has an `onDeath` event, we can also replace the Player's `Life` check from the `WavesGameMode` to use the event by doing the following:

8. Create an `OnLifeChanged` function on the `WavesGameMode` script and move the life checking condition from `Update` to this function.

9. In `Awake`, subscribe to this new function to the `onDeath` event of the Player's `Life` component reference:

```
void Awake()
{
    playerLife.onDeath.AddListener(OnPlayerLifeChanged);
}

void OnPlayerLifeChanged()
{
    if (playerLife.amount <= 0)
    {
        SceneManager.LoadScene("LoseScreen");
    }
}
```

Figure 16.21 – Checking the lose condition with events

As you can see, creating custom events allows you to detect more specific situations other than the defaults in Unity, and keeps your code clean, without needing to constantly ask conditions in the `Update` function, which is not necessarily bad, but the event approach generates clearer code.

Remember that we can lose our game also by the Player's Base Life reaching 0, and we will explore the concept of the Player's base later in this book, but for now, let's create a cube that represents the Object that Enemies will attack to reduce the Base Life, like the Base Core. Taking this into account, I challenge you to add this other lose condition to our script. When you finish, you can check the solution in the following screenshot:

```
[SerializeField] Life playerLife;
[SerializeField] Life playerBaseLife;

void Start()
{
    playerLife.onDeath.AddListener(OnPlayerLifeChanged);
    playerBaseLife.onDeath.AddListener(OnPlayerBaseLifeChanged);
}

void OnPlayerLifeChanged()
{
    if (playerLife.amount <= 0)
    {
        SceneManager.LoadScene("LoseScreen");
    }
}

void OnPlayerBaseLifeChanged()
{
    if (playerBaseLife.amount <= 0)
    {
        SceneManager.LoadScene("LoseScreen");
    }
}
```

Figure 16.22 – Complete WavesGameMode lose condition

As you can see, we just repeated the life event subscription: remember to create an Object to represent the Player's Base damage point, add a `Life` script to it, and drag that one as the Player Base Life reference of `WavesGameMode`.

Now, let's keep illustrating this concept by applying it in the Managers to prevent the Game Mode from checking conditions every frame:

1. Add an `UnityEvent` field to `EnemyManager` called `onChanged`. This event will be executed whenever an Enemy is added or removed from the list.

2. Create two functions, `AddEnemy` and `RemoveEnemy`, both receiving a parameter of the `Enemy` type. The idea is that instead of `Enemy` adding and removing itself from the list directly, it should use these functions.

3. Inside these two functions, invoke the `onChanged` event to inform others that the enemies list has been updated. The idea is that anyone who wants to add or remove enemies from the list needs to use these functions:

```
public UnityEvent onChanged;

public void AddEnemy(Enemy enemy)
{
    enemies.Add(enemy);
    onChanged.Invoke();
}

public void RemoveEnemy(Enemy enemy)
{
    enemies.Remove(enemy);
    onChanged.Invoke();
}
```

Figure 16.23 – Calling events when enemies are added or removed

> **Important note**
>
> Here, we have the problem that nothing stops us from bypassing those two functions and using the list directly. You can solve that by making the list private and exposing it using the `IReadOnlyList` interface. Remember that this way, the list won't be visible in the Editor for debugging purposes.

4. Change the `Enemy` script to use these functions:

```
public class Enemy : MonoBehaviour
{
    void Start()
    {
        EnemyManager.instance.AddEnemy(this);
    }

    void OnDestroy()
    {
        EnemyManager.instance.RemoveEnemy(this);
    }
}
```

Figure 16.24 – Making the Enemy use the Add and Remove functions

5. Repeat the same process for WaveManager and WaveSpawner, create an onChanged event, and create the AddWave and RemoveWave functions and call them in WaveSpawner instead of directly accessing the list. This way, we are sure the event is called when necessary as we did with EnemyManager. Try to solve this step by yourself and then check the solution in the following screenshot, starting with WavesManager:

```
public class WavesManager : MonoBehaviour
{
    public static WavesManager instance;

    public List<WaveSpawner> waves;
    public UnityEvent onChanged;

    public void AddWave(WaveSpawner wave)
    {
        waves.Add(wave);
        onChanged.Invoke();
    }

    public void RemoveWave(WaveSpawner wave)
    {
        waves.Remove(wave);
        onChanged.Invoke();
    }

    void Awake()
    {
        if (instance == null)
            instance = this;
        else
            Debug.LogError("Duplicated WavesManager", gameObject);
    }
}
```

Figure 16.25 – Wave Manager On Changed event implementation

Also, `WavesSpawner` needs changes:

```csharp
public class WaveSpawner : MonoBehaviour
{
    public GameObject prefab;
    public float startTime;
    public float endTime;
    public float spawnRate;

    void Start()
    {
        WavesManager.instance.AddWave(this);
        InvokeRepeating("Spawn", startTime, spawnRate);
        Invoke("EndSpawner", endTime);
    }

    void Spawn()
    {
        Instantiate(prefab, transform.position, transform.rotation);
    }

    void EndSpawner()
    {
        WavesManager.instance.RemoveWave(this);
        CancelInvoke();
    }
}
```

Figure 16.26 – Implementing the AddWave and RemoveWave functions

6. In `WavesGameMode`, rename `Update` to `CheckWinCondition` and subscribe this function to the `onChanged` event of `EnemyManager` and the `onChanged` event of `WavesManager`. The idea is to check for the number of enemies and waves being changed only when it is necessary. Remember to do the subscription to the events in the `Start` function due to the Singletons being initialized in `Awake`:

```csharp
void Start()
{
    playerLife.onDeath.AddListener(OnPlayerLifeChanged);
    playerBaseLife.onDeath.AddListener(OnPlayerBaseLifeChanged);
    EnemyManager.instance.onChanged.AddListener(CheckWinCondition);
    WavesManager.instance.onChanged.AddListener(CheckWinCondition);
}

void CheckWinCondition()
{
    if (EnemyManager.instance.enemies.Count <= 0 && WavesManager.instance.waves.Count <= 0)
    {
        SceneManager.LoadScene("WinScreen");
    }
}
```

Figure 16.27 – Checking the win condition when the enemies or waves amount is changed

Yes, this way, we have to write more code than before, and in terms of functionality, we didn't obtain anything new, but in bigger projects, managing conditions through `Update` checks will lead to different kinds of problems as previously discussed, such as race conditions and performances issues. Having a scalable code base sometimes requires more code, and this is one of those cases.

Before we finish, something to consider is that Unity events are not the only way to create this kind of event communication in Unity; you will find a similar approach called **Action**, the native C# version of Unity events, which I recommend you to look for if you want to see all of the options out there.

Summary

In this chapter, we finished an important part of the game, the ending, either by victory or by defeat. We discussed a simple but powerful way to separate the different layers of responsibilities by using Managers created through Singletons, to guarantee that there's not more than one instance of every kind of manager and simplifying the connections between them through static access (something to consider the day you discover code testing). Also, we visited the concept of events to streamline the communication between Objects to prevent problems and create more meaningful communication between Objects.

With this knowledge, you are now able not only to detect the victory and lose conditions of the game but to also do that in a better-structured way. These patterns can be useful to improve our game code in general, and I recommend you to try to apply it in other relevant scenarios.

In the next chapter, we are going to explore how to create visual and audio feedback to respond to our gameplay, combining scripting and the assets we integrated in *Part 2* of this book.

17
Scripting the UI, Sounds, and Graphics

In a game, even if the player sees the game through the camera, there is important information that is not visible in plain sight, such as the exact number of remaining bullets, their health, the enemies, whether there's an enemy behind them, and so on. We have already discussed how to tackle those issues with the UI, sounds, and **visual effects** (**VFX**), but as we start to move on with scripting in our game, those elements also need to adapt to the game. The idea of this chapter is to make our UI, sounds, and VFX react to the game situation through scripting, reflecting what is happening in the world.

In this chapter, we will examine the following feedback scripting concepts:

- Scripting the UI
- Scripting feedback

By the end of this chapter, you will be able to make the UI react to the game situation, showing relevant information in form of text and bars, and also be able to make the game react to interactions with the UI, such as with buttons. Also, you will be able to make the game inform the user of this information through other mediums, such as sound and particle graphics, which can be as effective as the UI, but more appealing.

Scripting the UI

We previously created a UI layout with elements such as bars, text, and buttons, but so far, they are static. We need to make them adapt to the game's actual state. In this chapter, we are going to discuss the following UI scripting concepts:

- Showing information in the UI

- Programming the Pause menu

We will start by seeing how to display information on our UI using scripts that modify the text and images that are displayed with Canvas elements. After that, we will create the Pause functionality, which will be used throughout the UI.

Showing information in the UI

As discussed earlier, we will use the UI to display information to the user to allow them to make informed decisions, so let's start by seeing how we can make the player's health bar react to the amount of life they have left in the `Life` script we created earlier:

1. Add a new script called **Life Bar** to the **HealthBar** Canvas child object, which is the UI `Image` component we created earlier to represent the life bar:

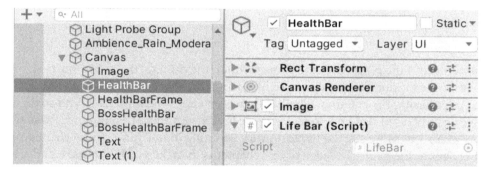

Figure 17.1 – The Life Bar component in the player's HealthBar Canvas

2. In the `Life Bar`, script adds a `Life` type field. This way, our script will ask the editor which `Life` component we will be monitoring. Save the script:

```
public class LifeBar : MonoBehaviour
{
    public Life targetLife;
}
```

Figure 17.2 – Editor-configurable reference to a Life component

3. In the Editor, drag the `Player` GameObject from the **Hierarchy** window to the `targetlife` property to make the life bar reference the player's life, and remember to have the `HealthBar` object selected before dragging **Player**.

    This way, we are telling our `LifeBar` script which `Life` component to check to see how much life the player has remaining. Something interesting here is that the enemies have the same `Life` component, so we can easily use this component to create life bars for every other object that has lives in our game:

Figure 17.3 – DraggingPlayer to reference its life component

4. Add the `using UnityEngine.UI;` line right after the `using` statements in the first few lines of the script. This will tell C# that we will be interacting with the UI scripts:

```
using System;
using System.Collections;
using System.Collections.Generic;
using UnityEngine;
using UnityEngine.UI;
```

Figure 17.4 – All the using statements in our script. We are not going
to use them all but let's keep them for now

5. Create a `private` field (without the `public` keyword) of the `Image` type. We will save the reference to the component here in a moment:

```
Image image;
public Life targetLife;
```

Figure 17.5 – Private reference to an image

6. Using `GetComponent` in `Awake`, access the reference to the `Image` component in our GameObject (`HealthBar`) and save it in the `image` field. As usual, the idea is to get this reference just once and save it for later use in the `Update` function. Of course, this will always work when you put this component in an object with an `Image` component. If not, the other option would be to create a public field of the `Image` type and drag the image component into it:

```
void Awake()
{
    image = GetComponent<Image>();
}
```

Figure 17.6 – Saving the reference to the Image component in this object

7. Create an `Update` event function in the `LifeBar` script. We will use this to constantly update the life bar according to the player's life.

8. In the `Update` event, divide the amount of life by `100` to have our current life percentage expressed in the `0` to `1` range (assuming our maximum life is `100`), and set the result in the `fillAmount` field of the `Image` component as in the following screenshot. Remember that `fillAmount` expects a value between `0` and `1`, with `0` signalling that the bar is empty and `1` that the bar is its full capacity:

```
void Update()
{
    image.fillAmount = targetLife.amount / 100;
}
```

Figure 17.7 – Updating the fill amount of the LifeBar script's
Image component according to the Life component

> **Important note:**
>
> Remember that putting `100` within the code is considered hardcoding (it is also known as a magic number), meaning later changes on that value would require us to look through the code for that value, which is a complicated task in big projects. That's why it is considered bad practice. It would be better to have a `Maximum Life` field in the `Life` component or at least have a constant with this value.

9. Save the script and in the Editor, select the player and play the game. During **Play** mode, press *Esc* to regain access to the mouse and change the player's health in the Inspector window to see how the life bar updates accordingly. You can also test this by making the player receive damage somehow, such as by making enemies spawn bullets (more on enemies later):

```csharp
using UnityEngine;
using UnityEngine.UI;

public class LifeBar : MonoBehaviour
{
    Image image;
    public Life targetLife;

    void Awake()
    {
        image = GetComponent<Image>();
    }

    void Update()
    {
        image.fillAmount = targetLife.amount / 100;
    }
}
```

Figure 17.8 – Full LifeBar script

> **Important note:**
> In the previous chapter, we explored the concept of events to detect changes in the state of other objects. The life bar is another example of using an event as we can change the fill amount of the image when the life actually changes. I challenge you to try to create an event when the life changes and implement this script using the one we looked at in the previous chapter.

You may be thinking that this UI behavior could be directly coded within the Life component, and that's completely possible, but the idea here is to create simple scripts with little pressure to keep our code separated. Each script should have just one reason to be modified, and mixing UI behavior and gameplay behavior in a single script would give the script two responsibilities, which results in two possible reasons to change our script. With this approach, we can also set the player's base life bar at the bottom by just adding the same script to its life bar but dragging the **Base Damage** object, which we created in the previous chapter, as the target life this time.

> **Important note:**
> The single object responsibility principle we just mentioned is one of the
> five object-oriented programming principles known as SOLID. If you don't
> know what SOLID is, I strongly recommend you look it up to improve your
> programming best practices.

Now that we have sorted out the player's life bar, let's make the `Bullets` label update
according to the player's remaining bullets. Something to consider here is that our current
Player Shooting script has unlimited bullets, so let's change that by following these steps:

1. Add a public `int` type field to the Player Shooting script called `bulletsAmount`.

2. In the `if` statement that checks the pressure of the left mouse button, add
   a condition to check whether the amount of bullets is greater than `0`.

3. Inside the `if` statement, reduce the number of bullets by `1`:

```
void Update()
{
    if (Input.GetKeyDown(KeyCode.Mouse0) && bulletsAmount > 0)
    {
        bulletsAmount--;

        GameObject clone = Instantiate(prefab);
        clone.transform.position = shootPoint.transform.position;
        clone.transform.rotation = shootPoint.transform.rotation;
    }
}
```

Figure 17.9 – Limiting the number of bullets to shoot

Now that we have a field indicating the number of remaining bullets, we can create
a script to display that number in the UI by doing the following:

4. Add a `PlayerBulletsUI` script to the bullet's `Text` GameObject. In my case,
   I called it `Bullets Label`.

5. Add the `using UnityEngine.UI` statement and add a private field of the `Text`
   type, saving it in the reference to our own `Text` component in `Awake`:

```
using UnityEngine;
using UnityEngine.UI;

public class PlayerBulletsUI : MonoBehaviour
{
    Text text;

    void Awake()
    {
        text = GetComponent<Text>();
    }
}
```

Figure 17.10 – Caching the reference to our own Text component

6. Create a `public` field of the `PlayerShooting` type called `targetShooting` and drag `Player` to this property in the Editor. As was the case for the life bar component, the idea is that our UI script will access the script that has the remaining bullets to update the text, bridging the two scripts (`Text` and `PlayerShooting`) to keep their responsibilities separated.

7. Create an `Update` statement and inside it, set the `text` field of the text reference (I know, confusing) with a concatenation of `"Bullets: "` and the `bulletsAmount` field of the `targetShooting` reference. This way, we will replace the text of the label according to the current amount of bullets:

```
void Update()
{
    text.text = "Bullets: " + targetShooting.bulletsAmount;
}
```

Figure 17.11 – Updating the bullet's text label

> **Important note:**
> Remember that concatenating strings allocates memory, so again, I urge you to only do this when necessary using events.

If you look at the two scripts, you will find a pattern. You can access the UI and Gameplay components and update the UI component accordingly, and most UI scripts will behave in the same way. Keeping this in mind, I challenge you to create the necessary scripts to make the **Score**, **Enemies**, and **Waves** counters work. Remember to add using UnityEngine.UI to use the Text component. After finishing this, you can compare your solution with the one in the following screenshot, starting with ScoreUI:

```
using UnityEngine;
using UnityEngine.UI;

public class ScoreUI : MonoBehaviour
{
    Text text;

    void Awake()
    {
        text = GetComponent<Text>();
    }

    void Update()
    {
        text.text = "Score: " + ScoreManager.instance.amount;
    }
}
```

Figure 17.12 – The ScoreUI script

Also, we need the WavesUI component:

```
using UnityEngine;
using UnityEngine.UI;

public class WavesUI : MonoBehaviour
{
    Text text;

    void Start()
    {
        text = GetComponent<Text>();
        WavesManager.instance.onChanged.AddListener(RefreshText);
    }

    void RefreshText()
    {
        text.text = "Remaining Waves: " + WavesManager.instance.waves.Count;
    }
}
```

Figure 17.13 – The WavesUI script

Finally, we need `EnemiesUI`:

```
using UnityEngine;
using UnityEngine.UI;

public class EnemiesUI : MonoBehaviour
{
    Text text;

    void Start()
    {
        text = GetComponent<Text>();
        EnemyManager.instance.onChanged.AddListener(RefreshText);
    }

    void RefreshText()
    {
        text.text = "Remaining Enemies: " + EnemyManager.instance.enemies.Count;
    }
}
```

Figure 17.14 – The EnemiesUI script

As you can see, we have used the events already coded in the managers to change the UI only when necessary. Now that we have coded the UI labels and bars, let's code the `Pause` menu.

Programming the Pause menu

Recall how we created a Pause menu in a previous chapter, but it is currently disabled, so let's make it work. First, we need to code `Pause`, which can be quite complicated. So again, we will use a simple approach for pausing most behaviors, which is stopping the time! Remember that most of our movement scripts use time functionality, such as **Delta Time**, as a way to calculate the amount of movement to apply, and there's a way to simulate time going slower or faster, which is by setting `timeScale`.

This field will affect Unity's time system's speed, and we can set it to 0 to simulate that time has stopped, which will pause animations, stop particles, and reduce **Delta Time** to 0, making our movements stop. So, let's do it:

1. Create a script called `Pause` and add it to a new object in the scene, also called `Pause`.

2. In `Update`, detect when the *Esc* key is pressed, and in that scenario, set `Time.timeScale` to 0:

```
public class Pause : MonoBehaviour
{
    void Update()
    {
        if (Input.GetKeyDown(KeyCode.Escape))
        {
            Time.timeScale = 0;
        }
    }
}
```

Figure 17.15 – Stopping time to simulate a pause

3. Save and test this.

    You will notice that almost everything will stop, but you can see how the shoot functionality still works. That's because the Player Shooting script is not time-dependent. One solution here could be to simply check whether `Time.timeScale` is greater than 0 to prevent this:

```
if (Input.GetKeyDown(KeyCode.Mouse0) && bulletsAmount > 0 && Time.timeScale > 0)
{
    bulletsAmount--;
```

Figure 17.16 – Checking pause in the PSlayer Shooting script

> **Important note:**
> As usual, we have pursued the simplest way here, but there is a better approach. I challenge you to try to create `PauseManager` with a Boolean indicating whether the game is paused or not, changing `timeScale` in the process.

Now that we have a simple but effective way to pause the game, let's make the **Pause** menu visible to unpause the game by doing the following:

4. Add a field of the `GameObject` type called `pauseMenu` in the `Pause` script. The idea is to drag the **Pause** menu here so that we have a reference to enable and disable it.

5. In `Awake`, add `pauseMenu.SetActive(false);` to disable the **Pause** menu at the beginning of the game. Even if we disabled the **Pause** menu in the editor, we add this just in case we re-enable it by mistake. It must always start disabled.

6. Using the same function but passing `true` as the first parameter, enable the **Pause** menu in the *Esc* key pressure check:

```
public class Pause : MonoBehaviour
{
    public GameObject pauseMenu;

    void Awake()
    {
        pauseMenu.SetActive(false);
    }

    void Update()
    {
        if (Input.GetKeyDown(KeyCode.Escape))
        {
            pauseMenu.SetActive(true);
            Time.timeScale = 0;
        }
    }
}
```

Figure 17.17 – Enabling the Pause menu when pressing the Esc key

Now, we need to make the **Pause** menu buttons work. If you recall, in the previous chapter, we explored the concept of events, implementing them with `UnityEvents` and the `Button` script. Our **Pause** menu buttons use the same class to implement the `OnClick` event, which is an event that informs us that a specific button has been pressed. Let's resume the game when pressing those buttons by doing the following:

7. Create a field of the `Button` type in our `Pause` script called `resumeButton`, and drag `resumeButton` to it; this way, our `Pause` script has a reference to the button.

8. In `Awake`, add a listener function called `OnResumePressed` to the `onClick` event of `resumeButton`.

9. Make the `OnResumePressed` function set `timeScale` to `1` and disable the **Pause** menu, as we did in `Awake`:

```
public GameObject pauseMenu;
public Button resumeButton;

void Awake()
{
    pauseMenu.SetActive(false);
    resumeButton.onClick.AddListener(OnResumePressed);
}

void OnResumePressed()
{
    pauseMenu.SetActive(false);
    Time.timeScale = 1;
}
```

Figure 17.18 – Unpausing the game

If you save and test this, you will notice that you cannot click the **Resume** button because we disabled the cursor at the beginning of the game, so make sure you re-enable it while in `Pause` and disable it when you resume:

```
void OnResumePressed()
{
    pauseMenu.SetActive(false);
    Time.timeScale = 1;
    Cursor.visible = false;
    Cursor.lockState = CursorLockMode.Locked;
}

void Update()
{
    if (Input.GetKeyDown(KeyCode.Escape))
    {
        Cursor.visible = true;
        Cursor.lockState = CursorLockMode.None;
        pauseMenu.SetActive(true);
        Time.timeScale = 0;
    }
}
```

Figure 17.19 – Showing and hiding the cursor while in Pause

Now that you know how to code buttons, I challenge you to code the **Exit** button's behavior. Again, remember to add `using UnityEngine.UI`. Also, you will need to call `Application.Quit();` to exit the game, but take into account that this will do nothing in the Editor; we don't want to close the Editor while creating the game. This function only works when you build the game. So for now, just call it and if you want to print a message to be sure that the button is working properly, a solution is provided in the following screenshot:

```csharp
using UnityEngine;
using UnityEngine.UI;

public class QuitButton : MonoBehaviour
{
    Button button;

    void Awake()
    {
        button = GetComponent<Button>();
        button.onClick.AddListener(Quit);
    }

    void Quit()
    {
        print("Quitting");
        Application.Quit();
    }
}
```

Figure 17.20 – The Quit button script

This solution proposes that you add this script directly to the **Quit** button GameObject itself so that the script listens to the `onClick` event on its `Button` sibling component, and in that case, executes the `Quit` function. You could also add this behavior to the `Pause` script, and while that will work, remember that if a script can be split into two because it does two unrelated tasks, it is always best to split it so that separate behavior is unrelated. Here, the Pause behavior is not related to the Quit behaviour.

Now that we have our Pause system set up using the UI and buttons, let's continue looking at other visual and audible ways to make our player aware of what has happened.

Scripting feedback

We just used the UI to pass on data to the user so that they know what is happening, but sometimes that's not enough. We can reinforce game events using other types of feedback, such as sound and explosions, which we integrated in previous chapters.

In this section, we will explore the following feedback concepts:

- Scripting visual feedback

- Scripting audio feedback

- Scripting animations

We will start seeing how to make our gameplay have more feedback, with different visuals used in the right moments, such as audio and particle systems. Then, we are going to make the animations of our characters match these moments, for example, we will create the illusion that they are actually walking.

Scripting visual feedback

Visual feedback is the concept of using different VFX, such as particles and a VFX Graph, to reinforce what is happening. For example, say right now we are shooting and we know that this is happening because we can see the bullet. It doesn't exactly feel like shooting as a proper shooting simulation needs our gun to show the muzzle flash effect. Another example would be the enemy dying—it just despawns! That doesn't feel as satisfying as it should be. We can instead add a little explosion (considering they are robots).

Let's start making our enemies spawn an explosion when they die by doing the following:

1. Create an explosion effect or download one from the Asset Store. It shouldn't loop and it needs to be destroyed automatically when the explosion is over (ensure **Looping** is unchecked and **Stop Action** is set to destroy in the main module).

2. Some explosions in the Asset Store might use non-URP-compatible shaders. You can fix them by setting the **Edit | Render Pipeline | Universal Render Pipeline | Upgrade Selected Materials** option to **UniversalRP Materials** while keeping the materials selected.

3. Manually upgrade the materials that didn't upgrade automatically.

4. Add a script to the Enemy prefab called ExplosionOnDeath. This will be responsible for spawning the particles Prefab when the enemy dies.

5. Add a field of the `GameObject` type called `particlePrefab` and drag the explosion Prefab to it.

> **Important note:**
>
> You may be expecting to add the explosion spawning to the `Life` component. In that case, you are assuming that anything to do with life will spawn a particle when dying, but consider scenarios where characters die with a falling animation instead, or maybe an object that just despawns with no effect whatsoever. If a certain behavior is not used in most scenarios, it is better to code it in a separate optional script to allow us to mix and match different components and get the exact behavior we want.

6. Make the script access the `Life` component and subscribe to its `onDeath` event.

7. In the `listener` function, spawn the particle system in the same location:

```csharp
public class ExplosionOnDeath : MonoBehaviour
{
    public GameObject particlePrefab;

    void Awake()
    {
        var life = GetComponent<Life>();
        life.onDeath.AddListener(OnDeath);
    }

    void OnDeath()
    {
        Instantiate(particlePrefab, transform.position, transform.rotation);
    }
}
```

Figure 17.21 – The explosion spawner script

As you can see, we are just using the same concepts we learned about in previous chapters, but combining them in new ways. This is what programming is all about. Let's continue with the muzzle effect, which will also be a particle system, but we will take another approach this time.

8. Download a weapon model from the Asset Store and instantiate it so that it is the parent of the hand of the player. Remember that our character is rigged and has a hand bone, so you should put the weapon there:

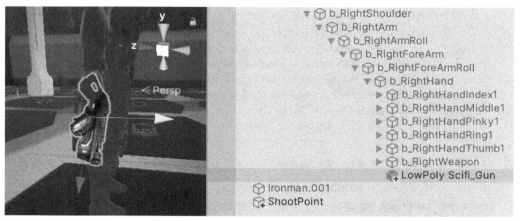

Figure 17.22 – Parenting a weapon in the hand bone

9. Create or get a muzzle particle system. In this case, my muzzle particle system was created as a short particle system that has a burst of particles and then automatically stops. Try to get one with that behavior because there are others out there that will loop instead, and the script to handle that scenario would be different.

10. Create an instance of the particle system Prefab in the Editor and parent it inside the weapon, locating it in front of the weapon, aligned with the barrel of the gun. Make sure the **Play On Awake** property of the main module of the particle system is unchecked; we don't want the muzzle to fire until we press the fire key:

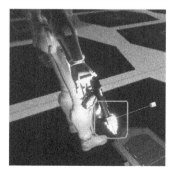

Figure 17.23 – The muzzle parented to the weapon

11. Create a field of the `ParticleSystem` type called `muzzleEffect` in `PlayerShooting` and drag the muzzle effect that is parented in the gun to it. Now, we have a reference to the `ParticleSystem` component of the muzzle to manage it.

12. Inside the `if` statement that checks whether we are shooting, execute `muzzleEffect.Play();` to play the particle system. It will automatically stop and is short enough to finish between key pressures:

```
public GameObject prefab;
public GameObject shootPoint;
public ParticleSystem muzzleEffect;
public int bulletsAmount;

void Update()
{
    if (Input.GetKeyDown(KeyCode.Mouse0) && bulletsAmount > 0 && Time.timeScale > 0)
    {
        bulletsAmount--;
        muzzleEffect.Play();

        GameObject clone = Instantiate(prefab);
        clone.transform.position = shootPoint.transform.position;
        clone.transform.rotation = shootPoint.transform.rotation;
    }
}
```

Figure 17.24 – The muzzle parented to the weapon

> **Important note:**
> Here, we again have the same question: Will all the weapons have a muzzle when shooting? In this scenario, I would say yes due to the scope of our project, so I will keep the code as it is. However, in the future, you can create an `onShoot` event if you need other components to know whether this script is shooting. This way, you can extend the shooting behavior. Consider using events as a way of enabling plugins in your script.

Now that we have some VFX in place, let's add sound effects.

Scripting audio feedback

VFX added a good depth of immersion to what is happening in the game, but we can improve this even further with sound. Let's start adding sound to the explosion effect by doing the following:

1. Download an explosion sound effect.

2. Select the explosion prefab and add **Audio Source** to it.

3. Set the downloaded explosion's audio clip as the **AudioClip** property of the audio source.

4. Make sure **Play On Awake** is checked and **Loop** is unchecked under **Audio Source**.

5. Set the **Spatial Blend** slider to **3D** and test the sound, configuring the **3D Sound** settings as needed:

Figure 17.25 – Adding sound to the explosion

As you can see here, we didn't need to use any script. As the sound is added to the Prefab, it will be played automatically in the very moment the prefab is instantiated. Now, let's integrate the shooting sound by doing the following:

6. Download a shooting sound and add it through an audio source to the weapon of the player, this time unchecking the **Play On Awake** checkbox and again setting **Spatial Blend** to **3D**.

7. In the `PlayerShooting` script, create a field of the `AudioSource` type called `shootSound` and drag the weapon to this property to connect the script with the `AudioSource` variable in the weapon.

8. In the `if` statement that checks whether we can shoot, add the `shootSound.Play();` line to execute the sound when shooting, using the same logic applied to the particle system:

```
public GameObject prefab;
public GameObject shootPoint;
public ParticleSystem muzzleEffect;
public AudioSource shootSound;
public int bulletsAmount;

void Update()
{
    if (Input.GetKeyDown(KeyCode.Mouse0) && bulletsAmount > 0 && Time.timeScale > 0)
    {
        bulletsAmount--;
        muzzleEffect.Play();
        shootSound.Play();
```

Figure 17.27 – Adding sound when shooting

Another approach to this would be the same as the one we did with the explosion; just add the shooting sound to the bullet, but if the bullet collides with a wall, soon enough the sound will be cut off. Or, if in the future we want an automatic weapon sound, it will need to be implemented as a single looping sound that starts when we press the relevant key and stops when we release it. This way, we prevent too many sound instances from overlapping when we shoot too many bullets. Take into account those kinds of scenarios when choosing the approach to script your feedback.

Now that we have finished with our audio feedback, let's finish integrating our animation assets, which we prepared in *Chapter 12, Creating Animations with Animator, Cinemachine, and Timeline*.

Scripting animations

In *Chapter 12*, *Creating Animations with Animator, Cinemachine, and Timeline*, we created an animator controller as a way to integrate several animations, and we also added parameters to it to control when the transitions between animations should execute. Now, it is time to do some scripting to make these parameters be affected by the actual behavior of the player and match the player's current state by doing the following:

1. In the `PlayerShooting` script, add a reference to `Animator` using `GetComponent` in `Awake` and cache it in a field:

```csharp
Animator animator;

void Awake()
{
    animator = GetComponent<Animator>();
}
```

Figure 17.28 – Caching the Animator reference

2. Call the `animator.SetBool("Shooting", true);` function in the `if` statement that checks whether we are shooting, and add the same function but pass `false` as a second argument in the `else` clause of the `if` statement. This function will modify the `"Shooting"` parameter of the animator controller:

```csharp
void Update()
{
    if (Input.GetKeyDown(KeyCode.Mouse0) && bulletsAmount > 0 && Time.timeScale > 0)
    {
        animator.SetBool("Shooting", true);
        bulletsAmount--;
        muzzleEffect.Play();
        shootSound.Play();

        GameObject clone = Instantiate(prefab);
        clone.transform.position = shootPoint.transform.position;
        clone.transform.rotation = shootPoint.transform.rotation;
    }
    else
    {
        animator.SetBool("Shooting", false);
    }
}
```

Figure 17.29 – Setting the Shooting Boolean depending on whether we are shooting

If you test this, you may notice an error—the animation is not playing. If you check the script, you will notice that it will be `true` just for one frame as we are using `GetKeyDown`, so the Shooting Boolean will immediately be set to `false` in the next frame. One solution of the several that we can implement here would be to make our shooting script repeat the shooting action while pressing the key instead of releasing and clicking again to shoot another bullet.

3. Check the following screenshot for the solution and try to understand the logic:

```
float lastShootTime;
public float fireRate;

void Update()
{
    if (Input.GetKey(KeyCode.Mouse0) && bulletsAmount > 0 && Time.timeScale > 0)
    {
        animator.SetBool("Shooting", true);

        var timeSinceLastShoot :float  = Time.time - lastShootTime;
        if(timeSinceLastShoot < fireRate)
            return;

        lastShootTime = Time.time;

        bulletsAmount--;
        muzzleEffect.Play();
        shootSound.Play();

        GameObject clone = Instantiate(prefab);
        clone.transform.position = shootPoint.transform.position;
        clone.transform.rotation = shootPoint.transform.rotation;
    }
    else
    {
        animator.SetBool("Shooting", false);
    }
}
```

Figure 17.30 – Repetitive shooting script

As you can see, our script now uses `GetKey` to keep shooting while keeping the shoot button pressed, and to prevent shooting in every frame, we compare the current time against the last shoot time to check how much time has passed since the last shot. We created the `fireRate` field to control the time between shots.

For the animator controller's `Velocity` parameter, we can detect the magnitude of the velocity vector of `Rigidbody`, in meters per second, and set that as the current value. This can be perfectly separated from the `PlayerMovement` script, so we can reuse this if necessary in other scenarios. So, we need a script such as the following, which just connects the `Rigidbody` component's velocity with the `animator Velocity` parameter:

```
using UnityEngine;

public class VelocityAnimator : MonoBehaviour
{
    Rigidbody rb;
    Animator animator;

    void Awake()
    {
        rb = GetComponent<Rigidbody>();
        animator = GetComponent<Animator>();
    }

    void Update()
    {
        animator.SetFloat("Velocity", rb.velocity.magnitude);
    }
}
```

Figure 17.31 – Repetitive shooting script

You may need to increase the `0.01` transitions threshold used so far a bit in the conditions of the transitions of the animator controller because `Rigidbody` keeps moving after releasing the keys. Using `1` worked perfectly for me. Another option would be to increase the drag and the velocity of the player to make the character stop faster. Pick whatever method works best for you.

As you can see, we can gather data about the actual movement and shooting action of our player to inform the animator controller of its state so that it can react accordingly.

Summary

Feedback is an important topic in video games. It gives valuable information to the player, such as the location of enemies if there is a 3D sound setup, distant shooting depicted by muzzle flashes in the background, life bars indicating that the player is about to die, animations that react according to the player's movements, and so on. In this chapter, we saw different forms of feedback, sounds, VFX, animations, and the UI, which we already created in *Part 2* of this book. Here, we learned how to use scripting to connect the UI to the game.

Now, you can script the UI, particle systems, and sounds to react to the game status, including changing the score text or the life bars of the UI or playing particle and sound effects when the character shoots. This improves the player's immersion experience in your game.

In the next chapter, we are going to discuss how to create a challenging AI for our enemies.

18
Implementing Game AI for Building Enemies

What is a game if not a great challenge to the player, who needs to use their character's abilities to tackle different scenarios? Each game imposes different kinds of obstacles to the Player, and the main one in our game is the enemies. Creating challenging and believable enemies can be complex, they need to behave like real characters and to be smart enough to not be easy to kill, but also easy enough that they are not impossible to kill either. We are going to use basic but good enough AI techniques to accomplish exactly that.

In this chapter, we will examine the following AI concepts:

- Gathering information with sensors
- Making decisions with FSMs
- Executing FSM actions

Gathering information with sensors

An AI works first by taking in info about its surroundings, then that data is analyzed to determine an action and finally, the chosen action is executed, and as you can see, we cannot do anything without information, so let's start with that part. There are several sources of information our AI can use, such as data about itself (life and bullets) or maybe some game state (winning condition or remaining enemies), which can be easily found with the code we saw so far, but one important source of information is also the AI senses. According to the needs of our game, we might need different senses such as sight and hearing, but in our case, sight will be enough, so let's learn how to code that.

In this section, we will examine the following sensor concepts:

- Creating Three-Filters sensors
- Debugging with Gizmos

Let's start seeing how to create a sensor with the Three-Filters approach.

Creating Three-Filters sensors

The common way to code senses is through a Three-Filters approach to discard enemies out of sight. The first filter is a distance filter, which will discard enemies too far away to be seen, then the angle check, which will check enemies inside our viewing cone, and finally a raycast check, which will discard enemies that are being occluded by obstacles such as walls. Before starting, a word of advice: we will be using vector mathematics here, and covering those topics in-depth is outside the scope of this book. If you don't understand something, feel free to just copy and paste the code in the screenshot and look up those concepts online. Let's code sensors the following way:

1. Create an empty GameObject called **AI** as a child of the **Enemy** Prefab. You need to first open the Prefab to modify its children (double-click the Prefab). Remember to set the transform of this Object to **position** (0,0,0), **rotation** (0,0,0), and **scale** (1,1,1) so it will be aligned to the Enemy. While we can certainly just put all AI scripts directly in the Enemy, we did this just for separation and organization:

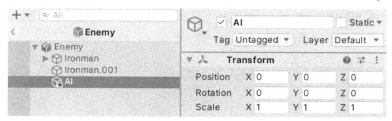

Figure 18.1 – AI scripts container

2. Create a script called `Sight` and add it to the AI child Object.

3. Create two fields of the `float` type called `distance` and `angle`, and another two of the `LayerMask` type called `obstaclesLayers` and `ObjectsLayers`. `distance` will be used as the vision distance, angle will determine the amplitude of the view cone, `ObstacleLayers` will be used by our obstacle check to determine which Objects are considered obstacles, and `ObjectsLayers` will be used to determine what types of Objects we want the sight to detect. We just want the sight to see enemies; we are not interested in Objects such as walls or power-ups. `LayerMask` is a property type that allows us to select one or more layers to use inside code, so we will be filtering Objects by layer. In a moment, you will see how we use it:

```
using UnityEngine;

public class Sight : MonoBehaviour
{
    public float distance;
    public float angle;
    public LayerMask objectsLayers;
    public LayerMask obstaclesLayers;
}
```

Figure 18.2 – Fields to parametrize our sight check

4. In `Update`, call `Physics.OverlapSphere` as in the next screenshot. This function creates an imaginary sphere in the place specified by the first parameter (in our case, our position) and with a radius specified in the second parameter (the `distance` property) to detect Objects with the layers specified in the third parameter (`ObjectsLayers`). It will return an array with all Objects Colliders found inside the sphere, these functions use Physics to do the check, so the Objects must have at least one collider. This is the way we will be using to get all enemies inside our view distance, and we will be further filtering them in the next steps.

> **Important Note**
>
> Another way of accomplishing the first check is to just check the distance to the Player, or if looking for other kinds of Objects, to a Manager containing a list of them, but the way we chose is more versatile and can be used in any kind of Object.
>
> Also, you might want to check the `Physics.OverlapSphereNonAlloc` version of this function, which does the same thing but is more performant by not allocating an array to return the results.

5. Iterate over the array of Objects returned by the function:

```
void Update()
{
    Collider[] colliders = Physics.OverlapSphere(transform.position, distance, objectsLayers);

    for (int i = 0; i < colliders.Length; i++)
    {
        Collider collider = colliders[i];
    }
}
```

Figure 18.3 – Getting all Objects at a certain distance

6. To detect whether the Object falls inside the vision cone, we need to calculate the angle between our viewing direction and the direction to the Object itself. If the angle between those two directions is less than our cone angle, we consider that the Object falls inside our vision. We can start detecting the direction toward the Object, which is calculated normalizing the difference between the Object position and ours, like in the following screenshot. You might notice we used bounds. center instead of transform.position; this way, we check the direction to the center of the Object instead of its pivot. Remember that the Player's pivot is in the ground and the ray check might collide against it before the Player:

```
Vector3 directionToCollider = Vector3.Normalize(collider.bounds.center - transform.position);
```

Figure 18.4 – Calculating direction from our position toward the collider

7. We can use the Vector3.Angle function to calculate the angle between two directions. In our case, we can calculate the angle between the direction toward the Enemy and our forward vector to see the angle:

```
float angleToCollider = Vector3.Angle(transform.forward, directionToCollider);
```

Figure 18.5 – Calculating the angle between two directions

> **IMPORTANT INFO**
>
> If you want, you can instead use `Vector3.Dot`, which will execute a dot product. `Vector3.Angle` actually uses that one, but to convert the result of the dot product into an angle, it needs to use trigonometry and this can be expensive to calculate. Anyway, our approach is simpler and fast while you don't have a big number of sensors (50+, depending on the target device), which won't happen in our case.

8. Now check whether the calculated angle is less than the one specified in the `angle` field. Consider that if we set an angle of 90 degrees, it will be actually 180 degrees, because if the `Vector3.Angle` function returns, as an example, 30, it can be 30 to the left or the right. If our angle says 90 degrees, it can be both 90 degrees to the left or to the right, so it will detect Objects in a 180-degree arc.

9. Use the `Physics.Line` function to create an imaginary line between the first and the second parameter (our position and the collider position) to detect Objects with the layers specified in the third parameter (the `obstacles` layers) and return `boolean` indicating whether that ray hit something or not. The idea is to use the line to detect whether there are any obstacles between ourselves and the detected collider, and if there is no obstacle, this means that we have a direct line of sight toward the Object. Again, remember that this function depends on the obstacle Objects having colliders, which in our case, we have (walls, floor, and so on):

```
if (angleToCollider < angle)
{
    if (!Physics.Linecast(transform.position, collider.bounds.center, obstaclesLayers))
    {

    }
}
```

Figure 18.6 – Using a Line Cast to check obstacles between the sensor and the target Object

10. If the Object passes the three checks that means that this is the Object we are currently seeing, so we can save it inside a field of the `Collider` type called `detectedObject`, to save that information for later usage by the rest of the AI scripts. Consider using `break` to stop `for` that is iterating the colliders to prevent wasting resources by checking the other Objects, and to set `detectedObject` to `null` before `for` to clear the result from the previous frame, so in case, in this frame, we don't detect anything, it will keep the null value so we can notice that there is nothing in the sensor:

```csharp
public float distance;
public float angle;
public LayerMask objectsLayers;
public LayerMask obstaclesLayers;

public Collider detectedObject;

void Update()
{
    Collider[] colliders = Physics.OverlapSphere(transform.position, distance, objectsLayers);

    detectedObject = null;
    for (int i = 0; i < colliders.Length; i++)
    {
        Collider collider = colliders[i];

        Vector3 directionToCollider = Vector3.Normalize(collider.bounds.center - transform.position);

        float angleToCollider = Vector3.Angle(transform.forward, directionToCollider);

        if (angleToCollider < angle)
        {
            if (!Physics.Linecast(transform.position, collider.bounds.center, obstaclesLayers))
            {
                detectedObject = collider;
                break;
            }
        }
    }
}
```

Figure 18.7 – Full sensor script

> **IMPORTANT INFO**
>
> In our case, we are using the sensor just to look for the Player, the only Object the sensor is in charge of looking for, but if you want to make the sensor more advanced, you can just keep a list of detected Objects, placing inside it every Object that passes the three tests instead of just the first one.

11. In the Editor, configure the sensor as you wish. In this case, we will set `ObjectsLayer` to `Player` so our sensor will focus its search on Objects with that layer, and `obstaclesLayer` to `Default`, the layer we used for walls and floors:

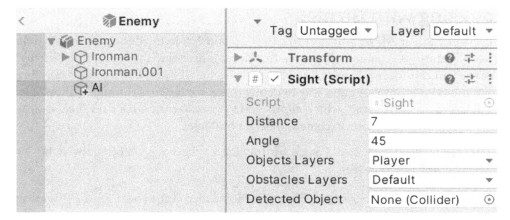

Figure 18.8 – Sensor settings

12. To test this, just place an Enemy with a movement speed of 0 in front of the Player, select its AI child Object and then play the game to see how the property is set in the Inspector. Also, try putting an obstacle between the two and check that the property says "None" (null). If you don't get the expected result, double-check your script, its configuration, and whether the Player has the Player layer and the obstacles have the Default layer. Also, you might need to raise the AI Object a little bit to prevent the ray from starting below the ground and hitting it:

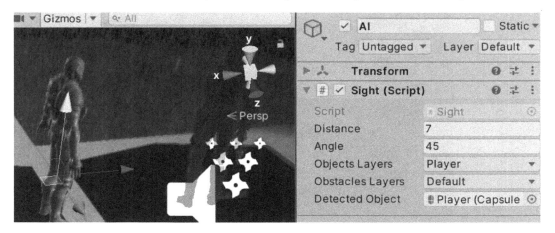

Figure 18.9 – The sensor capturing the Player

Even if we have our sensor working, sometimes checking whether it's working or configured properly requires some visual aids we can create using Gizmos.

Debugging with Gizmos

As we will create our AI, we will start to detect certain errors in edge cases, usually related to misconfigurations. You may think that the Player falls inside the sight of the Enemy but maybe you cannot see that the line of sight is occluded by an Object, especially as the enemies move constantly. A good way to debug those scenarios is through Editor-only visual aids known as Gizmos, which allows you to visualize invisible data such as the sight distance or the line casts executed to detect obstacles.

Let's start seeing how to create Gizmos by drawing a sphere representing the sight distance by doing the following:

1. In the Sight script, create an event function called OnDrawGizmos. This event is only executed in the Editor (not in builds) and is the place Unity asks us to draw Gizmos.

2. Use the Gizmos.DrawWireSphere function passing our position as the first parameter and the distance as the second parameter to draw a sphere in our position with the radius of our distance. You can check how the size of the Gizmo changes as you change the distance field:

Figure 18.10 – Sphere Gizmo

3. Optionally, you can change the color of the Gizmo, setting Gizmos.color prior to calling the drawing functions:

```
void OnDrawGizmos()
{
    Gizmos.color = Color.red;
    Gizmos.DrawWireSphere(transform.position, distance);
}
```

Figure 18.11 – Gizmos drawing code

> **IMPORTANT INFO**
>
> Now you are drawing Gizmos constantly, and if you have lots of enemies,
> they can pollute the scene view with too many Gizmos. In that case, try the
> OnDrawGizmosSelected event function instead, which draws Gizmos
> only if the Object is selected.

4. We can draw the lines representing the cone using Gizmos.DrawRay, which
    receives the origin of the line to draw and the direction of the line, which can be
    multiplied by a certain value to specify the length of the line, as in the following
    screenshot:

```
Vector3 rightDirection = Quaternion.Euler(0, angle, 0) * transform.forward;
Gizmos.DrawRay(transform.position, rightDirection * distance);

Vector3 leftDirection = Quaternion.Euler(0, -angle, 0) * transform.forward;
Gizmos.DrawRay(transform.position, leftDirection * distance);
```

Figure 18.12 – Drawing rotated lines

5. In the screenshot, we used Quaternion.Euler to generate a quaternion based
    on the angles we want to rotate. If you multiply this quaternion by a direction,
    we will get the rotated direction. We are taking our forward vector and rotating it
    according to the angle field to generate our cone vision lines. Also, we multiply this
    direction by the sight distance to draw the line as far as our sight can see; you will
    see how the line matches the end of the sphere this way:

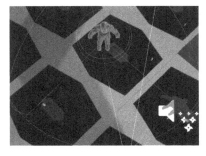

Figure 18.13 – Vision Angle lines

We can also draw the line casts, which check the obstacles, but as those depend on the current situation of the game, such as the Objects that pass the first two checks and their positions, we can use `Debug.DrawLine` instead, which can be executed in the `Update` method. This version of `DrawLine` is designed to be used in runtime only. The `Gizmos` we saw also executes in the Editor. Let's try them the following way:

1. First, let's debug the scenario where `LineCast` didn't detect any obstacles, so we need to draw a line between our sensor and the Object. We can call `Debug.DrawLine` in the `if` statement that calls `LineCast`, as in the following screenshot:

```
if (!Physics.Linecast(transform.position, collider.bounds.center, obstaclesLayers))
{
    Debug.DrawLine(transform.position, collider.bounds.center, Color.green);
    detectedObject = collider;
    break;
}
```

Figure 18.14 – Drawing a line in Update

2. In the next screenshot, you can see `DrawLine` in action:

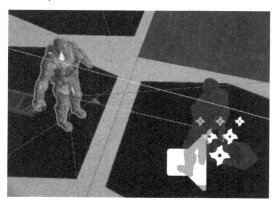

Figure 18.15 – Line toward the detected Object

3. We also want to draw a line in red when the sight is occluded by an Object. In this case, we need to know where the Line Cast hit, so we can use an overload of the function, which provides an `out` parameter that gives us more information about what the line collided with, such as the position of the hit and the normal and the collided Object, as in the following screenshot:

```
if (!Physics.Linecast(transform.position, collider.bounds.center, out RaycastHit hit, obstaclesLayers))
{
```

Figure 18.16 – Getting information about Linecast

> **IMPORTANT INFO**
>
> Consider that `Linecast` doesn't always collide with the nearest obstacle but with the first Object it detects in the line, which can vary in order. If you need to detect the nearest obstacle, look for the `Physics.Raycast` version of the function.

4. We can use that information to draw the line from our position to the hit point in the `else` clause of the `if` sentence, when the line collides with something:

```
if (!Physics.Linecast(transform.position, collider.bounds.center, out RaycastHit hit, obstaclesLayers))
{
    Debug.DrawLine(transform.position, collider.bounds.center, Color.green);
    detectedObject = collider;
    break;
}
else
{
    Debug.DrawLine(transform.position, hit.point, Color.red);
}
```

Figure 18.17 – Drawing a line in case we have an obstacle

5. In the next screenshot, you can see the results:

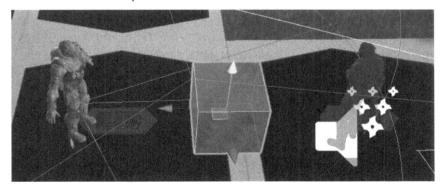

Figure 18.18 – Line when an obstacle occludes vision

Now that we have our sensors completed, let's use the information provided by them to make decisions with **Finite State Machines (FSMs)**.

Making decisions with FSMs

We explored the concept of FSMs in the past when we used them in the Animator. We learned that an FSM is a collection of states, each one representing an action that an Object can be executing at a time, and a set of transitions that dictates how the states are switched. This concept is not only used in Animation but in a myriad of programming scenarios, and one of the common ones is in AI. We can just replace the animations with AI code in the states and we have an AI FSM.

In this section, we will examine the following AI FSM concepts:

- Creating the FSM
- Creating transitions

Let's start creating our FSM skeleton.

Creating the FSM

To create our own FSM, we need to recap some basic concepts. Remember that an FSM can have a state for each possible action it can execute and that only one can be executed at a time. In terms of AI, we can be Patrolling, Attacking, Fleeing, and so on. Also, remember that there are transitions between States that determine conditions to be met to change from one state to the other, and in terms of AI, this can be the user being near the Enemy to start attacking or life being low to start fleeing. In the next screenshot, you can find a simple reminder example of the two possible states of a door:

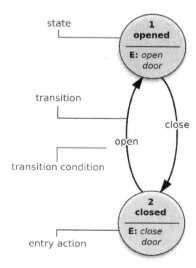

Figure 18.19 – FSM example

There are several ways to implement FSMs for AI; you can even use the Animator if you want to or download some FSM system from the Asset Store. In our case, we are going to take the simplest approach possible, a single script with a set of If sentences, which can be basic but is still a good start to understand the concept. Let's implement it by doing the following:

1. Create a script called EnemyFSM in the AI child Object of the Enemy.

2. Create enum called EnemyState with the GoToBase, AttackBase, ChasePlayer, and AttackPlayer values. We are going to have those states in our AI.

3. Create a field of the EnemyState type called currentState, which will hold, well, the current state of our Enemy:

```
public class EnemyFSM : MonoBehaviour
{
    public enum EnemyState { GoToBase, AttackBase, ChasePlayer, AttackPlayer }

    public EnemyState currentState;
```

Figure 18.20 – EnemyFSM states definition

4. Create three functions named after the states we defined.

5. Call those functions in Update depending on the current state:

```
void Update()
{
    if(currentState == EnemyState.GoToBase)
        GoToBase();
    else if(currentState == EnemyState.AttackBase)
        AttackBase();
    else if(currentState == EnemyState.ChasePlayer)
        ChasePlayer();
    else if(currentState == EnemyState.AttackPlayer)
        AttackPlayer();
}

void GoToBase() {print("GoToBase"); }
void AttackBase() { print("AttackBase"); }
void ChasePlayer() { print("ChasePlayer"); }
void AttackPlayer() { print("AttackPlayer"); }
```

Figure 18.21 – If-based FSM

> **IMPORTANT INFO**
> Yes, you can totally use a switch here, but I just prefer the regular `if` syntax.

6. Test in the Editor how changing the `currentState` field will change which state is active, seeing the messages being printed in the console:

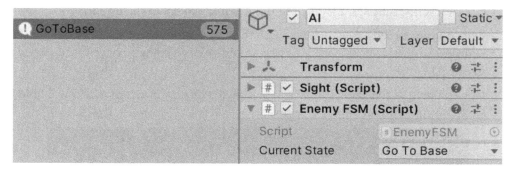

Figure 18.22 – States testing

As you can see, it is a pretty simple but totally functional approach, so let's continue with this FSM, creating its transitions.

Creating transitions

If you remember the transitions created in the Animator Controller, those were basically a collection of conditions that are checked if the state the transition belongs to is active. In our FSM approach, this translates simply as If sentences that detect conditions inside the states. Let's create the transitions between our proposed states as follows:

1. Add a field of the `Sight` type called `sightSensor` in our FSM script, and drag the AI GameObject to that field to connect it to the `Sight` component there. As the FSM component is in the same Object as `Sight`, we can also use `GetComponent` instead, but in advanced AIs, you might have different sensors that detect different Objects, so I prefer to prepare my script for that scenario, but pick the approach you like the most.

2. In the `GoToBase` function, check whether the detected Object of the `Sight` component is not `null`, meaning that something is inside our line of vision. If our AI is going toward the base but detects an Object in the way there, we must switch to the `Chase` state to pursue the Player, so we change the state, as in the following screenshot:

```
public Sight sightSensor;

void GoToBase()
{
    if (sightSensor.detectedObject != null)
    {
        currentState = EnemyState.ChasePlayer;
    }
}
```

Figure 18.23 – Creating transitions

3. Also, we must change to `AttackBase` in case we are near enough the Object that must be damaged to decrease the base life. We can create a field of the `Transform` type called `baseTransform` and drag the Base Life Object there so we can check the distance. Remember to add a `float` field called `baseAttackDistance` to make that distance configurable:

```
public Transform baseTransform;
public float baseAttackDistance;

void GoToBase()
{
    if (sightSensor.detectedObject != null)
        currentState = EnemyState.ChasePlayer;

    float distanceToBase = Vector3.Distance(transform.position, baseTransform.position);
    if (distanceToBase <= baseAttackDistance)
        currentState = EnemyState.AttackBase;
}
```

Figure 18.24 – Go to Base Transitions

4. In the case of `ChasePlayer`, we need to check whether the Player is out of sight to switch back to the `GoToBase` state or whether we are near enough the `Player` to start attacking it. We will need another `distance` field, which determines the distance to attack the Player, and we might want different attack distances for those two targets. Consider an early return in the transition to prevent getting `null` reference exceptions if we try to access the position of the sensor-detected Object when there is none:

```
void ChasePlayer()
{
    if (sightSensor.detectedObject == null)
    {
        currentState = EnemyState.GoToBase;
        return;
    }

    float distanceToPlayer = Vector3.Distance(transform.position, sightSensor.detectedObject.transform.position);
    if (distanceToPlayer <= playerAttackDistance)
        currentState = EnemyState.AttackPlayer;
}
```

Figure 18.25 – Chase Player Transitions

5. For `AttackPlayer`, we need to check whether `Player` is out of sight to get back to `GoToBase` or whether it is far enough to go back to chasing it. You can notice how we multiplied `PlayerAttackDistance` to make the stop-attacking distance a little bit larger than the start-attacking distance; this will prevent switching back and forth rapidly between attack and chase when the Player is near that distance. You can make it configurable instead of hardcoding `1.1`:

```
void AttackPlayer()
{
    if (sightSensor.detectedObject == null)
    {
        currentState = EnemyState.GoToBase;
        return;
    }

    float distanceToPlayer = Vector3.Distance(transform.position, sightSensor.detectedObject.transform.position);
    if (distanceToPlayer > playerAttackDistance * 1.1f)
        currentState = EnemyState.ChasePlayer;
}
```

Figure 18.26 – Attack Player Transitions

6. In our case, `AttackBase` won't have any transition. Once the Enemy is near enough the base to attack it, it will stay like that, even if the Player starts shooting at it. Its only objective once there is to destroy the base.

7. Remember you can use `Gizmos` to draw the distances:

```
void OnDrawGizmos()
{
    Gizmos.color = Color.blue;
    Gizmos.DrawWireSphere(transform.position, playerAttackDistance);

    Gizmos.color = Color.yellow;
    Gizmos.DrawWireSphere(transform.position, baseAttackDistance);
}
```

Figure 18.27 – FSM Gizmos

8. Test the script selecting the AI Object prior to hitting play and then move the Player around, checking how the states change in the inspector. You can also keep the original print messages in each state to see them changing in the console. Remember to set the attack distances and the references to the Objects. In the screenshot, you can see the settings we use:

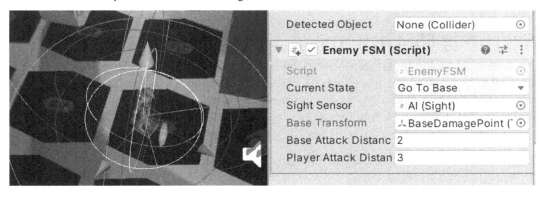

Figure 18.28 – Enemy FSM settings

A little problem that we will have now is that the spawned enemies won't have the needed references to make the distance calculations toward the Base Transform. You will notice that if you try to apply the changes on the Enemy of the scene to the Prefab (**Overrides | Apply All**), the Base Transform will say `None`. Remember that Prefabs cannot contain references to Objects in the scene, which complicates our work here. One alternative would be to create `BaseManager`, a Singleton that holds the reference to the damage position, so our `EnemyFSM` can access it. Another one could be to make use of functions such as `GameObject.Find` to find our Object.

In this case, we will try the latter. Even if it can be less performant than the Manager version, I want to show you how to use it to expand your Unity toolset. In this case, just set the `baseTransform` field in `Awake` to the return of `GameObject.Find`, using `BaseDamagePoint` as the first parameter, which will look for an Object called like that, as in the following screenshot. Also, feel free to remove the private keyword from the `baseTransform` field; now that is set via code, it makes little sense to display it in the Editor other than to debug it. You will see that now our wave-spawned enemies will change states:

```
Transform baseTransform;

void Awake()
{
    baseTransform = GameObject.Find("BaseDamagePoint").transform;
}
```

Figure 18.29 – Searching for an Object in the scene by name

Now that our FSM states are coded and transition properly, let's make them do something.

Executing FSM actions

Now we need to do the last step—make the FSM do something interesting. Here, we can do a lot of things such as shoot the base or the Player and move the Enemy toward its target (the Player or the base). We will be handling movement with the Unity Pathfinding system called `NavMesh`, a tool that allows our AI to calculate and traverse paths between two points avoiding obstacles, which needs some preparation to work properly.

In this section, we will examine the following FSM action concepts:

- Calculating our scene Pathfinding
- Using Pathfinding
- Adding final details

Let's start preparing our scene for movement with Pathfinding.

Calculating our scene Pathfinding

Pathfinding algorithms rely on simplified versions of the scene. Analyzing the full geometry of a complex scene is almost impossible to do in real time. There are several ways to represent Pathfinding information extracted from a scene, such as Graphs and NavMesh geometries. Unity uses the latter—a simplified mesh similar to a 3D model that spans over all areas that Unity determines are walkable. In the next screenshot, you can find an example of a NavMesh generated in a scene, that is, the light blue geometry:

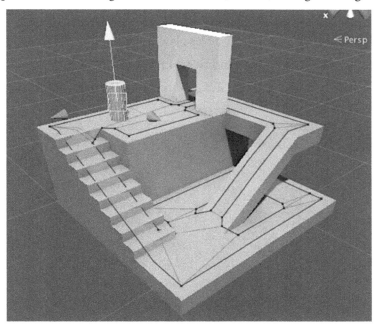

Figure 18.30 – NavMesh of walkable areas in the scene

Generating a NavMesh can take from seconds to minutes depending on the size of the scene. That's why Unity's Pathfinding system calculates that once in the Editor, so when we distribute our game, the user will use the pre-generated NavMesh. Just like Lightmapping, a NavMesh is baked into a file for later usage. Like Lightmapping, the main caveat here is that the NavMesh Objects cannot change during runtime. If you destroy or move a floor tile, the AI will still walk over that area. The NavMesh on top of that didn't notice the floor isn't there anymore, so you are not able to move or modify those Objects in any way. Luckily, in our case, we won't suffer any modification of the scene during runtime, but remember that there are components such as NavMeshObsacle that can help us in those scenarios.

To generate a NavMesh for our scene, do the following:

1. Select any walkable Object and the obstacles on top of it, such as floors, walls, and other obstacles, and mark them as **Static**. You might remember that the **Static** checkbox also affects Lightmapping, so if you want an Object not to be part of Lightmapping but contribute to the NavMesh generation, you can click the arrow at the left of the static check and select **Navigation Static** only. Try to limit Navigation Static Objects to only the ones that the enemies will actually traverse to increase NavMesh generation speed. Making the Terrain navigable, in our case, will increase generation time a lot and we will never play in that area.

2. Open the NavMesh panel in **Window | AI | Navigation**.

3. Select the **Bake** tab and click the **Bake** button at the bottom of the window and check the generated NavMesh:

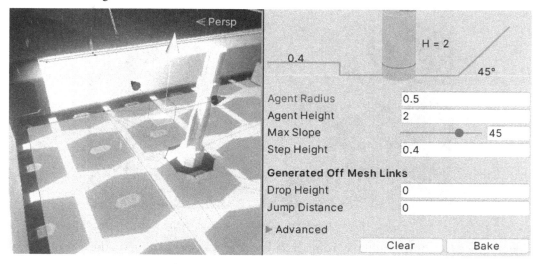

Figure 18.31 – Generating a NavMesh

And that's pretty much everything you need to do. Of course, there are lots of settings you can fiddle around with, such as **Max Slope**, which indicates the maximum angle of slopes the AI will be able to climb, or **Step Height**, which will determine whether the AI can climb stairs, connecting the floors between the steps in the NavMesh, but as we have a plain and simple scene, the default settings will suffice.

Now, let's make our AI move around the NavMesh.

Using Pathfinding

For making an AI Object that moves with `NavMesh`, Unity provides the `NavMeshAgent` component, which will make our AI stick to the `NavMesh`, preventing the Object to go outside it. It will not only calculate the Path to a specified destination automatically but also will move the Object through the path with the use of Steering behavior algorithms that mimic the way a human would move through the path, slowing down on corners and turning with interpolations instead of instantaneously. Also, this component is capable of evading other `NavMeshAgents` running in the scene, preventing all of the enemies from collapsing in the same position.

Let's use this powerful component by doing the following:

1. Select the Enemy Prefab and add the `NavMeshAgent` component to it. Add it to the root Object, the one called Enemy, not the AI child—we want the whole Object to move. You will see a cylinder around the Object representing the area the Object will occupy in the `NavMesh`. Remember that this isn't a collider, so it won't be used for physical collisions:

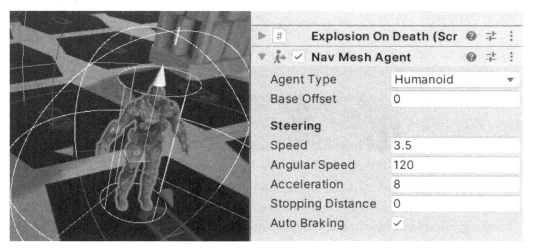

Figure 18.32 – The NavMeshAgent component

2. Remove the `ForwardMovement` component; from now on, we will drive the movement of our Enemy with `NavMeshAgent`.

3. In the `Awake` event function of the `EnemyFSM` script, use the `GetComponentInParent` function to cache the reference of `NavMeshAgent`. This will work similar to `GetComponent`—it will look for a component in our `GameObject`, but if the component is not there, this version will try to look for that component in all parents. Remember to add the `using UnityEngine.AI` line to use the `NavMeshAgent` class in this script:

```
NavMeshAgent agent;

void Awake()
{
    baseTransform = GameObject.Find("BaseDamagePoint").transform;
    agent = GetComponentInParent<NavMeshAgent>();
}
```

Figure 18.33 – Caching a parent component reference

IMPORTANT INFO

As you can imagine, there is `GetComponentInChildren`, which searches components in `GameObject` first and then in all its children if necessary.

---

4. In the `GoToBase` state function, call the `SetDestination` function of the `NavMeshAgent` reference, passing the position of the base Object as the target:

```
void GoToBase()
{
    agent.SetDestination(baseTransform.position);
}
```

Figure 18.34 – Setting a destination of our AI

5. Save the script and test this with a few enemies in the scene or with the enemies spawned by the waves. You will see the problem where the enemies will never stop going toward the target position, entering inside the Object, if necessary, even if the current state of their FSMs changes when they are near enough. That's because we never tell `NavMeshAgent` to stop, which we can do by setting the `isStopped` field of the agent to `true`. You might want to tweak the Base Attack Distance to make the Enemy stop a little bit nearer or further:

```
void AttackBase()
{
    agent.isStopped = true;
}
```

Figure 18.35 – Stopping agent movement

6. We can do the same for `ChasePlayer` and `AttackPlayer`. In `ChasePlayer`, we can set the destination of the agent to the Player position, and in Attack Player, we can stop the movement. In this scenario, Attack Player can go back again to `GoToBase` or `ChasePlayer`, so you need to set the `isStopped` agent field to `false` in those states or before doing the transition. We will pick the former, as that version will cover other states that also stop the agent without extra code. We will start with the `GoToBase` state:

```
void GoToBase()
{
    agent.isStopped = false;
    agent.SetDestination(baseTransform.position);
```

Figure 18.36 – Reactivating the agent

7. Then, continue with Chase Player:

```
void ChasePlayer()
{
    agent.isStopped = false;

    if (sightSensor.detectedObject == null)
    {
        currentState = EnemyState.GoToBase;
        return;
    }

    agent.SetDestination(sightSensor.detectedObject.transform.position);
```

Figure 18.37 – Reactivating the agent and chasing the Player

8. And finally, continue with Attack Player:

```
void AttackPlayer()
{
    agent.isStopped = true;
```

Figure 18.38 – Stopping the movement

9. You can tweak the **Acceleration, Speed,** and **Angular Speed** properties of
    `NavMeshAgent` to control how fast the Enemy will move. Also, remember
    to apply the changes to the Prefab for the spawned enemies to be affected.

Now that we have movement in our Enemy, let's finish the final details of our AI.

Adding final details

We have two things missing here, the Enemy is not shooting any bullets and it doesn't
have animations. Let's start fixing the shooting by doing the following:

1. Add a `bulletPrefab` field of the `GameObject` type to our `EnemyFSM` script
    and a `float` field called `fireRate`.

2. Create a function called `Shoot` and call it inside `AttackBase` and
    `AttackPlayer`:

```
void AttackPlayer()
{
    agent.isStopped = true;

    if (sightSensor.detectedObject == null)
    {
        currentState = EnemyState.GoToBase;
        return;
    }

    Shoot();

    float distanceToPlayer = Vector3.Distance(transform.position, sightSensor.detectedObject.transform.position);
    if (distanceToPlayer > playerAttackDistance * 1.1f)
        currentState = EnemyState.ChasePlayer;
}

void AttackBase()
{
    agent.isStopped = true;
    Shoot();
}

void Shoot()
{

}
```

Figure 18.39 – Shooting function calls

3. In the Shoot function, put a similar code as the one used in the PlayerShooting script to shoot bullets at a specific fire rate, as in the following screenshot. Remember to set the Enemy layer in your Enemy Prefab, in case you didn't before, to prevent the bullet from damaging the Enemy itself. You might also want to raise the AI script a little bit to shoot bullets in another position or, better, add a shootPoint transform field and create an empty Object in the Enemy to use as a spawn position. If you do that, consider making the empty Object to not be rotated so the Enemy rotation affects the direction of the bullet properly:

```
void Shoot()
{
    if (Time.timeScale > 0)
    {
        var timeSinceLastShoot :float = Time.time - lastShootTime;
        if(timeSinceLastShoot < fireRate)
            return;

        lastShootTime = Time.time;
        Instantiate(bulletPrefab, transform.position, transform.rotation);
    }
}
```

Figure 18.40 – Shooting function code

IMPORTANT INFO

Here, you find some duplicated shooting behavior between PlayerShooting and EnemyFSM. You can fix that by creating a Weapon behavior with a function called Shoot that instantiates bullets and takes into account the fire rate, and call it inside both components to re-utilize it.

4. When the agent is stopped, not only does the movement stop but also the rotation. If the Player moves while the Enemy is attacked, we still need the Enemy to face it to shoot bullets in its direction. We can create a `LookTo` function that receives the target position to look and call it in `AttackPlayer` and `AttackBase`, passing the target to shoot at:

```
    LookTo(sightSensor.detectedObject.transform.position);
    Shoot();

    float distanceToPlayer = Vector3.Distance(transform.position, sightSensor.detectedObject.transform.position);
    if (distanceToPlayer > playerAttackDistance * 1.1f)
        currentState = EnemyState.ChasePlayer;
}

void AttackBase()
{
    agent.isStopped = true;
    LookTo(baseTransform.position);
    Shoot();
}

void LookTo(Vector3 targetPosition)
{

}
```

Figure 18.41 – LookTo function calls

5. Complete the `LookTo` function by getting the direction of our parent to the target position, we access our parent with `transform.parent` because, remember, we are the child AI Object, the Object that will move is our parent. Then, we set the `Y` component of the direction to `0` to prevent the direction pointing upward or downward—we don't want our Enemy to rotate vertically. Finally, we set the forward vector of our parent to that direction so it will face the target position immediately. You can replace that with interpolation through quaternions to have a smoother rotation if you want to, but let's keep things as simple as possible for now:

```
void LookTo(Vector3 targetPosition)
{
    Vector3 directionToPosition = Vector3.Normalize(targetPosition - transform.parent.position);
    directionToPosition.y = 0;
    transform.parent.forward = directionToPosition;
}
```

Figure 18.42 – Looking toward a target

Finally, we can add animations to the Enemy using the same Animator Controller used in the Player and setting the parameters with other scripts in the following steps:

6. Add an `Animator` component to the Enemy, if it's not already there, and set the same Controller used in the Player; in our case, this is also called `Player`.

7. Create and add a script to the Enemy root Object called `NavMeshAnimator`, which will take the current velocity of `NavMeshAgent` and will set it to the Animator Controller. This will work similar to the `VelocityAnimator` script and is in charge of updating the Animator Controller `velocity` parameter to the velocity of our Object. We didn't use that one here because `NavMeshAgent` doesn't use `Rigidbody` to move. It has its own velocity system. We can actually set `Rigidbody` to `kinematic` if we want because of this, since it moves but not with Physics:

```csharp
using UnityEngine;
using UnityEngine.AI;

public class NavMeshAnimator : MonoBehaviour
{
    Animator animator;
    NavMeshAgent agent;

    void Awake()
    {
        animator = GetComponent<Animator>();
        agent = GetComponent<NavMeshAgent>();
    }

    void Update()
    {
        animator.SetFloat("Velocity", agent.velocity.magnitude);
    }
}
```

Figure 18.43 – Connecting the NavMeshAgent to our Animator Controller

8. Cache a reference to the parent `Animator` in the `EnemyFSM` script. Just do the same thing we did to access `NavMeshAgent`:

```
Animator animator;

void Awake()
{
    baseTransform = GameObject.Find("BaseDamagePoint").transform;
    agent = GetComponentInParent<NavMeshAgent>();
    animator = GetComponentInParent<Animator>();
}
```

Figure 18.44 – Accessing the parent's Animator reference

9. Turn on the `Shooting animator` parameter inside the `Shoot` function to make sure every time we shoot, that parameter is set to `true` (checked):

```
void Shoot()
{
    animator.SetBool("Shooting", true);
```

Figure 18.45 – Turning on the shooting animation

10. Turn off `boolean` in all non-shooting states, such as `GoToBase` and `ChasePlayer`:

```
void GoToBase()
{
    animator.SetBool("Shooting", false);
    agent.isStopped = false;

    agent.SetDestination(baseTransform.position);

    if (sightSensor.detectedObject != null)
        currentState = EnemyState.ChasePlayer;

    float distanceToBase = Vector3.Distance(transform.position, baseTransform.position);
    if (distanceToBase <= baseAttackDistance)
        currentState = EnemyState.AttackBase;
}


void ChasePlayer()
{
    animator.SetBool("Shooting", false);
    agent.isStopped = false;
```

Figure 18.46 – Turning off the shooting animation

With that, we have finished all AI behaviors. Of course, this script is big enough to deserve some rework and splitting in the future, and some actions such as stopping and resuming the animations and `NavMeshAgent` can be done in a better way. But with this, we have prototyped our AI, and we can test it until we are happy with it, and then we can improve this code.

Summary

I'm pretty sure AI is not what you imagined; you are not creating any SkyNet here, but we have accomplished a simple but interesting AI for challenging our Player, which we can iterate and tweak to tailor to our game's expected behavior. We saw how to gather our surrounding information through sensors to make decisions on what action to execute using FSMs, and using different Unity systems such as Pathfinding and Animator to make the AI execute those actions.

With this, we end *Part 2* of this book, about C# scripting. In the next short part, we are going to finish our game's final details, starting with optimization.

19

Scene Performance Optimization

Welcome to the third part of this book—I am glad you have reached this part as it means that you have almost completed a full game! In this chapter, we are going to discuss optimization techniques to review your game's performance and improve it, as having a good and constant framerate is vital to any game. Performance is a broad topic that requires a deep understanding of several Unity systems and could span several books. We are going to look at how to measure performance and explore the effects of our changes to systems to learn how they work through testing.

In this chapter, we will examine the following performance concepts:

- Optimizing graphics
- Optimizing processing
- Optimizing memory

By the end of this chapter, you will be able to gather performance data of the three main pieces of hardware that run your game—the GPU, CPU, and RAM. You will be able to analyze that data to detect possible performance issues and understand how to solve the most common ones.

Optimizing graphics

The most common cause of performance issues is related to the misuse of assets, especially on the graphics side, due to not having enough knowledge of how Unity's graphic engines work. We are going to explore how a GPU works at a high level and how to improve its usage.

In this section, we will examine the following graphics optimization concepts:

- Introduction to graphic engines
- Using Frame Debugger
- Using batching
- Other optimizations

We will start by looking at a high-level overview of how graphics are rendered to better understand the performance data that we will gather later in Frame Debugger. Based on the debugger's results, we are going to identify the areas that we can apply batching to (which is a technique to combine the rendering process of several objects, thereby reducing its cost), along with other common optimizations to keep in mind.

Introduction to graphic engines

Nowadays, every gaming device, whether it is a computer, a mobile device, or a console, has a video card—a set of hardware that specializes in graphics processing. It differs from a CPU in a subtle but important way. Graphics processing involves the processing of thousands of mesh vertices and the rendering of millions of pixels, so the GPU is designed to run short programs for a massive length of time, while the CPU can handle programs of any length but with limited parallelization capabilities. The reason for having those processing units is so that our program can use each one when needed.

The problem here is that graphics don't just rely on the GPU. The CPU is also involved in the process, making calculations and issuing commands to the GPU, so they must work together. For that to happen, both processing units need to communicate, and because they are (usually) physically separated, they need another piece of hardware to allow this—a bus, the most common type being the **Peripheral Component Interconnect Express** (**PCI Express**) bus.

PCI Express is a type of connection that allows massive amounts of data to be moved between the GPU and CPU, but the problem is that even if it's very fast, the communication time can be noticeable if you issue a lot of commands between both units. So, the key concept here is that graphics performance is improved mainly by reducing the communications between the GPU and CPU:

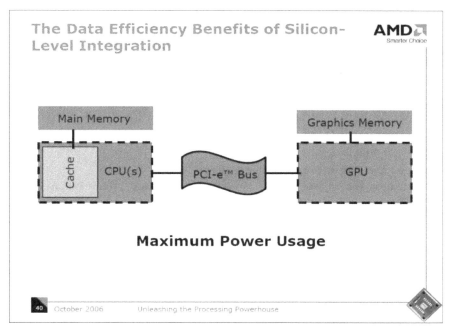

Figure 19.1 – CPU/GPU communication through a PCI Express bus

> **Important note**
>
> Nowadays, new hardware architecture allows the CPU and GPU to coexist in the same chipset, reducing its communication time and even sharing memory. Sadly, that architecture doesn't allow the necessary processing power needed for video games. It is likely that we will only see it applied to high-end gaming, but not in the near future, or even ever.

The basic algorithm of a graphics engine is to determine which objects are visible using culling algorithms, sorting and grouping them according to their similarities, and then issuing drawing commands to the GPU to render those groups of objects, sometimes more than once (as in *Chapter 8, Lighting Using Universal Render Pipeline*). Here, the main form of communication are those drawing commands, usually called **draw calls**, and our main task when optimizing graphics is to reduce them as much as we can. The problem is that there are several sources of draw calls that need to be considered, such as the lighting, and the scale of objects to see whether they are static or not. Studying every single one of them will take a long time, and even so, new versions of Unity can introduce new graphic features with their own draw calls. Instead, we will explore a way to discover these draw calls using Frame Debugger.

Using Frame Debugger

Frame Debugger is a tool that allows us to see a list of all the drawing commands or draw calls that the Unity rendering engine sends to the GPU. It not only lists them but also provides information about each draw call, including the data needed to detect optimization opportunities. By using **Frame Debugger**, we can see how our changes modify the number of draw calls, giving us immediate feedback on our efforts.

> **Important note**
> Note that reducing draw calls is sometimes not enough to improve performance, as each draw call can have different processing times; but usually, that difference is not big enough to consider. Also, in certain special rendering techniques, such as ray tracing or ray marching, a single draw call can drain all of our GPU power. This won't be the case in our game, so we won't take that into account right now.

Let's use Frame Debugger to analyze the rendering process of our game by doing the following:

1. Open Frame Debugger (**Window | Analysis | Frame Debugger**).

2. Play the game and if you want to analyze the performance, click the **Enable** button in the top-left corner of the window (press *Esc* to regain control of the mouse while playing):

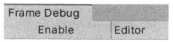

Figure 19.2 – Enabling Frame Debugger

3. Click on the **Game** tab to open the Game view.

> **Important note**
> Sometimes, it is useful to have both the **Scene** and **Game** panels in sight, which you can accomplish by dragging one of them to the bottom of Unity to have them separated and visible.

4. Drag the slider to the right of the **Disable** button slowly from left to right to see how the scene is rendered. Each step is a draw call that is being executed in the CPU for that given game frame. You can also observe how the list in the left part of the window highlights the name of the executed draw call at that moment:

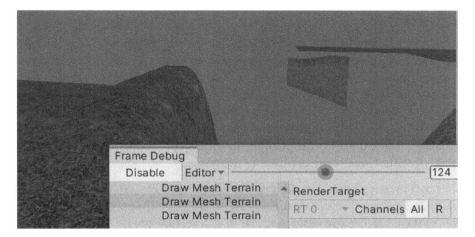

Figure 19.3 – Analyzing our frame's draw calls

5. Click on any draw call from the list and observe the details in the right part of the window.

    Most of them can be confusing to you if you are not used to code engines or shaders, but you can see that some of them have a human-readable part called **Why this draw call can't be batched with the previous one,** which tells you why two objects weren't drawn together in a single draw call. We will examine those reasons later:

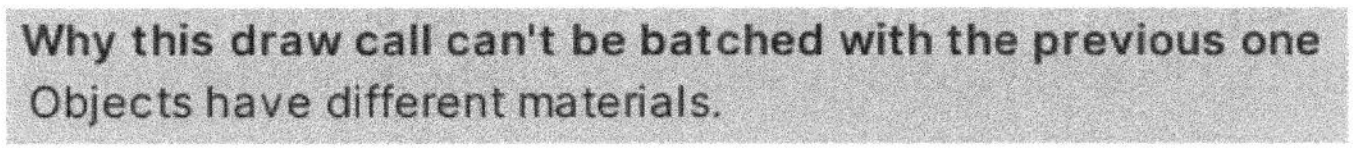

Figure 19.4 – The batching break reasons in Frame Debugger

6. With the window open in **Play** mode, disable the terrain and see how the amount of draw calls changes immediately. Sometimes, just turning objects on and off can be enough to detect what is causing performance issues. Also, try disabling postprocessing and other graphics-related objects, such as particles.

Even if we are not fully aware of what each one of these draw calls came from, we can at least start by modifying the settings throughout Unity to see the impact of those changes. There's no better way of discovering how something as massive as Unity works than going through every toggle and seeing the impact of those changes through a measuring tool.

Now, let's discuss the basic techniques for reducing draw calls and see their effects in Frame Debugger.

Using batching

We discussed several optimization techniques in previous chapters, with lighting being the most important one. If you measure the draw calls as you implement the techniques, you will notice the impact of those actions on the draw call count. However, in this section, we will focus on another graphics optimization technique known as batching. Batching is the process of grouping several objects to draw them together in a single draw call. You may be wondering why we can't just draw everything in a single draw call, and while that is technically possible, there is a set of conditions that need to be met in order to combine two objects, the usual case being combining materials.

Remember that materials are assets that act as graphic profiles, from specifying a **Material** mode or Shader and a set of parameters to customizing the aspect of our objects, and remember that we can use the same material in several objects. If Unity has to draw an object with a different material than the previous one, a SetPass call needs to be called before issuing its draw call, which is another form of CPU/GPU communication used to set the **Material** properties in the GPU, such as its textures and colors. If two objects use the same materials, this step can be skipped. The SetPass call from the first object is reused by the second, and that opens the opportunity to batch the objects. If they share the same settings, Unity can combine the meshes into a single one in the CPU, and then send the combined mesh in a single draw call to the GPU.

There are several ways to reduce the number of materials, such as removing duplicates, but the most effective way is through a concept called texture atlasing. This means merging textures from different objects into a single one. This way, several objects can use the same material due to the fact that the texture used there can be applied to several objects and an object that has its own texture requires its own material. Sadly, there's no automatic system in Unity to combine the textures of three-dimensional objects, such as the **Texture Atlas** object we used in 2D. There are probably some systems in the Asset Store, but automatic systems can have several side effects. This work is usually done by an artist, so just keep this technique in mind when working with a dedicated 3D artist (or if you are your own artist):

Figure 19.5 – Pieces of different metallic objects

Let's explore batching with Frame Debugger by doing the following:

1. Search for the **Render Pipeline** asset that we currently want to use (**Edit | Project Settings | Graphics | Scriptable Render Settings**):

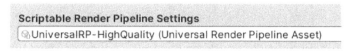

Figure 19.6 – Scriptable Render Pipeline settings

2. Uncheck **SRP Batcher** in the **Advanced** section. We will discuss this later:

Figure 19.7 – Disabling SRP Batcher

3. Create a new empty scene for testing (**File | New Scene**).

4. Create two materials of different colors.

5. Create two cubes and put one material into the first and the other into the second.

6. Open Frame Debugger and click **Enable** to see the call list for the draw calls of our cubes:

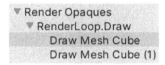

Figure 19.8 – The draw calls for the cubes

7. Select the second **Draw Mesh Cube** call and look at the batch-breaking reason. It should say that the objects have different materials.

8. Use one of the materials on both cubes and look at the list again. You will notice that now we just have one **Draw Mesh Cube** call. You might need to disable and enable Frame Debugger again for it to refresh properly.

Now, I challenge you to try the same steps but create spheres instead of cubes. If you do that, you will probably notice that even with the same materials, the spheres are not batched! Here is where we need to introduce the concept of dynamic batching.

Remember that GameObjects have a **Static** checkbox, which serves to notify several Unity systems that the object won't move so that they can apply several optimizations. Objects that don't have this checkbox checked are considered dynamic. So far, the cubes and spheres we used for our tests have been dynamic, so Unity needed to combine them in every frame because they can move, and combining is not "free." Its cost is associated directly with the number of vertexes in the model. You can get the exact numbers and all the required considerations from the Unity manual, which will appear if you search **Unity Batching**. However, it is enough to say that if the number of vertexes of an object is big enough, that object won't be batched, and doing so would require more than issuing two draw calls. That's why our spheres weren't batched; a sphere has too many vertices.

Now, things are different if we have static objects because they use a second batching system—the static batcher. The concept of this is the same. Merge objects to render them in one draw call, and again these objects need to share the same material. The main difference is that this batcher will batch more objects than the dynamic batcher because merging is done once at the time that the scene loads and is then saved in memory to use in the next frames, costing memory but saving lots of processing time each frame. You can use the same approach we used to test the dynamic batcher to test the static version just by checking the **Static** checkbox of the spheres this time and seeing the result in **Play** mode; in **Edition** mode (when it is not playing), the static batcher won't work:

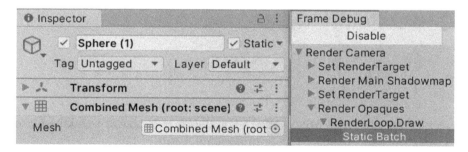

Figure 19.9 – A static sphere and its static batch

Before moving on, let's discuss why we disabled SRP Batcher and how that changes what we just discussed. In its 2020 edition, Unity introduced URP (Universal Render Pipeline), a new Render Pipeline. Along with several improvements, one that is relevant right now is SRP Batcher, a new batcher that works on dynamic objects with no vertex or material limits (but with other limits). Instead of relying on sharing the same material with batch objects, SRP Batcher can have a batch of objects with materials that use the same Shader, meaning we can have, for example, 100 objects with 100 different materials for each one, and they will be batched regardless of the number of vertexes, as long as the material uses the same Shader and Variant:

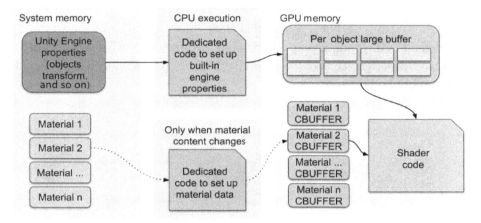

Figure 19.10 – GPU data persistence for materials, which allows SRP Batcher to exist

One Shader can have several versions or Variants, and the selected Variant is chosen based on the settings. We can have a Shader that doesn't use normal mapping and a Variant that doesn't calculate normals will be used, so that can affect SRP Batcher. So, there's basically no drawback to using SRP Batcher, so go ahead and turn it on again. Try creating lots of spheres with as many materials as you can and check the number of batches it will generate in Frame Debugger. Just consider that if you need to work on a project done in a pre-URP era, this won't be available, so you will need to know the proper batching strategy to use.

Other optimizations

As mentioned before, there are lots of possible graphics optimizations, so let's discuss briefly the basic ones, starting with **Level of Detail (LOD)**. LOD is the process of changing the mesh of an object based on its distance to the camera. This can reduce draw calls if you replace, for example, a house with several parts and pieces with a single combined mesh with reduced detail when the house is far. Another benefit of using LOD is that you reduce the cost of a draw call because of the reduction in the vertex count.

To use this feature, do the following:

1. Create an empty object and parent the two versions of the model. You need to use models that have several versions with different levels of detail, but for now, we are just going to test this feature using a cube and a sphere:

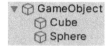

Figure 19.11 – A single object with two LOD meshes

2. Add an LOD group component to the parent.

3. The default LOD group is prepared to support three LOD mesh groups, but as we only have two, right-click on one and click **Delete**. You can also select **Insert Before** to add more LOD groups:

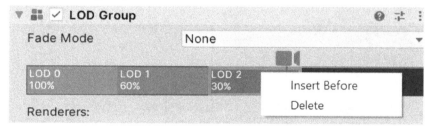

Figure 19.12 – Removing an LOD group

4. Select **LOD 0**, the highest detail LOD group, and click on the **Add** button in the **Renderers** list below this to add the sphere to that group. You can add as many mesh renderers as you want.

5. Select **LOD 1** and add the cube:

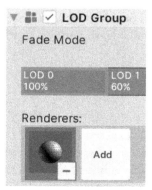

Figure 19.13 – Adding renderers to LOD groups

6. Drag the line between the two groups to control the distance range that each group will occupy. As you drag it, you will see a preview of how far the camera needs to be to switch groups. Also, you have the culled group, which is the distance from where the camera will not render any group.

7. Just move the camera around in **Edit** mode to see how the meshes are swapped.

8. Something to consider here is that the colliders of the objects won't be disabled, so just have the renderers in the LOD sub-objects. Put the collider with the shape of LOD 0 in the parent object, or just remove the colliders from the LOD group objects, except group 0.

Another optimization to consider is frustum culling. By default, Unity will render any object that falls into the view area or frustum of the camera, skipping the ones that don't. The algorithm is cheap enough to always use, and there's no way to disable it. However, it does have a flaw. If we have a wall hiding all the objects behind it, even if they are occluded, they fall inside the frustum, so they will be rendered anyway. Detecting whether every pixel of a mesh occludes every pixel of the other mesh is almost impossible to do in realtime, but luckily, we have a workaround: occlusion culling.

Occlusion culling is a process that analyzes a scene and determines which objects can be seen in different parts of the scene, dividing them into sectors and analyzing each one. As this process can take quite a long time, it is done in the editor, as is done with lightmapping. As you can imagine, it only works on static objects. To use it, do the following:

1. Mark the objects that shouldn't move as static, or if you only want this object to be considered static for the occlusion culling system, check the **Occluder** and **Ocludee** checkboxes of the arrow to the right of the **Static** checkbox.

2. Open the **Occlusion Culling** window (**Window | Rendering | Occlusion Culling**).

3. Save the scene and hit the **Bake** button at the bottom of the window, and then wait for the baking process. If you don't save the scene before the baking process, it won't be executed.

4. Select the **Visualization** tab in the **Occlusion Culling** window.

5. With the **Occlusion Culling** window visible, select the camera and drag it around, seeing how objects are occluded as the camera moves:

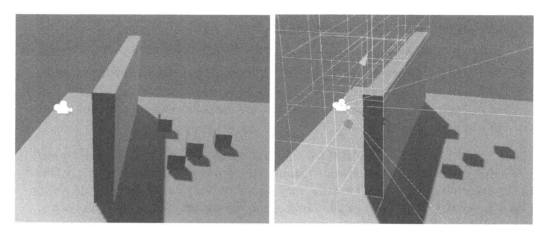

Figure 19.14 – On the left is the normal scene and on the right is the scene with occlusion culling

Take into account that if you move the camera outside the calculated area, the process won't take place, and Unity will only calculate areas near the static objects. You can extend the calculation area by creating an empty object and adding an **Occlusion Area** component, setting its position and size to cover the area that the camera will reach, and finally, rebaking the culling. Try to be sensible with the size of the cube. The larger the area to calculate, the larger the space needed in your disk to store the generated data. You can use several of these areas to be more precise—for example, in an L-shaped scene, you can use two of them:

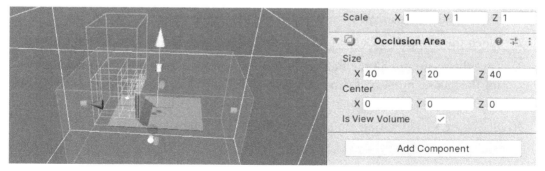

Figure 19.15 – Occlusion Area

If you see that the objects are not being occluded, it could be that the occluder object (the wall in this case) is not big enough to be considered. You can increase the size of the object or reduce the **Smallest Occluder** setting in the **Bake** tab of the window. Doing that will subdivide the scene further to detect smaller occluders, but that will take more space in the disk to store more data. So again, be sensible with this setting.

There are still some more techniques that we can apply to our game, but the ones we have discussed are sufficient. So now, let's start discussing other optimization areas, such as the processing area.

Optimizing processing

While graphics usually take up most of the time that a frame needs to be generated, we should never underestimate the cost of badly optimized code and scenes. There are several parts of the game that are still calculated in the CPU, including part of the graphics process (such as the batching calculations), Unity Physics, audio, and our code. Here, we have a lot more causes of performance issues than on the graphics side, so again, instead of discussing every optimization, let's learn how to discover them.

In this section, we will examine the following CPU optimization concepts:

- Detecting CPU- and GPU-bound
- Using the CPU Usage Profiler
- General CPU optimization techniques

We will start by discussing the concepts of CPU- and GPU-bound, which focus on the optimization process, determining whether the problem is GPU- or CPU-related. Later, as with the GPU optimization process, we will look at how to gather the performance data of the CPU and interpret it to detect possible optimization techniques to be applied.

Detecting CPU- and GPU-bound

As with Frame Debugger, the Unity Profiler allows us to gather data about the performance of our game through a series of Profiler modules, each one designed to gather data about different Unity systems per frame, such as Physics, audio, and, most importantly, CPU usage. This last module allows us to see every single function that Unity called to process the frame—that is, from our script's executed functions to other systems, such as Physics and graphics.

Before exploring CPU usage, one important bit of data that we can gather in this module is whether we are CPU- or GPU- bound. As explained before, a frame is processed using both CPU and GPU, and those pieces of hardware can work in parallel. While GPU is executing drawing commands, the CPU can execute Physics and our scripts in a very efficient way. But now, let's say that the CPU finishes its work while the GPU is still working. Can the CPU start to work on the next frame? The answer is no. This would lead to a de-synchronization, so in this scenario, the CPU will need to wait. This is known as CPU-bound, and we have also the opposite case, GPU-bound, when the GPU finishes earlier than the CPU.

> **Important note**
>
> It is worth mentioning that on mobile devices, it is sometimes preferable to reduce the framerate of our game to reduce battery consumption, making the game idle for a moment between frame to frame, but that could lead to a slower response in our commands and input. To solve that, Unity has created a package that adds the ability to skip the rendering process after a configurable number of frames, which keeps the processing working but skips rendering. So, naturally, those frames will be CPU-bound only.

It is important to concentrate our optimization efforts, so if we detect that our game is GPU-bound, we will focus on GPU graphics optimization, and if it is CPU-bound, then we will focus on the rest of the systems and the CPU side of graphics processing. To detect whether our game is one or the other, do the following:

1. Open **Profiler** (**Window | Analysis | Profiler**).

2. In the **Profiler Modules** dropdown in the top-left corner, tick **GPU** to enable the GPU profiler:

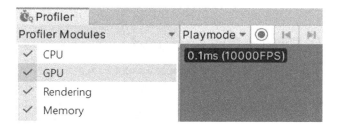

Figure 19.16 – Enabling the GPU profiler

3. Play the game and select the **CPU Usage** profiler, clicking on its name in the left part of the **Profiler** window.

4. Observe the bar with the **CPU** and **GPU** labels in the middle of the window. It should say how many milliseconds are being consumed by the CPU and GPU. The one with the higher number will be the one that is limiting our framerate and will determine whether we are GPU- or CPU-bound:

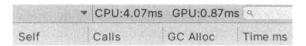

Figure 19.17 – Determining whether we are CPU- or GPU-bound

5. Click the button that says Timeline and select Hierarchy instead:

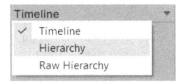

Figure 19.18 – Selecting Hierarchy

6. There is a chance that when you try to open the GPU profiler, you will see a not supported message, and this can happen in certain cases (such as on some mac devices). In that scenario, another way to see whether we are GPU-bound is by searching waitforpresent in the search bar right next to the CPU/GPU labels while selecting the CPU Usage profiler:

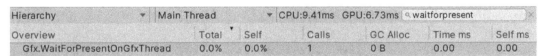

Figure 19.19 – Searching waitforpresent

7. Here, you can see how long the CPU has been waiting for the GPU. Check the **Time ms** column to get the number. If you see 0.00, this is because the CPU is not waiting for the GPU, meaning we are not GPU-bound. In the preceding screenshot, you can see that my screen displays 0.00 while the CPU is taking 9.41ms and the GPU is taking 6.73ms. So, my device is CPU-bound.

Now that we can detect whether we are CPU- or GPU-bound, we can focus our optimization efforts. So far, we discussed how to profile and optimize part of the GPU process. Now, if we detect that we are CPU-bound, let's see how to profile the CPU.

Using the CPU Usage profiler

Profiling the CPU is done in a similar way to profiling the GPU. We need to get a list of actions the CPU executes and try to reduce them, and here is where the CPU Usage profiler module comes in—a tool that allows us to see all the instructions that the CPU executed in one frame. The main difference is that the GPU mostly executes draw calls, and we have a few types of them, while the CPU can have hundreds of different instructions to execute, and sometimes some of them cannot be deleted, such as Physics Update or audio processing. In these scenarios, we are looking to reduce the cost of these functions in case they are consuming too much time. So, again, an important note here is to detect which function is taking too much time and then reduce its cost or remove it, which requires a deeper understanding of the underlying system. Let's start detecting the function first.

When you play the game with the **Profiler** tab opened, you will see a series of graphics showing the performance of our game, and in the CPU Usage profiler, you will see that the graphic is split into different colors, each one referring to different parts of frame processing. You can check the information to the left of the profiler to see what each color means, but let's discuss the most important ones. In the following screenshot, you can see how the graphic should look:

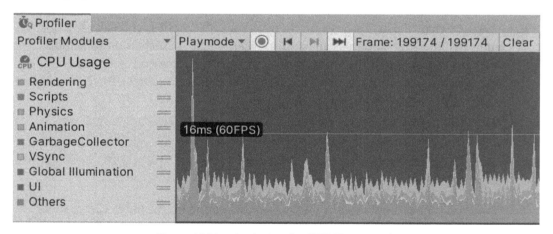

Figure 19.20 – Analyzing the CPU Usage graph

If you check the graphic, you will probably assume that the dark-green part of the graph is taking up most of the performance time, and while that is true, you can also see from the legend that dark green means **Others**, and that's because we are profiling the game in the editor. The editor won't behave exactly like the final game. In order for it to run, it has to do lots of extra processing that won't be executed in the game, so the best you can do is profile directly in the build of the game. There, you will gather more accurate data. We are going to discuss how to do builds in the next chapter, so for now, we can ignore that area. What we can do now is simply click on the colored square to the left of the **Others** label to disable that measurement from the graph in order to clean it up a little bit. If you also see a large section of yellow, it is referring to VSync, which is basically the time spent waiting for our processing to match the monitor's refresh rate. This is also something that we can ignore, so you should also disable it. In the next screenshot, you can check the graphic color categories and how to disable them:

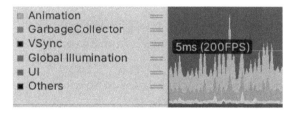

Figure 19.21 – Disabling VSync and Others from the profiler

Now that we have cleaned up the graph, we can get a good idea of our games potential framerate by looking at the line with the ms label (in our case, **5ms (200 FPS)**), which indicates that frames below that line have more than 200 FPS, and frames above that line have less. In my case, I have excellent performance, but remember, I am testing this on a powerful machine. The best way to profile is not only in the build of the game (as an executable) but also in the target device, which should be the lowest spec hardware we intend our game to run on. Our target device depends a lot on the target audience of the game. If we are making a casual game, we are probably targeting mobile devices, so we should test the game on the lowest spec phone we can, but if we are targeting hardcore gamers, they will probably have a powerful machine to run our game on.

> **Important note**
>
> If you are targeting hardcore gamers, of course, this doesn't mean that we can just make a very unoptimized game because of that, but it will give us enough processing space to add more detail. Anyway, I strongly recommend you avoid those kinds of games if you are a beginner as they are more difficult to develop, which you will probably realize. Stick to simple games to begin with.

Looking at the graphics colors, you can observe the cost on the CPU side of rendering in light green, which the graph shows is taking up a significant portion of the processing time, which is actually normal. Then, in blue, we can see the cost of our scripts' execution, which is also taking up a significant portion, but again, this is quite normal. Also, we can observe a little bit of orange, which is Physics, and also a little bit of light blue, which is Animation. Remember to check the colored labels in the profiler to remember which color refers to what.

Now, those colored bars represent a group of operations, so if we consider the **Rendering** bar to be representing 10 operations, how do we know which operations that includes? Also, how do we know which of these operations is taking up the most performance time? Out of those 10 operations, a single one could be causing these issues. Here is where the bottom part of the profiler is useful. It shows a list of all the functions being called in the frame. To use it, do the following:

1. Clear the search bar we used earlier. It will filter function calls by name, and we want to see them all. Remember to switch from Timeline to Hierarchy mode if not already there.

2. Click on the **Time ms** column until you see an arrow pointing downward. This will order the calls by cost in descending order.

3. Click on a frame that is taking your attention in the graph—probably one of the ones with the biggest height that consumes more processing time. This will make the profiler stop the game straight away and show you information about that frame.

> **Important note**
>
> There are two things to consider when looking at the graph. If you see peaks that are significantly higher than the rest of the frames, that can cause a hiccup in your game—a very brief moment where the game is frozen—which can break the performance. Also, you can look for a long series of frames with higher time consumption. Try to reduce them as well. Even if this is only temporary, the impact of it will be easily perceived by the player.

4. **PlayerLoop** will probably appear as the most time-consuming frame, but that's not very informative. You can explore it further by expanding it by clicking on the arrow to its left.

5. Click on each function to highlight it in the graph. Functions with higher processing times will be highlighted with thicker bars, and those are the ones we will focus on:

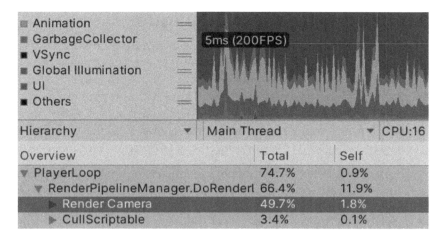

Figure 19.22 – The Render Camera function highlighted in the graph

6. You can keep click on the arrows to further explore the functions until you hit a limit. If you want to go deeper, enable the **Deep Profiler** mode in the top bar of the profiler. This will give you more details, but take into account that this process is expensive and will make the game go slower, altering the time shown in the graph, making it appear much higher than the real time. Here, ignore the numbers and look at how much of the process a function is taking up based on the graph. You will need to stop, enable **Deep Profile**, and play it again to make it work:

Figure 19.23 – Enabling Deep Profile

With this knowledge, we can start improving our game performance (if it's below the target framerate), but each function is called by the CPU and is improved in its own unique way, which requires a greater knowledge of Unity's internal workings. That could span several books, and anyway, the internals change on a version-to-version basis. Instead, you could study how each function works by looking up data about that specific system on the internet, or again, by just disabling and enabling objects or parts of our code to explore the impact of our actions, as we did with Frame Debugger. Profiling requires creativity and inference to interpret and react accordingly on the data obtained, so you will need some patience here.

Now that we have discussed how to get the profiling data relating to the CPU, let's discuss some common ways to reduce CPU usage.

General CPU optimization techniques

In terms of CPU optimizations, there are lots of possible causes of high performance, including the abuse of Unity's features, a large amount of Physics or audio objects, improper asset/objects configurations, and so on. Our scripts can also be coded in an unoptimized way, abusing or misusing expensive Unity API functions. So far, we have discussed several good practices of using Unity Systems, such as audio configurations, texture sizes, batching, and finding functions such as `GameObject.Find` and replacing them with managers. So, let's discuss some specific details about common cases.

Let's start by seeing how a large number of objects impacts our performance. Here, you can just create lots of objects with `Rigidbody` configured in **Dynamic Profile**, and observe the results in the Profiler. You will notice, in the following screenshot, how the orange part of the profiler just got bigger and that the `Physics.Processing` function is responsible for this increase:

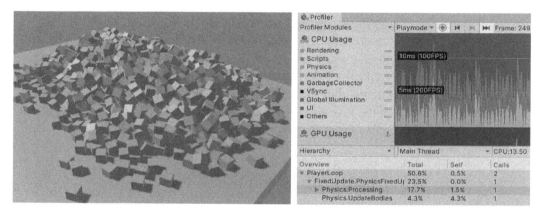

Figure 19.24 – The Physics processing of several objects

Another test to see the impact of several objects could be to create lots of audio sources. In the following screenshot, you can see that we needed to re-enable **Others** because audio processing comes under that category. We mentioned earlier that **Others** belongs to the editor, but it can encompass other processes as well, so keep that in mind:

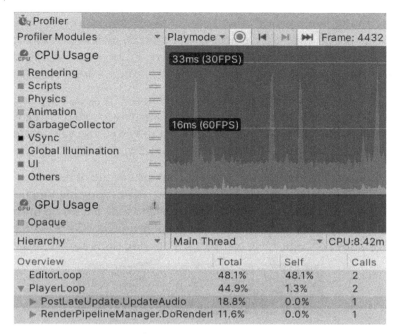

Figure 19.25 – The Physics processing of several objects

So, to discover these kinds of problems, you can just start disabling and enabling objects and see whether they increase the time. A final test is on particles. Create a system that spawns a big enough number of particles to affect our framerate and check the profiler. In the following screenshot, you can check how the particle processing function is highlighted in the graph, showing that it takes a large amount of time:

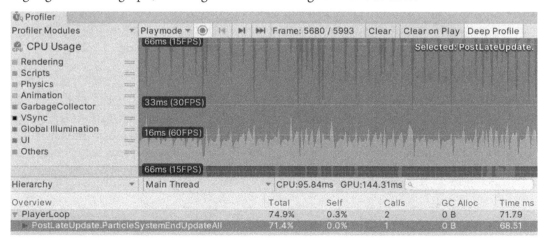

Figure 19.26 – Particle processing

Then, on the scripting side, we have other kinds of things to consider, some of which are common to all programming languages and platforms, such as iterating long lists of objects, the misuse of data structures, and deep recursion. However, in this section, I will mainly be discussing Unity-specific APIs, starting with `print` or `Debug.Log`.

This function is useful to get debugging information in the console, but it can also be costly because all logs are written onto the disk immediately to avoid losing valuable information if our game crashes. Of course, we want to keep those valuable logs in the game, but we don't want it to affect performance, so what can we do?

One possible approach is to keep those messages but disable the non-essential ones in the final build, such as informative messages, keeping the error-reporting function active. One way to do this is through compiler directives, such as the ones used in the following screenshot. Remember that this kind of `if` statement is executed by the compiler and can exclude entire portions of code when compiling if its conditions are not met:

```
#if UNITY_EDITOR || DEVELOPMENT_BUILD
print("Informative Message");
#endif
```

Figure 19.27 – Disabling code

In the preceding screenshot, you can see how we are asking whether this code is being compiled by the editor or for a development build, which is a special kind of build intended to be used for testing (more on that in the next chapter). You can also create your own kind of logging system with functions with the compiler directives, so you don't need to use them in every log that you want to exclude.

There are a few other script aspects that can affect performance not only on the processing side but also on the memory side, so let's discuss them in the next section.

Optimizing memory

We discussed how to profile and optimize two pieces of hardware—the CPU and GPU—but there is another piece of hardware that plays a key role in our game—RAM. This is the place where we put all of our game's data. Games can be memory-intensive applications, and unlike several other applications, they are constantly executing code, so we need to be especially careful about that.

In this section, we will examine the following memory optimization concepts:

- Memory allocation and the garbage collector
- Using the Memory Profiler

Let's start discussing how memory allocation works and what role garbage collection plays here.

Memory allocation and the garbage collector

Each time we instantiate an object, we are allocating memory in RAM, and in a game, we will be allocating memory constantly. In other programming languages, aside from allocating the memory, you need to manually deallocate it, but C# has a garbage collector, which is a system that tracks unused memory and cleans it. This system works with a reference counter, which tracks how many references to an object exist, and when that counter reaches 0, it means all references have become null and the object can be deallocated. This deallocation process can be triggered in several situations, the most common situation being when we reach the maximum assigned memory and we want to allocate a new object. In that scenario, we can release enough memory to allocate our object, and if that is not possible, the memory is expanded.

In any game, you will probably be allocating and deallocating memory constantly, which can lead to memory fragmentation, meaning there are small spaces between alive object memory blocks that are mostly useless because they aren't big enough to allocate an object, or maybe the sum of the spaces are big enough, but we need continuous memory space to allocate our objects. In the following diagram, you can see a classic example of trying to fit a big chunk of memory into the little gaps generated by fragmentation:

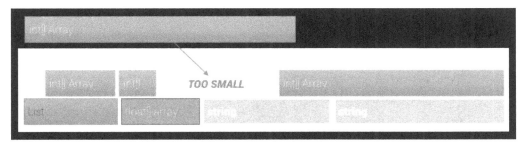

Figure 19.28 – Trying to instantiate an object in a fragmented memory space

Some types of garbage collection systems, such as the one in regular C#, are generational, meaning memory is split into generation buckets according to the "age" of its memory. Newer memory will be placed in the first bucket, and this memory tends to be allocated and deallocated frequently. Because this bucket is small, working within it is fast. The second bucket has the memory that survived a previous deallocation sweep process in the first bucket. That memory is moved to the second bucket to prevent it from being checked constantly if it survived the process, and it is possible that that memory will last the length of our program's lifetime. The third bucket is just another layer of bucket 2. The idea is that most of the time, the allocation and deallocation system will be working in bucket 1, and as it is small enough, it is quick to allocate, deallocate, and compact memory in a continuous fashion.

The problem here is that Unity uses its own version of the garbage collection system, and that version is non-generational and non-compacting, meaning memory is not split into buckets and memory won't be moved to fill the gaps. This suggests that allocating and deallocating memory in Unity will still result in the fragmentation problem, and if you don't regulate your memory allocation, you might end up with an expensive garbage collection system being executed very often, producing hiccups in our game, which you can see in the Profiler CPU Usage module as a pale yellow color.

One way to deal with this is by preventing memory allocation as much as you can, avoiding it when is not necessary. There are a few tweaks here and there that you can make to prevent memory allocation, but before looking at those, again, it is important to first get data about the problem before start fixing things that may not be an issue. This advice applies to any type of optimization process. Here, we can still use the CPU Usage profiler to see how much memory is allocated to each function call that the CPU executes in each frame, and that is simply done by looking at the **GC Alloc** column, which indicates the amount of memory that the function allocated:

Overview	Total	Self	Calls	GC Alloc
▼ Update.ScriptRunBehaviourUpdate	6.4%	0.0%	1	2.3 KB
▼ BehaviourUpdate	6.4%	1.2%	1	2.3 KB
▼ Sight.Update()	2.0%	0.5%	69	2.2 KB
Physics.OverlapSphere	1.4%	1.4%	69	0 B
GC.Alloc	0.0%	0.0%	69	2.2 KB
Physics.Raycast	0.0%	0.0%	1	0 B

Figure 19.29 – The memory allocation of the Update event function of Sight

In the preceding screenshot, we can see how our function is allocating too much memory, which is produced because there are a large number of enemies in the scene. But that's no excuse; we are allocating that much RAM at every frame, so we need to improve this. There are several things that can contribute to our memory being claimed by allocations, so let's discuss the basic ones, starting with array-returning functions.

If we review the Sight code, we can see that the only moment where we are allocating memory is in the call to `Physics.OverlapSphere`, and that is evident because it is an array-returning function, which is a function that returns a varying amount of data. To do this, it needs to allocate an array and return that array to us. This needs to be done on the side that created the function, Unity, but in this case, Unity gives us two versions of the function—the one that we are using and the `NonAlloc` version. It is usually recommended to use the second version, but Unity uses the other one to make coding simpler for beginners. The `NonAlloc` version looks as in the following screenshot:

```
static Collider[] colliders = new Collider[100];

void Update()
{
    int detectedAmount= Physics.OverlapSphereNonAlloc(transform.position, distance, colliders, objectsLayers);

    detectedObject = null;
    for (int i = 0; i < detectedAmount; i++)
```

Figure 19.30 – Memory allocation of the Update event function of Sight

This version requires us to allocate an array with enough space to save the largest amount of colliders our `OverlapSphere` variable can find and pass it as the third parameter. This allows us to allocate the array just once and reuse it on every occasion that we need it. In the preceding screenshot, you can see how the array is static, which means it is shared between all the Sight variables as they won't execute in parallel (no `Update` function will). This will work fine. Keep in mind that the function will return the number of objects that were detected, so we just iterate on that count. The array can have previous results stored within it.

Now, check your profiler and notice how the amount of memory allocated has been reduced greatly. There might be some remaining memory allocation within our function, but sometimes there is no way to keep it at `0`. However, you can try to look at the reasons for this using deep profiling or by commenting some code and seeing which comment removes the allocation. I challenge you to try this. Also, `OverlapSphere` is not the only case where this could occur. You have others, such as the `GetComponents` functions family, which, unlike `GetComponent,` finds all the components of a given type, not just the first one, so pay attention to any array-returning function of Unity and try to replace it with a non-allocating version, if there is one.

Another common source of memory allocation is string concatenation. Remember that strings are immutable, meaning they cannot change if you concatenate two strings. A third one needs to be generated with enough space to hold the first ones. If you need to concatenate a large number of times, consider using `string.Format` if you are just replacing placeholders in a template string, such as putting the name of the player and the score they got in a message or using `StringBuilder`, a class that just holds all the strings to be concatenated in a list and, when necessary, concatenates them together, instead of concatenating them one by one as the + operator does. Also, consider using the new string interpolation functionality of C#. You can see some examples in the following screenshot:

```csharp
string name = "John";
string score = "100";
string template = "{0} has won {1} points";

print(string.Format(template, name, score)); //John has won 100 points
print($"{name} has won {score} points."); //John has won 100 points


StringBuilder builder = new StringBuilder();
builder.Append("My ");
builder.Append("name ");
builder.Append("is ");
builder.Append("Neo.");
print(builder.ToString()); //My name is Neo.
```

Figure 19.31 – String management in C#

Finally, a classic technique to consider is object pooling, which is suitable in cases where you need to instantiate and destroy objects constantly, such as with bullets or effects. In that scenario, the use of regular `Instantiate` and `Destroy` functions will lead to memory fragmentation, but object pooling fixes that by allocating the maximum amount of required objects possible. It replaces `Instantiate` by taking one of the preallocated functions and it replaces `Destroy` by returning the object to the pool. A simple pool can be seen in the following screenshot:

```
public class Pool : MonoBehaviour
{
    List<GameObject> storedObjects = new List<GameObject>();

    [SerializeField] GameObject prefab;

    public GameObject Get()
    {
        if (storedObjects.Count > 0)
        {
            var obj :GameObject  = storedObjects[0];
            storedObjects.RemoveAt(0);
            obj.SetActive(true);
            return obj;
        }
        else
        {
            return Instantiate(prefab);
        }
    }

    public void Return(GameObject obj)
    {
        obj.SetActive(false);
        storedObjects.Add(obj);
    }
}
```

Figure 19.32 – A simple object pool

There are several ways to improve this pool, but it is fine as it is for now. Note that objects need to be reinitialized when they are taken out of the pool, and you can do that with the OnEnable event function or by creating a custom function to inform the object to do so.

Now that we have explored some basic memory allocation reduction techniques, let's look at a new Memory Profiler tool, introduced in the latest version of Unity, to explore memory in greater detail.

Using the Memory Profiler

With this profiler, we can detect memory allocated on a frame per-frame basis, but it won't show the total memory allocated so far, which would be useful to study how we are using our memory. This is where the Memory Profiler can help us. This relatively new Unity package allows us to take memory snapshots of every single object allocated both on the native and managed side—native meaning the internal C++ Unity code, and managed meaning anything that belongs to the C# side (that is, both our code and Unity's C# engine code). We can explore snapshots with a visual tool and rapidly see which type of object is consuming the most RAM and how they are referenced by other objects.

To start using the Memory Profiler, do the following:

1. Install the **Memory Profiler** package from `Package Manager` (**Window |
    Package Manager**). Remember to set **Packages Mode** to **Unity Registry** and
    enable the preview packages (**Wheel Icon | Advanced Project Settings | Enable
    Preview Packages**).

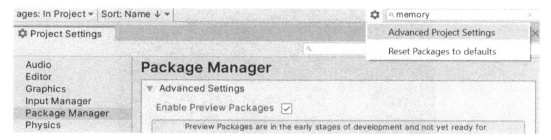

Figure 19.33 – Enabling preview packages

2. Open `Memory Profiler` in **Window | Analysis | Memory Profiler**.

3. Play the game and click on the **Capture Player** button in the **Memory
    Profiler** window:

Figure 19.34 – Enabling preview packages

4. Click on the **Open** button next to the snapshot that was captured to open the tree
    view, where you can see the memory split into blocks by type:

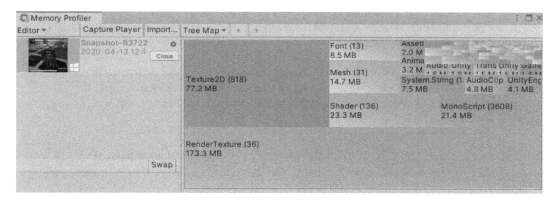

Figure 19.35 – Memory blocks

5. In our case, we can see that `RenderTexture` uses up the most memory, which belongs to the image that is displayed in the scene, as well as some textures used by postprocessing effects. Try to disable the `PPVolume` object and take another snapshot to detect the difference.

6. In my case, that dropped off 130 MB. There are other textures needed for other effects, such as HDR. If you want to explore where those remaining MBs came from, click on the block to subdivide it into its objects and take your own guesses based on the names of the textures:

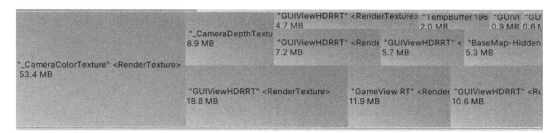

Figure 19.36 – Memory blocks in detail

7. You can repeat the same process in the `Texture2D` block type, which belongs to the textures used in the materials of our models. You can look at the biggest one and detect its usage—maybe it is a big texture that is never seen close enough to justify its size. Then, we can reduce its size using the Max Size of the Texture import settings.

> **Important note**
>
> As with any profiler, it is always useful to carry out the profiling directly in the build (more on that in the next chapter) because taking snapshots in the editor will capture lots of memory that is used by the editor and will not be used in the build. An example of this is the loading of unnecessary textures because the editor probably loaded them when you clicked them to see their previews in the Inspector window.

Take into account the fact that due to the Memory Profiler being a package, its UI can change often, but its basic idea will remain. You can use this tool to detect whether you are using the memory in unexpected ways. Something useful to consider here is how Unity loads assets when loading a scene, which consists of loading all assets referenced in the scene at load time. This means that you can have, as an example, an array of prefabs that have references to materials that have references to textures, and even if you don't instantiate a single instance of them, the prefabs must be loaded in memory, causing them to occupy space. In this scenario, I recommend that you explore the use of addressables, which provide a way to load assets dynamically. But let's keep things simple for now.

You can do more with the profiler, such as access a list view of all objects and observe every field of it and its references to see which objects are using it (from the main menu, go to **TreeMap | Table | All objects**), but for beginners, I found that view a little bit confusing. A good alternative to the Memory Profiler reference navigation system is using the Memory module of the profiler. This is a basic version of the Memory Profiler that won't show you the memory with a nice tree view or in the amount of detail that the Memory Profiler can provide, but provides a simpler version of a reference navigator, which can be enough most of the time.

To use it, do the following:

1. Open the profiler (**Window | Analysis | Profiler**).

2. While in play mode, scroll down through the list of profiler modules and select **Memory**.

3. With the **Gather object references** toggle turned on, click on **Take Sample Playmode**.

4. Explore the list that pops up, open the categories, and select an asset. In the following screenshot, you can see that I have selected the texture and on the right panel, I can explore the references. This texture is used by a material named base color, which is referenced by a mesh renderer in a GameObject called floor_1_LOD0. You can even click on an item in the reference list to highlight the referencer object:

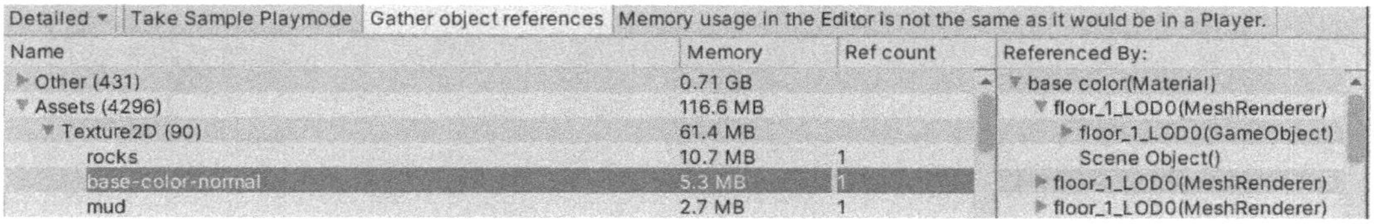

Figure 19.37 – Reference list

As you can see, both the Memory Profiler and the Memory module in the profiler do similar things. They can take snapshots of memory for you to analyze them. I believe that with time, Unity will unify those tools, but for now, use one or the other based on their strong and weak points, such as the ability of the Memory Profiler to compare two snapshots to analyze differences, or its ability to explore low-level data of the memory, such as seeing which managed object is using which native object (which is pretty advanced and most times unnecessary). You can use the Memory module to analyze references to see which object is using which texture and why.

Summary

Optimizing a game is not an easy task, especially if you are not familiar with the internals of how each Unity system works. Sadly, this is a Titanic task and no one knows every single system in its finest details, but with the tools learned in this chapter, we have a way to explore how changes affect systems through exploration. We learned how to profile the CPU, GPU, and RAM and what the key hardware in any game is, and also covered some common good practices to avoid abusing them.

Now you are able to diagnose performance issues in your game, gathering data about the performance of the three main pieces of hardware—the CPU, GPU, and RAM—and then use that data to focus your optimization efforts into applying the correct optimization technique. Performance is important as your game needs to run smoothly to give your users a pleasant experience.

In the next chapter, we are going to see how to create a build of our game to share with other people without needing to install Unity.

20
Building the Project

So, we have reached a point where the game is mature enough to test it with real people. The problem is that we can't pretend people will install Unity, open a project, and hit Play. They want to receive a nice executable file to double-click and play right away. In this chapter, we are going to discuss how we can convert our project into an easy-to-share executable format.

In this chapter, we will examine the following build concepts:

- Building a project
- Debugging the build

Building a project

In software development (including video games), the result of taking the source files of our project and converting them into an executable format is called Build. The generated executable files are optimized to get the maximum performance possible. We can't get performance while editing the game due to the changing nature of a project. It would be time-consuming to prepare the assets in their final form while editing the game. Also, the generated files have a difficult-to-read format. They won't have the textures, audios, and source code files just there for the user to look at. They will be formatted in custom file structures, so in a way, it's protected from users stealing them.

> **Important note**
>
> Actually, there are several tools to extract source files from video games, especially from a widely used engine such as Unity. You can extract assets such as textures and 3D models, and there are even programs that extract those assets directly from the VRAM, so we cannot guarantee that the assets won't be used outside the game. In the end, users have the data of those assets in their disks.

The build process is pretty simple when you target desktop platforms such as PC, Mac, or Linux, but there are a few settings we need to keep in mind before building. The first configuration we are going to see is the scenes list. We have already discussed this, but it's a good moment to remember that it is important to set the first element of this list to the Scene that will be loaded first. Remember, you can do this by going to **File | Build Settings** and dragging your desired starter scene to the top of the list. In our case, we defined the Game scene as the first scene, but in a real game, it would be ideal to create a Main Menu scene using UI and some graphics:

Figure 20.1 – The Scenes list order

Another setting you can change here is the target platform – the target operating system that the build will be created for. Usually, this is set for the same operating system you are developing on, but if you are, as an example, developing on a Mac, and you want to build for Windows, just set the **Target Platform** setting to Windows. That way, the result will be `exe` instead of `app`. You may see Android and iOS as other target platforms, but making mobile games requires other considerations that we are not going to discuss in this book:

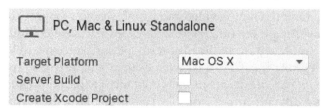

Figure 20.2 – Target Platform

In the same window, you can click the **Player Settings** button at the bottom left, or just open the **Edit | Project Settings** window and click on the **Player** category to access the rest of the Build Settings. Unity calls the generated executable files the game Player. Here we have a set of configurations that will affect how the build or Player behaves, and here is a list of the basic ones:

- **Product Name**: This is the name of the game in the window title bar and executable file.

- **Company Name**: This is the name of the company that developed the game, which is used by Unity to create certain file paths and will be included in the executable information.

- **Default Icon**: Here, you can select a texture to act as the executable icon.

- **Default Cursor**: You can set a texture to replace the regular system cursor. If you do that, remember to set the **Cursor Hotspot** property to the pixel of the image you want the cursor to do the clicks.

- **Resolution and Presentation:** Settings about how our game's resolution is going to be handled.

- **Resolution and Presentation | Default is Native Resolution**: With this checked and when the game is running in full-screen mode, the resolution currently used in the system will be the one used by Unity. You can uncheck this and set your desired resolution.

- **Splash Image:** Settings about the splash image the game will show after loading for the first time.

- **Splash Image | Show Splash Screen**: This will enable a Unity splash screen that will display logos as an introduction to the game. If you have the Unity Pro license, you can uncheck this to create your custom splash screen, if you want to.

- **Splash Image | Logos List**: Here, you can add a set of images that Unity will display when launching the game. If you are using Unity for free, you are forced to have the Unity logo displayed in this list.

- **Splash Image | Draw Mode**: You can set this to **All Sequential** to show each logo, one after the other, or to Unity logo Below to show your custom introductory logos with the Unity logo always present below yours:

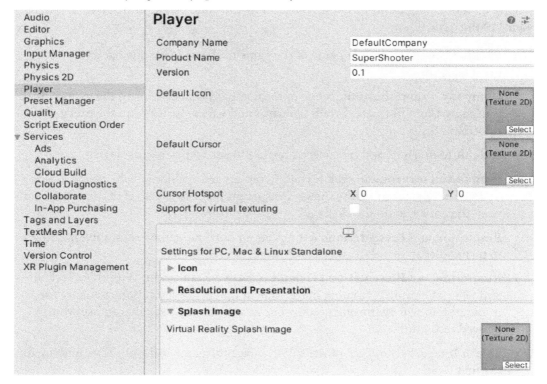

Figure 20.3 – Player settings

After configuring these settings as you wish, the next step is to do the actual build, which can be accomplished by hitting the **Build** button in the **File | Build Settings** window. This will ask you to set where you want the build files to be created. I recommend you create an empty folder on your desktop to have easy access to the result. Be patient—this process can take a while according to the size of the project:

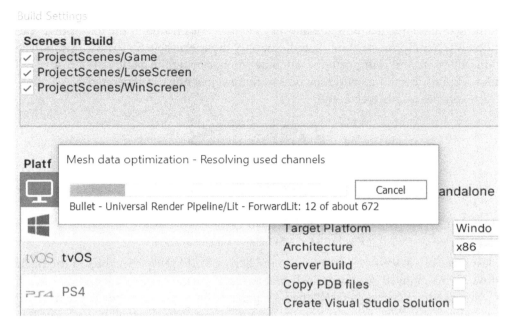

Figure 20.4 – Building the game

Something that can fail here is having non-build compatible scripts—scripts that are intended to be executed only in the editor, mostly editor extensions. We haven't created any of those, so if you have an error message in the console after building, similar to the following screenshot, that can happen because of some script in some Asset Store package. In that case, just delete the files that are shown in the console before the Build Error message. If, by any chance, there is one of your scripts there, be sure you don't have any `using UnityEditor;` lines in any of your scripts. That would try to use the Editor namespace, the one that is not included in the build compilation to save space in the disk:

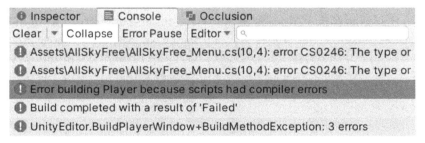

Figure 20.5 – Build errors

And that's pretty much everything you need to know. You have generated your game! Something to take into account is that every file that was created in the folder that you specified when building must be shared, not only the executable file. The `Data` folder contains all assets and is important to include when sharing the game in the case of Windows builds. For Linux and Mac builds, there is just one file generated (`x86/x86_64` and `app packages` respectively):

Figure 20.6 – A Windows-generated folder

One last piece of advice—pay attention to the **Script Build Only** checkbox in the **Build** window. If you changed only code and want to test that change, check it and do the build. This will make the process go faster than a regular build. Just remember to uncheck this if you changed anything else in the editor because those changes won't be included if you have it checked.

Now that we have the build, you can test it by double-clicking the executable file. Now that you have tried your build, we can discuss how we use the same Debug and Profiling tools we used in the editor to test our build.

Debugging the build

In an ideal world, the editor and the build will behave the same, but sadly that isn't true. The editor is prepared to work in a fast-iteration mode. Code and assets have minimum processing prior to being used to make changes often and fast, so we can test our game easily. When the game is built, a series of optimizations and differences from the editor project will be applied to ensure the best performance we can get, but those differences can cause certain parts of the game to behave differently, making the profiling data of the player differ from the editor. That's why we are going to explore how we can debug and profile our game in the build.

In this section, we will examine the following Build Debugging concepts:

- Debugging Code
- Profiling Performance

Let's start discussing how to debug the code of a build.

Debugging code

As player code is compiled differently, we can get errors in the build that didn't happen in the editor, and we need to debug it somehow. We have two main ways to debug—by printing messages and through breakpoints. So, let's start with the first one, messages. If you ran your executable file, you may have noticed that there's no console available. It's just the Game view in fullscreen, which makes sense; we don't want to distract the user with annoying testing messages. Luckily, the messages are still being printed, but in a file, so we can just go to that file and look for them.

The location varies according to the operating system. In this list, you can find the possible locations:

- **Linux**: `~/.config/unity3d/CompanyName/ProductName/Player.log`
- **Mac**: `~/Library/Logs/Company Name/Product Name/Player.log`
- **Windows**: `C:\Users\username\AppData\LocalLow\CompanyName\ProductName\Player.log`

In these paths, you must change `CompanyName` and `ProductName` with the values of the properties in the `Player` settings we set before, which are called the same, **Company** and **Product Name**. In Windows, you must replace `username` with the name of the Windows account you are executing the game in. Consider that the folders might be hidden, so enable the option to show hidden files in your operating system:

Figure 20.7 – Showing hidden files

Inside that folder, you will find a file called `Player`; you can open it with any text editor and look at the messages. In this case, I have used Windows, so the directory path looks like the following screenshot:

Figure 20.8 – Debugging directory

Aside from downloading any custom package from the Asset Store, there is a way to see the messages of the console directly in the game, at least the error messages—by creating a development build. This is a special build that allows extended debugging and profiling capabilities in exchange for not fully optimizing the code as the final build does, but it will be enough for general debugging. You can create this kind of build by just checking the **Development Build** checkbox in the **File | Build Settings** window:

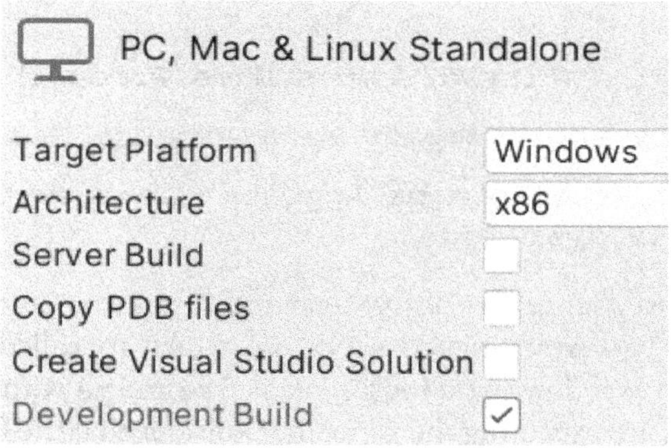

PC, Mac & Linux Standalone

Target Platform   Windows
Architecture   x86
Server Build   ☐
Copy PDB files   ☐
Create Visual Studio Solution ☐
Development Build   ☑

Figure 20.9 – The Development Build checkbox

Remember that just the error messages will be displayed here, so a little trick you can do is to replace the `print` and `Debug.Log` function calls with `Debug.LogError`, which will also print the message in the console but with a red icon. Consider that this is not a good practice, so limit the usage of this kind of message for temporal debugging. For permanent logging, use the log file or find a custom debugging console for runtime in the Asset Store.

Remember that for **Development Build** to work you need to build the game again; luckily, the first build is the one that takes the most time, and the next will be faster. This time, you can just click the **Build and Run** button to do the build in the folder in which you did the previous build:

```
public class PlayerShooting : MonoBehaviour
{
    void Start()
    {
        Debug.LogError("Testing Player Shooting Start");
    }
}
```

Figure 20.10 – Debugging error messages

In the next screenshot, you can see the error being displayed in the runtime:

Figure 20.11 – Error messages in a development build

Also, you can use regular breakpoints the same way as we explained in *Chapter 13, Introduction to Unity Scripting with C#*. Attaching the IDE to the player, it will show up in the list of targets. But for that to work, you must not only check **Development Build** in the Build window but also **Script Debugging**. Here, you have an additional option shown when that is checked that allows you to pause the entire game until a debugger is attached, the one called **Wait for Managed Debugger**. This is useful if you want to test something that happens immediately at the beginning and doesn't allow you enough time to attach the debugger:

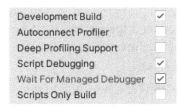

Figure 20.12 – Enabling script debugging

We have another way to see the messages, but that will require the Profiler to work, so let's use this as an excuse to also discuss how to profile the editor.

Profiling performance

We are going to use the same tools as we saw in the previous chapter, but to profile the player this time. Luckily, the difference is minimal. As we did in the previous section, you need to build the player in **Development** mode, checking the **Development Build** checkbox in the Build window, and then the profilers should automatically detect it.

Let's start using the Profiler on the build by doing the following:

1. Play the game through the build.

2. Switch to Unity using *Alt + Tab* (*command + tab* on Mac).

3. Open the Profiler.

4. Click the menu that says **Playmode** and select the item that contains **Player** in it. Because I have used Windows, it says **WindowsPlayer**:

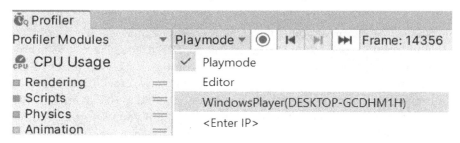

Figure 20.13 – Profiling the player

Notice that when you click a frame, the game won't stop like in the editor. If you want to focus your attention on the frames at a specific moment, you can click the record button (the red circle) to make the Profiler stop capturing data, so you can analyze the frames captured so far.

Also, you can see that when the Profiler is attached to the player, the console will also be attached, so you can see the logs directly in Unity. Consider that this version requires Unity to be opened, and we cannot expect our friends who are testing our game to have it. You might need to click on the **Player** button that appears on the **Console** and check **Player Logging** for this to work:

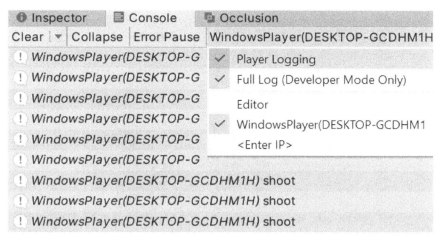

Figure 20.14 – Enabling Player Logging after attaching the Profiler

The Frame Debugger is also enabled to work with the player. You need to click the **Editor** button in the Frame Debugger and again, you will see the player in the list of possible debugging targets; after selecting it, hit **Enable** as usual. Consider that the preview of the Draw Calls won't be seen in the Game view but in the build itself. If you are running the game in full screen mode, you might need to switch back and forth between Unity and the build:

Figure 20.15 – Debugging the frames of our game's player

You may also run the game in **Windowed** mode, setting the **Fullscreen Mode** property in the Player settings to **Windowed**, and establishing a default resolution that is smaller than your desktop resolution, to have both Unity and the player visible:

Figure 20.16 – Enabling Windowed mode

Finally, **Memory Profiler** also supports profiling the Player, and as you might guess, you can just select the player in the list that is displayed when you click the first button of the top bar of the window and then click **Capture Player**:

Figure 20.17 – Taking memory snapshots of the player

And that is it. As you can see, Unity Profilers are designed to be easily integrated with the player. If you start to take data from them, you will see the difference compared to editor profiling, especially in **Memory Profiler**.

Summary

In this chapter, we saw how to create an executable version of the game and properly configure it so you can share it with not only your friends but potentially the world! We also discussed how to profile our build; remember that doing that will give us more accurate data than profiling the editor, so we can better improve the performance of our game.

But before doing that, let's discuss some final details. These are not Unity-related details, but game-related ones; things you need to consider before and after showing your game to people other than yourself or any person that saw your game while it was being developed. We will do this in the next chapter.

21
Finishing Touches

Here we are! We now have a fully developed game, so can we get some money now? Sadly not. A successful game relies on heavy refinement; the devil is in the details! Also, don't get too hyped about earning money yet; this is your first game and there are a lot of non-development-related tasks to accomplish. It's time to discuss what can we do now with what we have achieved so far.

In this chapter, we will examine the following concepts:

- Iterating your game
- Releasing your game

Iterating your game

We are about to finish our first game iteration. We had an idea, we implemented it, and now it's time to test it. After this test, we will get feedback on the things that can be improved, so we will formulate ideas to improve them, implement them, test them, and repeat. That is iteration.

In this section, we will examine the following iteration concepts:

- Testing and feedback
- Solving feedback

Let's start by discussing how to properly test the game on people.

Testing and feedback

Apart from a strong marketing strategy, the success of your game relies on the first 10 minutes of gameplay. If you can't get the attention of the player in that time, you will certainly lose them. The first impression of your game is important. Those first 10 minutes must be flawless and sadly, our perception of the game is not relevant here. You spent several hours playing it and you know every inch of the levels and how to properly control your character, as well as all the mechanics and dynamics of your game—it is YOUR game. You love it as it is. It's a big accomplishment. Now, someone who has never played the game won't feel the same way. That's why testing is so important.

The first time you make someone play your game, you will be shocked—believe me, I've been there. You will notice that the player probably won't understand the game. They won't understand how to control the player or how to win the game and will be stuck in parts of the level that you never imagined to be difficult. There will be bugs everywhere and it will be a total mess—and that is great! That is the exact purpose of testing your game, to get valuable information or feedback. This feedback is what will make your game better if you tackle it properly.

In a testing session, there are two main sources of feedback—observation and user feedback. Observation is the act of silently looking at the person who is playing the game and seeing how they play it—which keys do they first press, what is their reaction when something happens, when do they start getting frustrated in an unexpected way (some games rely on frustration, such as *Dark Souls*), and generally checking that the player is getting the exact experience you expected.

The silent part of the observation is crucial. You must *not* talk to the player, especially not give them any hints nor help, at least not unless they are completely lost and the testing session can't progress without help—a situation that is also a form of useful feedback in itself. You must observe the player in their natural state in the same situation that they will be playing your game in their house. If not, the feedback gathered will be biased and won't be useful. When testing big games, they even carry out tests in Gesell chambers. These are rooms with a pane of glass that can be seen from one side only—like an interrogation room but less scary. This way, the player won't feel any kind of pressure about being observed:

Figure 21.1 – Gesell chamber

The second source is direct feedback, which is basically asking the tester about their impressions of the game after the session. Here, you can first let the tester tell you their experience and provide any feedback that they have, if any, and then you can start asking questions related to that feedback or other questions relating to the test. This could include questions such as *how did you find the controls? Which part of the game did you find most frustrating? Which part was the most rewarding? Would you pay for this game?*

Something important to consider when taking feedback from the tester is who they are. Are they a friend, a relative, or a total stranger? When testing with people close to you, it's probable that the feedback won't be useful. They will try to water down the poor parts of the game as they might think that you asked them to play the game to receive compliments, but that cannot be farther from the truth. You want real, harsh, objective feedback—that's the only way you can really improve your game.

So, unless your friends are really honest with you, try to test your game on unknown people. This could be other students in your educational institution, or at your workplace, or random people in the street. Try to go to game conventions with spaces to showcase indie games. Also, consider your target audience when testing. If your game is a casual mobile game, you shouldn't be taking it to a Doom meet-up as you will mostly receive unrelated feedback. Know your audience and look for them. Also, consider that you will probably need to test your game on at least 10 people. You will notice that maybe one person didn't like the game and the other 9 did. As in statistics, your sample must be big enough to be considered valid.

Also, even though we said that our perception doesn't count, if you apply common sense and be honest with yourself, you can get feedback from your own playtesting. But now that we have gathered feedback, what we can do with it?

Interpreting feedback

You got what you wanted—lots of information about your game. What do you do now? Well, that depends on the feedback. You have different types and different ways to solve it. The easiest feedback to tackle is errors—for example, the door didn't open when I put in the key, the enemy won't die no matter how many bullets I shot at it, and so on. To solve these, you must carry out what the player did step by step so that you can reproduce the issue. Once you reproduce it, debug your game to see the error—maybe it's caused by a null check or a misconfiguration in the scene.

Try to gather as much detail about the situation as possible, such as when the issue occurred and at what level, which gear the player had, the number of lives the player had left, or if the player was in the air or crouched down—any data that allows you to get to the exact same situation. Some bugs can be tricky and can sometimes happen in the strangest situations. You might think that strange bugs that happen 1% of the time can be ignored, but remember that if your game is successful, it will be played by hundreds, maybe thousands, of players—that 1% can really affect your player base.

Then, you have to balance the feedback. You could get feedback such as there weren't enough bullets, I had too many lives, the enemies are tough, the game is too easy, or the game is too hard. This must be considered alongside your objectives. Did you really want the player to be short on bullets or lives? Did you want the enemies to be hard to defeat? In this scenario, things that the player found difficult might be the exact experience you desired, and here is where you need to remember the target audience. Maybe the user that gave you that feedback is not who you expect to play the game (again, think of the example of *Dark Souls*, a game that is not for everyone). But if the player is the target audience, you might need to balance.

Balancing is when you need to tweak the game numbers, the amount of bullets, the amount of waves, the enemies, the enemies' lives, the enemies' bullets, and so on. That's why we exposed lots of properties of our scripts—so that they can be easily changed. This can be an extensive process. Getting all those numbers to work together is difficult. If you increase a property too much, another one might need to be reduced. Your game is basically a big spreadsheet of calculations. Actually, most game designers master the use of spreadsheets to do exactly this—balance the game, make calculations, and see how changing one cell changes the other—and before testing it the hard way, play the game.

In the following screenshot, you can see how we prepared our `Player` object to be easily configured in the Editor:

Figure 21.2 – Some of the properties that affect gameplay

You can also get some feedback such as *"I don't understand why the player does what it does," "I don't understand the motives of the villains,"* and so on. This can be easy to underestimate, but remember that your game mechanics, aesthetics, and story (if any) must be in sync. If one of those elements fails, there is the risk of the rest of them also failing. If you have a futuristic history setting but your main weapon is a metal sword, you need to justify its existence somehow, perhaps with a story point. If your enemy wants to destroy the world but appears to be a kind person, you need to justify that somehow. These details are what make the game believable.

Finally, you have perception feedback, such as *"the game didn't entertain me"* or *"I didn't enjoy the game."* That feedback can be converted into the other feedback if you ask the right questions, but sometimes, the tester doesn't know what the problem is; the game can just feel wrong in their eyes. This, of course, is not useful by itself, but don't underestimate it. It might be a hint that you need to do further testing.

In game development, when you think you are finished with the game, you will discover that you have just started to develop it. Testing will make you realize that the game is not finished until the players are happy with the game, and that can take even more time than preparing the first version, so prepare for having to iterate the game a lot.

Big games, where the first prototype could take years, carry out testing in the early stages of their game, sometimes with fake assets to hide sensitive information that can spoil the game or make the competitors aware of their plans. Some developers even release a mini-game based on the main game, with a different story and aesthetics, just to test an idea. Also, there is the soft launch, where the game is released but to a restricted audience—maybe to a specific country that will not be your main audience and source of income—to test and iterate the game before releasing it to the rest of the world.

So, have patience. Testing is where the real development of the game starts, but after all those extensive testing sessions have ended and the game is finished, what is the next step? Release!

Releasing your game

We are here— the big moment! We have the gold build, which is the final version of the game. Do we just throw it at our target store (such as Steam, the Google Play Store, the Apple App Store, and so on)? Well…no—actually, we still have lots of work to do, work that we should have started before getting to the gold build. So, let's explore what that extra work is and in which phase it should be carried out.

In this section, we will examine the following release phases:

- Pre-release
- Release
- Post-release

Let's start by discussing the pre-release phase.

Pre-release

One thing to do before pre-release, and ideally before you start developing your game, is to decide where you are going to sell your game. Nowadays, that means choosing a digital store—selling physical copies of games is not an option for newly starting independent developers. You have several options, but for PCs, the most common place for this is Steam, a well-known platform that allows you to upload your game to the platform for the price of 100 USD. After it is reviewed, it can then be published. On iOS, the only way is using the App Store, which charges 100 USD per year for you to publish on it. Finally, on Android, you have the Play store, which allows you to publish on it for a one-off payment of 25 USD. Consoles have harder requisites, so we are not going to mention them.

After picking a digital store, if you just release your game without any preparation, your game can be easily lost in the sea of releases that happen on the same day. Nowadays, the competition is strong, and dozens of games might be released on the same day as yours, so you must highlight your game somehow. There are lots of ways of doing this, but it requires experience in digital marketing, which can be difficult. It requires skills other than regular developer ones. If you insist on doing it by yourself without hiring someone, here are some things you can do.

First, you can create a game community, such as a blog or group, where you can post information about your game regularly. This includes updates on its development, screenshots of new features, new concept art, and so on. Your job here is to capture the interest of players and keep them interested in your game even if it's not released yet, just to prepare them to buy your game as soon as it's released. Here, you need to be creative to keep their interest in the game—vary the content you post, maybe share some mini-games with your community with the opportunity to win prizes, or post questionnaires or giveaways; really, do anything that captures the attention of your audience.

Also, try to develop a community when you are not too near but not too far from the release date. That way, you won't lose the attention of the players due to long wait times and you can be honest with the expectations of your game. They will change a lot during the development and the scope is likely to be reduced from its initial design. You will need to deal with the hype, which can be dangerous.

Of course, we need people to join the community, so you must publish it somewhere. You can pay for ads, but aside from the cost and difficulty to make them relevant, there are other free ways of doing this. You might send a free copy of your game to an influencer, such as a YouTuber or an Instagrammer, so that they can play your game and give a review to their audience. This can be difficult if the influencer doesn't like the game as they will be honest, and that can be bad for you. So, you really need to be sure to give them a polished version, but not necessarily a final version. There are also paid influencers that you can approach, but again, that requires money.

You have other free options, such as going onto forums or groups and posting information about your game, but be sensible here. Don't make your post feel like cheap advertising—know where you are publishing. Some groups don't like those kinds of posts and will reject them. Try to look for places that allow that kind of self-advertising. There are groups intended just for that, so just avoid being invasive in certain communities.

Finally, another option you have is to contact a publisher, a company that specializes in doing this kind of marketing. They will allocate money for publishing and will have people that work to manage your communities, which can be a big relief. You have more time to create your game, but it also has some drawbacks. First, of course, they will get a cut of your game revenue, and depending on the publisher, this can be really high. However, you need to contrast that with the revenue you will get by doing your own marketing. Also, publishers will ask you to change your game to meet their criteria. Some ask for your game to be localized (supporting several languages) or ask for your game to support certain controllers, to have a certain way to do tutorials, and so on. Finally, consider that certain publishers are associated with certain types of games, so if you are creating an intense action game, you wouldn't publish it with a casual-games publisher. Find the right publisher for you:

Figure 21.3 – Some well-known publishers, some of which don't develop their own games, just publish them

Now that we have the foundations prepared for release, how do we release the game?

Release

Aside from all the setup and integrations your game might need to have to the selected digital store platform (which again depends on your audience), there are some things to consider when releasing it.

Some stores might have a review process, which consists of playing your game and seeing whether it meets the criteria of the store. As an example, at the time of writing this book, the Apple App Store requires every game they publish to have some kind of social sign-in option (such as Facebook, Google, and so on) and to also support Apple sign-in. They will simply not admit your game if you do not comply. Another example is PS Vita, which asks your game to support some kind of interaction with its front or rear touchpads. So, be aware early on about these requirements. They can affect the release of your game a lot if you don't take care of it.

Aside from these requirements, of course, there are other criteria to be met, such as whether there is adult or violent content. Consider a platform that supports the kind of game you have created. Some can even ask you to get ratings from the **Entertainment Software Rating Board** (**ESRB**) or similar rating boards. Another common requirement that you need to be aware of is that the game should not crash, at least not in the usual workflow of the game. Also, the game must perform well, can't have intense performance issues, and sometimes, your initial game download size can't exceed a specified maximum limit, which you can usually solve by downloading the content in the game itself (look for the **Addressables** Unity package for this). Again, all of these requirements vary depending on the store.

Now, even if these requirements are met, the process to check them can take time—days, weeks, or sometimes even months. So, keep this in mind when defining a release date. In big consoles where this process can take months, sometimes the developers use that time to create the famous day-1 patch, a patch that fixes bugs that won't stop the game from being released but help with the overall game experience. It's a questionable but understandable practice.

Finally, remember that the first day of the release is critical. You will be in the **New Releases** section of the store, and here is where you will have the most exposure. After that, all exposure will mostly rely on your marketing and sales. Some stores allow you to be featured. You can talk directly with representatives of the store and see how you can do this. If the store is interested in your game, they might feature you (or you might have to pay for that). The first day is important, so be prepared for that.

Now, the game is out and in the hands of the people. Have we finished our work? A few years ago, that might have been true, but not today. We still have the post-release work to do.

Post-release

Even if the game is released, this is not an excuse to stop testing it. You can actually get even more feedback if your game is played by thousands of people. Sadly, you can't be there to observe them, but you can automate the information-gathering process. You can do this by making your code report analytics to a server, as the Unity Analytics package does. Even if this information is not as direct as in-person testing, a massive amount of data and statistics can be gathered this way, and you can improve the game on the fly thanks to updates, something that old games couldn't do as easily as they can today. No game is released perfect, and sometimes, due to time pressures, you might need to roll out an early release, so prepare your game to be updated regularly after release. There are some cases of games that had a bad launch but were resurrected from the grave. Don't underestimate that last course of action. You have already spent too much to give up on your badly released game.

Also, if your monetization model relies on in-app purchases, which means people spend money on loot boxes or cosmetic items, you will need to have constant content updates. This will keep the players playing your game. The more they play the game, the more money will be spent on it. You might take advantage of the information you gather through analytics not only to fix your game but also to decide which content is being consumed most by your players and focus on that. You can also carry out A/B testing, which consists of releasing two versions of the update to different users and seeing which one is the most successful. This allows you to test ideas on a live game. As you can see, there is still plenty of work to do. Also, use metrics to track whether players are losing interest in your game, and if so, why—is there a difficult level? Is the game too easy? Pay attention to your player base. Ask them questions in the communities you created, or just look at the reviews—users are usually willing to tell you how they would like their favorite game to be improved.

Summary

Developing the game is just one part of the work; releasing it to be successful can be a huge task. Sometimes, it can cost more than the game itself. So, unless you are making a game for fun, if you want to make your game for a living, you will need to learn how to manage releases or hire people that are capable of helping with the pre-release, release, and post-release phases of your game, which can be a smart move.

Of course, this chapter just provides a simple introduction to this big topic, so I would recommend that you read some extra material if you want to take this part of game development seriously. A very well-explained and bite-sized source of information on this topic is the *Extra Credits* YouTube channel, which provides short videos to convey valuable information. Also, there is a great book called *The Art of Game Design: A Book of Lenses*, which provides a thorough introduction to game design.

Congratulations, you have finished *part 3* of this book! You have gained the basic knowledge to start your game development career and choose some of the several roles you can do in it. I recommend you put what you've learned into practice before reading more books on this topic. Gaining information is important, but the only way to convert that information into knowledge is through experimentation. Just be sure to balance theory and practice.

In the next part of this book, we are going to explore some extra topics that might be of interest to you, starting with an introduction to extended reality applications.

22
Augmented Reality in Unity

Nowadays, new technologies expand the fields of application of Unity, from gaming to all kinds of software, such as simulations, training, apps, and so on. In the latest versions of Unity, we saw lots of improvements in the field of **augmented reality (AR)**, which allows us to add a layer of virtuality on top of our reality, thereby augmenting what our device can perceive to create games that rely on real-world data, such as the camera's image, our real-world position, and the current weather. This can also be applied to work environments, such as when viewing the building map or checking the electrical ducts inside a wall. Welcome to the extra section of this book, where we are going to discuss how to create AR applications using Unity's AR Foundation package.

In this chapter, we will examine the following AR Foundation concepts:

- Using AR Foundation
- Building for mobile devices
- Creating a simple AR game

By the end of this chapter, you will be able to create AR apps using AR Foundation, and will have a fully functional game that uses its framework so that you can test the framework's capabilities.

Let's start by exploring the AR Foundation framework.

Using AR Foundation

When it comes to AR, Unity has two main tools to create applications: Vuforia and AR Foundation. Vuforia is an AR framework that can work on almost any phone and contains all the needed features for basic AR apps, but with a paid subscription for more advanced features. On the other hand, the completely free AR Foundation framework supports the latest AR native features of our devices but is supported only by newer devices. Picking between one or the other depends a lot on the type of project you're going to build and the target audience. However, since this book aims to discuss the latest Unity features, we are going to explore how to use AR Foundation to create our first AR app for detecting the positions of images and surfaces in the real world. So, we'll start by exploring its API.

In this section, we will examine the following AR Foundation concepts:

- Creating an AR Foundation project
- Using tracking features

Let's start by discussing how to prepare our project so that it can run AR Foundation apps.

Creating an AR Foundation project

Something to consider when creating AR projects is that we will not only change the way we code our game, but also the game design aspect. AR apps have differences, especially in the way the user interacts, and also limitations, such as the user being in control of the camera all the time. We cannot simply port an existing game to AR without changing the very core experience of the game. That's why, in this chapter, we are going to work on a brand new project; it would be too difficult to change the game we've created so far so that it works well in AR.

In our case, we are going to create a game where the user controls a player moving a "marker", a physical image you can print that will allow our app to recognize where the player is in the real world. We will be able to move the player while moving that image, and this virtual player will automatically shoot at the nearest Enemy. Those enemies will spawn from certain spawn points that the user will need to place in different parts of the home. As an example, we can put two spawn points on the walls and place our player marker in a table in the middle of the room so that the enemies will go toward them. In the following image, you can see a preview of what the game will look like:

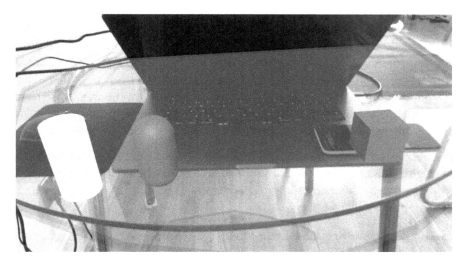

Figure 22.1 – Finished game. The Cylinder is an Enemy Spawner, the Capsule is the Enemy, and the Cube is the Player. These are positioned in a marker image displayed by the cellphone

We'll start creating a new URP-based project in the same manner we created our first game. Something to consider is that AR Foundation works with other pipelines, including built-in ones, in case you want to use it in already existing projects. If you don't remember how to create a project, please refer to *Chapter 2, Setting Up Unity*. Once you're in your new blank project, install the AR Foundation package from the Package Manager, just like we've installed other packages previously; that is, from **Window | Package Manager**. Remember to set the Package Manager so that it shows all packages, not only the ones in the project (the **Packages** button at the top-left part of the window needs to be set to **Unity Registry**). At the time of writing this book, the latest version is 4.0.2. Remember you can use the **See other Versions** button that appears clicking the triangle at the left of the package under **Package Item** in the list to display other version options. If you find a newer version than mine, you can try using that one, but as usual, if something works differently to what we want, please install this specific version:

Package Manager		
✚ ▼ Packages: In Project ▼ Sort: Name ↓ ▼		⚙ ⌕ ar
▼ Unity		**AR Foundation**
▶ AR Foundation	4.0.2	Unity Technologies Inc.
▶ ARCore XR Plug...	4.0... ✓	**Version 4.0.2 - June 16, 2020**

Figure 22.2 – Installing AR Foundation

Before we install any other needed packages, now is a good moment to discuss some core ideas of the AR Foundation framework. This package, by itself, does nothing; it defines a series of AR features that mobile devices offer, such as image tracking, cloud points, and object tracking, but the actual implementation of how to do that is contained in the **Provider** packages, such as AR Kit and AR Core XR plugins. This is designed like this because, depending on the target device you want to work with, the way those features are implemented changes. As an example, in iOS, Unity implements those features using AR Kit, while in Android, it uses AR Core; they are platform-specific frameworks.

Something to consider here is that not all iOS or Android devices support AR Foundation apps. You might find an updated list of supported devices when searching for AR Core and AR Kit supported devices on the internet. At the time of writing, the following links provide the supported devices lists:

- iOS: `https://www.apple.com/lae/ios/augmented-reality/` (at the bottom of the page)

- Android: `https://developers.google.com/ar/discover/ supported-devices`

Also, there isn't a PC Provider package, so the only way to test AR Foundation apps so far is directly on the device, but testing tools are going to be released soon. In my case, I will be creating an app for iOS, so aside from the **AR Foundation** package, I need to install the **ARKit XR** plugin. However, if you want to develop for Android, install the **ARCore XR** plugin instead (or both if you're targeting both platforms). I will be using the 4.0.2 version of the ARKit package, but at the moment of writing this book, the ARCore recommended version is 4.0.4 Usually, the versions of the **AR Foundation** and **Provider** packages match, but apply the same logic as when you picked the **AR Foundation** version. In the following screenshot, you can see the **ARKit** package in the Package Manager:

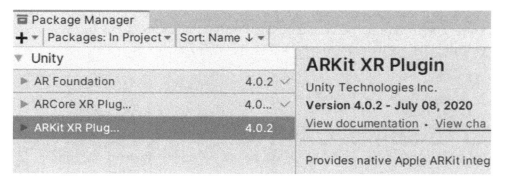

Figure 22.3 – Installing the platform-specific AR provider package

Now that we have the needed plugins, we need to prepare a scene for AR, as follows:

1. Create a new Scene in **File | New Scene**.

2. Delete **Main Camera**; we are going to use a different one.

3. In the **GameObject | XR** menu, create an **AR Session** Object.

4. In the same menu, create an **AR Session Origin** Object that has a **Camera** inside it:

Figure 22.4 – Creating the Session objects

5. Your hierarchy should look as follows:

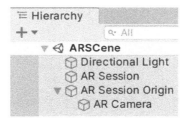

Figure 22.5 – Starter ARSCcene

The **AR Session** object will be responsible for initializing AR Framework and will handle all the update logic for the AR systems. The **AR Session Origin** object will allow the framework to locate tracked objects such as images and point clouds in a relative position to the scene. The devices inform the positions of tracked objects relative to what the device considers "the origin". This is usually the first area of your house you were pointing at when the app started detecting objects, so the AR Session Origin object will represent that area. Finally, you can check the camera inside the origin, which contains some extra components, with the most important being **AR Pose Driver**, which will make your **Camera** object move along with your device. Since the device's position is relative to the Session Origin object's point, the camera needs to be inside the origin object.

One extra step in case you are working in a URP project (our case) is that you need to set up the render pipeline so that it supports rendering the camera image in the app. To do that, go to the `Settings` folder that was generated when we created the project, look for the `Forward Renderer` file, and select it. In the **Renderer Features** list, click the **Add renderer feature** button and select **AR Background Renderer Feature**. Consider that this option might be unavailable if you are working on versions older than 4.0.0 of the AR Foundation and Provider plugins. In the following screenshot, you can see what the Forward Renderer asset should look like:

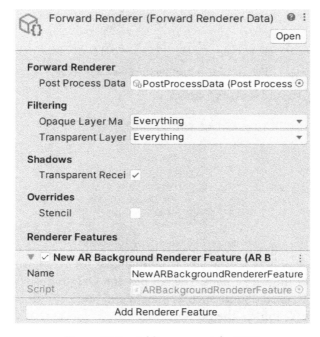

Figure 22.6 – Adding support for URP

And that's all! We are ready to start exploring the AR Foundation components so that we can implement tracking features.

Using tracking features

For our project, we are going to need two of the most common tracking features in AR (but not the only ones): image recognition and plane detection. The first one consists of detecting the position in the real world of a specific image so that we can place digital objects on top of it, such as the player. The second one, plane detection, consists of recognizing real-life surfaces, such as floors, tables, and walls, so that we have a reference of where we can put objects such as the enemies' spawn points. Only horizontal and vertical surfaces are recognized (just vertical surfaces on some devices).

The first thing we need to do is tell our app which images it needs to detect, as follows:

1. Add an image to the project that you can print or display in a cellphone. Having a way to display the image in the real world is necessary to test this. In this case, I will use the following image:

Figure 22.7 – Image to track

> **Important Note**
>
> Try to get an image that contains as many features as you can. This means an image with lots of little details, such as contrasts, sharp corners, and so on. Those are what our AR systems use to detect it; the more detail, the better the recognition. In our case, the Unity logo we are using doesn't actually have too many details, but there's enough contrast (just black and white) and sharp corners for the system to recognize it. If your device has trouble detecting it, try other images (the classic QR code might help).

Consider that some devices might have trouble with certain images, such as the image suggested in this book. If this generates issues when testing, please try using another one. You will be testing this on your device in the upcoming sections of this chapter, so just keep this in mind.

2. Create a Reference Image Library, an asset containing all the images we wish our app to recognize, by clicking the + button in **Project Panel** and selecting **XR | Reference Image Library**:

Figure 22.8 – Creating a Reference Image Library

3. Select the library asset and click the **Add Image** button to add a new image to the library.

4. Drag the texture to the texture slot (the one that says **None**).

5. Turn **Specify Size** on and set **Physical Size** to the size that your image will be in real life, in meters. Try to be accurate here; on some devices, not having this value right might result in the image not being tracked:

Figure 22.9 – Adding an image to be recognized

Now that we've specified the images to be detected, let's test this by placing a cube on top of the real-life image:

1. Create a prefab of a cube and add the **AR Tracked Image** component to it.

2. Add the **AR Tracked Image Manager** component to the **AR Session Origin** object. This will be responsible for detecting images and creating objects in its position.

3. Drag the **Image Library** asset to the **Serialized Library** property of the component to specify the images to recognize.

4. Drag the **Cube** prefab to the **Tracked Image** Prefab property of the component:

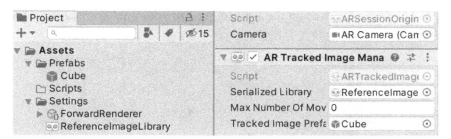

Figure 22.10 – Setting up the Tracked Image Manager

And that's all! We will see a cube spawning in the same position the image is located at in the real world. Remember that you need to test this in the device, which we will do in the next section, so for now, let's keep coding our test app:

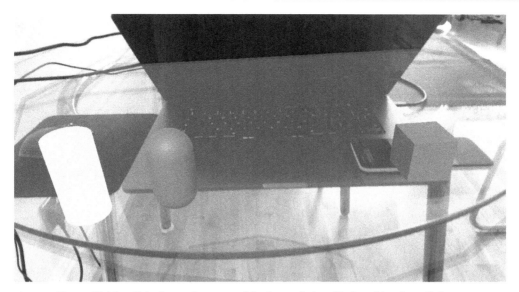

Figure 22.11 – Cube located on top of the image being displayed by the cellphone

Let's also prepare our app so that it can detect and display the plane surfaces the camera has recognized. This is simply done by adding the **AR Plane Manager** component to the **AR Session Origin** object:

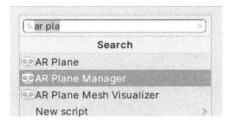

Figure 22.12 – Adding the AR Plane Manager component

This component will detect surface planes over our house as we move the camera over it. It can take a while to detect them, so it's important to visualize the detected areas to get feedback about this to ensure it's working properly. We can manually get information about the plane from a component reference to the AR Plane Manager, but luckily, Unity allows us to visualize planes easily. Let's take a look:

1. Create a prefab of a plane, first by creating the plane in **GameObject |
    3D Object | Plane**.

2. Add a **Line Renderer** to it. This will allow us to draw a line over the edges of the detected areas.

3. Set the **Width** property of **Line Renderer** to a small value such as `0.01`, the **Color** property to black, and uncheck **Use World Space**:

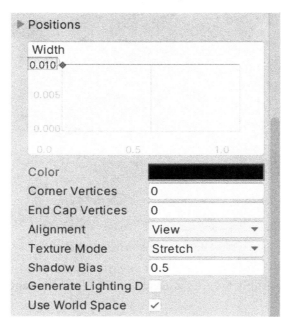

Figure 22.13 – Setting the Line Renderer

4. Remember to create a material for **Line Renderer** with the proper shader and set it as the material of the renderer:

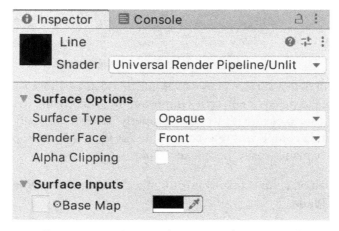

Figure 22.14 – Creating the Line Renderer Material

5. Also, create a transparent material and use it in the **MeshRenderer** plane. We want to see through it so that we can easily see the real surface beneath:

Figure 22.15 – Material for the detected plane

6. Add the **AR Plane** and **AR Plane Mesh Visualizer** components to the **Plane** prefab.

7. Drag the prefab to the **Plane Prefab** property of the **AR Plane Manager** component of the **AR Session Origin** object:

Figure 22.16 – Setting the plane visualization prefab

Now, we have a way to see the planes, but seeing them is not the only thing we can do (sometimes, we don't even want them to be visible). The real power of planes resides on placing virtual objects on top of real-life surfaces, tapping in a specific plane area, and getting its real-life position. We can access the plane data using the AR Plane Manager or by accessing the AR Plane component of our visualization planes, but something easier is to use the **AR Raycast Manager** component.

The **AR Raycast Manager** component provides us with the equivalent to the `Physics.Raycast` function of the Unity Physics system, which, as you may recall, is used to create imaginary rays that start from one position and go toward a specified direction in order to make them hit surfaces and detect the exact hit point. The version provided by **AR Raycast Manager**, instead of colliding with Physics Colliders, collides with tracked objects, mostly Point Clouds (we are not using them) and the "Planes" we are tracking. We can test this feature by following these steps:

1. Add the **AR Raycast Manager** component to the **AR Session Origin** object.

2. Create a custom script called `InstanceOnPlane` in the **AR Session Origin** object.

3. In the **Awake** cache, add the reference to ARRaycastManager. You will need to add the `using UnityEngine.XR.ARFoundation;` line to the top of the script for this class to be usable in our script.

4. Create a private field of the `List<ARRaycastHit>` type and instantiate it; the Raycast is going to detect every plane our ray hit, not just the first one:

```
List<ARRaycastHit> hits = new List<ARRaycastHit>();
```

Figure 22.17 – List to store hits

5. Under **Update**, check if the Left Mouse Button (`KeyCode.Mouse0`) is being pressed. In AR apps, the mouse is emulated with the device's touch screen (you can also use the `Input.touches` array for multi-touch support).

6. Inside the `if` statement, add another condition for calling the `Raycast` function of **AR Raycast Manager**, passing the position of the mouse as the first parameter and the list of hits as the second.

7. This will throw a raycast toward the direction the player touches the screen and store the hits inside the list we provided. This will return `true` if something has been hit, and `false` if not:

```
if (Input.GetKeyDown(KeyCode.Mouse0) && raycastManager.Raycast(Input.mousePosition, hits))
{

}
```

Figure 22.18 – Throwing AR raycasts

8. Add a public field to specify the prefab to instantiate in the place we touched. You can just create a Sphere prefab to test this; there's no need to add any special component to the prefab here.

9. Instantiate the prefab in the **Position** and **Rotation** fields of the **Pose** property of the first hit stored in the list. The hits are sorted by distance, so the first hit is the closest one. Your final script should look as follows:

```
using System.Collections.Generic;
using UnityEngine;
using UnityEngine.XR.ARFoundation;

public class InstanceOnPlane : MonoBehaviour
{
    List<ARRaycastHit> hits = new List<ARRaycastHit>();
    ARRaycastManager raycastManager;
    public GameObject prefab;

    void Awake()
    {
        raycastManager = GetComponent<ARRaycastManager>();
    }

    void Update()
    {
        if (Input.GetKeyDown(KeyCode.Mouse0) && raycastManager.Raycast(Input.mousePosition, hits))
        {
            Instantiate(prefab, hits[0].pose.position, hits[0].pose.rotation);
        }
    }
}
```

Figure 22.19 – Raycaster component

In this section, we learned how to create a new AR project using AR Foundation. We discussed how to install and set up the framework, as well as how to detect real-life image positions and surfaces, and then how to place objects on top of them.

As you may have noticed, we never hit play to test this, and sadly at the time of writing this book, we cannot test this in the Editor. Instead, we need to test this directly on the device. Due to this, in the next section, we are going to learn how to do builds for mobile devices such as Android and iOS.

Building for mobile devices

Unity is a very powerful tool that solves the most common problems in game development very easily, and one of them is building the game for several target platforms. Now, the Unity part of building our project for such devices is easy to do, but each device has its non-Unity-related nuances for installing development builds. In order to test our AR app, we need to test it directly in the device. So, let's explore how we can make our app run on Android and iOS, the most common mobile platforms.

Before diving into this topic, it is worth mentioning that the following procedures change a lot over time, so you will need to find the latest instructions on the internet. The Unity Learn portal site (`https://learn.unity.com/tutorial/building-for-mobile`) may be a good alternative in case the instructions in this book fail, but try the steps here first.

In this section, we will examine the following mobile building concepts:

- Building for Android
- Building for iOS

Let's start by discussing how to build our app so that it runs on Android phones.

Building for Android

Creating Android builds is relatively easy compared to other platforms, so we'll start with Android. Remember that you will need an Android device capable of running AR Foundation apps, so please refer to the link regarding Android supported devices we mentioned in the first section of this chapter. The first thing we need to do is check if we have installed Unity's Android support and configured our project to use that platform. To do that, follow these steps:

1. Close Unity and open **Unity Hub**.

2. Go to the **Installs** section and locate the Unity version you are working on.

3. Click the three dots button at the top-right corner of the Unity version and click **Add Modules**:

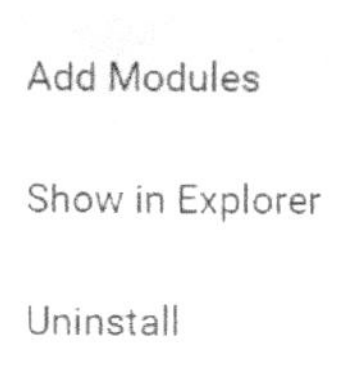

Add Modules

Show in Explorer

Uninstall

Figure 22.20 – Adding modules to the Unity version

4. Make sure **Android Build Support** and the sub-options that are displayed when you click the arrow on its left are checked. If not, check them and click the **Done** button at the bottom-right to install them:

∨ ☑ Android Build Support	Installed	1.1 GB
☑ Android SDK & NDK Tools	Installed	2.9 GB
☑ OpenJDK	Installed	70.5 MB

Figure 22.21 – Adding Android support to Unity

5. Open the AR project we created in this chapter.

6. Go to **Build Settings** (**File | Build Settings**).

7. Select the **Android** platform from the list and click the **Switch Platform** button at the bottom-right part of the window:

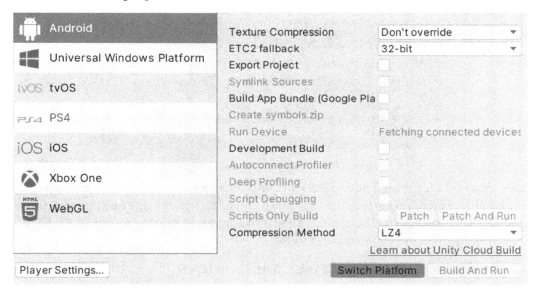

Figure 22.22 – Switching to Android builds

To build an app on Android, there are some requirements we need to meet, such as having the Java SDK (not the regular Java runtime) and Android SDK installed, but luckily, the new versions of Unity take care of that. Just to double-check that we have installed the needed dependencies, follow these steps:

1. Go to **Unity Preferences** (**Edit | Preferences** on Windows, **Unity | Preferences** on Mac).

2. Click **External Tools**.

3. Check that all the options that say …**Installed with Unity** on the Android section are checked. This means we will be using all the dependencies installed by Unity:

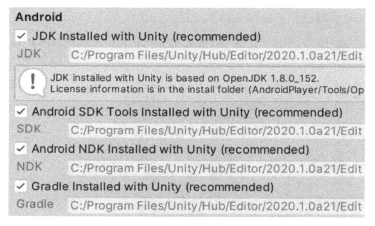

Figure 22.23 – Using installed dependencies

There are some additional Android AR Core-specific related settings to check that you can find at https://developers.google.com/ar/develop/unity-arf/ quickstart-android. These can change if you are using newer versions of AR Core. You can apply them by following these steps:

1. Go to **Player Settings** (**Edit | Project Settings | Player**).

2. Uncheck **Multithreaded Rendering** and **Auto Graphics API**.

3. Remove **Vulkan** from the **Graphics APIs** list.

4. Set **Minimum API Level** to **Android 7.0**:

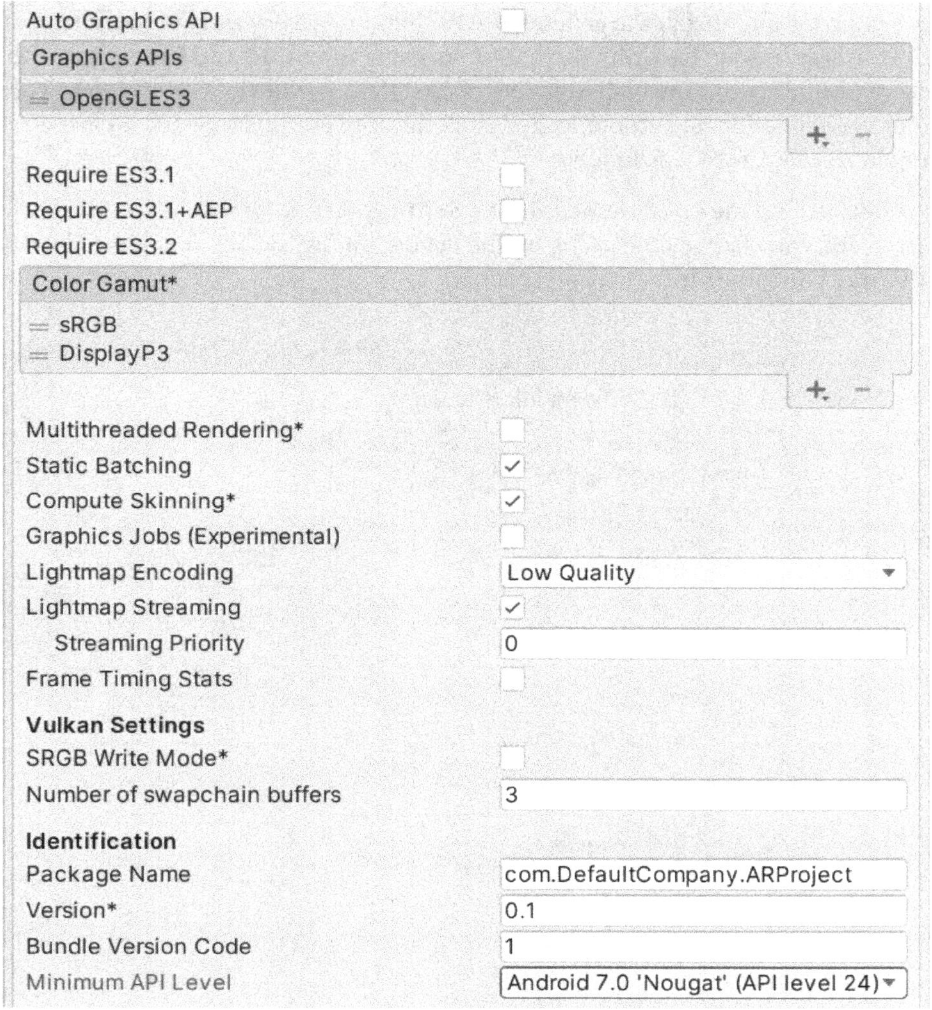

Figure 22.24 – AR Core settings

Now, you can finally build the app from **File | Build Settings** like usual, by using the **Build** button. This time, the output will be a single APK file that you can install by copying the file to your device and opening it. Remember that in order to install APKs that weren't downloaded from the Play Store, you need to set your device to allow **Install Unknown Apps**. The location for that option varies a lot, depending on the Android version and the device you are using, but this option is usually located in the **Security** settings. Some Android versions prompt you to view these settings when installing the APK.

Now, we can copy and install the generated APK build file every time we want to create a build. However, we can let Unity do that for us using the **Build and Run** button. This option, after building the app, will look for the first Android device connected to your computer via USB and will automatically install the app. For this to work, we need to prepare our device and PC, as follows:

On your device, find the build number in the **Settings** section of the device, whose location, again, can change depending on the device. On my device, it is located in the **About Phone | Software Information** section:

Figure 22.25 – Locating the build number

1. Tap it a few times until the device says you are now a programmer. This procedure enables the hidden developer option in the device, which you can now find in the settings.

2. Open the developer options and turn on **USB Debugging**, which allows your PC to have special permissions on your device. In this case, it allows you to install apps.

3. Install the USB drivers from your phone manufacturer's site onto your computer. For example, if you have a Samsung device, search for `Samsung USB Driver`. Also, if you can't find that, you can look for `Android USB Driver` to get the generic drivers, but that might not work if your device manufacturer has their own. On Mac, this step is usually not necessary.

4. Connect your device (or reconnect it if it's already connected). The option to **Allow USB Debugging** for your computer will appear on the device. Check **Always Allow** and click **OK**:

Figure 22.26 – Allowing USB debugging

5. Accept the **Allow Data** prompt that appears.

6. If these options don't appear, check that the **USB Mode** of your device is set to **Debugging** and not any other.

7. In Unity, build with the **Build and Run** button.

8. Please remember to try another image if you have trouble detecting the image where we instantiate the player (the Unity logo, in my case). This might vary a lot, according to your device's capabilities.

And that's all! Now that you have your app running on your device, let's learn how to do the same for the iOS platform.

Building for iOS

When developing on iOS, you will need to spend some money. You will need to run Xcode, a piece of software you can only run on OS X. Due to this, you'll need a device that can run it, such as a MacBook, a Mac mini, and so on. There may be ways to run OS X on PCs, but you will need to find this out and try it for yourself. Besides spending on a Mac and on an iOS device (iPhone, iPad, iPod, and so on), you'll need to pay for an Apple Developer account, which costs 99 USD per year, even if you are not planning to release the application on the App Store (there may be alternatives, but, again, you will need to find them).

So, to create an iOS build, you should do the following:

1. Get a Mac computer.

2. Get an iOS device.

3. Create an Apple Developer account (at the time of writing this book, you can create one at `https://developer.apple.com/`).

4. Install Xcode from the App Store onto your Mac.

5. Check if you have iOS build support in Unity Install on the Unity Hub. Please refer to the *Building on Android* section for more information about this step:

Figure 22.27 – Enabling iOS build support

6. Switch to the iOS platform under **Build Settings**, selecting iOS and clicking the **Switch Platform** button:

Figure 22.28 – Switching to iOS build

7. Click the **Build** button in the **Build Settings** window and wait.

You will notice that the result of the build process will be a folder containing an Xcode project. Unity cannot create the build directly, so it generates a project you can open with the Xcode software we mentioned previously. The step you need to follow to create a build with the Xcode version being used in this book (11.4.1) are as follows:

1. Double-click the `.xcproject` file inside the generated folder:

Figure 22.29 – Xcode project file

2. Go to **Xcode | Preferences**.

3. In the **Accounts** tab, hit the + button at the bottom-left part of the window and log in with the Apple account you registered as an Apple developer:

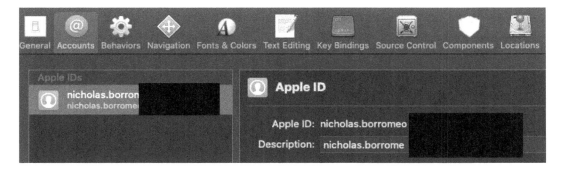

Figure 22.30 – Account Settings

4. Connect your device and select it from the top-left part of the window, which should now say **Generic iOS device**:

Figure 22.31 – Selecting the device

5. In the left panel, click the folder icon and then the **Unity-iPhone** settings to display the project settings.

6. From the **TARGETS** list, select **Unity-iPhone** and click on the **Signing & Capabilities** tab.

7. In the **Team** settings, select the options that says Personal Team:

Figure 22.32 – Selecting a team

8. If you see a **Failed to register bundle identifier** error, just change the **Bundle Identifier** setting for another one, always respecting the format (com.XXXX. XXXX), and then click on **Try Again** until it is solved. Once you find one that works, set it in Unity (**Bundle Identifier** under **Player Settings**) to avoid needing to change it in every build.

9. Hit the **Play** button at the top-left part of the window and wait for the build to complete. You might be prompted to enter your password a couple of times in the process, so please do so.

10. When the build completes, remember to unlock the device. A prompt will ask you to do that. Note that the process won't continue unless you unlock the phone.

11. After completion, you may see an error saying that the app couldn't be launched but that it was installed anyway. If you try to open it, it will say you need to trust the developer of the app, which you can do by going to the settings of your device.

12. From there, go to **General | Device Management** and select the first developer in the list.

13. Click the blue **Trust …** button and then **Trust**.

14. Try to open the app again.

15. Please remember to try another image if you're having trouble detecting the image where we instantiate the player (the Unity logo, in my case). This might vary a lot, depending on your device's capabilities.

In this section, we discussed how to build a Unity project that can run on iOS and Android, thus allowing us to create mobile apps–AR mobile apps, specifically. Like any build, there are methods we can follow to profile and debug, as we saw when we looked at PC builds, but we are not going to discuss that here. Now that we have created our first test project, we will convert it into a real game by adding some mechanics to it.

Creating a simple AR game

As we discussed previously, the idea is to create a simple game where we can move our player while moving a real-life image, and also put in some Enemy Spawners by just tapping where we want them to be, such as a wall, the floor, a table, and so on. Our player will automatically shoot at the nearest Enemy, and the enemies will shoot directly at the player, so our only task will be to move the Player so that they avoid bullets. We are going to implement these game mechanics using scripts very similar to the ones we used in this book's main project.

In this section, we will develop the following AR game features:

- Spawning the Player and Enemies
- Coding the Player and Enemy behavior

First, we are going to discuss how to make our Player and Enemies appear on the app, specifically in real-world positions, and then we will make them move and shoot each other to create the specified gameplay mechanics. Let's start with spawning.

Spawning the Player and Enemies

Let's start with the Player, since that's the easiest one to deal with: we will create a prefab with the graphics we want the player to have (in my case, just a cube), a `Rigidbody` with **Is Kinematic** checked (the Player will move), and an **AR Tracked Image** script. We will set that prefab as **Tracked Image Prefab** of the **AR Tracked Image Manager** component in the **AR Session Origin** object. This will put the Player on the tracked image. Remember to set the size of the Player in terms of real-life sizes. In my case, I scaled the Player to $(0.05, 0.05, 0.05)$. Since the original cube is 1 meter in size, this means that my player will be *5x5x5* centimeters. Your Player prefab should look as follows:

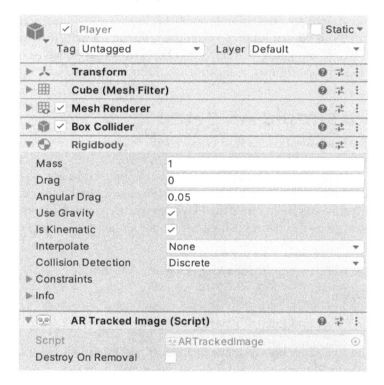

Figure 22.33 – The starting "Player" prefab

The enemies will require a little bit more work, as shown here:

1. Create a prefab called `Spawner` with the graphic you want your Spawner to have (in my case, a cylinder) and its real-life size.

2. Add a custom script that spawns a prefab every few seconds, such as the one shown in the following screenshot.

3. You will notice the usage of `Physics.IgnoreCollision` to prevent the Spawner from colliding with the `Spawner` object, getting the colliders of both objects and passing them to the function. You can also use the **Layer Collision Matrix** to prevent collisions, just like we did with this book's main project, if you prefer to:

```
using UnityEngine;

public class Spawner : MonoBehaviour
{
    public GameObject prefab;
    public float frequency;
    void Awake()
    {
        InvokeRepeating("Spawn", frequency ,frequency);
    }

    void Spawn()
    {
        var obj :GameObject = Instantiate(prefab, transform.position, transform.rotation);
        Physics.IgnoreCollision(GetComponentInChildren<Collider>(), obj.GetComponentInChildren<Collider>());
    }
}
```

Figure 22.34 – Spawner script

4. Create an `Enemy` prefab with the desired graphic (a Capsule, in my case) and a `Rigidbody` component with the **Is Kinematic** checkbox checked. This way, the Enemy will move but not with physics. Remember to consider the real-life size of the Enemy.

5. Set the **Prefab** property of the Spawner so that it spawns our Enemy at your desired time frequency:

Figure 22.35 – Configuring the Spawner

6. Add a new `SpawnerPlacer` custom script to the **AR Session Origin** object that instantiates a prefab in the place the player tapped using the AR Raycast system, as shown in the following screenshot:

```csharp
using System.Collections.Generic;
using UnityEngine;
using UnityEngine.XR.ARFoundation;

public class SpawnerPlacer : MonoBehaviour
{
    List<ARRaycastHit> hits = new List<ARRaycastHit>();
    public GameObject spawnerPrefab;

    void Update()
    {
        if (Input.GetKeyDown(KeyCode.Mouse0) &&
            GetComponent<ARRaycastManager>().Raycast(Input.mousePosition, hits))
        {
            Instantiate(spawnerPrefab, hits[0].pose.position, hits[0].pose.rotation);
        }
    }
}
```

Figure 22.36 – Placing the Spawners

7. Set the prefab of `SpawnerPlacer` so that it spawns the **Spawner** prefab we created earlier.

And that's all for the first part. If you test the game now, you will be able to tap on the detected planes in the app and see how the Spawner starts creating enemies. You can also look at the target image and see our Cube Player appear.

Now that we have the objects in the scene, let's make them do something more interesting, starting with the Enemies.

Coding the Player and Enemy behavior

The Enemy must move toward the player in order to shoot at them, so it will need to have access to the player position. Since the Enemy is instantiated, we cannot drag the Player reference to the prefab. However, the Player has also been instantiated, so we can add a `PlayerManager` script to the player that uses the Singleton pattern (as we did with managers). To do that, follow these steps:

1. Create a `PlayerManager` script similar to the one shown in the following screenshot and add it to the Player:

```
using UnityEngine;

public class PlayerManager : MonoBehaviour
{
    public static PlayerManager instance;

    void Awake()
    {
        instance = this;
    }
}
```

Figure 22.37 – Creating the PlayerManager script

2. Now that the Enemy has a reference to the player, let's make them look at the player by adding a `LookAtPlayer` script, as shown here:

```
using UnityEngine;

public class LookAtPlayer : MonoBehaviour
{
    void Update()
    {
        if(PlayerManager.instance == null) return;

        transform.forward = PlayerManager.instance.transform.position - transform.position;
    }
}
```

Figure 22.38 – Creating the LookAtPlayer script

3. Also, add a simple `MoveForward` script like the one shown in the following screenshot to make the **Enemy** not only look at the player but also move toward them. Since the `LookAtPlayer` script is making the Enemy face the Player, this script moving along the z axis is just enough:

```csharp
using UnityEngine;

public class MoveForward : MonoBehaviour
{
    public float speed;

    void Update()
    {
        transform.Translate(0, 0, speed * Time.deltaTime);
    }
}
```

Figure 22.39 – Creating the MoveForward script

Now, we will take care of the Player movement. Remember that our player is controlled through moving the image, so here, we are actually referring to the rotation, since the player will need to automatically look and shoot at the nearest Enemy. To do this, follow these steps:

1. Create an `Enemy` script and add it to the **Enemy** prefab.

2. Create an `EnemyManager` script like the one shown in the following screenshot and add it to an empty `EnemyManager` object in the scene:

```csharp
using System.Collections.Generic;
using UnityEngine;

public class EnemyManager : MonoBehaviour
{
    public static EnemyManager instance;

    public List<Enemy> all = new List<Enemy>();

    void Awake()
    {
        instance = this;
    }
}
```

Figure 22.40 – Creating the EnemyManager script

3. In the `Enemy` script, make sure to register the object in the **all** list of
`EnemyManager`, as we did previously with `WavesManager` in this book's
main project:

```
using UnityEngine;

public class Enemy : MonoBehaviour
{
    void OnEnable()
    {
        EnemyManager.instance.all.Add(this);
    }

    void OnDisable()
    {
        EnemyManager.instance.all.Remove(this);
    }
}
```

Figure 22.41 – Creating the Enemy script

4. Create a `LookAtNearestEnemy` script like the one shown in the following
screenshot and add it to the **Player** prefab to make it look at the nearest Enemy:

```
using UnityEngine;

public class LookAtNearestEnemy : MonoBehaviour
{
    void Update()
    {
        if(EnemyManager.instance.all.Count <= 0) return;

        var nearestEnemy = EnemyManager.instance.all[0];

        for (var i = 1; i < EnemyManager.instance.all.Count; i++)
        {
            var enemy = EnemyManager.instance.all[i];
            var distToNearest float = Vector3.Distance(nearestEnemy.transform.position, transform.position);
            var distToEnemy float = Vector3.Distance(enemy.transform.position, transform.position);

            if (distToEnemy < distToNearest)
                nearestEnemy = enemy;
        }

        if (nearestEnemy)
            transform.forward = nearestEnemy.transform.position - transform.position;
    }
}
```

Figure 22.42 – Looking at the nearest Enemy

Now that our objects are rotating and moving as expected, the only thing missing is shooting and damaging:

5. Create a `Life` script like the one shown in the following screenshot and add it to both the **Player** and **Enemy** components. Remember to set a value for the amount-of-life field. You will see this version of `Life` instead of needing to check if the life has reached zero every frame. We have created a `Damage` function to check that damage is dealt (the `Damage` function is executed), but the other version of this book's project also works:

```csharp
using UnityEngine;

public class Life : MonoBehaviour
{
    public int amount;

    public void Damage(int damageAmount)
    {
        amount -= damageAmount;
        if(amount <= 0)
            Destroy(gameObject);
    }
}
```

Figure 22.43 – Creating a Life component

6. Create a `Bullet` prefab with the desired graphics, the collider with the **Is Trigger** checkbox on the collider checked, a `Rigidbody` component with **Is Kinematic** checked (a Kinematic Trigger Collider), and the proper real-life size.

7. Add the `MoveForward` script to the **Bullet** prefab to make it move. Remember to set the speed.

8. Add a `Spawner` script to both the **Player** and the **Enemy** components and set the **Bullet** prefab as the prefab to spawn, as well as the desired spawn frequency.

9. Add a `Damager` script like the one shown in the following screenshot to the **Bullet** prefab to make bullets inflict damage on the objects it touches. Remember to set the damage:

```
using UnityEngine;

public class Damager : MonoBehaviour
{
    public int amount;

    void OnTriggerEnter(Collider other)
    {
        other.GetComponent<Life>()?.Damage(amount);
        Destroy(gameObject);
    }
}
```

Figure 22.44 – Creating a Damager script – part 1

10. Add an AutoDestroy script like the one shown in the following screenshot to the **Bullet** prefab to make it despawn after a while. Remember to set the Destroy time:

```
using UnityEngine;

public class AutoDestroy : MonoBehaviour
{
    public float time;

    void Awake()
    {
        Destroy(gameObject, time);
    }
}
```

Figure 22.45 – Creating a Damager script – part 2

And that's all! As you can see, we basically created a new game using almost the same scripts we used in the main game, mostly because we designed them to be generic (and the game genres are almost the same). Of course, this project can be improved a lot, but we have a nice base project upon which to create amazing AR apps.

Summary

In this chapter, we introduced the AR Foundation Unity framework, explored how to set it up, and how to implement several tracking features so that we can position virtual objects on top of real-life objects. We also discussed how to build our project so that it can run on both iOS and Android platforms, which is the only way we can test our AR apps at the time of writing. Finally, we created a simple AR game based on the game we created in the main project but modified it so that it's suitable for use in AR scenarios.

With this new knowledge, you will be able to start your path as an AR app developer, creating apps that augment real objects with virtual objects by detecting the positions of the real objects. This can be applied to games, training apps, and simulations. You may even be able to find new fields of usage, so take advantage of this new technology and its new possibilities!

Other Books You May Enjoy

If you enjoyed this book, you may be interested in these other books by Packt:

Unity Certified Programmer: Exam Guide

Philip Walker

ISBN: 978-1-83882-842-4

- Discover techniques for writing modular, readable, and reusable scripts in Unity
- Implement and configure objects, physics, controls, and movements for your game projects
- Understand 2D and 3D animation and write scripts that interact with Unity's Rendering API
- Explore Unity APIs for adding lighting, materials, and texture to your apps
- Write Unity scripts for building interfaces for menu systems, UI navigation, application settings, and much more
- Delve into SOLID principles for writing clean and maintainable Unity applications

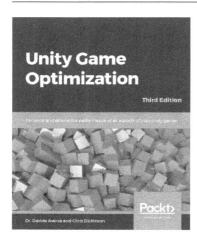

Unity Game Optimization - Third Edition

Dr. Davide Aversa, Chris Dickinson

ISBN: 978-1-83855-651-8

- Apply the Unity Profiler to find bottlenecks in your app, and discover how to resolve them

- Discover performance problems that are critical for VR projects and learn how to tackle them

- Enhance shaders in an accessible way, optimizing them with subtle yet effective performance tweaks

- Use the physics engine to keep scenes as dynamic as possible

- Organize, filter, and compress art assets to maximize performance while maintaining high quality

- Use the Mono framework and C# to implement low-level enhancements that maximize memory usage and prevent garbage collection

Leave a review - let other readers know what you think

Please share your thoughts on this book with others by leaving a review on the site that you bought it from. If you purchased the book from Amazon, please leave us an honest review on this book's Amazon page. This is vital so that other potential readers can see and use your unbiased opinion to make purchasing decisions, we can understand what our customers think about our products, and our authors can see your feedback on the title that they have worked with Packt to create. It will only take a few minutes of your time, but is valuable to other potential customers, our authors, and Packt. Thank you!

Index

3D

A

F

G

CPSIA information can be obtained
at www.ICGtesting.com
Printed in the USA
LVHW101938020921
696794LV00006B/615